# Vegetarianism

# Vegetarianism
## A History

Colin Spencer

Four Walls Eight Windows
New York/London

Copyright © 1993, 2000 Colin Spencer

Published in the United States by
Four Walls Eight Windows
39 West 14th Street
New York, NY 10011
http://www.4w8w.com

Originally published as *The Heretic's Feast* by Fourth Estate, London, 1993.
Published as *Vegetarianism* by Grub Street, London, 2000.

First Four Walls Eight Windows printing September 2002

**Library of Congress Cataloging-in-Publication Data:**
Spencer, Colin.
  Vegetarianism: a history / by Colin Spencer.
    p. cm.
  Originally published under title: The heretic's feast. Hanover, NH:
University Press of New England, 1996.
  Includes bibliographical references and index.
  ISBN: 1-56858-238-2 (hc.)
  1. Vegetarianism—History. I. Spencer, Colin. Heretic's feast. II. Title.

TX392.S722 2002
613.2'62'09—dc21
2002069298

Printed in the United States
Typeset by Pearl Graphics, Hemel Hempstead

10    9    8    7    6    5    4    3    2    1

# Contents

# Foreword
# for 2nd Edition

The nature of our diet in the last decade of the twentieth century became headline news. For many months at a time 'mad cow disease', and later in the decade 'frankenstein' foods, were issues of enormous dramatic power which involved the consumer in a debate on the nature of the food upon our plates. Parents began to enquire anxiously what was it they were feeding their infants and in an age when these same children were struck down suddenly with allergies or made terminally ill by a farm visit, parents were made vividly aware that the national diet could no longer be trusted. Consumers began to ask questions demanding information and when they received answers they often found them inadequate and failed to be reassured.

In this uncertain climate there was an upsurge of interest in vegetarianism, or what it is increasingly called in nutritional and scientific circles 'the plant diet', allied with a knowledge that even this diet was only safe if it was wholly organic. Yet government trials of GE crops which officially began in the year 2000, but some of which began at least four years earlier, have even threatened the future existence of organic agriculture in the British Isles.

In the light of this new public awareness in the problems which beset our food supply this history was revised. Not only have I needed to update the last chapter, but I have also totally rewritten the first chapter which deals with our evolution. This is partly because new discoveries are made every year about our distant past which spawn new theories, but also because many epidemiologists now consider that our metabolism born from 7 million years' evolution on the plant diet of vast bio-diversity (see p. 34-35) is hugely significant and should be recognised and followed as best we can in our nutritional practice.

Also, within this last decade the meaning of the term vegetarianism has changed. It means a diet less pure and rigid than it did when it was coined in 1848. It means an emphasis on plants while a small amount of protein from fish and perhaps poultry could possibly be in the background. This new definition is distressing to vegetarian purists who have a natural hatred of the slaughter of sentient creatures for the human diet. Nevertheless, this shift in meaning has occurred and the result is that the diet is now far more mainstream socially than it ever was before. People who choose to eat this way in public do not hide the fact or apologise, as they once did; in fact, such people are now commonplace and every banqueting function that is held automatically caters for a percentage who require the vegetarian option.

In the light of all this a detailed history of the diet seemed even more timely now than it was eight years ago. In these years almost every month we have had the results of more research which goes to prove that a low fat vegetable diet is by far the healthiest one for human survival. In addition the effects of industrial agriculture have polluted our environment to such a degree that there is a perceptible rise in diseases of the nervous system as well as a decline in male potency.

This new edition has also given me the opportunity to correct some minor errors and to add more detail about the actual foods that were eaten.

Colin Spencer

Winchelsea, 2000

# Foreword

I have to confess that before I began work on this book I was only vaguely aware of vegetarian history. I knew that there were people in the past, like Pythagoras and Leonardo da Vinci, who rejected meat-eating and espoused a vegetarian ideal but exactly why they should have done so remained obscure. I knew also that Tolstoy was committed to such a cause in his latter years. I knew that Hinduism in India made the cow sacred and had created probably the most delicious vegetarian cuisine in the world; that Buddhism had, as its first precept, not to kill or injure any human, animal, bird, fish or insect, yet Buddhist priests would accept the gift of a morsel of meat in their begging bowls, as the spirit of the giving counted more than the object itself. Of course, I could not help but know also that George Bernard Shaw was a vegetarian and often mildly amused about it. He wrote to Ellen Terry: 'The odd thing about being a vegetarian is not that the things that happen to other people don't happen to me – they all do – but that they happen differently: pain is different, pleasure different, fever different, cold different, even love different.'[1] This book explores that difference.

Like many others I thought that the vegetarian movement was a very contemporary phenomenon. I had no idea that the issues which agitate so many today – a hatred of unnecessary slaughter, the concept of animal welfare, our own physical health, the earth's balance and hence its ecology – would have been perfectly understood in the ancient world, certainly as early as 600 BC.

So much in the pages that follow was as new to me as it will be to most readers. Much I found at first astonishing, but then as I read on I began to see a strong pattern which distinguished the movement of Pythagoreanism as much as it did the historical figures that came after. What people eat is a symbol of what they believe. It is in fact much more than a symbol, because food is life and people cannot survive without it. Hence the living food which supplies energy becomes invested with all manner of hidden meanings.

At a certain point in prehistory it obviously became clear to some people, and these would have most likely been priests, that the living food which sustains the body and spirit logically could not come from dead flesh. We know now that meat is nutritionally a perfectly acceptable food, but to the ancients it was very obviously something that contains blood, and blood very early on had a powerful mystical significance. So inevitably this book became a history of the ideas behind the decision to adopt a meat-free diet. It is the psychology of abstention from flesh which I hope it explores, and why this decision so often seems outrageous to the rest of society.

Ideas do not spring to the forefront of public awareness without having evolved in the shadows for great lengths of time. Though I suspect a vegetable diet is as old as humankind – even older, for it comprised the central nutrients in that hominid interval before apes and human beings diverged into the various species that we are still unearthing today – it took many thousands of years after domestication of livestock and early agriculture for ideas on abstention from food to become part of the metaphysical language of religious devotion. This book, then, is an attempt to explore the reasons why omnivorous humans should at times voluntarily have abstained from an available food that was often acceptable to their companions, and why this abstention was always an integral part of an ideology. For diet, from the earliest times, was but one factor in a structure of concepts that interpreted the world.

The vegetarian ideal as a concept which embodied a moral imperative – 'thou shalt not kill for food' – made its first impact on history in India and Greece at around the same time, 500 BC, within the lifetimes of both Buddha and Pythagoras (but see footnote, p.77). It was linked with two other ideas; the wider of the two forbade all killing and hence opposed murder, strife and war, while at the heart of the philosophy was a belief in metempsychosis, or the transmigration of souls – more popularly thought of as reincarnation. Yet this moral concept can be traced back further: from Buddha to Hinduism and the Rig-Veda, the Indus civilisation perhaps, and then to Mesopotamia and Egypt; while the Pythagorean school owed much to the Orphic religion, the Eleusinian Mysteries and the cult of Dionysus, which, again, can be traced back to Egypt.

So many of the writers throughout history who have expressed passionate views on the morality of human diet, and are quoted in the pages of this book, made assumptions about the nature of the diet of prehistoric humankind. Very often these assumptions were made on the basis of little or no evidence and were coloured by fantasy and wishful thinking. It therefore seemed essential to present what evidence we now have on the human diet throughout our evolution; and further, to present such evidence (which can change as new archaeological finds are made) without being biased towards the idea of our early ancestors as either carnivores or herbivores. We know, of course, that human beings are omnivores yet can survive on a much smaller range of foods if necessity insists. What the ancient writers were not aware of was the dental archaeological evidence which allows us to trace the development of our ability to survive on a broad-spectrum diet.

Naturally, humans will eat anything they can to preserve life. Perhaps our omnivorousness was what led to our becoming the dominant species. The ability to adjust to new climatic conditions by exploration of new habitats and their food, migration to new lands and the will to taste a variety of strange and alien foods are aspects of the singularity of human beings. When an animal's biology depends on a precise nutritional equation, as is the case for the panda or the koala bear, for example, the species is severely limited. These animals can only live and thrive where a particular food grows, and if the availability of that food declines, the animal species declines with it. Independence from a particular food, or rather the ability to gain nutrients from a wide variety of highly different foods, must have offered an obvious evolutionary advantage.

But these pages are not, I must stress, a history of involuntary vegetarianism, the diet which most of the human race has lived on since we first emerged because poverty or scarcity dictated it. (The word 'vegetarianism' was not coined until the 1840s, but I have tended for the sake of clarity to use it throughout.) Taboos against particular foods must have occurred very early, long before domestication, as a means of distinguishing a community or individuals. A taboo is only an ideal in another form and ideals, when they involve the voluntary sacrifice of a particular food, can only flourish in a well-fed community, where people have enough leisure to reflect on the meaning of existence.

We shall see that throughout early history it was ecological changes which influenced the amount of food available, and it was these changes which dictated human evolution, provoking emigration to the shoreline, to estuaries and to new lands, and with it the consumption of new foods. It seemed to me, then, necessary to review the evidence of the food which early humans consumed and to see whether it could tell us anything new; also, to try to understand the context in which the decision by certain Egyptian priests and later by both Pythagoras and Buddha to forgo meat altogether was made.

But not only did I want to know how our prehistoric ancestors became omnivores, I also wanted to discover if abstention from meat excited resentment and ridicule in antiquity as it has done later in history, when those who eschewed meat and dairy products often provoked surprisingly virulent anger in others. Today, meat has become a symbol combining various meanings to do with power, orthodoxy and dominance, and these, in turn, evoke highly complicated emotional responses in us. Abstention from meat cannot be studied without these meanings being explored.[2]

The diets of primates and hominids are fascinating and much can be learnt of them from dental records. Yet this information is limited – it cannot tell us precisely the number of insects, say, the primate ate in a week while it was grazing on fruit, or what type of insect they were. What such records do tell us is the nature of the bulk of their diet – not only whether they were herbivores or carnivores, but sometimes the type of vegetable matter they ate. For example, the huge quern-like cheek teeth of *Australopithecus robustus* were used for grinding roots, seeds and nuts.

That a pattern eventually emerged which was characteristic of both diet and ideology came as a surprise. Was there much difference between the breakfasts of Pythagoras and Dr Bircher-Benner over two thousand years later? – very little (though the similarity could be explained by the involuntary vegetarianism of the poor which kept some highly nutritious dishes in daily use). Was there much difference between the words of Mani, the founder of Manicheanism, who described how light itself could sustain, and those of Ms Caddy, the founder of the Findhorn Community in the 1960s? – very little (though the Findhorn Community could not have read Mani, because the relevant papers had not been published then).

The various ideologies whose ethos included vegetarianism have been much researched and much written about, but the diet itself has usually been ignored, even though the history of the vegetarian ideal is a long, complex and dramatic one. Very seldom does it appear in the indexes of books, as if historians have considered the diet to be unimportant to their survey of a chosen subject. For example, in sixty biographies of Leonardo da Vinci only two bothered to mention his vegetarianism, which was, after all, a central part of his beliefs. Now that the subject is slowly gaining some credibility and respect, perhaps historians might give it more attention. There are, of course, honourable exceptions, which are referred to in the text.

What this study hopes to show are the factors that have to be present within a society before the vegetarian creed can be taken up, those which stimulate its growth and the nature of the ideology which forms it. Inevitably this involves pacifism but also the questioning of received wisdom and established mores. Often the vegetarian creed has been one of dissidence, comprising rebels and outsiders, individuals and groups who find the society they live in to lack moral worth. They have been strong individualists, often pilloried and ridiculed for what they said. There is nothing new about turning vegetarians into figures of fun: the disciples of Pythagoras became stock characters in Attic comedy, certain to raise a laugh. But other societies felt such criticism was no laughing matter and the outsiders were reviled. Vegetarians then became criminalised and were considered blasphemers and heretics.

Abstainers from meat came in all permutations and persuasions from heretics, humanists and Christian fundamentalists (the Seventh Day Adventists) to the most radical Quakers, agnostics like Edward Carpenter, philosophers like Epicurus, founders of religion like John Wesley and even an emperor – Asoka. These pages outline a history, largely unexplored,* of dissidence and revolt which often led to persecution and death, punishments which are only understandable once we comprehend the central and unifying role of meat within society.

---

*The first and only comprehensive history, until now, of vegetarianism was published in 1883, *The Ethics of Diet* by Howard Williams. *The Vegetable Passion*, described as a history of the vegetarian state of mind, by Janet Barkas, is sketchy on ancient history but still the most recent book of this kind. See A Select Bibliography, pp.368–72, for details of these books, and for other works which deal fleetingly with various aspects of the story.

# Acknowledgements

My thanks are due to:

Christopher Potter of Fourth Estate who first suggested that such a history should be written;

Dr Alan Long of VEGA, who very kindly lent me his file on human evolution;

Dr Germaine Greer for introducing me to the Cambridge University Library;

Professor Peter J. Wilson, who generously read Chapter 1 and gently criticised my research;

The Vegetarian Society, who opened their files and library to me; Professor Michael A. Crawford, who clarified some queries of mine on prehistoric nutrition;

Dr Gordon Latto, who kindly put me in touch with the Order of the Cross;

Anne Cox, who has assisted me patiently with typing the first edition. Finally, to Anne Dolamore and Grub Street for their enthusiasm in seeing that the time was right for a new edition.

# 1

# In the Beginning

A medieval scholar would have had no trouble at all in starting this history: Adam and Eve in Paradise; that state before the Fall when beasts were tame, there was no killing, and Adam and Eve – and all creation – were inevitably herbivores. But we, in the post–Darwinian era, see humankind in the context of an ancestry so varied and so distant that time itself becomes a colossus, an obstacle to understanding the far distant past. Yet how living organisms survive is the same now as it was then. Humans and our hominid ancestors have depended on the same metabolic process for a thousand million years, from that pre–Cambrian period when the evidence of fossils shows us that multi–cellular animals appear for the first time. Tracing back that relationship between food and life, we see that it stems from a chemical reaction. By means of photosynthesis, sunlight builds up complex compounds within plants which can be used by animals when consumed and then stored by them as energy to grow and breed. All flesh is grass, indeed;[1] a symbol of human fragility and transience: The grass withereth and the flower thereof falleth away. Yet the quintessence of our existence is in that stem of grass: 'With the aid of the sun's energy, biological evolution marches up hill, producing increased variety and higher degrees of organisation.'[2]

To see that our destiny is to become a component of fertile soil highlights the metabolic process by which a living organism puts off the onset of decay, but what precisely is this process? Merely the facts of eating, drinking, breathing and 'assimilating', from the Greek meaning 'change' or 'exchange'. So what is it in food and breath that we exchange? The answer is forms of energy. Organisms consume food and exude waste, and this is the basic equation true of all life. Our life begins, continues and ends because of an exchange of energy and this includes the act of eating itself. Nutrition is a determinant 'in evolution which operated on – even directed – the basic plan of living systems'.[3]

The consumption of food is the primary concern of all living organisms and each organism is designed for a specific diet – a lion will quickly grow sick and die if given a diet of salad, while a rabbit will thrive – and the type of food consumed makes possible various specialisations within both the plant and the animal kingdoms. But to identify what made up diets millions of years ago must surely be impossible? Not quite, for the climate and the environment tell us much and fossilised teeth, skulls, jaws and limbs tell us still more. But to explore such distant times is to become immersed in a world of supposition and conjecture based on scanty fossil evidence, where new archaeological findings often change our understanding and where there is sometimes little agreement among learned anthropologists. None the less, as more archaeological discoveries are made, the origin of humankind seems to recede ever further on a time-scale so immense that our minds find it difficult to grasp. The ancestry of the homininae, i.e. both hominoids and hominids, from which humankind itself emerged, can be traced back twenty-four million years. But as we are mammals, and modern mammals can be traced back seventy-five million years, the origin of humankind cannot be determined absolutely. Hominids and *Homo sapiens* merge in such a way that a study of the latter must include the former. The dietary natures of the various types of hominid are each fascinating, and each reveals more of our distant ancestors.

It is perhaps difficult as well for our minds to grasp the gradualness of evolution, how for half a million years nothing much seems to change. How insignificant those tiny adjustments by creatures to new problems in their living context must have seemed at the time. The change, for example, from clawed paw to recognisable hand, or when the thumb and index finger first met at the tip to form a circle, thereby allowing a more precise grip – these alterations in that arboreal creature swinging from branch to trunk in thick forest glades still fill us with profound astonishment, while all the further changes (bipedalism, loss of body hair, the manner by which body temperature is controlled, the growth of the cerebral cortex, development of language) which distinguish us from the primates have an audacity that takes the breath away.

It is the popular assumption, but alas a crude one, that evolution works through a simple interaction between the needs of an organism and the impact of external forces, in a quite arbitrary manner. This assumption posits a passive organism – a feather blown by the wind and does not allow for the organism having preferences or aims. This contrasts with the theory of 'organic evolution', which assumes that the higher organisms have a varied repertoire of reactive behaviour at their disposal. Professor Popper points out that an animal

> may adopt a preference for a new kind of food consciously as the result of trial and error. This means changing its environment to the extent that new aspects of the environment take on a new biological (ecological) significance. In this way individual preferences and skills may lead to the selection, and perhaps even the construction, of a new ecological niche by the organism.[4]

Immediately we admit that an organism may have preferences, we must admit that it also has consciousness, i.e. an awareness of options which necessitate a choice. The following pages document how humankind at certain times in its history has denied that any other creature is possessed of consciousness. Consciousness was somehow confused with divinity or the light of God and, therefore, denied to other animals. Such historical prejudices are slow to vanish: even in 1963 Sir Alistair Hardy in his Gifford Lectures, 'The Living Stream', allows consciousness to mammals, persuaded by Joy Adamson's books on her lioness, but not to insects or invertebrates – though even a cursory glance at an ants' nest is surely a convincing illustration of aims and preferences. Today, as we edge towards a holistic concept of the universe, it is not bizarre to perceive the possibility of mind in everything, as some of the Pre-Socratic philosophers did. Hardy goes on to quote from Sherrington in another set of Gifford Lectures, 'Man on His Nature':

> Mind as attaching to any unicellular life would seem to me to be unrecognisable to observation; but I would not feel that permits me to affirm it is not there. Indeed, I would think, that since mind appears in the developing soma (the body as distinct from the reproductive germ cells) that amounts to showing that it is potential in the ovum (and sperm) from which the soma sprang.

Consciousness then, I would argue, becomes a positive but unknowable and indirect factor in evolution. Scientists have now located cells similar to ours in the frontal lobe of the brains of primates which are responsible for self-consciousness. They have named them 'self-awareness neutrons', and they integrate the work of various parts of the brain and create a sense of individuality.★ These neurons in humans disappear in cases of Alzheimer's disease. Thus, primates have a sense of self and though that self is primarily concerned in searching for food, consumption and then procreation, this activity itself is imbued with a sense of 'who I am' and 'which direction I am choosing to go.' One of the magical facts of our existence is that all living creatures are individuals. Pet owners know that cat or dog siblings have completely different natures and close observers of primates know this to be true in often a startling manner. Our primate cousins are, in fact, very like ourselves.

'Plants rooted to the spot are certainly at the mercy of their environment; but animals which can move about have an opportunity to choose their habitat,' says Hardy, also in his lectures on 'The Living Stream'. Choice of habitat is dictated, of course, by the type and amount of food which is found there. Food is the propelling force which produces the adaptive changes to the creature. Popper, in contrast to Hardy's description of the plant at the mercy of the environment, points out that 'even a tree may push a root into a fissure between two rocks, force the rocks apart, and thus get access to soil of a chemical composition differing from that of its immediate surroundings'.[5] Thus you might add that the plant is at the mercy

---

★Research done by Professor John Allman of the California Institute of Technology.

of its own nature as well as of the environment, which moves the vegetable world even closer to our own varied psyche.

## The Decisive Primate

We, of course, cannot gauge to what degree animals and living creatures are self-conscious, but observation of primates in the wild, as well as laboratory research with chimpanzees, has given us many illustrations of problem-solving, hence reasoning, of the most astonishing character, as is seen in the work of Jane Goodall. One might argue, then, that those species of apes who are our distant ancestors made a choice not to kill other creatures for meat and to live on a vegetarian diet. This sounds like a gross simplification – they were built to browse among tree tops where their main diet was fruit, berries, nuts and leaves; and in that environment there is no opportunity for a kill. But once they began to live part of their life on the ground which opened up a much greater range of plant foods, animal proteins must have also offered themselves as potentially desirable. Termites for example are now considered by chimps to be an enormous delicacy and sticks are employed to go fishing for them. Other insects would surely have been eaten; beetles and cicadas, I am told, once the hard shell is cracked taste sweet. But we know that, occasionally, modern chimpanzees can collectively kill another smaller primate or other baby mammals for food. Yet this behaviour has never become habitual; nor did it change the physical attributes of those creatures to turn them into efficient carnivores. The carnivore moves on all fours, has articulated claws, eyes with acute night vision, a skin without pores, small salivary glands, a rasping tongue, a short intestinal canal only three times the length of the body, a smooth colon, slightly developed incisor teeth and pointed molars. Carnivores are also able to move at great speed when in pursuit of their prey – the cheetah can even maintain a speed of 100 kph for sixty seconds. Hence there is an element of choice in the behaviour of these early primates, though choice in such a limited and restricted form that we would hardly be inclined to name it as such. What choice does a tree shrew have? But if its forest is burned down it has either to adapt itself to live on the ground or to cross the ground in search of a new forest. At some levels and at some times options must occur and choices have to be made.

Our hominoid ancestors evolved over a period of 24 million years and, for all but one and a half million of these years, the evidence we have leaves little doubt that their diet was almost completely vegetarian, except for insects and grubs. It might be argued that a small primate choosing to eat a grub, beetle or fly is killing for food. However, the amounts must have been small in the context of their whole diet, for the teeth remained more suitable for grinding vegetation, and cannot reasonably turn this herbivore into a carnivore with the specialised evolutionary pedigree outlined above.

The term hominoid, meaning 'of those species of apes by which types of both man and ape evolved', is used to cover those primates which carry the genetic material of ape and man and which flourished as several different hominoid species for an inordinate length of time – the first signs of the beginnings of man, costumed as it were as a very small ape, appeared 25 million years ago, in the Miocene period, when the rain forest first began to recede and savannah grasslands appeared.

An extraordinary amount of microscopic detective work is undertaken whenever a find of early fossils is made, work which because of genetic research with DNA* and other technologies becomes more and more specific, illuminating the distant past and turning it into a more familiar yesterday. The fossil remains of teeth and jaws tell us about the diet of those primates and from their bones we can understand how they moved. Also, because pollen passes through the digestive tract, fossilised faecal material when it is discovered on site can tell us what vegetation was consumed, though such coprolitic evidence is extremely rare.

A diversity of arboreal creatures, apes and monkeys, developed in the Miocene 15-25 million years ago: *Pliopithecus*, an early gibbon; *Dryopithecus*, a small arboreal monkey-like creature, thought possibly to be the stock from which both apes and humans grew; *Proconsul*, the earliest known ape; and *Sivapithecus*, possibly the ancestor of the modern orang-utan. Because there was a primate population explosion in these ten million years we can deduce that environment and organism were well suited. The earth was covered in rain forest and the climate was warm and wet. The great dinosaurs had disappeared and it was the day of the mammal. Because of their smallness and their fur (the *Aegyptopithecus* of 35 million years ago, thought to be the prototype of all monkeys and apes, was about the size of a large cat) they could maintain a constant body temperature throughout climatic changes. Living in trees demands a different set of skills from being on the ground. Moving from tree to branch over considerable distances in search of food necessitates that the animal be able to judge space and distance if it is not to fall. Watch a gibbon and see the exactness of its aim as it swings across space and unerringly hits the branch it needs. In mastering these skills, tree-dwellers inevitably developed both their hands and their eyes: the opposable thumb made for dexterity, as useful for finding food and grasping branches as it would be for making tools, while eyesight became stereoscopic, allowing vision in three dimensions, and gradually able to perceive colour – how useful for seeing ripe fruit in the dense green shade or the approach of predators. The teeth and jaws of these hominoids have been studied and found little different from those of modern apes, their habitat being forest and open woodland intersected by streams on the lower slopes of volcanoes.

The remains of one in particular, *Ramapithecus*, who lived 10-14 million years ago, had teeth which show changes from all the hominoids before,

---

*For example, four letters in the DNA sequences represent units of chemical codes. As genes change at a rate of 2-4% per million years, geneticists are able to consult a 'molecular clock'. Thermoluminescence (TL) estimates the age of objects from the energy they have accumulated through internal radioactivity.

particularly the abundant fossils of *Dryopithecus*. The dental arcade is slightly curved, the canines are smaller,★ while the molars have a larger grinding surface with a thicker enamel covering. These indicate a jaw which worked as a powerful chewing apparatus, suitable for crushing and grinding. The jaw shows evidence of lateral as well as vertical movement, meaning rotary chewing rather than the vertical chomping of apes. These teeth and jaws represent the earliest evidence of possible hominid chewing equipment. Professor Bilsborough[6] interprets the remains as showing that an ecological shift had taken place by early ape populations towards a diet different from that of their *Dryopithecus* contemporaries. *Ramapithecus* lived in woodland, open glades and streams near grasslands. There is no evidence at all that their diet would have included meat, no evidence of tools or any indication of social organisation as the diet would have been composed of leaves, fruit, nuts, berries, bark and grasses. 'Such primates are competent to adapt to diverse environments and to accommodate changes in the availability of foods, coping with some scarcity, even of staples; these animals will have populations with a diet that varies from place to place.'[7]

Woodlands encourage a diversity of form, so more varied primates flourished in forests rather than grasslands. Living in trees demands a different pattern of locomotion, swinging, leaping, climbing rather than mere quadrupedalism – walking on four limbs – the manner of locomotion which the savannahs impose.

Within the Miocene epoch large glaciers formed at 13 million and ten million years ago. When glaciers spread from the poles they caused not only cooling of the atmosphere and the decline of some plants, causing migration of the animals that lived off them, but also fluctuations in the sea level, which changed the contours of the land; lakes appeared where dry land existed before, dry regions appeared where once there were swamps, but the soil itself also became less rich in minerals and so less fertile, because the rocks themselves, becoming frozen, no longer eroded, no longer washed into rivers to be deposited in the lowlands. Everything was halted beneath a solidifying mass of ice. The Ice Ages as we know them occurred much later, in the Pleistocene, so these Miocene glaciers (and the ecological changes they brought), forming in the midst of an explosion in the evolution of primates, could have stimulated the first impulse towards the true hominid, as opposed to the pongids (the ape genus). There is no agreement when the divergence occurred, but it would have involved choice, a decision to explore the ground, to live and gather food from that source as well as from the trees. 'When the conditions of the environment are changed, we are able to see more clearly how food preferences motivate intelligence by demanding the application of thought and ingenuity as a guide for action to obtain ends, to realize preferences.'[8]

---

★When I was at school during the Second World War canine teeth were considered evidence of meat-eating. It is now known that they are like the fangs, tusks and antlers common in many species, which in the males serve as equipment in territorial contests and bouts of supremacy over females.

*Ramapithecus* shows dental and cranial features different from those of the earlier primates of the Miocene, owing, it is thought, to the habitat of mixed grassland and forest. There is still much debate on whether this creature is a hominid ancestor of humankind or whether it is a hominoid and therefore a pongid ancestor, but everyone agrees that it was an amiable fructivore, though a small quantity of insect life might have been present and eaten in the fruit. Whether these early apes consumed their food in the same manner as contemporary apes we cannot know, but logic inclines us to think there would be little if any difference. Yet what the teeth and jaw of *Ramapithecus* do tell us is that a much larger amount of grass and grass seed was consumed. The larger cheek teeth and thicker enamel are adaptations for chewing hard, resistant food objects such as grass and covered seeds, a source of food which at that time other animals were unable to consume. More extensive grasslands could have appeared in the Miocene because of the growth of glaciers. Thus the very first impetus towards humankind was as a reaction to change and hardship. The survival of a species demands a tenacious grip upon the most tenuous thread of existence through gruelling experiences that contemporary city-dwellers can hardly envisage.

Though we have always believed apes to be herbivorous, we now have some clues from the remains of the fruit and leaves they have consumed that they are also very fond of fruit containing maggots or other insects. Yet such meat composes only a tiny percentage of their diet. Some observers of the manner by which monkeys eat claim that much sniffing, feeling and exploratory nibbling occurs before they pick and consume the fruit they want, which will be the one with the bugs inside. Some Amazonian species, it would appear, are more interested in the insect larva than in the fruit. They open a weevil-infested fig, eat the weevil, and discard the fig.[9] But sniffing the fruit, it is thought, is largely a means of discovering how ripe it is, just as we inspect fruit we buy by touching and sniffing it. Insect-eating may also occur because insects are sweet, i.e. they resemble fruit more than meat.

There is also the example of chimpanzees who will sometimes work together as a group to hunt down monkeys (generally the vegetarian colobus), then tear the creatures apart and settle down to eat them. Peter Wilson has this to say: 'The business of hunting among chimpanzees seems to develop more from stress than from necessity, but the stress may well be allayed in the course of the activity itself – the cooperation and killing.'[10]

When Jane Goodall first observed her chimps eating meat it came as an astonishing revelation to the world of anthropology. Her findings are fascinating, as is the close observation of the chimps' behaviour.

As I watched I saw that one of them was holding a pink-looking object from which he was, from time to time, pulling pieces with his teeth. There was a female and a youngster and they were both reaching out towards the male, their hands actually touching his mouth. Presently the female picked up a piece of the pink thing and put it to her mouth: it was at this moment that

I realised the chimps were eating meat. After each bite of meat the male picked off some leaves with his lips and chewed them with the flesh. Often, when he had chewed for several minutes on this leafy wodge, he spat out the remains into the waiting hands of the female. Suddenly he dropped a small piece of meat and, like a flash, the youngster swung after it to the ground. But even as he reached to pick it up, the undergrowth exploded and an adult bushpig charged towards him. Screaming, the juvenile leapt back into the tree. The pig remained in the open, snorting and moving backwards and forwards. Presently I made out the shapes of three small striped piglets. Obviously the chimps were eating a baby pig.[11]

A little later Jane Goodall comments: 'Previously scientists had believed that, whilst these apes might occasionally supplement their diet with a few insects or small rodents and the like, they were primarily vegetarians and fruit-eaters. No one had suspected that they might hunt larger mammals.'[12]

At first it was thought, and it still is argued, that this conclusively destroys any idea that our near ancestors, the apes, were peaceful vegetarians. The following exemplified a common view:

Since we mankind evolved from the primate world, then these tendencies for meat must be bred in us. Meat animals are the only means of utilising the protein in plant sources growing in poor ground. Meat clearly is an important source of the essential nutrients needed for sustenance. People need no conversion. Long live meat![13]

The group killing of a colobus monkey, observed by Goodall, needed foresight, planning, alert observation and an ability to grasp the potential of a situation: 'as though at a signal, the chimpanzees who had been resting and grooming peacefully on the ground had got up and stationed themselves close to trees that would act as escape routes for the intended victim'.[14] The more one reads the Goodall accounts, the more the picture of the peaceful ape is shattered. The account of the kill shows nature very deeply red in tooth and claw. The chimpanzees feed only on the young of bushpigs, bush-bucks and baboons, as well as both young and adult red colobus monkeys, redtail monkeys and blue monkeys. These victims are pounced upon when slightly separated from the rest of their group and either they are instantly torn to pieces while alive or their heads are dashed against a rock or tree. The catch is often kept by the killer, who may dispense tidbits to the others or very likely keep the bulk of the carcase to itself. They eat slowly, chewing leaves with each mouthful, and the brain appears to be a special delicacy.

But when we look at the actual amount of meat eaten, our picture of the carnivorous chimpanzee is somewhat altered. Goodall tells us first that the Gombe Stream chimpanzees are efficient hunters, then that a group of forty chimps may catch over twenty animals in one year. When later the chimpanzees were observed over a span of ten years the fifty-odd chimpanzees 'killed and ate no fewer than ninety-five individual mammals'.[15] But it is the size of the carcases which is important:

> There is no evidence that chimpanzees capture or even pursue an animal that weighs more than about 20 lbs. For example, most captured baboons were infants or juveniles with an estimated weight of 10 lbs or less. Similarly the bushbucks and bushpigs that the chimpanzees kill are either newborn or very young. Few of the adult mammals killed by the Gombe chimpanzees weighed as much as 20 lbs.[16]

These figures led John Hawthorn to make some interesting calculations:

> Now 950 lbs of meat, or 95 lbs [per animal] per annum, is not much split between a group of fifty animals. It averages out at around 2.4 g per individual per day, or less than 1 g of animal protein. For a chimp weighing 100 lbs this is not much when compared with a typical UK human intake of about 30 g per head per day for an individual weighing half as much again. Would chimps eat more if they could get it? Perhaps so for Teleki notes that about a third of the capture attempts were unsuccessful.[17]

A third of the attempts being unsuccessful contradicts the statement by Goodall, who worked with Teleki, that the chimps were efficient hunters. If they were, then they chose to eat only this small amount of meat, a sliver per day and no more. Hawthorn compiled a list from Walker's *Mammals of the World* to show the diet of living primates:[18]

| | |
|---|---|
| Number of known genera of living primates | 62 |
| Fruit-, vegetable- and nut-eaters | 60 |
| Insect-eaters | 42 |
| Eaters of birds or their eggs | 23 |
| Eaters of carrion | 4 |
| Hunters of small animals | 16 |
| Eaters of large animals | 1 (man) |

The table shows how animal protein is a minor and opportunistic part of primates' diet. The latter adjective is important, since, as Goodall herself observed, many of the baby pigs killed were stumbled over by accident. If the chimpanzees ate meat that particular day, it was fortuitous.

So although chimpanzees have been observed to eat meat, this cannot be assumed to have been true for any hominoid ancestors, or for their descendants, many of the hominids. Dental evidence shows no pattern of persistent meat-eating in these early creatures. Hence the argument remains valid that overall a choice was made not to kill for food (though that choice does not preclude the arbitrary killing we have seen, for primate nature is quite as inconsistent as human nature), and we can say quite confidently that meat-eating arrived much later in the evolution of humankind, and to a much smaller degree than was thought before.

## The Aquatic Ape?

One of the most striking clues to when the hominid diverged from the pongid, finally leaving its ape cousins behind, is offered by the herpes virus (HSV). We share with monkeys and apes that form of the virus, HSV 1, which is transmitted by genital contact, but HSV 2, the form which is transmitted orally, by kissing, is unique to humans. Apes rarely 'kiss', and of course would not when copulating as the female is in the kneeling position. Thus face-to-face copulation in the human race can be dated from the emergence of HSV 2, about ten million years ago.'[19] Face-to-face copulation would also seem to indicate bipedalism, hence dating of HSV 2 also gives a clue to when our ancestors began walking erect upon two feet, with hands free for gathering and carrying food, and perhaps for erecting some crude form of shelter.

The bonobo or pigmy chimp is an outstanding example of an oscular ape, in fact, one almost addicted to the energetic sensuality of the use of the tongue in kissing. Many a bonobo keeper has experienced it. Not surprisingly, this tiny ape which enjoys water and bipedalism, shares 98% of our genetic make up. So our resemblance to the bonobo is as near as is a dog to a fox. They live in a peaceful matriarchal society, consuming a wide range of fruits, leaves and plants, where any disputes are settled by sexual favours homosexual and heterosexual in all possible permutations. They are herbivorous in the wild but in captivity, like other primates, will eat almost anything. They are, in fact, sexually insatiable and omnivorous like ourselves.

There is an inexplicable hiatus in the archaeological record between ten and four and a half million years ago. The earliest fossil discovered was *Ardipithecus ramidus* dated 4.4. million years ago,[20] in size and appearance it must have resembled very closely the bonobo chimp. They lived in a forest or woodland area where there were plenty of glades and open spaces between the trees, they were also close to water, though aquatic remains – turtle, fish and crocodile – found with them were not so common as the land mammals. There were plenty of primates, the small colombine monkey being the most common. This is the favourite prey of chimps in the wild today. Larger mammals were rare, – hippo, rhinos, giraffids and bovines. But there were plenty of small creatures, bats, small squirrels, dwarf mongoose, bush rats and mole rats. The most common seed discovered was that of Canthium, a thorny shrub which still grows in Africa and now also in the East, the leaves fruits and seeds of which are eaten.*

*Ramidus* walked erect; we do not know whether he had a hairy pelt or not, but there is a theory which could explain his upright posture so much in variance with the other primates. This is the Aquatic Ape Theory or ATT

---

*It is used in curry dishes as a seasoning.

first postulated by Sir Alistair Hardy and others, including the writer Elaine Morgan. The theory suggests that we took to the sea and that, when successive Ice Ages had receded, the sea rose to its present level, obliterating any archaeological evidence upon the shoreline of this possibly semi-aquatic existence. This theory would explain several unusual features which humans share with aquatic mammals such as dolphins: a naked skin, tear ducts and subcutaneous fat to insulate the body. Obviously fish and shellfish would have been prominent in our diet. The theory is also given support and a highly sympathetic and detailed analysis by the authors of *The Driving Force*.[21] They look at evolution from a nutritionist's standpoint and say that the human brain needs in its growth a consistent balance of 1:1 between Omega 3 and Omega 6 neural fatty acids. It is this balanced combination which promotes encephalisation, in particular the growth of the cerebral cortex, that frontal lobe which is the site of intellect and reasoning, and which in evolution must have stimulated brain size in some hominids. Land mammals have 3-6 times more Omega 6 than Omega 3 fatty acids, while fish have more Omega 3 (cod has a ratio of 1:40 in its muscle membranes), but dolphins have the same 1:1 ratio as ourselves. The sea would have provided hominids with the food containing the Omega 3 fatty acids, while the land would have supplied sources of Omega 6, in the form of bushes, trees and grasses. In Africa today there are over two hundred wild plants which are rich in Omega 6 fatty acids. Balanites Egyptaecica, for example, has a large almond-sized seed which comprises over 50% oil, 70% of which is Omega 6 linoleic acid.[22] Thus, only in the sea and land interface is it possible to obtain a rich supply of both types of fatty acids, especially around the river estuaries, which are particularly rich in minerals (washed down by the rains from rocky uplands) and where an astonishing wealth of shoreline food abounds.

The piscine organisms that could be gathered easily, would of course, have been shellfish: limpets, clams, mussels, sea urchins (the favourite food of sea otters) which cling to rocks and roots of trees in river estuaries. Birds prise these from the rocks then drop them on rocks to open. Primates, hominoids or hominids would have discovered that they were good to eat by snatching scraps from the birds, and would quickly learn to prise clams away from rocks themselves, then break them open by using stones. Chimps are adept at using objects as tools. The soft interior of oysters, mussels and clams would have slipped down easily, and would have been a rich source of protein and minerals, especially calcium, necessary for making strong bones. For there is no source of calcium in the rain forest.

But for fish eating to be a significant event, it would have to become the staple part of the diet over a length of time like one million years and the hominoids would inevitably be living on the water's edge. An archipelago, a group of small islands would be a perfect habitat for such a diet and necessary for this group to be stranded from all the other apes. We first split from the primate line between 8 and 6 million years ago. Is there any possibility that a water or a sea context could have existed at this time in any part of the African continent?

Yes, is the short answer and not far away from where the earliest fossil discoveries are being made. Many of the remains that have been discovered of our ancestors have been found in the Olduvai Gorge which is part of the rift valley of East Africa. Rift valleys mark faults in the earth's crust where two or more plates move apart or crash together. In north east Africa we have a situation where three plates converge, the Arabian, the Nubian and the Somalian; the centre of the highest amount of disturbance is one part of Ethiopia called Afar, which gave its name to the hominid nicknamed Lucy, called *Australopithecus afarensis*. Until the late Miocene, that is seven million years ago, Arabia was joined to Africa by the Afar Isthmus. Interestingly enough in the oral tradition of the Somali they tell of their ancestors who crossed from Southern Arabia to Somaliland (which occupies the Horn of Africa) for the two countries were connected by land. (They were connected by land again in the Ice Ages.)

When the three plates converged the sea rushed into Afar and further movements of the earth's crust sealed the Sea of Afar from the ocean. Over millions of years this water evaporated and left salt deposits thousands of feet deep. (Much the same is happening to the Dead Sea in Israel which is evaporating away.) Before this happened that part of Africa and Asia was unbroken dense rain forest populated by a range of creatures including primates and hominoids. Once the sea had rushed into that forest the highland regions, the Danakil Alps, became islands. The creatures that were stranded had to live with the sea and from it in order to survive. The split between the primate line and the human line occurred around this time, so if hominoids were amongst the ones stranded, it is logical that shellfish would become a staple part of the diet; also wading into the shallows to gather shellfish would have induced bipedalism. Nor would it be unreasonable to also assume that once the taste for shellfish existed then the hominid learnt to dive and swim so as to gather more food from the sea bed. 'Some of the richest food sources in the world are found in tropical wetlands and off-shore waters. The food supply, in quantity, variety and ease of procurement, would far exceed what the savannah could offer to a small unspecialised primate.'[23]

*Ardipithecus ramidus* was found in Ethiopia, west of the River Awash about three hundred kilometres from the present Danakil Alps. Seventeen hominid individuals were found in fragments; they have been dated at 4.4 million years ago, that is two and a half million years after the Sea of Afar was formed. They lived in a forest or woodland area where there were plenty of glades and open spaces between the trees, they were also close to water. The Awash runs into a series of lakes which follow the rift valley ending in the lakes of Rudolph and Turkana where early hominid finds have been made.

Let me now turn to the idea that a diet of fish rich in Omega 3 fatty acids would achieve that ratio with Omega 6 of one to one which is necessary in the human nervous system. Omega 6 is found in seeds, nuts and plants (land mammals have about three to six times as much Omega 6 as they do Omega 3). Omega 3 is found in all marine life and in the green parts of plants,phytoplankton and algae. It is possible for a marine animal to have an equal ratio, but the dolphin has to work hard at it finding the Omega 6 – squid contains arachidonic acid which is their main source of it. It is thought that dolphins because they began existence as land mammals still retained their dependence upon Omega 6. Biochemically, they were still land mammals living in a marine habitat.[24]

It is also possible for a herbivorous land mammal that never visits the sea to retain the ratio of 1 to 1, but again it would have to search for the food source of Omega 3. It would have difficulty in finding the nutrient require-ments for the brain and visual system. But it is not impossible, it might, for example, find it in algae – the Aztecs dried algae and made cakes out of it.

But at the sea's edge there is a rich source of both fatty acids; all forms of shellfish as well as the squid contain arachidonic acid, Omega 6, while the base of the food chain in the sea as algae, plankton and all seaweeds starts with long chain Omega 3 acids very close to those used in the human brain.

Is it then feasible that a group of hominoids were stranded upon what we now call the Danakil Alps,in the Sea of Afar which around seven million years ago would have become a series of islands? That once there a diet of sea creatures was the only way to survive? The sea was landlocked, they could not as happened to the whales, dolphins and seals up to five million years ago take to the ocean and become solely marine. They were stranded on small islands in an inland sea. Once there, their bodies gradually adapted, they learnt to hold their breath under water, to dive great depths, to collect huge clams and oysters from the sea bed, to use branches as traps for fish, to dry sea weed until it was brittle and easily digestible, and this new diet stimulated their mental and visual system. It would have enabled a small herbivore primate to move towards an omnivorous diet without needing to learn the skills and weapons necessary for hunting in the savannah.

The evidence for believing that our bodies today show that a phase of living from the sea seems to me thoroughly reasonable. My explanation relies on the extensive work done upon the theory by Elaine Morgan.[25]

(1) **Sex.** We mate face to face, almost unknown in land mammals, but common among aquatic mammals. Whales, dolphins, beavers, sea otters and others all mate face to face. Loss of oestrus. All primate females like other animals have a time when they go on heat. At sometime in our evolution the female moved towards being permanently receptive. Genitals. Average size of penis in humans at 13 cm compared to chimpanzee at 8 cm and gorilla at 3 cm is large, while the female genitals have retracted inside the body wall and are protected by thick folds of skin. Both these changes reflect similar genitalia arrangement in aquatic species. The longer penis is necessary in the missionary position.

(2) **Loss of hair.** Darwin commented. 'The loss of hair is an inconvenience and probably an injury to man, for he is thus exposed to the scorching of the sun and to sudden chills, especially due to wet weather. No one supposes that the nakedness of the skin is any direct advantage to man; his body therefore cannot have been divested of hair through natural selection.' Darwin has no explanation for it then. If the primates left the trees for the savannah and lost their hairy pelts it would have made life far more difficult for them. In fact, to shield their skin from the sun ray's their pelts should have become longer. Darwin later came up with the explanation that *homo sapiens* found hairless women more sexually attractive[26], which is on the par of John Ruskin being so horrified when he found his bride had pubic hair that the marriage remained unconsummated. (Thus Darwin's idea has more to do with Victorian concepts of female beauty than scientific reasoning.)[27]

But nakedness is an obvious advantage for gliding through the water (whales, dolphins, porpoises, dugongs and the hippopotamous are all naked). Small aquatic animals rely on an oily pelt which is waterproof and traps a bubble of air around the body. Many of these sea animals once lived on land. Unknown quadrupeds turned into whales and dolphins, primitive dogs turned into seals, a bear-like creature turned into the walrus and so it continues.

(3) **Breathing.** Darwin again: 'It is a strange fact that every particle of food and drink we swallow has to pass over the orifice of the trachea with some risk of falling into the lungs.' In land mammals the tube for air and for food are divided, air is taken in through the nostrils to a tube to the lungs, while a separate tube descends from the throat to the stomach. Animals can breathe and drink simultaneously. We cannot without choking; this is due to the descended larynx which we share with diving mammals. It allows large amounts of air to be inhaled or exhaled, thus allowing us to swim under water for a length of time.

(4) **The fat layer we have no other primate has.** Subcutaneous fat would not have been a help but a hazard living in the savannah. But in the water it is efficient as protection against heat loss.

(5) **Bipedalism.** The mammalian spine evolved over a hundred million years on the principle of having one leg at each corner. The vertebral column is like an arch supported by two pairs of movable pillars, and the internal organs are suspended from that arch and evenly distributed along the length of it. Our ancestors converted themselves into walking towers with a high centre of gravity and a narrow base. We can observe in the wild four legged animals when they want to see further, or to reach food, raise themselves up on two legs. It is a position which is difficult for them to keep for longer than a few moments. Yet in water it is easy, the buoyancy of the water holds the body up. A group of primates which had to forage for food at the sea's edge could easily spend the whole day in the water foraging and eating as they waded along. It would not take many generations for a variety

of changes to begin to occur which would help the creature to adapt to such an environment. But because sea foods are high in protein and rich in all manner of nutrients the foragers would not have to spend all their time at it, as they would have done living just on vegetation. Such extra time allows for social mobility, home building, ingenuity and tool making.

(6) **Our enjoyment of water is unique among land mammals.** Babies are natural swimmers if they go into water before they walk. We love the sea, we take long holidays near and upon it, coastal resorts are favoured places to live, we also have a natural fondness for islands. If there was no watery interlude in our evolution, one would think that our atavistic yearnings might lead us to holiday amidst forests, but thankfully there are no package tours to such places.

What else but a dramatic change in the environment for one group of primates could stimulate such radical differences? The primate line continued, the chimp and the gorilla, our nearest cousins became what they are today. But we, only a little larger, a brain a little bigger, walked upright. But we were not to remain isolated in this inland sea on the Horn of Africa.

Our new world began to fade one or one and a half million years after we colonised it, for the Sea of Afar as it gradually evaporated became saltier and saltier. We had to migrate southwards along the rift valley where there was fresh water. Whatever changes began to occur before now slowed down again. It would suggest to me that a change of diet, a lack of marine sustenance, is responsible.

But there is no archaeological proof that such hominids existed. We know where to look for the proof, but no palaeontologist would consider digging in the Danakil Alps for remains of the Aquatic Ape, for the theory is not considered seriously.

Apart from the lack of archaeological evidence I have one other serious criticism of the theory. It all happened far too early in our evolution. If brain encephalisation began because of the one to one dietary balance achieved, this aquatic phase should have occurred four million years later in order to produce homo sapiens. Yet I believe something akin to it did.

## Toolmakers and Gatherers

Though the preceding may be considered supposition, such is true of all theories about prehistory. Some suppositions rest on archaeological finds and after four million years ago there is plenty of evidence from sites in East Africa of our distant ancestors. Here at last we see a reflection almost of ourselves, or rather two: one small and slight, *Australopithecus afarensis* (Lucy being the most complete skeletal evidence, and so called because Donald Johanson, the anthropologist, discovered the fossil while listening to the Beatles song 'Lucy in the Sky with Diamonds'); the other, *Australopithecus robustus*, much larger with a bony ridge on its cranium. And there is plenty of evidence of what those ancestors ate.

By four million years ago the African rain forest had receded to reveal vast areas of savannah grassland. Various hominids (more types are being discovered every few years) had now left the forest to exist in this new habitat. Walking upright is a far more efficient method of keeping cool and bipedalism was hominids' accepted means of locomotion. Lucy's skeleton is very similar to ours, except for her skull, which resembles that of a modern chimpanzee, with a strong jaw and thick enamel teeth. The microscopic wear pattern on these teeth indicates that she ate mostly fruit and that she died when she was about twenty. Her remains were found in Ethiopia and are dated at 3.2 million years ago. *Australopithecus afarensis* tend to be between 3 feet 6 inches and 4 feet in height and to weigh between 30 and 40 kg, the size of a modern eight-year-old child.

*Australopithecus robustus* arrived on the scene later, appearing 2.5 million years ago, and were about 5 feet in height. They survived for a million years and then they petered out. All signs of Lucy also disappear at the same time. Stockier and heavier, the *A. robustus* males' distinctive crest at the top of the skull (the sagittal crest) held large muscles to work the most powerful jaw yet seen among our ancestors. The cheek teeth are enormous, thick, rounded enamel querns, while crowded at the front of the jaw are small peg-like incisors and canines. This jaw is a munching and grinding machine, but there is no sign again of bone-munching or meat-eating: these powerful jaws and teeth were made for pulverising roots, grains, nuts, seeds and bark.

This robust hominid calls up visions of a hunter and slayer of beasts, and, indeed, was considered to be a violent and aggressive killer because some of the cave sites where *A. robustus* remains were discovered were littered with animal bones. This view was shared by Raymond Dart and Robert Ardrey and had a pervasive influence in the fifties and sixties. The truth, however, may have been that *A. robustus* was eaten – hundreds of their skulls have been found in limestone caves at Swartkrans, in South Africa, showing signs of attack by carnivores, such as sabre-tooth tigers and leopards. Besides, neither *A. afarensis* or *A. robustus* made killing tools for hunting and they were certainly not strong enough for a Herculean combat. But a recent discovery of the hands and fingers of *A. robustus* shows a great similarity with our hands and greater flexibility in the fingers than was generally thought. Near these were found broken bones which were obviously digging tools, useful for digging up roots. The diet of *A. robustus* was limited compared with other species and a climatic change which deprived their territory of a particular range of plants could have hastened their weakening and demise. With such a jaw there was no possibility of adapting. Survival is about flexibility – the days of omnivorous humans were getting closer.

However, it is impossible to say that both *A. robustus* and the more graceful and tiny *A. afarensis* never ate meat. They could have easily supplemented their diet with termites, snails, freshwater clams and lizards, for such a small amount of flesh would not change or show up on the dental fossils; but there is certainly no evidence of these two hominids as predators or hunters. This, I believe, was a conscious decision. They must have observed carnivores killing and gorging on their prey, must have known that meat counted as food and that creatures flourished on such a diet, yet they refused to kill even small mammals – certainly within the power of *A. robustus*. 'Nothing that we know of prehistoric primates, including hominids, precludes us from thinking that they did not possess comparable competences [to chimpanzees] and were not faced with similar problems of choice, selection, and preference.'[28] Dental evidence overwhelmingly shows a broad-spectrum vegetable diet, obtainable mostly from the plains and grasslands which were growing greater in area with the approaching aridity of the Pliocene era. Nutritionally the diet would have been adequate: nuts, berries, leaves, fruits, grasses, seeds, roots, tubers, fungi, insects, grubs and reptiles.

But at two million years ago, living at the same time as the vegetarian *A. afarensis* and *A. robustus*, was *Homo habilis*: handyman, the toolmaker, marking the earliest beginnings of the stone age, and with a larger brain than any ape so far. Though *habilis* was thought the first tool maker, we have already seen this to be untrue. Modern chimps use sticks to go termite fishing, hence we can be pretty certain that hominids like the very early *ramidus* would have used stout pointed sticks as digging tools, long tapering sticks as hooking tools for getting at fruit hanging at the end of branches and would have made dams for trapping fish. After all, hominids were the most intelligent beings upon the earth, for they were to survive and flourish for a few million years. Remains of their tools have been found at Olduvai Gorge – mostly primitive axes the size of tennis balls – amidst signs of meat-eating, though there are still no signs of hunting.

It is thought that *Homo habilis* was a scavenger, either from supplies left in the trees by leopards or from the carcases which lions had stripped bare. The stone tools would extract the marrow from the bones and the brain from the skulls, which is all a lion will leave, but they are highly nutritious remnants. Professor Blumenschine commented: 'The rich source of fat in bone marrow would have provided an easily acquired high yield, low risk and predictable energy supplement to a predominantly plant food diet.'[29] Leopards are inclined to leave the kill or parts of it in the trees for up to two days and to be out of sight of the tree for several hours. *Homo habilis* was adept at climbing trees, and as leopards tend to use the same tree and hiding-place, stealing such food would not be difficult, though it would demand planning that involved foresight and group co-operation.

Recent excavations of fossils in eastern and southern Africa suggest that there was more than one kind of *Homo habilis*, and that there may even have been as many as five. The fossils all had human features that distinguished them from *Australopithecus*, yet they were different from each other. So the link between *Homo habilis* and *Homo erectus* is blurred. The crucial period, the 'humanising' period between two and 1.6 million years ago, appears more complex than previously thought. *Homo habilis* was small; the puzzle is, how did *Homo erectus*, with long limbs and larger brain, come about?

Signs of the brain power and skill of *Homo erectus* are found in their tools. At 1.5 million years ago stone tools became more varied, including hand-axes and cleavers at Olduvai. At the site, which is a long narrow lake, the remains of a large population of small animals have been found: tortoises, frogs, toads, rodents, fish and birds. Larger forms are also present: pigs, antelopes, bovids and giraffids. This is certainly striking evidence of the first hunters, requiring social organisation and greater intelligence to plan a hunt and kill. This change in diet shows in the dental records: gone are the large cheek teeth, those millstones for grinding grasses and roots, while the front teeth grow sharper and longer, useful for nipping raw flesh. At the same time the brain has become larger and the cranium itself slowly evolves into a spherical shape. It has been claimed that meat-eating was vital to humankind's early development; that without the consumption of raw flesh, the mental development of humans would have been diminished. Meat is a concentrated source of protein in comparison with fruit and vegetables. Though eggs, seeds and nuts are comparable proteins which would have been part of the diet. Besides, we now know that the emphasis on a large amount of protein being a vital part of the diet is wrong. The argument runs that hunters, once they began to eat meat regularly would have had more time free from the search for food to learn new skills. Meat must have freed humans from bondage to their stomachs, allowing them to apply themselves to new puzzles and problems, leading to an ever-greater brain capacity. (And some people still hold that red steak is essential to mental agility and growth from adolescence to maturity.) The survival and evolution of *Homo habilis* and *H. erectus*, while *Australopithecus afarensis* and *A. robustus* died out, have added ammunition to this argument.

But this emphasis on early man, the hunter, underestimates the role of his mate and mother, woman, the gatherer. Rosalind Miles points out that the role of women was fundamental to social organisation and the development of the brain:

> women's invention of food-sharing as part of the extended care of their children must have been at least as important a step towards group cooperation and social organization as the work of man the hunter leader running his band. Women's work as mothers of human infants who need a long growing space for post-natal development also involves them in numerous other aspects of maternal care (sheltering, comforting, diverting), in play, and in social activity with other mothers and other young. All these are decisively shown by modern psychology to enhance what we call IQ, and must have been of critical value in assisting our branching away from the great apes in mental and conceptual ability. Female parents are not the only ones who can comfort, stimulate or play. But all these activities are very far removed from the supposed role of hunting, killing, primitive man.[30]

Further, it should be clear that meat in itself as protein is not much superior to eggs or nuts and could not alter the evolution of the brain; if this were so this miracle food would have continued to enlarge humans' brain size in succeeding years when much greater amounts of meat were consumed. Indeed, if meat promoted encephalisation, presumably the world's carnivorous animals would have become far more intelligent and might by now have been the dominant species. Meat, as we have already discussed, contains the Omega 6 fatty acids obtained from seeds, nuts and plants which are vital for encephalisation, but they must be balanced by an equal amount of Omega 3, which is found in leaves, other green parts of plants, phytoplankton and algae. Hence, a diet largely comprising raw meat without sufficient Omega 3 would not increase encephalisation.

Although evidence of hunting (the bones of the animals often being preserved while plant foodstuffs are not) can give a picture of a solely meat-eating community, this would be a grave distortion as it is thought that the Olduvai communities would have survived by gathering plant foods for the bulk of their diet. Rosalind Miles also points out:

> Of women's duties, food gathering unquestionably came top of the list, and this work kept the tribe alive ... women regularly produce as much as eighty per cent of the tribe's total food intake, on a daily basis. One interpretation of these figures is that in every hunter/gatherer society, the male members were and are doing only one-fifth of the work necessary for the group to survive, while the other four-fifths is carried out entirely by the women.[31]

This view of the hunter males leaving the females behind to gather berries, roots and leaves may be a prejudiced one – it is more likely that hunting was a group activity, with both sexes relying on each other's skills – but the point is that hunting provided only a relatively small proportion of a tribe's food.

★   ★   ★

The traditional interpretation that humankind's evolution reflects its needs as a hunting carnivore is now disproved. The aspects of humans which distinguish them from the primate – upright posture, bipedal locomotion, thumb and index finger precision, expansion of brain power – were all in existence before humans, as hunters and carnivores, really flourished. There is no doubt that humankind came into being sustained on a diet that was almost wholly vegetarian and that afterwards remained substantially so. Jon Wynne Tyson[32] points out various differences between ourselves and carnivores which have developed and persisted over these 23 million years. Carnivores have a short bowel to permit the expulsion of toxins. Vegetarian animals have long bowels to allow for slow digestion and fermentation. Flesh-eaters have long sharp teeth and retractable claws, while their jaws open straight up and down, unlike vegetarians, whose jaws can move in a circular motion for slow mastication. We and other vegetarian mammals sweat through the skin while carnivores keep cool by rapid breathing and extrusion of the tongue.

Throughout these millions of years females must have gathered a huge encyclopaedia of natural knowledge, gathering herbs, flowers and seeds, recognising where they grew, the time of year and the effect on the human body, knowledge which would have been passed on from generation to generation by signs and noises which were the beginning of language. They would have recognised the effect of certain hallucinogens, parts of plants which gave to the people that ate them trances and dreams. They would have recognised the starchy roots and the flavouring seeds, known what was sweet, bitter, peppery or fiery, recognised the leaves that were sedative or the ones that were stimulating. The botanical knowledge must have been vast, passed on to each generation, knowledge that could not be written down; language itself then must have first come about to describe the food that lay in and around the earth, its characteristics and what part of it was to be eaten.

Today, the Amerindian tribes of the Amazon and Orinoco basins have an intimate knowledge of the plants of the rain forest. A few shamans and tribal elders are able to put names on a thousand or more species of plants. European and American botanists not only agree with these species distinctions but also learn a great deal from the Indians themselves. Throughout this early African evolution there were nearly a thousand species of plants which could have been eaten for food.

Hunting animals for meat came very late in our evolution. If you imagine the lifetime of a seventy year old, then it was only nine days before they were seventy that meat eating began and another two and a half days before they ate it cooked.

So how did humans become hunters, willing to kill other creatures for food? It is not difficult to imagine how, over the years and generations, a growing liking for tiny creatures that were easily caught, such as snails, lizards and frogs, could have led to the pursuit of larger birds and animals. Such hunting would have been aided by the human skill of throwing rocks and stones with force and accuracy, a skill that was learnt, it is now believed, by the early hominids, possibly as protection against predators. But Peter Wilson points out that the hominid species evolved the largest and most complex brain relative to body size and that these changes must have come about as adaptive responses to problems in the environment; solving problems is a sign of a growing intelligence and power of reasoning. Food and its acquisition being the main problem, it was in this area that decisions were made:

Early hominids in Africa seem to have been primarily vegetarian and probably preferred grasses, grains, and seeds. But they could equally well have subsisted on leaves and fruits. Either way, any such preference for a staple would bring early hominids into competition with baboons (if they preferred seeds) or with the great apes (if they preferred fruits and leaves). Modern *Homo sapiens* is nowhere near as strong as a chimpanzee or as agile. It is of considerable interest that a large number of baboon bones have been found at australopithecine sites, the implication being that the latter killed the former.[33]

It would seem then that early humans began hunting other creatures not simply out of preference but because they were competing for the main food supply. Wilson goes on:

> Hominids are no more 'naturally' hunters than they are fishers. They are simply competent to hunt, but to turn a dormant competence into a successful performance, early hominids would have had to develop and improve their ability to stalk, hide, and kill.[34]

In other words, killing is not natural to humans, it does not fit either their physical or their dietary nature. Ways and means of hunting and killing were devised simply through necessity and the urge to survive:

> Since nonhuman primates placed in comparable situations quickly develop their competence for tactical thinking and organization when faced with problems of securing a preferred food, it is hardly too far-fetched to suggest that early hominids performed in the same way. We can assert that early hominids had the capacity to develop such a response because we have the evidence of encephalization. Further, there is the circumstantial evidence of Oldowan tools and weapons found in association possibly with *Australopithecus* and indubitably with *Homo habilis* and *erectus*.[35]

Competition for food may also have prompted another response, suggests Wilson:

> the genus *Homo* . . . came into competition with other species, including those of *Australopithecus*, for preferred staple foods (probably vegetable) and found the solution in evading the competition by migration. The pressure was not so much on wants as on tastes, as Hegel succinctly put it. This might have happened because of the very characteristics of the genus that put it at a disadvantage in direct competition. As a generalized creature it could take advantage of environments beyond the reach of more specialized and limited species, but it would have been the weaker opponent of species that were specialized herbivores or carnivores.[36]

## Migration
Indeed, the search for food was to provoke whole populations to migrate further east across the Arabian peninsula to Southern Asia. Migration from central Africa and the gradual colonisation of the rest of the world must have primarily been due to radical climatic changes due to the ice age and the disappearance of food sources. But in this migration humankind discovered

an abundance of marine life for the very first time. Or if you are a believer in the Aquatic Ape theory it would have been for the second time and a return to a natural birthright. Because of the solidifying mass of ice that had crept down from the polar caps the sea's level around the African coast had dropped by a hundred metres; this exposed land bridges between what were once islands which led to other continents. But it also led them to molluscs and seas teeming with fish. It is now that brain encephalisation took place and it is obvious that it was now that the dietary one to one intake of Omega 6 and 3 occurred. Fish was to enter the diet and to remain there. Fish is the important element in the dietary intake which was largely missing before. Any fossils and signs of habitation by *erectus* in that time has, since 6000 BC, been under water. It was only by hugging the coastlines that *erectus* could explore ways of travelling further. Then, when the glaciers melted, as the sea's level rose again, some of the groups of *homo erectus* would have become stranded, surrounded by sea, they would be adapting to its limitations and rediscovering its nutritional wealth.

The search for food – the hunt and new pastures to forage – generates mental activity. The nomadic mind is far more alert, with greater and more acute powers of observation, able to make connections and act upon them swiftly. The nomad also has a keener sense of the past, of what was lived through and what has been left behind, and in such regret or nostalgia are the seeds of legend and myth.

Memory, in the nomadic mind, needs to be reliable. The details of a journey must be accurately observed, to allow its route to be retraced if necessary, but also for signs of favoured pastures and food – often a single plant will tell, in its position in relation to wind, sun, earth and rock, where others might be. Migration exerts far greater pressure on the intellectual response than the known and familiar habitat, for what is alien breeds enquiry and the need to understand and conquer. Also, in this changing environment, there is greater scope and need to teach. Wilson wisely points out the difference between the intelligence of humans and that of the chimpanzees in Goodall's experiments who could learn various tasks, yet could never teach the same tasks to others of their species. He suggests it is reasonable to assume that hominids were not greatly different in their intelligence from primates, that they, too, lacked the ability to impart information, and that it is the ability to teach which signals the divide between human and hominid. Culture is not learned behaviour, he says, but 'taught behaviour', adding: 'it is the development of the art of teaching as an art (or a science or a skill) of culture as a whole that seems to me to be a significantly human accomplishment.'[37]

## The Emergence of Humans

*Homo erectus* had a larger brain and lived as a collection of small families with, it is surmised, a leader. *Homo erectus* also had the power to communicate with each other, though when language as such came into being we cannot tell.

The only clue we find in the hominids and pongids is the position of the larynx relative to the rest of the respiratory tract. In humans, compared with primates, the larynx is low, allowing a long tubular resonating cavity. The structure of the chimpanzee larynx, for example, does not allow it to make many of the sounds needed for human speech. It has been suggested that the hominids were able to make vowel sounds and non-linguistic vocalisations and that consonants were added as the hominids developed more control by manipulating tongues, lips and teeth. As *Australopithecus afarensis* flourished for over four million years, mainly as fructivores, their speech must have been fairly well developed to have enabled them to organise life around a lake, with gathering expeditions and defence against predators; though no doubt language as we know it, a complex system of symbols with countless combinations, a means by which we can store and transmit knowledge, allowing us to gain from experience and plan for the future, developed gradually over millions of years.

It would appear true that progress is not constant. For millions of years, if climate, environment and the social context are favourable, a species can remain almost stable. Then some change in that environment can radically alter the climate and food supply, thus stimulating the organism into a challenge to find new pastures, new homes. The larger brain size of *Homo erectus*, the first hunters, implies a radical change that involved decisions and planning which sharply divided them from the vegetarian hominids before. One concise theory states that *Homo erectus* thought their way out of trouble, while *Australopithecus robustus* chewed and in that docility declined and vanished.

We now live in a time when progress is rapid. The surge of knowledge since the Renaissance, culminating in advanced technology, the exploration of space and the manipulation of DNA, seems to have partially blinded us to a more profound truth about our relationship with the earth. Professor Popper comments:

> The greatest achievements of humanity lie in the past. They include the invention of language and of the use of artificial tools for making other artefacts; the use of fire as a tool; the discovery of the consciousness of self and of other selves, and the knowledge that we all have to die.[38]

It is impossible to say whether *Homo erectus* discovered the consciousness of self but they achieved the rest. There are remains of *Homo erectus* in southern France at Terra Amata. They hunted in organised bands and shared food with the rest of the group, even the weak. The skeleton of a twelve-year-old boy, 5 feet 6 inches tall, would point to an adult height of six feet. Its healthy bones and teeth suggest a plentiful and balanced diet. Hunting skills kept *Homo erectus* well fed in a variety of environments: Europe, Asia, China, Java. Fire kept them warm, and cooked their meat, which they were now skilled at butchering. Dental evidence shows that *Homo erectus* had a less powerful jaw, for cooked meat is easier to consume than raw. At Terra Amata shells of limpets, oysters and mussels were found, as well as the bones of red deer, elephants, wild boars, mountain goats and even rhinoceroses. It is also possible that the discovery of fire (around 500,000 years ago, it is thought) could have provided a further stimulus to migration into colder climes and more meat-eating because there was a great deal less edible plant food; that humans as carnivores only came into real maturity once meat could be cooked.

It was never clear in evolutionary terms how *Homo erectus* could possibly have merged into *Homo sapiens neanderthalensis* (so named after the site where their remains were first discovered, in 1856, the Neander Valley, near Düsseldorf). Now it is thought that, like *Australopithecus*, *neanderthalensis* were an independent and co-existing branch, thriving in the same areas as *Homo erectus* as distinct species though their beginnings are as recent as 250,000 years ago. *Homo sapiens neanderthalensis* also migrated across Europe and Asia, and there is no doubt that they represent the zenith of humankind as carnivores. These strong, vigorous people, with larger brains than our own, lived throughout the Ice Ages and survived by being inventive and resourceful – and by hunting and the use of fire. Evidence in caves shows that fires were kept alive all the time, and that shelters were made from animal skins stretched across a framework of mammoth bones and tusks. There was not much opportunity to be vegetarian for ice and snow would have covered the ground for most of the year. (In fact, this high-protein diet, with few fresh vegetables or green leaves, led to scurvy, rickets and arthritis. Lack of sunlight, from living in caves through long bleak winters, must also have been a primary cause of afflictions. Their life expectancy was twenty-nine.\*) Though meat was primarily a source of food, it was also attractive as part of a structure of newly learnt skills. Animals which kept to particular tracks and pastures at different times of the year, returning at the same times each year, added form and detail to the known cosmos of early humans, and came to be manipulated and dominated by them. Nothing is more comforting than the thought of power and control over one's environment. Not to make tools, not to migrate and trek, not to hunt and kill other creatures, would seem like a return to a lesser, more primitive state of development. For early humans this godlike power over the lives of other creatures may have led, too, to a belief in 'gods' that had such power over themselves.

It is certainly thought that *Homo sapiens neanderthalensis* were aware of their own mortality, for they buried their dead together with gifts. We have evidence from the Shanidar caves in northern Iraq of several bodies buried on beds of twigs entwined with flowers. In the same cave skeletons of the very old and handicapped seem to show a compassion for the weak and

---

\*Life expectancy has always been, until recently, very low: Neanderthal, 29; Cro-Magnon, 32; Neolithic, 38; Roman, 32; medieval, 48; until 1900, 48; until 1940, 69.

infirm. The burial objects indicate a belief in an after-life and in the existence of a soul, or at least of another world, where the shades of the dead are sustained by their burial gifts. They must have seen eternity much as the ancient Egyptians did.

It is impossible to say when the first myths about the role of humankind, their creation and destiny, were generated as explanations of the enigma of existence. The most tentative ideas on dating have suggested that myth-making must have begun after the advent of agriculture, as so many myths explain the seasonal fertility of the soil. Yet there is surely in these Neanderthal burials a belief in the continuance of life, and stories and events must have been recounted and depicted in dramas and ritual. The birth of legend may be even more distant, but at least here in the caves of Shanidar are our first intimations of it.

Common to all religions is the idea of the Golden Age, the paradise before the Fall. This period of peaceful co-existence between early humankind and the other creatures of the earth would have been non-violent and vegetarian, so there must have been within the race memory of early humans a knowledge of their herbivore past when no blood was shed, a distant memory of peace and plenty. Indeed, the rain forests of the Miocene, in those flourishing days of mammal expansion, might even have been free of dangerous predators. Wilson argues that the Golden Age could just as likely represent an impossible ideal never attained, but I strongly believe that myths stem from a wish to explain phenomena, suffering and distant memories which are passed through story-telling from one generation to the next. If killing, aggression and the consumption of raw, bloody meat were the only truth of our distant past, that vision of a Golden Age would never have appeared in legend.

At some time from 100,000 years ago humankind appears, whether in the guise of Neanderthal, *Homo erectus* or Cro-Magnon: humans as migrators and myth-makers; with a soul, rituals, a sense of aesthetics and a sense of mission; humans as teachers and survivors – survivors perhaps because they are also omnivores. The evidence now points to the possibility that humans would not have survived if at this crucial time of climatic change they had not augmented their diet with meat. The consumption of salt by hominid or *Homo* would tell us whether raw meat was eaten as an integral part of the diet or not, for all herbivores have to eat salt, while the Inuit, who exist on a diet of raw meat, have an aversion to salt. Salt will give us a clue to later meat-eating habits even if this crucial prehistoric era keeps its secrets.

As mentioned above, it is now thought in some quarters that *Homo sapiens neanderthalensis* were not a direct ancestor of *Homo sapiens* but, like *Australopithecus robustus* and *A. afarensis*, were an evolutionary cul-de-sac which died out. Neanderthal burial remains in the Kebara Cave in Israel have been dated to between 60,000 and 48,000 years ago, at which time

Cro-Magnon* or *Homo sapiens sapiens* were already living in the southern
Levant. Why should Neanderthals die out while Cro-Magnon, our direct
ancestors, lived on? Anthropologists are inclined to say that they were better
adapted to their environment, without saying exactly how. Diet must surely
be one factor. Cro-Magnon living in the Middle East in a more temperate
clime would have eaten greater amounts of plants and fruit than
Neanderthals in the icy wastes of Europe. This better-balanced diet may
explain why Cro-Magnon thrived, but not how, in Europe, about 40,000
years ago, Neanderthals began to decline. Dr Christopher Stringer has little
doubt that the Cro-Magnon were far more clever in the competition for the
limited food resources of the Ice Age and in the organisation of their
communities to cope with the environment. One theory proposed by Ezra
Zubrow (of the State University of New York, Buffalo) is that an increase in
the mortality rate in a community of 1% is all that is needed for their
extinction within thirty generations or one millennium. But Colin Tudge
has touched on another fundamental truth, namely that hunter-gatherers
need to know the natural history of several thousand plants (where they
grow and which part of the plant is edible at which time of year) and of
several hundred animals (their feeding habits and migrating patterns).[39] All
this information must be remembered, learnt by the young and passed on by
the old. The theory of morphic resonance[40] is of some help in explaining
how this vast knowledge is stored, stating that some knowledge is so inherent
within us that it must be passed on genetically like a data bank. This theory
has caused controversy and has attracted fierce criticism.

Tudge suggests an explanation for the unchanging stability of some
periods. He thinks that early humans, like modern aborigines, regarded
knowledge as finite, accepting the mysteries around them without
intellectual enquiry. This would explain those huge periods when the
archaeological record shows human culture to have changed very little.
*Homo erectus* appeared two million years ago and stayed much the same for
one million years. The first signs of archaic *Homo sapiens* appeared 250,000
years ago, but there was little cultural progress until 35,000 years ago, when
better tools were developed and experiments were possibly made with
cultivation and domestication. (It is thought dogs became part of the human
community at this time.) Tudge says: 'It must have dawned on them that
knowledge was not finite, but that they could find out things by thinking
. . . they realised that their brains were far more powerful than they had
hitherto acknowledged.'[41] This attitude, he points out, was essential to set
humankind on the road to cultivation rather than hunting. Hence it was the
new thinkers amongst *Homo sapiens sapiens*, who migrated across Asia and

---

*So-called because the first skeleton was discovered, in 1868, in a rock shelter at Cro-
Magnon, in the Dordogne, France. Considered to be a modern variety of *Homo sapiens*
characteristically European in skeletal anatomy, it is said that the Guanches of the Canary
Islands represent the last pure Cro-Magnon stock. In discussions of prehistory, Cro-Magnon
is a term applied only to those remains of *Homo sapiens sapiens* found in Europe.

Europe bringing a new technology and new solutions to old problems, that slowly ousted sturdy Neanderthal.

Any study of hunter-gatherer tribes gives us many clues as to how our ancestors would have behaved. Of particular interest are hunter-gatherer practices of the American Indians, which were highly motivated by a sense of conservation. It was a law among them, for example, not to kill more game than was necessary for their consumption. For a society to plan wisely for the future a detailed knowledge of the past is necessary, not only through acute observation of the habits and details of animals and plants, but also through empathy with the creatures themselves, a feeling of kinship with the plants. None of the hunter-gatherers studied make maximum use of all the potentially available food. Custom and belief proscribe certain foods or limit their consumption; taboos are thought to have magical consequences for the individual – to observe them will ensure health and strength. Food taboos are particularly apposite at crucial times for the individual or the group: pregnancy, illness or a threat from an enemy. Quite often prohibitions are placed upon foods which are difficult or dangerous to procure – the greater the danger, the more rare, desirable and magical the food and the greater its benefit to the consumer.

We are generally led to see only the advantages of being an omnivore. Being able to select from a wide range of foods is a major contributory factor to our survival, yet there is also the major disadvantage that within us is no overall genetic prerecognition of which foods will harm us or not. We are unlike other creatures whose jaws, digestive systems and whole bio-chemistry can work only with particular nutrients. For example, the bodies of the large cat carnivores are built up from biochemicals which plant foods cannot supply. The genetic blueprint grows inside the seed, egg or womb. Diet is so important to the particular living organism that if, for example, a gene change programmed a cow to see in the dark like a cat, such a change would be nullified by the dearth of nutrients which are needed to build complex eyes before it left the womb. Our genetic imprint allows for a wide range of foods which supply a mix of nutrients (carbohydrates, fats and protein). Deficiencies in any of them or an imbalance between them in the diet of a pregnant mother will affect the embryo. But in the search for food our genetic imprint is of little help. Anything possible is consumed and we have to rely on experience, to learn to accept or reject a food on the basis of its later metabolic reactions in our bodies. Hunger, propelling us to eat, and fear of poisoning telling us not to, are the two opposing forces still within human nature. The empirical diet of early humans must have discovered deadly toxins as well as medicines and hallucinogens. Our only guides were the impulse to sweetness, the longing for salt and an initial revulsion to bitterness, the last often a warning of toxicity – hence our caution with new foods, our reluctance to try anything strange and our obstinacy in sticking to foods we know. These preferences must have determined what came to be seen as beneficial or harmful to the social group. Conventions and taboos, concerning both meat and plants, still exist today, of course, though in a far more complex form than would have been the case for these early hunter-gatherers. But what is pertinent is that conventions and taboos cannot exist without an abundance of food; nor can the choice not to eat meat be made without a range of alternative foods on which to survive.

Placing the evolution of humankind in the context of its ecology has not been popular until very recently. But Robert Foley[42] suggests that though shifts in habitat promote change in the organism, those shifts must not be too rapid or severe, for the indigenous species either migrates or dies out. He looks at two of the characteristics of humans today which separate us from our ancestors: large social groups with a considerable kin-based substructure and high dietary selectivity. He then asks what ecological circumstances might promote such differences, and concludes: 'These characteristics are most likely to occur in patchy environments where food is both of high quality and predictable.' To ensure the predictability of food, a community must plan ahead, polish and invent new technology, organise foraging. All this, which needs intellectual expertise, will reduce the unpredictability of the environment.

## Gathering Food

We can speculate on what the early gatherer consumed because of ethnographic evidence from tribes that still eat from the wild.[43] In the early spring foods are limited, but there are a range of plants that store their nutrition over the winter for their growing season which is about to begin. The onion family, for example, what a boon those sharp fiery aromatic bulbs must have been and we find many myths attached to both onion and garlic as to their magical and healing properties. They were right, as we now know. Plants of the lily family, its close cousin, the rhizomes of Solomon's Seal lie near the surface. The liking for bulbs continued for centuries, they were certainly eaten in Classical Greece. The rhizomes of bracken can be dried and ground into a flour. Water plants were also a rich source of flour, the tubers of the yellow water-lily in Ancient Egypt were all dried, ground, mixed and baked. Fireweed, a common enough herb, the core of the stem can be used as flour, the gelatinous pith is sometimes eaten raw, later cooked as a soup and the roots can be eaten as a vegetable

In early spring, as soon as the first frost fades, the roots of the trees begin to take up water and then the sap starts to flow up the trunks. Sap is rich in sugars from the starch that has been stored over winter, and this is a valuable food source. Hominids must have discovered this by peeling the outer layer of bark away and licking the sweet layer beneth. We are familiar with maple syrup, but other species of trees: birches, lime, aspen, as well as other maples, all produce abundant sap. A week or so later in spring plants start to send up their shoots; these are highly nutritious as we know when we sprout seeds or beans, for they contain the growing energy of the plant. Asparagus is one of the few plants we still eat at this stage, sea kale is another, Good King

Henry should also be blanched and eaten then and not later as some Herbals advise. In the forest many shoots would blanch naturally beneath a covering of leaves. Bellwort, common pokeberry, sea holly, bracken, all have edible shoots. Also, baby pine cones and buds of trees, such as lime, were a rich source of protein.

Deciduous forests, at this time of year, contain an important food, called cambium. In the spring, the trunks of trees begin to widen due to a single layer of cells – the cambium – which ensheaths the trunk. These young cells are rich in protein and carbohydrate, the exterior bark of the tree would have been cut away and the new moist cambium scraped off. Such removal of living tissue, if scraped away in a ring, would of course have killed the tree; no doubt this was learnt through trial and error. Cambium is still eaten today, we know it as Slippery Elm. Up to very recent times a bark bread was made from cambrium in Scandinavia from an elm (*Ulmus Glabra*). Bark is often mentioned as being eaten by primates; no one bothers to tell you that it is this highly sweet moist substance, like maple syrup toffee, which is consumed so greedily. There is a tendency in our modern world to make out that eating from the wild is both difficult and unappetising, yet when we try it we all think how delicious it is.

In late spring and early summer new green leaves could be eaten, roots were pounded into a paste, the mucilaginous leaves like mallow, were useful in holding disparate ingredients together long before fire was discovered. For I am sure that composing a dish, mixing say herbs, onions and a pounded root together, using a natural rock or stone basin long predates cooking over a flame.

Particular families of plants have been always favoured, (*Umbelliferae*), the parsley family, which includes the wild carrot and parsnip, rock samphire, fennel and another member, never eaten now, the Earth-nut or Pig-nut (*Conopodium majus*); this is a small edible tuber which has never been cultivated but it has always been considered delicious. The seeds of the buckwheat family (*Polygonaceae*) are highly nutritious, rhubarb and dock were eaten and sorrel, with its astringent fruity flavour, must have delighted early foragers. Another member of this family, the root and leaves of bistort (*Polygonum bistorta*) was still used until recently in Yorkshire as the major ingredient in Dock Pudding – though this only uses the leaves. The root is soaked to steep out the tannin, then it was dried and ground into a flour, but the first young shoots were eaten as well.

Throughout the spring and summer, flowerbuds were gathered, especially the largest like the water-lily (*Nympaea*). Then once flowering is over, it is the seeds which become a rich source of food, the dandelion, the vetches and all of the grasses. Berries and soft fruits are almost too obvious to mention but their sweetness one imagines would have been welcomed, for we have no idea how early the gathering of wild honey began. However fossilised bees have been found in Baltic amber some 50 million years ago. Honey is also mentioned in all the myths as one of the foods that the heroes were given by the gods.

Then in late summer the miraculous mushroom appeared where nothing existed before. Plants growing near the sea and the estuaries were rich in minerals, as these were washed down from the mountains and then used by the plants. For example Rock Samphire, still growing around our coasts and now ignored, was for centuries pickled and sent to London, and was highly prized.

When winter is threatening the problem is to find foods that store – nuts are the obvious answer. Hazel nuts, walnut, sweet chestnut, pine nuts, hickories, beechnuts and of course acorns. For the oak was the dominant tree of all the temperate forests. Roasting or boiling acorns destroys their bitterness, and the tannin has to be extracted, so acorns as a winter staple could only appear after the discovery of fire. If the ground was not frozen hard, bulbs and tubers could be dug up; there is also evidence of winter storage of seeds as well as nuts and the drying of fruits, currants and wild strawberries. The fungi were also of immense value at this time, especially the large ones like (*Fistulina hepatica*) a massive bracket fungus which grows on trees. We must not also forget lichens like the reindeer moss (*Cladonia rangiferina*) which is one of the staple foods of reindeer and caribou. There were algae too growing over ponds and lakes, the Aztecs gathered a blue-green algae (*Cyanophyta*) and dried it making it into cakes which stored well.

But of course gathering and foraging is haphazard, there is an enormous element of luck, food sources can so easily be wiped out by floods, frosts and earthquakes, or by herds of grazing animals. How much more preferable it would be for humankind if they could control their food supply, if it could be grown near their shelter. The impulse to settle and garden must have been there among small clans and individuals worldwide long before it actually began. Indeed, the years when domestication began have steadily in the last few decades receded from 9000 BC to 14000 BC and they were certainly herding moufflon sheep (therefore milking them for cheese) from the caves of North Africa as early as 35,000 BC.

## Taming the Environment

The first settlements were by the seashore where the food supply was constant. One might think that in an environment where food was plentiful and its supply predictable it would be but a short step to cultivation and the domestication of animals. However, such radical changes tend to occur so slowly that they are quite imperceptible to those involved.

First, the environment bore the imprint of travelling peoples: tracks through forest, temporary settlements near the seashore, rivers and lakes. Then the plants to be cultivated needed the particular environment which humans created. These plants all had 'weedy tendencies'; they were unable to grow in dense forest among perennial trees and shrubs, needing open and disturbed habitats with thin, bare soil and little competition from other plants. They had to have soil high in nitrogen, to germinate and grow quickly and to be able to mature their seeds before the height of summer would dry out the ground, so their growth had to occur between the rains of spring and the middle of summer. Those plants growing around settlements where the thin soil was manured by people and animals more or less offered themselves to be tended and eaten. They were there for the picking. Hawkes comments:

> To primitive man it must have seemed little short of miraculous to find that plants needed for food sprang up by his very huts and paths. Perhaps it is not too far-fetched to suggest that this situation might have been the basis for so many folk legends which attributed the beginnings of agriculture and the introduction of useful plants to gods or supernatural beings.[44]

It is thought that a relatively rapid climatic change was a direct or indirect factor in domestication. A general warming in south-western Asia was noticeable by 12,000 BC. Trees such as oak and pistachio were beginning to invade the foothills of this area and this continuous shift of vegetation moved upward to hill and mountain while animals gradually populated areas which were too cold for them before. In the Near East it took little more than a thousand years for people to move out of caves and build villages and to begin reaping and milling wild cereals while domesticating animals.

Village life cannot be sustained unless there is an established water supply and a food source. A small society could depend upon some highly nutritious plant, cereal grains or nuts like acorns, which could be gathered, dried, reduced to powder and stored over winter. The first plants to be domesticated were cereals, wheat★ and barley. In Thessaly oats and millet may also have come into cultivation very early. Pulses such as peas and lentils, vetch, as well as flax were all activated before 5,000 BC. But it is thought that before all these plants flourished there was a long period of experimentation.

As the voluntary abstinence from killing animals and eating their meat is based in the ancient world on spiritual values and beliefs, on the world that was invisible but which controlled the material, visible world, it is necessary then to examine how such beliefs could possibly have come into existence. I would suggest that they are entwined with dominance and power and that both domestication and architecture are integral to them. It was at this time that the eating of meat became a convention, part of the structure of social life, and was elevated to the top of the hierarchy of consumption as a celebration meal surrounded by dogma and ritual. It is likely that meat-eating has always tended to occupy this position. Hunter-gatherer societies always share meat with everyone in the group, but not plant foods, which appear to be consumed by those people that collected them. Hunter-gatherers would only occasionally have eaten meat, for there would not

---

★Three species of wheat became established – *Triticum monococcum*, *Triticum dicoccum* and *Triticum aestivum* – and both hulled and naked varieties of two- and six-row barley.

always have been a ready supply. With the domestication of animals this would change, but only for the ruling elite.

What stimulus could have persuaded hunter–gatherers to modify their way of life and to adopt agriculture? Only, one would imagine, the discovery of an abundance of food in their midst. Wild cereals were gathered and roasted in northern Israel at least 33,000 years ago, though the first signs of vegetable preparation are in upper Egypt, where stone pestles and mortars, used for grinding up wild tubers and roots, have been found dated at 20,000 years ago.

Around 20,000 BC, in the Upper Palaeolithic period, a much greater variety of food was consumed: fish, crabs, water turtles, molluscs, land snails, partridges, migratory water fowl and wild cereal grains. Though nearly everything was viewed as food and a variety of small game was eaten, the hunting of hoofed mammals still provided 90% of human meat intake. At the same time small grinding stones, used for grinding wild cereals, and storage facilities have been found in caves. These storage pits were suitable for grains, acorns or pistachios, though grain might also have been roasted in the pits over heated pebbles.

The first signs of agriculture, also from northern Israel, date back 13,000 years. Flint sickle blades have been unearthed which were used to cut wild barley and emmer wheat. These sickles were used by the Natufians, who made tools out of flint and bone, lived in small villages in houses with stone foundations and lived up to the astonishing age of fifty (see footnote, p.24). Although their development of agriculture was accidental rather than by design,[45] the cultivation of crops was an insurance against the inadequacy of food gathering, as at this period planted and unplanted cereals were of the same wild genetic type. However, their diet was not restricted to cereals: they ate gazelle, deer, ibex, acorns, pistachio nuts, fish and snails.

There is no sign of voluntary vegetarianism in the beginnings of agriculture. But, because of hardship, inexperience and the fact that everything had to be learnt by trial and error, it is likely that the majority of the first farmers were involuntary vegetarians for much of the time. Even after the domestication of animals meat would have been kept for sacrifice, ritual and celebration (they would hardly have wanted to kill their herds or flocks off regularly), eaten more often perhaps by the ruling elite.★ The latter, too, were the ones who had the time and leisure for hunting and ensuring a steady supply of wild game.

In the history of the human decision whether to eat meat, the change from hunter to domesticator was a major behavioural shift: by selecting the plants to be cultivated and the animals to be reared, humans were now

---

★Wilson comments that the first farmers were almost certainly predominantly vegetarian, using milk and blood and keeping meat for ritual occasions. He recalls: 'I lived with the cattle-keeping Tsimihety in Madagascar and they did not even milk their cows and ate meat solely on ritual occasions, about twelve times a year.'[46]

limiting the range of their diet. The first domestic animals were all mammals: the dogs, pigs, sheep, goats and cattle. The first two eat a wide variety of plants and animal material including offal and carrion, while the rest eat materials like leaves and grass which we cannot digest. So three of the first four domestic animals did not compete with humans for the food supply, but ate food we could not use ourselves. All of the animals could interbreed quite successfully with their wild ancestors and all, if treated kindly when young, could be easily tamed. The dog and the pig are in direct competition with man for food, particularly at times of scarcity, so it is likely that in order for them to be domesticated as they were there must have been a considerable surplus of food in those Middle Eastern areas where domestication first occurred.

The domestic bovid (cow, sheep and goat) can convert such unpromising foods as dry grass, leaves, straw, twigs and green fodder when it is available – foods high in cellulose which humans cannot digest – into carbohydrates, fats and proteins, in the form of animal milk and flesh, that humans can use. Further, they are valuable as a source of hides, horn, hair and wool. The domestication of animals marks the legitimising of regular slaughter. Animals were bred for specific purposes, and some inevitably were killed before they reached sexual maturity. In the harsher conditions of the wild the weak and the sick of any herd are isolated more quickly and grow sick or die. Males without females either fight for the right to have one, get killed or go rogue and wander off. But with domesticated animals the problem is always what to do with the males, the first priority being to select the strongest and finest specimens for stud purposes and to castrate the rest. Modern ethnographists have recorded a number of horrific castration practices[47] which illustrate how domesticated animals have suffered untold cruelty from the earliest times. Domestication was a logical extension of the dominance of humans. To keep other creatures in captivity and to govern their lives from birth through breeding and feeding to slaughter bestows a sense of power upon the owner. It is not difficult to see how the man who collected the largest herds would become the most influential and most powerful in the community.

One can also see how, in a community structured around the number of cattle owned by its inhabitants, the idea that their meat was unnecessary to human survival would seem heretical – it would be not simply a criticism of meat-eating but a criticism of power. Power itself would also come to mean moral worth and therefore to deserve reverence. Not to eat meat, or to frown on the captivity and killing of animals, went to the heart of society.

## Surplus Food

The first crops were not all edible, for both they and livestock yield natural fibres for making rope, nets, wool for spinning, clothing and blankets. A surplus in this and in food is highly significant. Once it exists new characters start to play a role within the group. A surplus provides one with rulers and bureaucrats.[48] Nomadic hunters and gatherers are egalitarian, each human performs part of the work of collecting food and helping the group to survive; they are all on equal terms. But once food can be stored, some members of the group have been freed to build houses or roads, to make tools and weapons, to count and make note of the food stockpile, to arrange for it to be guarded from thieves, to form an army, to build ships to cross rivers and seas, explore and invade different territory.

The first written record we have are the clay tablets unearthed in Crete which were deciphered in the 1950's. These do not tell the tale of myths and legends and dwell on the mystery of existence, no, they are simply lists, the account books of a lost society. Inscribed here are lists of women, children, tradesmen, rowers, troops, flocks of sheep and goats, grain, oil, spices, land leases and yields, tribute, ritual offerings, cloth, vessels, furniture, bronze, chariots and helmets.[49]

All of this complicated social activity is itself organised by bureaucrats and finally controlled by a ruler. They, of course, live off the stored food surplus. Once beasts of burden had been domesticated humankind could travel and colonise territory with more speed and efficiency. Cows and horses were hitched to carts, while camels could carry huge loads and go great distances without water. One of the most urgent motivations to travel into the unknown, to cross deserts, oceans and high mountain ranges, was the desire for new and exciting foods. I believe trade routes in foods and cloth began early, soon after the discovery of pack animals and their control by humankind. Lastly, but very importantly, a central constant food supply meant a huge population explosion, babies no longer had to be carried for the first few years of their life, so women could bear children more frequently. A surplus of food and goods marks the first step towards our modern society.

There is no doubt that successful domestication radically changed our diet, some would say not always for the good. Daily sustenance was now at hand. In the settlement of Catal Huyuk (around 6500 BC) two kinds of wild vetch were grown as fodder for the goats, sheep and cattle. They grew barley, emmer wheat and einkorn and had saddle querns for grinding those grains, out of them they made porridge and flat breads. They probably used acorns for starting the yoghourt and the fermented goat's milk that is still drunk in Turkey. They grew field peas and lentils (both can be dried and stored throughout the winter) and obtained oil from shepherd's purse (*Capsella bursa pastoris*) and another crucifer (*Erysimum sisymbriodes*). There was plenty of wild game and wild fruits, apples, olives, grape, figs and date, for these were not domesticated until later, there was also wild cabbage, fava bean, rocket, onions and garlic. Many other vegetables and herbs must have been grown in the garden plots around the settlement. This is a society which has a lively and organised trade, religious ritual, crafts and ceramics.[50]

What was lost in this diet was diversity. The wild foods that were abandoned with domestication were mostly wild seeds and nuts, at the site of Abu Hureyra on the Middle Euphrates (10,500 to 6,500 BC) the hunter gatherers of the early Mesolithic used at least 120 seed foods, but by the end of the Neolithic, the farmers used only 5 seeds, 3 cereals and 2 pulses.[51] Apparently such a reduction in the range of foods affected human stature and some authorities can cite evidence of malnutrition in skeletal remains. Deficiencies could have occurred in the essential fatty acids and in amino acids like lysine. As only 200 generations separate us from the last hunter gatherers we are in evolutionary terms still adapted to the broad spectrum hunter gatherer diet.

## Altars and Gardens

There can be little doubt that regular and celebratory meat-eating was fused indissolubly with power. Meat consumption was the conspicuous display of dominant ruling power. The more cattle slaughtered, cooked and eaten, the greater the man and hence the greater the community. Not to invest this display of greatness, of the right to kill or not to kill, with greater ritual was to ignore a major part of what impressed society most. For killing was not a simple matter; death, after all, had enormous significance. How to kill, where to kill and in what manner – in private, among a select group, or in public, in front of everyone? With words and music, prayers and dance? And, most important of all, if not outside, in which building? Killing needed a suitable setting.

Peter Wilson, in a powerful argument, suggests the importance of buildings in the domestication of humans, that in fact even the most primitive of shelters clustered together became a language read by the group: 'In domesticated societies the house and the village are the fusion of microcosm and macrocosm, body and world, individual and collective, and at the same time, they are the presentation of these abstractions to everyday life.'[52] He goes on to quote Levi-Strauss on the Bororo of Brazil, who were persuaded by missionaries to abandon their circular villages and to build new huts in parallel rows:

> Once they had been deprived of their bearings and were without the plan which acted as confirmation of their native lore, the Indians soon lost any feeling for tradition; it was as if their social and religious systems ... were too complex to exist without the pattern which was embodied in the plan of the village and of which their awareness was constantly being refreshed by their everyday activities.[53]

Very early remains of settlements show that around each hut there was a space for a walled or fenced garden, enough perhaps to grow some vegetables or to keep a few animals: 'The enclosed yard or garden was in many parts of the prehistoric world the primary mode of economic domestication. In most New World areas gardening preceded agriculture and, as in the island civilizations of Polynesia, was the primary subsistence mode.'[54]

Gardens close to or adjacent to the dwelling where food plants were grown were necessary to the care with which families were reared. Plants for specific ailments would be fostered with particular tenderness; such places would be enclosed by fences or walls to stop livestock or predators trampling and eating the plants. These fences and walls and the buildings themselves provided for the first time an area of privacy, where an individual could hide from the sight of the neighbours. The new physical privacy must also have given time for private thought, for deliberation over the great enigmas of life.

Domestication brought a shift in the spiritual emphasis which humans bequeathed to animals. Firstly, animals must be sacrificed to the gods before man could eat them:

> The consumption of meat actually coincides with the offering to the gods of a domestic animal whose flesh is reserved for men, leaving to divinity the smoke of the calcined bones and the scent of spices burned for the occasion. The division is thus clearly made on the alimentary plane between men and gods. Men receive the meat because they need to consume perishable flesh, of which they themselves consist, in order to live. Gods have the privilege of smells, perfumes, incorruptible substances that make up the superior foods reserved for the deathless powers.[55]

Killing and by extension the meat itself are invested with spiritual significance, and blood, spilt in the act of killing, takes on the mystical semblance of the source of life.

The immediate ancestors of domesticated humans were the hunter-gatherers who, it is reasonable to suppose, were either animistic believing all plants and animals had spirit, like humans – or totemistic – so that an animal or plant becomes a focal symbol for the tribe or community, which entails that various forms of behaviour are prohibited and so become taboo. Before a hunt the American Indian would pray for the spirit of the animal. We still do not know what the cave paintings at Lascaux and other places signify, but even across 30,000 years they strike us as having religious significance, as if the painter has somehow transferred the animals' spirits on to the wall to render them immortal. Wild animals to the prehistoric hunter must have seemed free spirits, creatures worthy of respect, gifted with senses – hearing, smell and vision – greater than those of humans.

As humans became more domesticated, meat did not have to be hunted – it grunted at the side of the dwelling or was rounded up at night. A captive animal was already half tamed and its mystery, an inherent spur to mysticism, had disappeared. Animals, once domesticated, were not seen as animals, but were investment, wealth, sustenance and survival, part of the human struggle to exist. Sacrifice on the bloody altar became the most significant fact of the animal's existence. Hence the family that slaughtered its last pig at the end of autumn, in order to survive through the winter, had stopped seeing the pig as a living creature; instead it was their own future.

When human survival is so wedded to animals, voluntarily to abstain from meat is actually to question human survival itself But when other food which makes slaughter unnecessary is abundant, some people feel uncertain that animals should be killed to feed themselves. Certainly, among some of those men and women who had chosen to become the priests of a community, who had taken a step away from it, an abstention from meat (even specific animals) began to creep into the tenets of religious belief. Not to eat meat, but simply to smell the aromas, was to become god-like, a sign of piety. Within the haven of religious institutions such behaviour was tolerated. We do not know for certain how early such taboos against flesh-eating began, but in Egypt there could have been vegetarian priestly sects that date back to the Old Kingdom – 3,200 BC (see Chapter 2). Meat-eating had, by then, become an integral part of the structure of society, manifest in methods of rearing, control of livestock, ritual slaughter, buildings – from barns to sacrificial altars – and in its sculpture and mythology.

Those who abstained from meat, if not religiously orthodox, would have to find a reason for their abstention that seemed not to be a condemnation of society itself. They had to find some divine sanction which would vindicate their behaviour in the eyes of the community. Nothing but a reinterpretation of the nature of god or of the gods would do, or, at least, an explanation of the invisible world which could gather all living things into it and give them equal spiritual value.

Yet for abstinence from meat to be practised at all, certain factors within a community had to exist. There had to be a plentiful and predictable supply of alternative foods to meat. Therefore abstention from the slaughter and consumption of animals could be possible only in a settled society with a tradition of domestication, with regular, if not always abundant, harvests of cereals, with soil fertile enough to grow fruit and vegetables, and with a temperate climate. In areas which are too cold to sustain much vegetable or cereal growth, animals or fish have to be eaten to survive.

A specific vegetarian ideology, therefore, cannot exist without a settled habitat with no foreseeable climatic changes, and it must have a view of the world and the destiny of humankind which earns respect from its community, even if it has few adherents. These factors were as true in 7,000 BC as they are in AD 2,000.

# 2

# Pythagoras
# and His Inheritance

One remarkable man at the end of the sixth century BC bequeathed to the diet which precludes meat his own name. This name was used throughout the Mediterranean countries and across Europe until the middle of the nineteenth century; it was used in Christian medieval Europe as a term of abuse and by the poet Shelley to describe an ideal way of life. The Pythagorean diet came to mean an avoidance of the flesh of slaughtered animals, but it was no more precise than that. It may originally have been vegan – what evidence we have suggests that Pythagoras' own diet was – but historically it often included dairy products and may also have included fish. At times historical records are vague on the actual ingredients of some diets, giving merely an impression of them.

But first let us look at the foods of Greece in that early period around the sixth millennium. We know that sheep and goats were herded and cows were used as draught animals, that the milk from sheep and goats was used to make cheese and yoghurt. Cows were too valuable as beasts of burden for their milk to be taken from the calves, after a lifetime's labour their meat, bones, horn and hides were used and treasured. We know that fish and shellfish played a central part in the diet, as would be expected in a country composed so much of islands. The remains of tunny, pike, carp, oysters, sea urchins and clams have all been discovered, snails too were an early food. They ate wild almonds, wild figs, pears, sloes, blackberries, arbutus and pistachios; they cultivated peas, wheat, lentils and barley. Wild pig, deer, ibex and hare were all hunted, ducks and geese were eaten as well as pigeon, partridge and peacock, the last two appearing in Minoan murals.[1] There was a large range of food and as slowly the olive tree and grapevines began to be cultivated in the second millennium food reached in the Golden Age heights of gastronomy that we would eagerly respond too. To abstain from any part of such a diet was a profoundly serious act.

To understand the significance of the Pythagorean abstention from meat we must first look at the society of early Greece and at the significance of meat itself.

## Meat in Homer

The *Iliad* portrays two worlds, one in which warrior heroes engage in fierce combat over Troy and another, pastoral, world of peace and agricultural productivity, where the community has no enemies. In reality an army in antiquity lived off the land, foraging expeditions were needed to provision the forces, and much of what the armies ate was stolen. Hard barley biscuit was the basic ration supplemented with onions, cheese and, if you were lucky, eggs and small game birds. Meat was eaten only at religious festivals or by the nobility who owned the great herds of cattle which betokened wealth.

The Greek and Trojan heroes in the *Iliad* are all great in courage and strength. Indeed, some are the offspring of a casual alliance between a deity and a mortal. The greater a hero's skill at war, the more esteem he is held in by his own city, and this esteem is marked by the choicest cuts of meat at table. The heroic diet consists of meat and little else except wine.[2]

In this respect it does not reflect the diet of the people, neither the elite nor the farming masses, Homer used food as symbols of valour.

When Achilles and his companion Patroclus prepare a meal for Ajax, Odysseus and Phoenix, they roast a sheep, a goat and a pig. (Thigh pieces were usually sacrificed to the gods, a detail Homer omits.) The meat has already been butchered for the heroes and is now cut into long strips, salted and wound around spits. Numerous vase paintings show successive steps in the preparation of meat for spit-roasting. Homer's description is reminiscent of many a suburban barbecue:

> Automedon held the meats, and brilliant Achilles carved them,
> and cut it well into pieces and spitted them, as meanwhile
> Menoitios' son, a man like a god, made the fire blaze greatly.
> But when the fire had burned itself out, and the flames had died down,
> he scattered the embers apart, and extended the spits across them
> lifting them to the andirons, and sprinkled the meats with divine salt.
> Then when he had roasted all, and spread the food on the platters,
> Patroklos took the bread and set it out on a table
> in fair baskets, while Achilles served the meats.[3]

Meat (not fowl or fish), bread and wine are the only foods the heroes ever eat, except for aged Nestor, who is given a restorative drink and a snack – onion, barley bread and honey. The drink was made from Pramneian wine, grated goat's milk cheese and white barley.

The life of Homer's heroes at war is described through metaphors drawn from rural crafts – weaving, pottery and carpentry – and from food and its preparation. A picture of a peaceful community is conjured up: bees hover over spring flowers, insects gather in spring about the stalls of the sheep-fold, when the milk splashes into the pails; grapes in woven baskets; orchards of figs and mulberries; olive trees and vineyards; vegetable gardens supply pulses, legumes and onions, while people care for herds of sheep, goats and cattle. The new shield forged by Hephaestus for Achilles is inlaid with a series of scenes of communal life: under an oak tree people prepare a picnic feast for the harvesters, girls make bread while an ox has been sacrificed, and the reapers are still hard at work cutting and binding the sheaves. The healing of Ares' wound is quick, 'as when the juice of the fig in white milk rapidly fixes that which was fluid before and curdles quickly for one who stirs it'.[4]

Wealth, power and leadership in Homer's world are directly connected with the number of livestock owned. Cattle are currency, in Book IV of the *Iliad* Diomedes – a Greek warrior – fools a Trojan by exchanging armour worth nine oxen for armour worth a hundred. Odysseus, on the mainland opposite Ithaca, owns twelve herds of cows, twelve flocks of sheep, and the same of goats and swine. This has been worked out as 30,000 head of animals.

Hunting wild animals was the main amusement of the lord and his companions. In the forests of Greece there were still lions, panthers, wolves and boars. The quarries that called for the greatest courage were, of course, the lion and panther, followed by the boar. The wolf ran away and, without horses, Homer's Greeks had no way to pursue it.* A noble went out after his quarry armed with spear and sword. Hunting the panther was considered the most dangerous, for the panther does not retreat but emerges from the thicket and confronts the huntsmen. Then it is a question of who strikes first. Even when pierced through by a spear the panther does not recoil but bravely fights on. Many a mauled and badly wounded hunter would later celebrate a heroic struggle.[5] When Odysseus was a young man he paid a visit to his maternal grandfather, Autolycus, who lived at the foot of Parnassus. At dawn the next day Odysseus and his uncles climbed the slopes of Parnassus to hunt boar. The dogs picked up a trail and were followed by the beaters. On a thick layer of leaves in the heart of a dense thicket an enormous solitary boar was found, sheltering from winds and mist, from the rain and sun. The boar sprang to its feet and burst from cover with bristling hair and blazing eyes. Odysseus leapt forward with his spear, the boar charged and hit the youth, tearing off a piece of flesh from his thigh. At the same time Odysseus struck in the right spot, the joint of the shoulder, and transfixed it through the heart. Odysseus carried the wound throughout his life, so that when he was disguised on his return home old Eurycleia recognised him when washing his feet.[6]

The slaughter of wild animals in the hunt was a dangerous and honourable pursuit. The more animals a lord killed and the greater the danger he underwent, the greater his worth and popularity in the eyes of his community.

But what of the tamed beasts, those great herds of domesticated creatures, how were they slaughtered? For the workers and labourers, the peasants, soldiers and craftsmen of Homeric Greece, meat would have been eaten at

---

*Horse-riding became general only at the end of the seventh century BC, after the Cimmerian invasion of Asia Minor.

the public festivals which fell at regular dates throughout the year. There were sacrifices to the gods officiated at by priests, but other sacrificial celebrations were also held – by cities, particular groups or a few individuals, in their own names and for their own purposes – where a magistrate or the head of a clan or lord of a great household might officiate.

On the religious festivals the priest organised the ritual. He specialised in the liturgy and this would have been his ancestral calling. It was his task to kill the animal, then to flay it and separate the entrails, and from these to 'read' the divination. The priest also dissected the flesh of the carcase and supervised the ritual which attended the cooking of it, although he might also be helped in these duties by the *mageiroi*, or 'butcher cooks', who were attached to the sanctuary. In the Homeric vocabulary the priest is the *hiereus* – meaning the sacrificer who makes the offering acceptable to the gods. He is also the *areter* who offers the prayer on behalf of the suppliant. The priest is the symbolic intermediary between the human and the divine.[7]

The first animal ever sacrificed was a pig, by one Clymenes. The oracle at Delphi declared it was permissible to sacrifice a victim but it must indicate its consent during the libation. When sprinkled with holy water the animal would shake its head and this would be interpreted as a gesture of consent.[8]

Odysseus offers a sacrifice in the name of the Achaean army to Apollo in his temple at Chryses in order to appease the god who at the request of his priest at Chryses has unloosed a plague upon the army. The sacrifice is a hundred head of cattle. The cattle are set around the altar in a ring. Odysseus addresses the priest. They all wash their hands and throw barley groats on to the fire. The priest prays to Apollo, then they raise the animals' heads and cut their throats, skin them and cut portions from the thighs:

> Wrapped them in fat, and laid raw meat on them;
> And these the old man burned upon the billets,
> And poured the red wine on them, while beside him
> The young men held in hand five-pointed forks.
> And when the thigh-pieces were wholly burned,
> And they had tasted of the inner meat,
> They cut the rest up small and spitted it
> And broiled it carefully, and drew off all.
> Now when their work was done, and they had made
> The banquet ready, then they fell to feasting,
> And lacked for nothing at the feast they shared.
> But when they wanted no more food or drink,
> The young men crowned the bowls with wine, and first
> Pouring libation-drops into the cups
> Served out to each. So all day long they soothed
> The god with song, the youths of the Achaeans,
> Raising a lovely paean, and extolling
> The Archer-god; and he took pleasure listening.[9]

Spices, which from the seventh century BC were sprinkled over the meat as it was roasting, had a vital meaning of their own. They represented the union between earth and sun, a gift of wild nature. Spices united the earth with the gods, whose attention it was their purpose to attract. Though the whole range of spices was used for culinary purposes and in aphrodisiacs, it was frankincense and myrrh that were used almost exclusively for sacrifices. A myth about the sun, who falls in love with the daughter of the King of the Persians, tells of the birth of the frankincense shrub,[10] and can be interpreted to mean that the product of this aromatic plant is born of the sun and is destined to be reunited with him. Thus, frankincense has the power to unite the Below with the Above.[11]

So it is not only meat itself which is powerfully venerated but also the spices thrown on to it in the shape of little loaves or as finely ground grains. Both together forge a pathway from humans to god. For any individual or group to avoid such communication with the divine is surely to court social opprobrium and disaster. This is what Wilkins has to say of the food and the sacrificial altar of the third century BC:

> The Greeks defined their culture by their foods – olives, wheat and barley, the vine, fish, all quintessential elements of the Mediterranean diet – and above all by the ritual of animal sacrifice in which a domesticated beast was led to the altar, had its throat cut and its blood poured over the altar in the presence of the worshippers. It was flayed; the vital organs were removed and a portion offered by burning to the gods, the rest roasted and tasted by the leading participants. The other meat was jointed and boiled and shared among all participants. The entrails and offcuts were made into black and other puddings. In this system the gods were honoured, the community expressed its solidarity, and a rare chance to eat meat was enjoyed. Solidarity was important, as now in the meat-eating codes of the Jewish and Muslim communities, and was expressed through public and private sacrifice. Anyone who was a vegetarian was not taking part and was in a sense opting out of society.[12]

Wilkins goes on to say in the same paper that if meat was to be eaten, religious rituals also came into play. It was difficult, in fact, for the Greeks to consume anything without first offering the best portions to a god. How then could Pythagoras and his closest followers, who abstained from all meat-eating, be accepted and revered by their society, how could they commune with and praise the gods? We shall return to this question later in the chapter.

From Athenaeus★ we learn about another aspect of meat-eating. Gorging on great amounts of meat was itself 'heroic' and was thought admirable. Milo

---

★An Egyptian (born in AD 200) and the author of *Deipnosophistai* (*The Gastronomers*), a work taking the form of an aristocratic symposium of learned men at a banquet discussing food.

of Croton in the lifetime of Pythagoras 'devoured a bull reclining in front of the altar of Zeus'. Athenaeus goes on to tell us that Milo lifted a four-year-old steer from the ground at the feast of Zeus and carried this monstrous beast around the stadium on his shoulders as if it was a newborn lamb. Athenaeus also mentions Herodorus who, 'only three and a half cubits tall, but strong in his ribs', confesses to eating twenty pounds of meat and the same amount of bread, washed down with three pitchers of wine, at a single sitting. If gorging on great amounts of meat was linked with Herculean strength and prowess in athletics, abstaining from it had a secular significance as well.

But firstly, who was Pythagoras,* whose name is really familiar to us only from his theorem?

## The Life of Pythagoras[13]

Pythagoras was born around 580 BC on Samos, an island which clings, limpet-like, to the coast of Turkey, known at that time as Ionia and at a peak of cultural and scientific civilisation, soon to be destroyed by the Persians. Born of well-to-do parents, he was educated first on the island but later moved away, partly no doubt to avoid the tyrant Polycrates who ruled Samos, but also by a desire to learn from the greatest teachers of his age. He was not to return to Samos for forty-five years.

As a youth Pythagoras first became the student of Pherekydes, on the island of Syros, in the centre of the Cyclades. Pherekydes was one of the most important influences on the young Pythagoras. He is credited with the doctrine of metempsychosis,† which holds the human soul to be immortal, passing on into another body, either human or animal, after death. Pherekydes at once recognised Pythagoras as the dead Aithalides, who had had the gift of recollecting all of his previous lives. Aithalides was reincarnated as Euphorbus – who recalled being plants and animals – who was killed by Menelaus, then as Hermotimus, who became a Delian fisherman, Pyrrhus.[14]

Pherekydes was supposed to have studied the secret books of the Phoenicians and originated the concept of the cosmic Eros: the creator of the cosmos combines all the opposites in the primeval mass of matter and blends them into a harmonious whole. Pherekydes believed also in psychic immortality and wrote a number of mythological and theological works. One work survives and that only in fragments, *Heptamychos*. Aristotle thought Pherekydes was a theologian who mixed philosophy with myth, but the student's devotion to his master must have been profound for Pherekydes

---

*See note 13 for the sources of the account of Pythagoras' life that follows. It is important for the reader to be aware of the particular sources I have used in this first section of the chapter because of the Pythagorean enigma and the controversy over the fourth-century Pythagoreans, both of which are explored later.
†Reincarnation beliefs must have been both common and popular in prehistory. One poignant example is the Tree of Life design at the Ggantija Temple of Gozo (3,600-3,300 BC).

was dying of phthiriasis, being eaten alive by lice, and it may have been Pythagoras who nursed the dying Pherekydes on the island of Delos.

Pythagoras next travelled to Ionia to study under Thales, and his pupil Anaximander, at Miletus, a thriving commercial city on the coast which had also given its name to the Milesian school of philosophy. Pherekydes had been one of the Sophai, the Seven Wise Men, and so too was Thales. This title meant inventiveness and practical wisdom rather than speculative insight. Thales was considered the first Greek philosopher. He explained the world in natural terms and said that all life had come from the sea, basing his claim on his discovery of sea fossils far inland. He is perhaps most famous for his concept of panpsychism, teaching that 'everything is full of gods', a concept mystics would adopt and develop down the ages. Aristotle suggests that Thales meant 'the soul is mingled with everything in the whole universe', but Thales believed that all inanimate matter was divine consciousness. This idea was to influence the thought of the young Pythagoras. Particularly useful to Pythagoras was the mathematical knowledge that Thales derived from the Babylonians, knowledge which he put to work in solving practical problems – the height of a pyramid or the distance of a ship as seen from the shore. Thales was very old at the time he taught Pythagoras and regretted he could not teach him everything he knew, but long after the sage was dead Pythagoras would sing his praises.

At the same time as Thales taught him, Pythagoras attended the lectures of Anaximander, Thales' pupil. Anaximander had learnt from the Babylonians how to construct horoscopes, so his pupil must also have learnt some astrology long before he visited Syria and Babylon on his extensive travels away from Samos. Anaximander taught geometry and expounded on the theory of evolution: he believed that humans had once been fish – we had to be derived from animals of a different sort, he reasoned, because humans have such a long infancy that they could not have survived originally. He was of course, close to the Aquatic Ape theory in this surmise. Anaximander believed in no one creator, but in an impersonal force. Creation had no beginning and no end; the infinite was the universal cause. Much of his creation theory was built on later by his pupil.

It is thought that Thales urged Pythagoras to go to Egypt and Babylon to learn mathematics. To visit both these places, centres then of an advanced scientific culture, must have seemed an urgent necessity. Pythagoras was twenty-two when he started on the voyage to Egypt. Isocrates, a friend of Socrates, wrote a few generations later that Pythagoras pursued philosophical theories relating to sacrifice and ritual in the Egyptian temples. Pythagoras was bound by an oath of silence not to speak of the secret rituals that he learnt there, but we know that they were magical rites to attract favours from the gods – the practice known as theurgy. But when he first arrived in Egypt Pythagoras was not made welcome by the Egyptian priests, and was refused at both Heliopolis and Memphis. Only after he had submitted to harsh tests was he admitted by the priests at Diospolis, and he had to observe with scrupulous care all of their taboos. Many of these demanded abstention from certain foods, but the Egyptian priests -were also particular about not wearing any clothing that derived from animals. Wool was banned, even as a shroud to be buried in; their clothes were made from linen and their sandals from papyrus. Pythagoras would have learnt the rites of purification, geometry and the rites of Osiris – his death, transfiguration, dismemberment, the search by his wife Setu for his parts and his restoration to life as King of the Underworld.

In 525 BC, when the Persians invaded Egypt, they imprisoned Pythagoras and took him to Babylon, possibly as part of a policy of deporting all Greeks living in Egypt. However, he was not a captive for long (his father was a rich merchant and may have paid a ransom), for he began his studies under the Chaldeans and a sage called Zaratas, who taught him secret Magian rites, which involved ritual cleansing through drugs and herbs. This teaching remained as an integral part of his own rituals, the use of hallucinatory drugs from plants being the preparation for mystic union with the gods. Purification involved not eating meat or beans. He also learnt of Iranian dualism, the contest between good and evil, a doctrine which caused controversy among later disciples. Pythagoras left Babylon and returned to his home on the island of Samos around 520 BC, where with a few companions he retired to a cave,★ thus beginning a certain style of ascetic meditation that found favour later with sects like the Essenes, John the Baptist and various Christian and Gnostic hermits. But Samos did not much appreciate Pythagoras or what he wished to teach. Polycrates the tyrant had been crucified by the Persians and fearing Persian rule Pythagoras left to travel in Greece, visiting Crete, Delphi and Eleusis and thence to southern Italy, to Croton, a city perched on the ball of the Italian boot. He would then have been about sixty. He had studied for forty-five years.

## The Teaching

The Greek cities of southern Italy were rich and prosperous. Sybaris just up the coast from Croton has given its name to our language as a synonym for excessive luxury and idle pleasures. Croton was as large, powerful and prosperous as its sister city. It was also famous for medicine and gave Pythagoras an enthusiastic welcome. One of his biographers, Iamblichus,† tells us he had an audience of 2,000 people and swayed the Council of Elders with many fine words. His fame spread rapidly. He made converts of rulers and princes in neighbouring regions and soon became the leader of a society numbering some 2,000 converts and 600 philosophers. He had a golden

---

★It was Pherekydes who taught that caves were receptacles for the divine hand of creation. Later Pythagoreans and Plato thought the cave was a source of mystical truths.
†A Syrian philosopher (AD 250-330) and one of the founders of Neoplatonism. He was in many ways more a follower of Pythagoras than Plato, for he stressed theurgy – ecstatic union with the one – rather than intellectual analysis. He wrote ten books on the Pythagorean sect, of which only five remain. The first was devoted to the life of the founder.

thigh (possibly a birthmark), which people thought invested him with the attributes of Apollo. His religion worshipped Apollo (Croton issued coins depicting the tripod of Apollo) but he also founded a school of mathematicians and a complete and compelling philosophy based on non-violence and mystic union with all living things. He was also credited with miraculous powers and was considered a magician. Bertrand Russell refers to him as 'a combination of Einstein and Mrs Eddy'. But science and magic were not poles apart then as they are now, and we have seen how theurgy was relevant to the religious experience.

For his new students at Croton the tests were rigorous. Pythagoras would question them about their relations and friends, enquire about their wishes and what they did with their day. He would observe their movements, the way they carried themselves and sat down, whether they laughed or smiled, were talkative or silent. He observed the neophytes for three years, testing out their stability and love of learning. If he or she passed (women were allowed into the school on equal terms, a surprising departure for the time but not one that became a precedent), a vow of silence would then be imposed for five years. It is thought that when Pythagoras was learning the priestly rites in Egypt he also was commanded by a five-year vow of silence, and much of his system at Croton was based on that of Diospolis. In this time all the belongings and any property of the neophyte were shared by the school. 'He first taught,' says Diogenes, 'that the property of friends was to be held in common – that friendship is equality – and his disciples laid down their money and goods at his feet, and had all things in common.'[15] The inner circle of 600 were stewards and law-makers, and if the neophytes or initiates were thought worthy after their five years of silence they were admitted and could now hear and see Pythagoras as he spoke. From the outer circle of 2,000 disciples Pythagoras was curtained off: they could hear him but not see him – possibly another practice learnt in Egypt.

The impact that Pythagoras had on science, mathematics and philosophy was considerable. He was the first to argue that the earth was a sphere and that the moon shone with reflected light; he suggested that light consisted of rays which travel in straight lines from the eye to the object and that the sensation of sight is obtained when these rays touch the object. (Modern geometrical optics reverses the direction of the rays.) 'All is number,' Pythagoras taught, meaning that the universe was governed by laws composed of mathematical formulas. Number could provide the answer to the origin of forms and qualities which up to then had perplexed the Pre-Socratic philosophers.

Pythagoras was the first musical numerologist and laid down the foundations of acoustics, discovering the connection between the pitch of a note and the length of a string. He discovered that a musical note produced by a string of fixed tension could be converted into its octave, if the length of the string was reduced by one half, and its fifth when reduced by two-thirds. The vibrating string also led Pythagoras to understand the mechanics of wave motion. Not only did he establish the notes which are still used in Western music but he derived from these the various modes – the particular form of a scale – which he named after Greek tribes: Dorian, Phrygian, Lydian, etc. Musical theory he regarded as a branch of philosophy.

Today the name of Pythagoras is most familiar to us because of his proposition about right-angled triangles, that the sum of the squares on the sides adjoining the right angle is equal to the square on the remaining side, the hypotenuse. Constructions such as Stonehenge and the pyramids that pre-date Pythagoras could not have been built without knowledge of the Pythagorean theorem, so it is now thought that these mathematical principles must have been learnt by Pythagoras when he was in Babylon or Egypt.

But it is his theory about the soul, life and death which interests us here, for these were inherently bound up with the Pythagorean diet. Pythagoras was the very first Greek to promulgate a dogma of the existence of the soul. Though the idea of soul permeates Homer, it is a much more fluid concept: *Thymos* is the stuff of life, vaporous breath, active, energetic feeling and thinking material very much related to blood. Pythagoras saw the soul as an abstract concept beyond all material metaphors. What is more, the soul was immortal and could be endlessly transformed into other living creatures. All life forms therefore should be treated as kindred. To kill and eat any living creatures, whether they be bird, reptile or fish, was to murder one's cousins and eat their flesh, for all people are reborn in the time-flow of life on earth and the notion that a human being has only one life is an illusion caused by lost memory. Such rebirth could recur any number of times unless a person should succeed in breaking the vicious circle by strenuous ascetic performances.

Michael Grant[16] considers Indian influences transmitted through Persia can be detected in the idea of the soul as 'a fallen, polluted divinity incarcerated within the body, as in a tomb, and destined to a cycle of reincarnations (metempsychosis) from which it can obtain release through ritual purgation, accompanied by ascetic abstinence associated with the worship of Apollo, "the purifier"'. Though this idea was flourishing in the Orphic cult, Grant goes on to write that Pythagoras also took the idea from Orphism that the soul could be temporarily detached from the body.

There is no doubt that Pythagoras was one of the great original thinkers. He co-ordinated and fused together ideas and knowledge from the different cultures he had studied, from Egypt and Babylon and possibly even further East; from Hinduism, Zoroaster and the Orphic cult which had flourished in Attica for nearly two hundred years. In particular, from the latter Pythagoras took the shaman aspects, the use of hallucinogenic herbs in the journey towards knowledge of God and the doctrine of individual immortality. The Egyptians were the first to claim the idea of the transmigration of souls into living creatures, whether bird, mammal, fish or reptile, and all the priestly sects abstained from eating various meats, fish and vegetables, the taboos being based upon sacred myths. Bernal says '. . . vegetarianism was current among Egyptian priests in Hellenistic and Roman times. It is impossible to say how ancient these abstinences were, but given the general conservatism of Egyptian religion, they could well date back to the Old Kingdom.'[17]

## Beans

There are a number of possible explanations for the Pythagorean abstention from bean-eating. It might partly be traced back to the Egyptian priests, as Herodotus observes. The authors of *Food: The Gift of Osiris*[18] remark that the priests merely wished to avoid the impurity of their emanations. A priest's dignity could suffer if he were to fart in the midst of holy ritual. But beans are not the only food to induce flatulence and these authors continue with a more symbolic explanation. The Egyptian word for bean, *iwryt*, is similar to the word *iwr*, meaning to conceive or to generate. This association for the Egyptian priests may have endowed the bean with a sacred aspect. Pythagoras also forbade them because, two theories suggest, beans were generated by the same putrefactive material that generates human beings or, according to Pliny, because he thought that the souls of the dead dwell in them. I would also suggest that fava beans, squinted at sideways, bear a resemblance to female pudenda; added to the similarity between the Egyptian words described above, this might have been seen as another indication that beans were indeed sacred and somehow fused with the act of creation. Pythagoras, according to Plutarch,[19] called eggs 'beans', making a pun on the word for conception. Porphyry tells us that Pythagoras buried some beans in mud in a pot, and when he dug them up ninety days later they had taken the shape of a woman's vagina. (Perhaps, as well, this is why throughout history, until very recently, beans have been thought to incite lustful thoughts.) A more prosaic explanation is that the bean was used as a voting token in elections; thus abstention from the eating of beans meant 'abstain from politics'. And another is that foods which can at times be toxic become taboo. Favism is a hereditary disorder which involves an allergic reaction to the broad bean. Sufferers can develop a blood disorder (haemolytic anaemia) by eating the beans or even walking through a field of them when they are in flower. The disease can affect people living around the Mediterranean shores.* Finally, the smell of foods was of great significance in the preparation and cooking for aromas made their way to the gods – and beans were held to smell of dung.

But the taboo against the fava bean is summed up best by Marcel Detienne,[20] who points out that the bean is the only plant whose stem is totally devoid of nodes, making it a means of communication between

---

*Quails were known to be lethal if eaten at a particular time of the year, after migration. The quail had eaten large amounts of henbane and hellebore, 'poisonous to men but good food for quails' (Aristotle, *On Plants*, 820b. 6–7).

Hades and the human world. He quotes from one of the Pythagoreans' Sacred Speeches: 'They serve as support and ladder for the souls [of men] when, full of vigour, they return to the light of day from the dwellings of Hades.' Detienne sees the beans' stems as the instruments of metempsychosis, the route through which there is a continuous exchange between the living and the dead. The practice of burying a bean in dung or earth for forty or ninety days before digging it up survived for some hundreds of years as a part of Graeco-Egyptian magic. The bean within this time would be transformed into a child's or man's head or sometimes a female sexual organ. The experiment aimed to prove that the bean generated life, but also putrefaction, death connected with inevitable rebirth. Porphyry reports how a bean would be lightly bitten or have its skin broken and then be left in the sun for a few moments. It would be found shortly afterwards to be giving off a smell of human semen or of blood shed in a murder.[21] Hence at some level eating beans was tantamount to murder; as one Pythagorean says: 'to eat beans is a crime equal to eating the heads of one's parents.' Detienne points out this is equivalent to cannibalism, summing up the Pythagorean revulsion as 'to eat the bean is to devour human flesh, to behave like a wild beast, to condemn oneself to a type of life that stands in extreme opposition to the Golden Age.'

Poor bean! In the ancient world it flourished under a huge weight of significance, a plant of profound mysticism, only its nutritional value ignored by the Pythagoreans. The taboo against beans was not observed by those who did not follow Pythagoras, or by the poor or slaves (Pythagoras had a personal slave from Thrace whom he later freed), who were only too glad to fill their bellies. It is clear from Athenaeus that some distinguished Greeks had a passion for beans – he mentions Telemachus as 'being a person who was constantly eating beans', as well as a bean soup enjoyed by the 'great philosopher' Pauson.

We might wonder what Pythagoras and his inner circle did eat. Consider: Pythagoras forbade all food that might cause flatulence or indigestion, plants and animals sacred to the gods, or anything which might defile the purity of the psyche and prevent the foretelling of the future. That left bread, honey, cereals, fruits and some vegetables.* A sparse diet, yet one now widely recognised as being the healthiest possible for body and mind.

## The School at Croton

The school at Croton was a flourishing religious school with its own buildings outside the city. It centred on Pythagoras and the cults of Apollo and the Muses, patron goddesses of poetry and culture. Identified with the god Apollo was the doctrine of the One, the source of all numbers, the idea of the Good, the supreme reality. The ritual was rigorous, silence being necessary over long periods, and the ethical observances were strict, but the magical rites and much of the wisdom were kept secret. At the end of

---

*Detienne argues that some animals were eaten by some Pythagoreans (see p.67).

Pythagoras' life various students rebelled and left to publish their Pythagorean lore – one of them, it is thought, was Empedocles (see p.64).

There were two classes of followers, with different regimes and different diets. The inner circle, the philosophers and guardians called *mathematikoi*, meaning 'scientists', ate their meals in silence and were total and strict abstainers from all flesh of sentient creatures. Nor did they drink wine. They were trained to contemplate the spirit while they ate, and were taught never to injure, harm or distress animals. It was thought that eating meat not only would block the ability to prophesy through dreams but also desensitise awareness of the psyche, making, as it were, brutes of us all.

The second class were the *akousmatikoi* meaning people listening to the esoteric teachings, who, surprisingly, considering Pythagoras' compassion for animals, were allowed to eat some animal flesh and drink some wine, but had to abstain on other days. For lunch they ate bread and honey. When they ate meat they were not allowed to eat bone marrow as it was considered a messenger from the gods. The *akousmatikoi* included whole families. Emphasis was placed on health and exercise: as well as listening to their leader, they wrestled, jumped and raced.

Pythagoras played the lyre, sang and composed, and employed music and dancing to cure the sick. He was also very fond of reading aloud from Homer and Hesiod.* The school sounds not dissimilar to many an ashram or retreat of today.

## Stories

The tales about Pythagoras are rather endearing. He stopped a man beating a dog because he recognised in the dog's cries the voice of an old friend. His teaching is passionate about not inflicting violence on animals. He seems to have been a Greek St Francis, and many of the stories about him prefigure not the saint of Assisi so much as the founder of Christianity himself.

It was believed that Pythagoras could walk on water and be in two places at once, in both Croton and Metapontium, that he could fly miraculously, heal the sick in an instant and make people recollect their previous incarnations. Another story has Pythagoras betting some fishermen that he would know the exact number of fish in their net when they drew it in. If

---

*Hesiod, one of the earliest Greek epic poets, flourished around 800 BC (some time after Homer, who is thought to have lived a century before). In contrast to the war epics of Homer, Hesiod celebrated agriculture and peace. His *Work and Days* must have been an influence upon Pythagoras in that it is the source of the myths of the Golden Age and of Pandora's Box, a myth which supports dualism. In the former the vegetarian life is extolled in lyrical terms:

All Nature's common blessings were their own
The life-bestowing tilth its fruitage bore,
The full, spontaneous and ungrudging store.

It was also Hesiod who told us what the gods ate: 'immortals inhabiting the Olympian mansions feast ever on the pure and bloodless food of Ambrosia'. They drank, of course, nectar, which appears to be a kind of refined dew.

he won he would take the catch. He did, of course, and allowed the fish back into the lake. Miraculously all the fish, though out of the water while being counted, were still alive and swam away. Pythagoras, in his quiet, amiable way, obviously had a way with animals. An ox obeyed his command to stop trampling a field of beans. He told a wild bear not to be so aggressive and fed it barley and acorns. Pythagoras, of course, believed that each of these creatures had a soul and that animals were capable of ethical virtues.

Iamblichus tells how Pythagoras was playing on the lyre and singing with his companions when they heard a drunken youth in love about to burn his rival's house down. The youth was encouraged by a flautist playing a Phrygian melody. Pythagoras commanded the flautist to change the music instantly to a slow and stately spondaic rhythm. This calmed the lad and he very soon returned home.

Pythagoras was never seen to weep or to laugh; his disposition was equable – he was neither relaxed and gleeful nor depressed and glum; his health was steady. A man of inner serenity obviously, of great strength of intellect and of character, one who was secure and rigorous in his own beliefs. He claimed knowledge of his own pre-existence and believed that through complete abstention from meat all of us could recall previous lives.

Porphyry, unlike other early biographers, actually tells us what Pythagoras ate: a breakfast of honey or honeycomb, for dinner millet or barley bread and either raw or boiled vegetables. This is true asceticism and Porphyry unsurprisingly tells us that Pythagoras was slim, lithe and energetic throughout his long life. Some say he died at the age of seventy, others at 104.

Pythagoras would sacrifice cakes, honey, mallow, asphodel, myrrh and frankincense to the gods. All of his biographers except one (Aristoxenus) say he sustained a vegetable diet for his whole life.* When he discovered the properties of the right-angled triangle he sacrificed an ox made out of dough. Small representations of animals made in bread were common at the sacrificial altar.

The dough or bread would have been made either from barley or emmer wheat. But Greek soil was not really suitable for wheat growing; much of it later was imported from the Ukraine or Egypt. However, some wheat was grown and that was kept for the elite. The majority ate a porridge made out of barley or it was made into flat cakes, these were dipped into sweet wine or honey. Pliny[23] thought barley was the oldest cereal, and as the gods dislike innovation, it was barley that was mostly used for sacrifices. Barley grew well on the thin limestone hills of Greece, it can cope with little rain and intense heat. By Pliny's time barley bread was the food of the very poor and fed to livestock. But when Pythagoras was alive barley was daily sustenance for the people. Barley grain was roasted; every Athenian bride was required by a law of Solon (630 BC c d. 560 ) to take to her wedding a *phrygeton*, a barley roaster, this was a shallow pan with a handle. Pliny tell us that the Greeks

---

*Williams thinks he became a vegetarian aged eighteen or twenty.[22]

soaked the barley grains in water, then left them for a night to dry by a fire before being ground. Another method is to roast the grains thoroughly, then sprinkle with water, then it is dried again before milling. Once ground it is mixed with salt, flax and coriander seed. This mixture would make an enormously tasty flat bread. If the barley is to be made into a paste it is soaked and left to ferment a little then ground, salted and flavoured, this would give a miso-like paste which would be both nutritious and delicious. Archestratos, the gastronome we hear of through Athenaeus, considered the barley grown on the isle of Lesbos to be supreme. He writes that 'if the gods eat barley-meal, then Hermes must go there and buy it for them.'

## Religious Practice

Pythagoras would travel to Eleusis to attend the Mysteries. The kings of Eleusis were also the priests of the two goddesses Penelope and Demeter, but that had been before the seventh century BC, when Eleusis was independent of Athens. Afterwards Eleusinian worship became the Athenian state religion. The Eleusinian Mysteries became one of the chief festivals of the Attic year. All Greeks, as long as they had been purified by washing in the sea before the onset of festivities, were welcome to celebrate the Mysteries at the shrine at Eleusis, even women and slaves. Famous religious agricultural festivals called the Greater and Lesser Eleusinian Mysteries celebrated the sowing, sprouting and reaping of the grain. The entire legend of Demeter and her daughter Kore was re-enacted in the Eleusinian ceremony. It is told in the Homeric hymn to Demeter.

When about to enter the Mysteries of Eleusis, Pythagoras prepared a special dish designed both to stimulate and eventually to cause hallucinations, the recipe of which he would probably have learnt in Babylon. The opium poppy was sacred to Demeter, and her statues were crowned with wreaths made from the blooms. The Eleusinian Mysteries involved the participants entering the caves and shrines of the gods. The ritual might continue from dusk onwards for long hours, even a day or more. The drugs induced a sense of timelessness and unreality where fantasies would appear and the celebrants would hardly know whether they were awake or dreaming, whether phantoms were real or illusions.

The actual dish eaten sounds like something between a hash cake and a particularly delicious bowl of muesli. Poppy and sesame seeds were crushed with the flower stalks of asphodel, the skin of squill,★ leaves of mallow, barley and chickpeas, chopped up in equal quantities with Hymettus honey. Another dish was designed to keep away thirst, learnt, Pythagoras claimed, from Hercules, who in turn had learnt it from the goddess Demeter herself when he was sent to the Libyan desert. It was made from cucumber seeds and stoned raisins, coriander flowers, seeds from mallow and purslane, a little grated cheese, wheatmeal and cream.

---

★Squill, an onion-like plant, is a stimulant and diuretic.

Pythagoreans abstained from meat in order to survive instead on foods which resembled more the aromatic spices which the gods lived on. The more insubstantial the foods, the more the body was purified and the closer it could come to the gods, and to this end mallow and asphodel were an important part of the Pythagorean diet. Both plants are wild and were considered 'primitive' foods, especially fit for Apollo, who generously provided the fruits of the earth. They are perfect foods, because they can be eaten directly and need no fire to alter them; thus they represented foods that humankind once shared equally with the gods. Mallow and asphodel were also thought to be miracle foods which could entirely suppress hunger and thirst. Another magus, sixth-century BC Cretan seer Epimenides, each day took only a pill composed of mallow and asphodel, for he refused to eat like other men as he needed to eat like the gods. He died supposedly at an advanced age – 157 or 299 years – and slept a miraculous sleep of fifty-seven years. He was also said to wander outside his body. In Plutarch's *Banquet*, Solon claims that Epimenides' diet was inspired by Hesiod: 'What great benefit there is in the mallow and the asphodel.'

At Delos there was an altar to Apollo where it was forbidden to make any animal sacrifice and it was this altar that Pythagoras revered most of all. Along with the cereals, mallow and asphodel, and barley cakes placed on this altar there were also spices, frankincense and myrrh. The spices are offered up and burnt by the flames, leaving nothing behind. The spices then are the principal foods of the gods, products of wild nature, inedible to men. Plutarch summarises a whole set of ancient tests in his *Dialogues* which describe beings that neither eat, nor drink, nor defecate, people without mouths or anuses who feed on smells alone. Pythagoras not only loathed blood sacrifice but also dismissed the reading and interpretation of the entrails of beasts. Rather would he see omens and signs in the flight of birds or in the trees and landscape.

Pythagoras, like Epimenides, is often described as part shaman. We associate this word with primitive medicine men who perform miraculous cures through their intervention with the spirits. Shamanism also has an element of showmanship, a sense of ritual and theatre, and is tinged in our minds with charlatanism. But there was a tradition of shamanism in Thrace, where Pythagoras travelled as a young man, and there are also in Greek legend many stories about shamans. Dodds[24] counts both Pythagoras and Empedocles (see p.64) as shamans.

Metempsychosis, the transmigration of souls, was at the heart of Pythagoras' vegetarianism, as we have seen, but Dombrowski[25] considers Pythagoras to have been a proponent of 'victory through vegetables', i.e. he believed that a vegetarian diet was a lot healthier than a meat-eating one. We have noted how well and vigorous Pythagoras was. He desired his disciples to be able to sustain themselves on easily gathered raw foods and the purest water, to be as healthy and strong as he was. Dombrowski also thinks that 'Pythagoras' vegetarianism was due to ethical considerations. He personally embodied what may be the cardinal insight of the Greeks: nothing in excess.

Perhaps another reason for his vegetarianism lies in this passage from Iamblichus: 'Amongst other reasons, Pythagoras enjoined abstinence from the flesh of animals because it is conducive to peace. For those who are accustomed to abominate the slaughter of other animals, as iniquitous and unnatural, will think it still more unjust and unlawful to kill a man or to engage in war'[26] (a thought reflected by Plato in *The Republic*).

In the Golden Age animals and humans could speak the same language. Pythagoras thought the only difference between us and the animals was that we had internal and external speech while the animals had only internal speech. Aristotle divides speech into three categories: (1) chaos – the sound of insects; (2) organised sounds, like bird song; and (3) language. Pythagoras tended to believe that both (1) and (2) were the same, a form of communication which, miraculously, he could understand. For Pythagoras humankind was intimately linked with the rest of creation. Humans were not kings or lords of everything that moved. The very concept of metempsychosis implies that all creatures are equal. We are clothed in the same crude physical body as the rest of creation, the divine spark of the soul embedded in the demands of the flesh, but able by ritual practices and observations of renouncement to allow that soul the freedom to illuminate existence. This is a crucial idea which, as we shall see, radically changed when first Plato then Judaeo–Christianity began to take hold of human minds and imaginations. It is clear, as Gorman says, that: 'Man was not the image of the Divine . . . real man was not his body but his psyche . . .'[27] The psychic self cannot be yoked to a sick and dying animal but must be purified and so become independent of the human animal. Only thus can it become one with the abstract harmony of numbers which resemble the gods and so escape being reincarnated in animal forms.

This concept, so basic to Pythagoras, emerges clearly again in Vedic Hinduism (see Chapter 3) and in the thoughts of many Christian mystics. Pythagoras in his ideas and life strikes us now as a very contemporary figure; we can not only sympathise with many of his beliefs and there has been in the last fifty years a growing and voluble number of people who fervently believe in them with as much passion as he and his followers once did. As we have seen in Chapter 1 the idea of the soul or self-awareness in animals is scientifically proven. We also know that the Pythagorean diet is ultimately the most healthy one, while the Pythagorean maxim, 'know yourself' has become the foundation stone of modern psychotherapy. There is a case for re-evaluating Pythagoras as the father of western philosphy.

## The Orphic Religion

In Greece the idea of the pure psychic self was alive and flourishing within the Orphic cult, and with it went a horror of murder and the slaughter of animals.

Dionysus is the son of Zeus and Persephone. Zeus gives him the kingdom of the universe when he is just a boy, but he is pursued by Titans. After many near-escapes he takes the form of a bull, but is caught and torn to pieces by the Titans. Athena saves his heart, which Zeus swallows. He then brings forth the new Dionysus. Through this second birth the Orphic religion distinguishes the new Dionysus from the old savage one of the Bacchic cult. Man was formed, so this legend tells us, by the Titans, wet with the blood of their victims, being struck by Zeus with lightning, the human race springing out of the ashes. Because it has both Titanic and Dionysian elements, human nature is both bad and good.

In their myth of the twice-born Dionysus the Orphics wished to awake in humankind the consciousness of their divine origin, so that humans might escape from the imprisonment of their bodies. In order to do so, the soul had to go through a cycle of incarnations. In the intervals between incarnations the soul would reside in Hades. To reach a final deliverance from this endless cycle of reincarnation they had to live an ascetic life full of restrictions including ceremonies of purification, complete abstinence from meat and other rules similar to those in the Pythagorean teaching. It is ironic that one of the strictest vegetarian cults should have stemmed from the cult of Dionysus, or Bacchus, whose worshippers would tear wild animals apart before eating them raw:

> Swept away by the 'eater of raw flesh' and his wild hunt, the devotees of Dionysos ōmēstēs cease to be tranquil diners on the flesh of an animal that has been cooked by the rules. They become savage themselves and behave like ferocious beasts. They escape the human condition by way of bestiality, taking the lower route among the animals, while Orphism proposes the same escape on the divine side, taking the upper route by refusing the meat diet that spills the blood of living beings and eating only perfectly pure food.[28]

The Bacchic movement came from Thrace and Phrygia and reached Greece around 800 BC. Some saw it as a reversion to the Minoan religion; it was a fertility rite and Bacchus/Dionysus was the god who promoted fertility. The celebrants were women who held wands tipped with ivy and vine and were known as the 'mad ones' – Maenads or Bacchants. They would roam the mountainsides, spending nights dancing and drinking beer or wine, believing that the intoxication was divine. They would dance themselves into frenzies when the sacrifice, in which a live animal was torn to pieces, took place.

Dionysus was believed to be actually within the substance of the wine and raw flesh that the worshippers consumed. A Persian Mithraic text reads: 'He who will not eat of my body and drink of my blood will not be made one with me or I with him, the same shall not know salvation.'[29] A host of scholars[30] have been fascinated by the similarities between the living sacrifice of Dionysus and of Christ: 'Was he not the god who saves by initiation in his mysteries, who delivers his faithful, be they women or slaves? Did he not appear in the "communal feast" of his initiates as the model of those gods who offer themselves as victims in the paroxysmal type of sacrifice?'[31]

Russell links this outbreak of primitive feelings to a reaction against prudence, pointing out that tilling of the soil requires foresight and planning, the sensible pragmatic approach. He sees the Dionysus cult as a reaction against such foresight:

> In intoxication, physical or spiritual, he recovers an intensity of feeling which prudence had destroyed; he finds the world full of delight and beauty, and his imagination is suddenly liberated from the prison of everyday preoccupations. The Bacchic ritual produced what was called 'enthusiasm', which means etymologically having the god enter the worshipper, who believed that he became one with the god.[32]

The Bacchic element, Russell believes, being passionate and ecstatic, influenced the religious philosophers, most importantly Plato.

Dionysus was, then, the god of fruitfulness, vegetation and wine. He began to be worshipped all over Greece and the Dionysus Festival was a time of wine drinking and sexual celebration. Every Greek joined in a kind of tribal initiation which also involved choral singing and mimes. Often the initiation into the mysteries of Dionysus was also an initiation into sexual life.

From these roots came the Orphic religion, named after Orpheus, the Greek hero with superhuman musical skills, who was also the author of sacred writings, the *Orphic Rhapsodies*. Traditionally Orpheus was another Thracian import like Bacchus, but it is more likely that he came from Crete and that the original source was Egypt, or 'perfumed Ethiopia', where Herodotus found 'holy Nysa'.[33] This is where a hundred perfumes emanate, distant birds bring cinnamon boughs and where the divine child, Dionysus, was born.

Martin Bernal[34] argues persuasively that the name Orpheus is the Egyptian form (') rp't (Hereditary Prince), transcribed in Greek as *Orpais*. The Hereditary Prince was a title given to the Egyptian god Geb, who was a deity of the earth and all the fauna and flora which covered it as well as of the Underworld. Bernal goes on to point out that (') rp't was written with an egg as a determinative,* related to the cosmogonic egg laid by Geb in his form as a goose, which is echoed by the primal egg at the beginning of the Orphic cosmogony.† Orpheus is also related to the *Book of the Dead*, which

---

*A determinative is an unpronounced sign.

†Orphism explained the creation of the world by saying that Time was the original principle. Ether and Chaos came into being and from these two elements Time formed a silver egg, from which sprang the first-born of the gods, Phanes, god of light. The whole development of the world was then the self-revelation of Phanes.

Up to that moment the myth is partially derived from Babylonian mythology, but it also incorporates psychological lessons. Seeing the whole world as the revelation of light leads to introspection and the Greek maxim 'know yourself', which was another Pythagorean concept. But the Orphic legend had also to connect with orthodox Greek theology. So Zeus swallows Phanes and becomes the original force by which the world now grows.

served in later Egypt as a guide for the soul through the perils of the Underworld. In Greece hymns and spells were inscribed on gold leaf and placed by the bodies of the Orphics. An Orphic sect flourishing from the sixth to the second centuries BC buried the following inscription:

> You will find in the well-built dwellings of Hades, on the right, a spring near a white cypress. The souls of the dead go down there seeking refreshment; but do not on any account approach it. You will find another whose chill waters flow from the Lake of Mnemosyne. Before it stand guardians, who will ask you why you come, searching the darkness of Hades. Say to them: 'I am a child of the earth and the starry heaven; I am dried up from thirst and I perish; but give me quickly the cold water which flows from the Lake of Memory.' And being servants of the King of the Underworld, they will have compassion on you and give you to drink of the Lake. And then you can follow on the sacred way the glorious procession of the other Mystai and Bacchoi.[35]

Martin Bernal[36] shows how Greek religious thought was entwined with the religion of Egypt. He points out that Classical and Hellenistic Greeks claimed that their religion came from Egypt, and Herodotus specified that the names of the gods were, with a few exceptions, Egyptian. There can be little doubt then that Pythagorean vegetarianism, through its Orphic influences, also has its roots deep in Ancient Egypt itself.

Orphism, though it merged into the philosophy of Pythagoras, still flourished in Greece as a separate, and probably highly subversive, religion. Aristophanes, in the *Frogs*, says: 'Orpheus taught men to abstain from murders.' It is clear that Orphic thought in the sixth century BC held that animal sacrifice was murder and that to eat meat was compounding that murder. Detienne says: 'To change one's diet is to throw into doubt the relationship between gods, men, and beasts upon which the whole politico-religious system of the city rests.'[37] And further: 'The so-called Orphic way of life is not reducible to an insipid vegetarianism. To abstain from eating meat in the Greek citystate is a highly subversive act.'[38]

But by 450 BC, when the Pythagorean order was attacked, the Orphic religion had begun to decline. It was the Pre-Socratic philosophers Parmenides and Heraclitus, following Xenophanes, who used rationalism to banish the elements of theurgy and mysticism in the Orphics. J.B. Bury wrote of rationalism: 'It meant the triumph of reason over mystery; it led to the discrediting of the Orphic movement; it ensured the free political and social progress of Hellas.'[39] Bury values Parmenides and Heraclitus for having established the study of philosophy over the doctrines of priests, which ignores, of course, the humanity and philosophy of Pythagoras, and the extraordinary psychic insight he had into human nature. The tendency of older Hellenic writers, with the exception of a few formidable thinkers, was to value Pythagorean mathematics but to disparage his mysticism and reject his vegetarianism as a matter of minor principle.

However, though Bury★ may have crowed over the decline of the Orphic religion in Greece, it continued to flourish in Asia Minor† up to the first few hundred years AD, where it sometimes merged quite seamlessly into Gnostic Christianity.‡ Within Ancient Rome it was one of the mystery religions, the figure of Orpheus being both ascetic and intellectual, having the power to sweeten all minds and temperaments, both men, gods and animals, with his music. This sound symbolised the music of the seven planets and the laws of the universe, this knowledge bequeathing a magical power over all living things.

## Egypt

A form of writing was in use in Egypt from 3,000 BC. It had come from Sumeria, where clay tablets had been used, but the Egyptians wrote with brush and ink on papyrus. Their hieroglyphs and a wealth of illustrations, carvings, reliefs and paintings have told us much about the Egyptians' avoidance of some foods.

Porphyry, in the third century AD, noticed that 'the Egyptians and Phoenicians would sooner taste human flesh than the flesh of a cow'.§40 This would seem to be explained by the fact that both the cow and the bull were considered sacred. The cow was associated with the goddess Hathor, who was mother goddess, the mother of humankind, nourishing the earth with her milk. Bulls were honoured as if they were gods, as Greek and Roman visitors would often observe. Sometimes the bull was an actual god, as was Apis; at other times it was just revered as sacred. The Israelites while enslaved in Egypt were seduced by bull and cow worship. They gave their gold jewellery to Aaron, who melted it down and made them their very own golden calf.

Apis was worshipped at Memphis, its cult introduced by the first pharaoh, Menes, the first to rule all the lands of the Nile around 2,750 BC. The Greek historian Diodorus (first century BC) believed that Apis worship stemmed from an association between agriculture, bulls and oxen, that it was a ritual to replenish the earth. But it was also believed that Osiris and Apis were one and that Osiris had taught humankind the methods of agriculture. Diodorus

---

★Perhaps it is unfair to quote from a distinguished Victorian historian, but his history became the definitive work for generations and the contemporary Macmillan paperback, though rewritten and brought up to date by Russell Meiggs, still leaves unchanged such anachronistic views of Bury as the one above.

†One of the rules of the cult of Dionysus-Bromius, from the second century AD in Smyrna, is that its worshippers should not eat eggs or broad beans. Another insists that purification consists in not eating meat or broad beans and in not shedding blood. If a blood sacrifice occurred, certain parts of the animal could not be eaten for specific Pythagorean reasons.

‡A gold ring from the fifth century AD at the British Museum bears a Greek inscription which reads: 'The Seal of John, the Pre-Eminent Saint', and depicts a seated Orpheus playing his lyre with two beasts at his feet.

§Cannibalism was looked upon as a sign of primitive bestiality, as a contradiction to civilisation itself.

wrote: 'at the death of Osiris his soul passed into the bull and therefore up to this day has always passed into its successor.'

The Apis bull was a product of divine conception. Fire came down from heaven upon the cow which then conceived Apis. The bull was carefully marked: he was black with a spot of white on the forehead; on his back was the figure of an eagle and beneath his tongue a beetle. Pliny says the beetle (*cantharis*) was a kind of knob under the tongue.

Apis was not allowed to become fat or senile. At a certain age he was drowned in the fountain of the priests and the whole of Egypt went into mourning. Then the search for the new Apis began. Every black male calf was closely inspected for the signs, which could take months. But the man whose herd the new Apis was found in was greatly admired. When the calf was discovered he was placed on a state barge in a gilded cabin and taken to the sanctuary at Memphis. Before, the priests had taken the bull to Nilopolis, where it was kept for forty days. Women were allowed to visit the bull and expose themselves. Apis was garlanded and at Memphis visitors were allowed to watch him cavort and skip and roll in the dust and play.

Apis also gave prophecies. Pliny records that companies of boys escorted Apis singing songs in his honour. But sometimes they were seized with a frenzy and chanted prophecies.

Bulls and bull-calves were also frequently sacrificed, but not cows, for they were sacred to Isis. The animals were scrupulously inspected – it would not have done to sacrifice Apis by mistake. Plutarch notes how reddish-brown cattle were sacrificed, but even they were carefully inspected too – if the animal had one black or white hair it could not be sacrificed, an attitude also reflected in the Bible: 'Speak unto the children of Israel, that they bring thee a red heifer without spot, wherein is no blemish.'[41]

All of the sacrificial animal could be certified pure except the head, which was seen as loathsome. Herodotus writes: 'heaping imprecations upon the head they take it to the market place and to Greek traders and sell it instantly. If there are no Greeks they throw the head into the river.' Again this is reflected in a passage from the Bible on how to get rid of impure meat: 'Thou shalt give it unto a stranger that he may eat it, or thou may sell it to an alien.'[42]

Herodotus considered that the whole of Egypt avoided eating the flesh of cows:

> . . . thus from Egypt as far as Lake Tritonis, Libya is inhabited by wandering tribes whose drink is milk and their food the flesh of animals. Cow's flesh, however, none of these tribes ever tastes, but abstain from it for the same reason as the Egyptians – even at Cyrene, the women think it wrong to eat the flesh of the cow – the Barcaean women abstain, not from cow's flesh only, but also from the flesh of swine . . .[43]

But the authors of *Food: The Gift of Osiris* think it erroneous to conclude that

Egyptians of all ages avoided beef. They believe that some kind of taboo operated at some periods.[44]

Not eating beef does not mean, of course, that the Egyptians did not eat meat of other kinds – game birds, duck, goose and chicken. But pork was also a taboo meat. Although in the Middle Kingdom there was no evidence of a codified taboo, there is by the time of the New Kingdom (1341 BC): there exists an illustration of a boar, the manifestation of Seth, being beaten by a baboon, Thoth, the god of knowledge and secret science. Later, Herodotus tells us: 'the pig is regarded among the Egyptians as an unclean animal, so much so that if a man in passing accidentally touches a pig, he instantly rushes to the river and plunges in with his clothes on . . .'[45] Swineherds were despised and not allowed to enter a temple or marry outside their group. Pigs were never sacrificed, as they were in Babylon, except to Bacchus and the moon. But the flesh had to be eaten on the day of the full moon. On the following day it was thrown away. There was an association between the eating of pork and leprosy. Plutarch wrote: 'the bodies of those who drink swine's milk break out with leprosy and scabrous things.'[46] Egyptian priests ate no pork, no mutton, no fish, no salt and, of course, no beans.

Returning to the taboo on beans that we discussed earlier, it is possible that the bean Pythagoras rejected so completely was not the bean the Egyptian priests refused to eat. The Greek bean *vicia faba* is the broad bean, the only legume in the ancient world until Columbus's discovery of the New World brought to Europe the haricot and other varieties. But the bean the Egyptians disliked, the theory goes, was not a legume at all but the fruit of the pink lotus, the pink Nile lily (*Nelumbium speciosum*), which grew wild at that time but does so no longer. This fruit was called the Egyptian bean by Herodotus. It was described as looking like a wasps' nest with thirty tubes running from the fruit down the stem. In each tube was a bean the size of an olive stone. The root was much prized and could be eaten raw or cooked, either boiled or roasted. The stem was also eaten, chewed and sucked like sugar cane. The bean was considered bitter and not eaten with as much enthusiasm as the rest of the plant. This fruit of the Nile lily may have been taboo because it springs from the Nile itself and therefore is closely associated with fish. The priests would have refused to eat fish because, as the Osiris myth tells us, the fish had fed upon the phallus of Osiris. The oxyrhynchus,* with its rather phallic snout, was one of the most commonly depicted fish of the Old Kingdom.

It is intriguing to speculate on how far back many of these religious ideas, stories and rituals go. Some – the images of a cow, the star goddess Hathor and Horus the falcon – can be traced back to prehistoric times. There are also close relations with north-east African religions. The bovine cults, the

---

*Not to be confused with the place where papyri and remnants of Greek literature have been discovered.

ritual dresses, masks and animal tails, the idea of the king as head ritualist, the despotic magician, and the position of the king's mother as a ruling matriarch are found in disparate tribes in surrounding areas of Africa. The roots of religion descend far back into the consciousness of humankind and obviously deep into the African heartland where our beginnings lie. These beliefs and customs continued to travel around the eastern Mediterranean and towards the East, and it is some semblance of these early beliefs that we see evoked with such grandeur in Ancient Egypt. Among all the very many complicated taboos were some directed against meat-eating. Whether some sects abstained from all flesh, in the Pythagorean way, for all of the time is a matter of debate. But remembering Martin Bernal's comment (see p.48) it would seem quite possible.

## Zoroaster

The founder of Zoroastrianism (known as Parseeism in India) was born in Iran around 628 BC and is thought to have lived until 550 BC. An abstainer from meat, he did much more than influence Pythagoras, for in his concepts of dualism and monotheism he influenced Judaeo-Christianity and in other ways Hinduism.

He promulgated the idea of one god, Ahura Mazda, the creator of heaven and earth, of the material and the spiritual worlds. The existence of God was proved from the evidence of the order of the world. Who could have created the heavens, the stars, the sun and the moon? Who could have made wind, water, fire and earth and all the life which existed, except one god? The source both of light and of darkness, he was also the sovereign lawgiver, the heart of the living spiritual world, the origin of moral order and judge. This supreme being is surrounded by seven beings called 'beneficent immortals'. Spenta Mainya (Holy Spirit), Asha Vahishta (Justice and Truth) and Vohu Manah (Righteous Thinking) are but three.

Zoroastrianism is monotheistic (the beneficent immortals are very much lesser gods and have to observe the same laws as mankind). Yet Zoroaster's other main concept was that of dualism. Hence the supreme god has a vigorous opponent who embodies the principle of evil – exactly the theological problem which Judaeo-Christianity landed itself with: how can you have a supreme being that cannot save its created world from evil, for how could it have created the principles of evil in the first place?

This difficulty is not answered by Zoroastrianism either. In the beginning there was a meeting of two spirits who were free to choose, in the words of the Gāthās (the holy hymns), 'life or not life', which gave birth to a good and to an evil principle. The Wise One having fathered these two spirits is still in control, though 'not life' has created the kingdom of the lie, filled with *daevas* – evil spirits (most of them borrowed from the old Indo-Iranian gods). Zoroaster states that the Wise Lord will vanquish the spirit of evil, which will mean the end of cosmic and ethical dualism. Humankind then has to choose between the rule of the Wise Lord and of Ahriman the Lie. Humans, in their freedom, are responsible for their fate. The righteous person will have the reward of integrity and immortality. Zoroaster tended to divide humanity up into the good and the bad and in his own time named them. Thus the good were settled herdsmen or farmers caring for their cattle and living in a definite social order. The bad, the followers of the Lie, were thieving nomads, the enemies of agriculture and careful animal husbandry (Russell's concept of men of prudence with foresight, in fact, rather than the Bacchic Maenads).

In these times the nomads were a constant problem unless the civilisation was strong and powerful along all its borders. A sad note is struck by an Egyptian scribe writing in the early years of the Middle Kingdom after attacks by Libyan tribesmen: 'all good things are ruined, the fishponds which shone with fish and wild fowl. All good things are passed away, the land is laid low in misery by reason of bedouins who traverse the land . . .'[47]

In the early hymns, the Gāthās, which were written by Zoroaster, there are constant references to the fate of people in the afterlife. Every act and thought in their lives will be judged by the Wise Lord, and the good will enter the kingdom of everlasting joy and light while the bad suffer horrors in darkness. There is also a last judgement, when evil will be finally destroyed, the world will be renewed and all will live in paradise. After Zoroaster's death later forms of the religion preach a resurrection of the dead.

Zoroaster forbade all animal sacrifice to the evil spirit, Ahriman, or to the lesser devils, the *daevas*, as well as all intoxicating drinks. The cock was a symbol of light, and was associated with the protection of good against evil because its crowing heralded the dawn, a belief held in the rest of the eastern Mediterranean.

The religion partly reflects the society that Zoroaster was born into of three distinct classes: the elite – the chiefs and priests – then the warriors and lastly the farmers, cattle breeders and husbandmen. Each class had a particular god or beneficent immortal nominated to care for them. The religion slowly moved southwards and became infiltrated by older ideas and more numerous gods. But Darius I (522–486 BC) worshipped the Wise Lord, Ahura Mazda, and later, in AD 224, Zoroastrianism became the official religion of the Persian dynasty.

The Avesta is the sacred book of Zoroastrianism, and includes the Gāthās. Most of this book is said to have been destroyed when Alexander the Great conquered Persia, so the present Avesta is assembled from remnants.

Through Pythagoras, who absorbed much of this teaching and its rites in Babylon, and the older complete Avesta, Zoroastrianism was a considerable influence on Greek thought: Anaximander's picture of the cosmos is borrowed from Zoroaster; Heraclitus was impressed by the priests of Zoroaster at Ephesus; the theory of the immortality of the soul and its going aloft to heaven, which emerged in Greece in the fifth century BC, is thought to have its roots in Zoroaster. Certainly Pythagoras' abstention from meat was stimulated by Zoroaster as well as by the Egyptians.

Descendants of the Zoroastrians who reached India and settled there, known as Parsees, still thrive. They were and still are known for their wealth, education and beneficence. In the nineteenth century they made contact with the surviving Zoroastrians in Iran, known as Gabars.

## The Pythagorean Enigma

The portrait of Pythagoras sketched out in this chapter reflects posterity's view of him and is best summed up by Barnes:

> Pythagoras, discoverer and eponym of a celebrated theorem, was a brilliant mathematician; by applying his mathematical knowledge, he made great progress in astronomy and harmonics, those sister sirens who together compose the music of the spheres; and finally, seeing mathematics and number at the bottom of the master sciences, he concocted an elaborate physical and metaphysical system and propounded a formal, arithmological cosmogony . . . Pythagoras was a Greek Newton; . . .
>
> If Greek science began in Miletus, it grew up in Italy under the tutelage of Pythagoras; and it was brought to maturity by Pythagoras' school, whose members, bound in fellowship by custom and ritual, secured the posthumous influence of their master's voice.[48]

But Barnes goes on to dismiss a picture of a vegetarian Pythagoras as mere fantasy. Elsewhere he discusses the vegetarianism of Empedocles, which he agrees is linked to the doctrine of metempsychosis, and I have made the same conjectural link when discussing the vegetarianism of Pythagoras. Barnes does not discuss the diet of Pythagoras because he claims we have no evidence of it. I would not be doing justice to the theme of this book, nor to the new works written in the last twenty years[49] which have attempted to analyse exactly what were the beliefs and ethics of Pythagoras himself, if I did not briefly explore the problem.

The difficulty first arises because nothing that Pythagoras taught was written down. All the evidence for the Newtonian Pythagoras comes from Iamblichus (AD 250–330) and Porphyry (AD 233–306), writing after an interval that would be comparable to a scientist today writing a biography of the thirteenth-century alchemist Roger Bacon. The first Pythagorean doctrines we see in written form appeared in a work, *Concerning Nature*, by Philolaus (*fl.* 475 BC), who was born either at Tarentum or at Croton in southern Italy. So there is a chance that Philolaus may actually have known Pythagoras himself and he would certainly have been reared and educated by people who did. At the least, one would think the writings of Philolaus could be trusted. But only fragments of this work have been preserved and these deal with astronomy, biology and psychology. But whether Philolaus speaks for himself, for Pythagoras or for his fellow Pythagoreans is still disputed. It was thought that *Concerning Nature* was so highly esteemed by Plato that he incorporated the principal part of it in *Timaeus*, but this is no help for there is nothing there on either diet or metempsychosis.

If we know very little in any absolute fashion about the teaching of Pythagoras, at least we can be certain that he was an impressive figure, for no other in the ancient world in the two hundred years after his death is mentioned so often: by Ion, Xenophanes, Herodotus, Isocrates, Plato and both Heraclitus and Empedocles. These last two lived within the lifetime of Pythagoras, and speak of his love of learning and his miraculous powers. Empedocles said that Pythagoras knew more than any man could learn in ten or twenty lives.

Barnes agrees that Plato and his followers were to some extent influenced by Pythagorean speculations in science and metaphysics which led to a syncretism of both Platonism and Pythagoreanism. This view, which can be traced back to Plato's nephew, Speusippus (successor to Plato as head of the Greek Academy), dominated later philosophical tradition and came to be regarded as Pythagoreanism pure and simple. Modern scholarship points out that each new biographer reinterpreted the material in the subjective light of his age and beliefs. Barnes admits that historians' ignorance of the real Pythagoras is not total, that there is one doctrine 'that we can ascribe with some confidence to Pythagoras'.[50] He quotes Dicaearchus, a pupil of Aristotle, who wrote two centuries after Pythagoras:

> What [Pythagoras] used to teach his associates, no one can tell with certainty; for they observed no ordinary silence. His most universally celebrated opinions, however, were that the soul is immortal; then that it migrates into other sorts of living creature; and in addition that after certain periods what has happened once happens again, and nothing is absolutely new; and that one should consider all animate things as akin. For Pythagoras seems to have been the first to have brought these doctrines into Greece.[51]

In the light of what Barnes says of Empedocles (see below) this would seem to be proof of Pythagoras' vegetarianism.

## Empedocles

Pythagorean ethics first became a philosophical morality in the life of Empedocles (490–430 BC), and the surviving fragments from *Purifications* attest to a desire to create a universal and absolute law in contrast to temporal and changing laws which vary from state to state. These universal laws amount to injunctions not to kill 'living creatures', to abstain from 'harsh-sounding bloodshed', in particular to avoid animal sacrifice, and 'never to eat meat, nor for that matter, beans or bay leaves'.[52]

Barnes comments that Empedocles' injunctions were both revolutionary and rational, for his town, Acragas, now modern Agrigento, was both rich and devout. Its streets must have resounded with the shrieks of dying animals, its air reeked with the stench of blood and burning carcases, as the normal accompaniment to the sacrifices in Greek religious practice. 'To advocate bloodless liturgy in such circumstances will have seemed both impious and absurd.'

Empedocles admits to previous lives, 'for already have I once been a boy, and a girl, and a bush, and a fish that jumps from the sea as it swims'.[53] Another fragment tells of a cycle of transmigrations lasting 30,000 seasons, imposed by necessity on spirits who 'sully their dear limbs with bloodshed'.[54]

It is clear how Empedocles sees animal sacrifice from another surviving fragment of *Purifications*:

> The father lifts up his own son in a different shape and, praying, slaughters him, in his great madness, as he cries piteously beseeching his sacrificer; but he, deaf to his pleas, slaughters and prepares in his halls an evil feast. Just so does son take father, and children mother: they tear out their life and devour their dear flesh.[55]

Athenaeus tells us that Empedocles won a horse race at Olympia and, being a Pythagorean and an abstainer from animal food, made an ox out of myrrh, frankincense and the most costly spices and divided it among the people who came to the festival.[56]

Empedocles discovered that air was a separate substance, having noticed that an upturned bucket placed into water does not allow the water to enter it. He also claimed that plants had gender and he formed a rather crude theory of evolution which nevertheless concluded that it was the fittest members of a species that would most likely survive. He said that the moon's light was reflected, that light takes very little time to travel, and that solar eclipses were caused by the moon. He believed that ancient humans had been perfect because of their vegetarianism, peacefulness and refusal to sacrifice animals. He harked back to the Golden Age when humankind offered to the gods nothing but perfumes and honey, when they were gentle towards animals and birds. He divided the world into Love and Strife. In the Golden Age, Strife was kept outside the world. Then gradually it entered the world, expelling Love. In a continuing process now Love becomes uppermost and Strife is vanquished, now Strife holds sway. Thus Empedocles interprets the changing world.

It is Aristotle who says that for Empedocles plants were endowed with sexual desire, that they felt pleasure and pain and had knowledge. Whether this belief in the sentience of plants challenges the foundations of his vegetarianism is a matter for debate, but his vegetarianism is obviously a direct result of his belief in the Pythagorean concept of metempsychosis. This concept was well known and even popular at the time, as a poem of Pindar's attests. Written in 476 BC, when Empedocles was a boy, Pindar's second Olympian Ode to Theron, the ruler of Acragas, depicts the delights of transmigration to an audience familiar with and enamoured of the doctrine.[57] Like Pythagoras, Empedocles is credited with miracles, the control of the winds and restoring the dead to life – birds, animals and a woman who had appeared dead for thirty days.

Russell sums him up thus: 'the mixture of philosopher, prophet, man of science and charlatan which we found in Pythagoras was exemplified very completely in Empedocles . . .'[58] He died, it is said, promising all he was a god and would return immediately, by jumping into the volcanic crater at Etna. Russell quotes an unattributed couplet:

> Great Empedocles, that ardent soul,
> Leapt into Etna, and was roasted whole.[59]

## The Pythagoreans

Let us now turn to the other main controversy which stems from one of the early biographies of Pythagoras, by Aristoxenus (fl. late fourth century BC) and written some two hundred years after the death of the founder of the sect.

What happened to the Pythagoreans in those years? In the last years of Pythagoras' life (we do not know for certain when he died*) a war broke out, in 510 BC, between Croton and Sybaris, in which the son-in-law of Pythagoras, Milo, a man with a gargantuan appetite for meat, appeared at the head of the Croton troops wearing a lion skin and bearing a club in the style of Heracles himself. Sybaris was defeated and the city totally destroyed. The reason given by Iamblichus for this war is that some people had fled from Sybaris to Croton. Pythagoras gave them his protection and refused Sybarite envoys demands for their return. Stories such as this have led later biographers to speculate that Pythagoras, in his last years, involved himself with politics, though this one seems to illustrate a simple respect for basic human rights. A few years later, in 508 or 500 BC, a Croton noble called Kylon led a mob to persecute the Pythagorean society at Croton. Pythagoras and his followers then moved to Metapontum. Aristoxenus gives the reasons for the persecution by Kylon:

> Kylon, a Crotoniate and leading citizen by birth, fame and riches, but otherwise a difficult, violent, disturbing and tyrannically disposed man, eagerly desired to participate in the Pythagorean way of life. He approached Pythagoras, then an old man, but was rejected because of the character defects just described. When this happened Kylon and his friends vowed to make a strong attack on Pythagoras and his followers. Thus a powerfully aggressive zeal activated Kylon and his followers to persecute the Pythagoreans to the very last man.[60]

---

*All the ancient biographers give different dates and reasons for his death: killed while trying to escape from Croton because he had refused to cross a field of beans, in 508 or 500 BC; suicide in the Temple of the Muses at Metapontum, disheartened by the persecution, also in 500 BC when he was about seventy; or living on to the age of either ninety-nine or 104.

The Pythagoreans suffered only a few years' exile from Croton because they were back there in the 490s BC. It is thought that during this time Pythagoras had travelled extensively through Sicily and the rest of Italy, starting small branches of followers of his philosophical teachings. We have already seen that in Sicily, when Empedocles was a child, the concept of the transmigration of souls was entirely acceptable and possibly even popular.

There is some indication that Iamblichus' dating of Pythagoras' death at shortly after 480 BC is true, for we know that Aristaeus of Croton became the head of the society at Croton at that time. He was already an old man and was, in turn, succeeded by the son of Pythagoras, Mnesarchus (named after his grandfather, a Hellenic custom), and then others, such as Boulagoras and Gartydas, who reputedly died of grief at the persecution that Croton was suffering at the time. In 455 BC the school was banned from Croton and its followers banished. It is said that the school was burned with forty followers still inside the building, only two of whom escaped: Lysis of Tarentum, who went to Thebes in Boeotia and became the teacher of Epaminondas,* and Philolaus, who established a Pythagorean school at Phlius in the Peloponnese which had close contacts with Socrates, and who published the Pythagorean work *Concerning Nature*.

A friend of Plato's, Archytas, formed a new centre of Pythagorean theory at Tarentum, Calabria, very near where the master had died. Archytas was a mathematician and his centre wielded considerable power – so much so in fact that it caused dissent and strife among the pupils. Archytas, being a mathematician, concentrated on scientific problems and excluded many of the original Pythagorean practices. There was little discipline, silence was not observed at meals, there was no five-year apprenticeship, and applicants were not screened. This was the society that Aristoxenus knew in 300 BC and on which he based many of his judgements about the original society.

## Aristoxenus

This writer of a critical biography of Pythagoras was a peripatetic philosopher who flourished around 310 BC. He had studied under Aristotle (384–322 BC) and wrote on musical theory, as well as writing biographies of Pythagoras, Archytas, Socrates and Plato. He was born at Tarentum, so must have known of and could even have been taught by the remnants of the Pythagorean school that still existed there. He also wrote on ethics; fragments attest to a Pythagorean cast of belief – for example, he wrote that the soul relates to the body as harmony to the parts of a musical instrument.

Aristoxenus gives a detailed account of the meals the Pythagoreans ate, which included barley and wheat bread, wine, seasoning, cooked and raw vegetables, and animal meats which were suitable for both sacrifice and eating. But he also called these Pythagoreans *akousmatikoi*, who were allowed to eat some meat.

---

*The Theban general who defeated the Spartans at Leuctra in 371 BC.

Dombrowski[61] explains the views of Aristoxenus by saying that his age, the Hellenistic era, was sceptical of Pythagoras and attempted increasingly to rationalise his teaching. Further, Aristoxenus was both a materialist and a sceptic and based his dietary views on the remnants of the Pythagorean society which he grew up with. But there were other Pythagoreans alive and teaching at the time of Aristoxenus and it is odd that he omitted them from his account. These were the wandering *Pythagoristai* or ascetic Pythagoreans who lived from day to day by begging, stopping to teach whenever they were asked. The Greek comedies of the fourth and third centuries BC poke fun at their vegetarianism: 'Some wretched Pythagorists chanced to be eating salt-wort* in the ravine, and, moreover, collecting poor bits of it in their bags' (Antiphanes, in *Memorials*); 'First of all, like a devotee of Pythagoras, he eats nothing that has life, but takes a sooty piece of barley-cake, the largest possible for a ha'penny and chews that' (Antiphanes); 'The devotees of Pythagoras, we hear, eat neither fish nor anything else that has life, and they are the only ones who drink no wine' (Alexis, in *Men of Tarentum*); 'Their entertainment will be dried figs and olive cakes and cheese, for to offer these in sacrifice is the Pythagorean custom' (*The Lady Devotee of Pythagoras*).[62]

By the time Aristoxenus was writing, a number of works praising Pythagoras already existed, including a biography by Timaeus (356–260 BC), a historian who had been born in Sicily and studied in Athens. It is Timaeus who first gave posterity its picture of a vegetarian Pythagoras. Aristoxenus, however, claims that Pythagoras ate all kinds of meat, except for sheep and working oxen. He is the only writer from antiquity to state such an opinion, one which, in the light of Pythagoras' known beliefs on metempsychosis, as we have already commented, seems unlikely to be accurate. Barnes comments:

> The sheep you slaughter and eat was once a man. Once, perhaps, your son or your father: patricide and filicide are evidently wrong; to avoid them you must avoid all bloodshed. And to avoid dining off your late relatives you must avoid eating meat or any of those select members of the vegetable kingdom which may receive once-human souls. The doctrine of transmigration, in short, shows that killing animals is killing people, and that eating animals is eating people; and eating people is wrong.[63]

To explain the influence that the work of Aristoxenus has had, Detienne[64] sees his point of view as a reflection of a fourth-century BC debate between vegetarians and meat-eaters, between Pythagoras – who fed exclusively upon strange substances 'which suppress hunger and thirst', like the mallow and asphodel in the pill that Epimenides took – and the son-in-law of Pythagoras, Milo of Croton – who consumed a whole ox at a sitting. At Croton, Milo is priest of Hera of Lacinia, the guardian deity and warrior

---

*Almost certainly marsh samphire.

power whose cult is closely linked with Heracles. It is as a warrior that Milo leads the men of Croton to victory against the Sybarites and thereby attains a position of central importance in the Pythagorean movement. Milo, the meat-eater, is the active citizen, the man of war and the politician, in contrast to the circle of ascetics, subject to rules of holiness aimed at purification of the soul, which is centred on Pythagoras.

Although Milo and the 'political' Pythagoreans ate meat, they did not eat all meats. It was strictly forbidden to eat the working ox, for Pythagoras said that to kill an ox was to slaughter a labourer. Why, then, was orthodox religious practice founded upon the ritual sacrifice of the ox? The reason was that, while pigs and goats lived in herds on open spaces of uncultivated land, the sheep and the ox lived close to the household – the ox, in particular, dwelled under the same roof as the farmer and worked in the fields with him – and it was this closeness of the ox to humankind which made it the perfect victim. The working ox was so valuable that it alone would ensure against drought and the onset of famine. So even when members of a Pythagorean group ate some meats, their refusal to partake of sacrificed ox or to sacrifice an ox themselves made them critical of the established values and beliefs within their society.

## The Heritage of Pythagoras

Whatever the truth about Pythagoras, his influence was enormous. His thought radically influenced philosophy, science and mathematics for centuries, and we are still in his debt. Russell[65] believes that Pythagoras has characterised religious philosophy in Greece, in the Middle Ages and in modern history down to the time of Kant. From Plato to Leibniz he sees an intimate blending of religion and reason, of moral aspiration with a logical admiration of what is timeless, all of which stems from Pythagoras. Much of what we regard as Platonism we find, upon analysis, to be in essence Pythagorean. Our whole conception of an eternal world revealed to the intellect but not to the senses is derived from Pythagoras.

$$\overline{\phantom{xxx}3\phantom{xxx}}$$

# India

The vegetarian tradition in the subcontinent of India is both renowned and extensive. It is accepted as part of the Hindu religion and inescapably linked to the concept of the sacred cow and the transmigration of souls. But was it always so and when exactly did the abstention from all flesh begin and how is it linked to both Buddhism and Jainism?

## *The Indus Valley*

The roots of Hinduism lie in a collection of writings, over a thousand hymns called the Rig-Veda. These comprise the earliest part of the Vedic literature produced by the Aryan people. There is some controversy over when the Rig-Veda was written, but a tentative consensus agrees around 1,500 BC. The Aryans honoured a vast number of gods, each governing some aspect of life. All of them represent nature: there are gods of the sky, sun, moon, dawn, wind and of fire. As we have seen in Chapter 2, reverence for the bull and cow was part of Egyptian fertility rituals and can be traced back into prehistory. The Rig-Veda came into India with the Aryan invasion which took place over several hundred years, from 1,500 to 1,200 BC. The Aryans came not as a horde, but in tribes, and as each new tribe crossed the Iranian plateau it pushed the older Dravidians down further and further inland. The Aryans gradually conquered the Ganges valley, developing a centre of Aryan power around the land of the Kurus, near Delhi, in the north and centre of India. By 500 BC the Aryans had spread all over northern India from the sea in the east to the sea in the west and from the Himalayas in the north to the Vindhya mountains in the south. The whole area was called Aryavarta. It was in the Ganges valley that Brahmanism grew out of the Aryans' Vedic religion and Sanskrit developed into India's national language.

The Aryans themselves, before the invasion, were thought to be tribal peoples living in the Caucasus mountains, in what is now Georgia, and in the Caspian Sea region. They invaded with horse and chariot. Other Aryan tribes travelled west and occupied central Europe, bringing with them the Indo-European language which spawned all other European languages. There are indications that they may also have had close links with Iran, for

Sanskrit has similarities with the earliest Iranian languages and the Aryan religion also shows basic Iranian roots. Within the Rig-Veda one can see influences from both Mesopotamia and Egypt, indicating not only the nomadic wanderings of the Aryans but also how they absorbed local customs and beliefs from wherever they went. Indeed, once within India itself the Aryan religions took on other indigenous concepts, some of which derived from the civilisation the Aryans had destroyed.

Of those three very early civilisations (Egypt, Mesopotamia and the Indus), that of the Indus valley remains the most intriguing, enigmatic and appealing. The script, though it was presumed to be an imitation of Sumerian, has not yet been deciphered. It is now thought that if it is related to any modern language at all, it must be to Dravidian, which is spoken in southern India. We know very little about the civilisation of the Indus; nor have we had much time to excavate its artefacts for it was the last of the early civilisations to be discovered, first identified in the remains of one of its great cities, Harappa, in 1921. Yet in size it was the most extensive of the three, larger than either Mesopotamia or Egypt. It reached from the Arabian Sea to north of Delhi, an area of 500,000 square miles, greater than modern Pakistan. It comprised a hundred towns and villages, as well as the cities of Mohenjo-Daro and Harappa, each of which was over three miles in circuit. The civilisation was intense and short – five centuries from 2,300 to 1,750 BC; yet, in its intensity, the style, flavour and character of much of India was formed and has endured to the present day.

The religion of these people emphasised the bull, the tiger and the elephant, while upon their seals the idiosyncratic figure of the seated yogi god first appears. Three figurines predominate: the bull, often standing before an altar; a horned male figure, who could represent the same deity as the bull; and a goddess, generally in hieratic poses. The horned god is thought to be a prototype of the Hindu god Siva, as in the Indus valley there was the same reverence for and celebration of the phallus as we find depicted in Hindu art.

A double grave found at Harappa of a man and a woman indicates the sacrifice of a widow on her husband's death, similar to the later self-sacrifice we know as suttee.

Their cities were composed of brick buildings around a central citadel. The streets were laid out on a grid pattern with the narrower streets running across the main thoroughfares. Many workshops have been discovered, belonging to metalworkers, gold- and coppersmiths, shellworkers and leadmakers, as well as potters' kilns and dyers' vats. The houses varied from one-room dwellings, with cooking and bathing areas partitioned off, to large houses with many rooms and courtyards, with their own private well, toilets and bathrooms. Nearly every house – however small – had some kind of bathroom of its own. These were in addition to public baths. The emphasis on bathing facilities also implies the importance of the purification ceremony. Brick stairways led to upper storeys and flat roofs. The cities also had a pottery drainage system, docks and canals. Perhaps the dock at Lothal is the most astonishing. Built beside the granary for easy unloading, at one end there are a sluice and locking device to control the flow of water to an artificial canal which joined the dock to the nearby estuary.

It is thought that the civilisation grew up in this area because agriculture was much simplified by the annual flooding of the Indus, as neither ploughing, manuring nor irrigation were necessary (which was also the case along the Nile in Egypt). All the main crops, and especially the cereals, were sown as the land emerged from the floods and were harvested a few months later. Wheat, barley and rice were grown, along with peas, mustard, sesame and dates, and as well as cotton. The Indus peoples had domesticated the cat and the dog, humped cattle (to become so vital to India's economy), shorthorns, some fowl, pigs, camels and buffaloes. The elephant too was very likely domesticated – certainly its ivory was used. Gold, silver, copper, lapis lazuli, turquoise and jade were imported: beads, gold, faience and cornelian found in Mohenjo-Daro show clear trading links with Mesopotamia, Crete and Egypt.

## The Aryan Invasion

When the Aryans first invaded it is thought the Indus civilisation was dying, weakened by flooding from the river Indus itself once its lifeblood, now its destroyer. The older books of the Rig-Veda tell of warriors attacking the great walled cities, while Indra, the supreme Aryan god, 'the one who had insight when he was born, who protected the gods with his power of thought, before whose breath the two world-halves tremble at the greatness of his manly powers,'[1] destroys citadels 'as age rents and consumes a garment'.[2]

But there were even earlier peoples* living in India before, throughout and after the Indus civilisation, people living in small rural groups, off the land, who survived after the Aryan invasion. These people had their own culture, their own beliefs and their own deities, and what we see in the originally Aryan Rig-Veda is a gradual absorption of the culture, the ideas and customs of the Indus valley and the Indian peoples elsewhere. The religion of these pre-Aryan peoples was totemism, a belief by which a clan or tribe know themselves to be united by kinship to some animal or plant from which they are descended.[3] This entails a oneness with animals and vegetables, indeed with the whole of creation, a belief in the unity of nature and that the life of humankind is inextricably bound up with the rest of creation (in modern parlance, holism). Though totemism is based on a reverence for a life pact between all living organisms, it has never appeared to halt tribal wars. Tribes are named after a plant or an animal, who is also the dead ancestor of the tribe. The totem is sacred, but also a friend and ally. Kinship with a particular animal means it is never eaten, except occasionally as a ritual sacrifice.

---

*They seem to have been dark-skinned, whereas the Aryans were light-skinned, and were slowly driven south. Under a caste system they eventually came to be regarded as inferior to all others.

Vegetable energy, as well as animal energy, is very widely venerated. Eating offers a way of capturing this force by absorption of the spiritual principle within the plants themselves. To early humans the spectacle of the vegetable world bore clearer witness to the polymorphism of nature than did the animal kingdom. That a tiny seed should produce verdant growth, which in turn would produce new seeds that humans could use or destroy, was a fact to be seen all about the jungle that was the normal environment of humans in India. India's prehistory reveals both a reverence for life, later to be termed *Ahimsa* in Hinduism, and a veneration of animal and plant life.

Other compositions were later added to the body of Vedic literature, such as Samhitas, Brahmanas and Upanishads,* but the hymns in the earlier Rig-Veda – which is an extraordinary Aryan inheritance considering that there is little else left of these first invaders – are always addressed to the high gods of the Aryan religion. They begin by praising the deity, offering sacrifices – grain or milk – by placing them in a fire. Then there are prayers with references to the myths of that particular deity. They conclude with a specific request which hopes for blessings, such as greater herds of cattle, more sons, better health and immortality.

The Aryans worshipped thirty-three gods, called *devas*, concepts made god, standing for various principles observed in nature, the cosmos and life. Later, after 1,000 BC, animals were sacrificed in the Brahmanas and the sacred verses were known as *mantras*. There was an element of blackmail in the spilling of blood to coerce the gods into giving what was asked. Slowly the priests became the elite of a society which had already been divided up into three social classes: warriors, farmers and cattle breeders, and, lastly, servants. Birth fixed people into their class for ever. Later, Hinduism created more classes and developed the caste system.

The hymns of the Rig-Veda may be formal but they are never dull; they are constantly irradiated by lyricism and mystical concepts. Of creation the Rig-Veda says: 'Death was not there, nor was there aught immortal, except for one thing breathless, yet breathed by its own nature.'[4] It is the first recorded mention of breath itself as life, and later, in the Upanishads (600 BC), the idea of breath becomes of even greater significance.†

The Vedic priests were called Brahmins and they, it is thought, learnt many disciplines and traditions from the earlier civilisation of the Indus valley. Yogic techniques of meditation, fasting, celibacy and physical isolation made up a style of devotional renunciation we think of as asceticism, a form of behaviour entirely new to the world. It was slowly

---

*The word means a sitting, an instruction, the sitting at the feet of the master. There are 112 Sanskrit Upanishads in all.

†Part of the Upanishads records the quest to find a co-ordinating principle which would underline aspects of the individual: speech, bearing, intellect. Breath appeared to be the essential attribute of the living. The word for 'soul', *atman*, is derived from *an*, 'breath', placing breath at the heart of the self or soul.

acknowledged that these techniques were useful as spiritual preparations before performing sacrifices.

'In the songs of the Vedas we find the wonder of man before nature: fire and water, the winds and the storms, the sun and the rising of the sun are sung with adoration.'[5] The idea of oneness with God is not yet fully developed in the Vedas (it is later fulfilled in the Upanishads) though it is near, as evinced by Varuna, the god of mercy: 'God made the rivers to flow. They feel no weariness, they cease not from flowing. They fly swiftly like birds in the air. May the stream of my life flow into the river of righteousness . . .'[6] Nor did the Rig-Veda shirk from asking those eternal questions: 'Who knows the truth? Who can tell whence and how arose this universe? The gods are later than its beginning: who knows therefore whence comes this creation?'[7]

The concept of the transmigration of souls later taken up so forcefully by Pythagoras first dimly appears in the Rig-Veda, but it is not expounded until later in the earliest Upanishad, the Brhadaranyaka. As a fervent belief in this idea leads logically to vegetarianism it would be illuminating to know how early it took hold. As we have seen, in the totemistic culture of the pre-Indus civilisation there was already a sense of oneness with creation.

In the Brahmanas (after 1,000 BC) is the idea that sacrifice might not be enough to ensure an afterlife. The Upanishads came out of the teachings of ascetics who in using the technique of physical isolation had begun to live in forests (a technique we shall later see used by early-Christian hermits). In these texts, full of mystical enchantment and psychological perception, the teachers saw that death is not conclusion but a rebirth into another existence and that it is the quality of our actions, our *karma*, which determines the character of the next life.

When the Rig-Veda was the only sacred text the reverence for the cow can be clearly deciphered. This is an allusion to the birth of speech at the beginning of creation: 'When the ancient Dawns first dawned, the great Syllable was born in the footsteps of the Cow.'[8] The idea that the cow preceded speech, and that language was modest enough to begin in a cow's footprints, points inevitably to the symbolism of agriculture, for sowing took place in the wet earth of the river valleys after the flooding and the seeds were placed in the indentations left by the hooves of the oxen.

The Aryans ate meat, but rarely. Meat was kept for sacrifice, for feasts and celebrations. Their diet was 'bread, milk, and products from milk, such as butter, cakes of flour and butter, vegetables and fruit'.[9] Their cooking medium was *ghi*, clarified butter which will keep for months in a hot climate. Barley was their main cereal: ground into flour, baked into cakes and dipped into clarified butter; made into a porridge, thick enough to be licked from the fingers; or diluted and taken as a drink. Both rice and wheat were grown a little later, introduced to the Aryans by the indigenous peoples. Boiled rice was eaten with curds, sesame, clarified butter, mung beans and other vegetables. Cakes were also made from rice flour mixed with sugar and spices. Soup was made from pulses, and pulses were also ground into flour, mixed with water and made into small cakes which were then fried. Milk, however, is the most important food mentioned in the Vedic writings. It was served fresh or boiled or as a cream of boiled milk. No milk was taken from a cow within ten days of calving. Milk was curdled (to make curds or yoghurt) either with the bark of a tree, a kind of creeper or an acid fruit called jujube.[10]

But the Aryans had no taboos about the eating of meat, however infrequent this tended to be. Guests, in fact, were called cow-killers, *goghna*, simply because they induced the host to slaughter an animal for the feast. The idea of an Indian, an orthodox Hindu, of this time killing and eating cows is nowadays deeply shocking to Hindus: 'there was a time when a supply of beef was deemed an absolute necessity by pious Hindus in their journey from this to another world, and a cow was invariably killed to be burnt with the dead.'[11]

The concept of unclean meat was an Aryan one. The flesh of dogs, domestic cocks or pigs, or camels – 'animals which had too much hair or no hair at all, carnivorous animals and animals having two rows of teeth'[12] – was forbidden. Yet it was agreed that when famine conditions existed all the rules could be relaxed and it was permissible to eat whatever was available.

The Aryans permitted animal slaughter only as a religious rite under the supervision of Brahmin priests. There is no way of telling how often ceremonial rituals took place. Killing meat was expensive (wealth was measured by the ownership of cattle) and only the very rich could afford it. The attention paid by the Brahmin priests to the size, shape and colour of cattle suitable for sacrifice was as detailed and precise as it is in the Book of Leviticus. One of the requirements was a white blaze on the forehead, a sign, as we have seen in Ancient Egypt, of the god Apis.

## Hinduism

Around 600 BC we find great changes have taken place. Two of the Upanishads have been written and have refined religious thought. But also, more importantly for those living at the time, war, drought and famine were increasingly common – the old Vedic gods appeared to be failing. Animal sacrifices were beginning to be disapproved of. Though the Brahmins went on sacrificing and eating beef, their habits began to be frowned on; Brahmanism was losing its hold on the people. Such a development can lead to two things: the old orthodoxy attempts to radicalise itself and fresh ideas appear which crystallise unspoken notions and claim the allegiance of the people. Thus the rules of Aryan conduct began to be codified in literature. There are instructions on the lesser sacrifices, and the Dharma-sutras spell out the details of day-to-day conduct, including what is to be eaten and why, all expressed in the most amiable manner:

He who gives no creatures willingly the pain of confinement or death, but

seeks the good of all, enjoys bliss without end. Flesh cannot be obtained
without injury to animals and the slaughter of animals obstructs the way to
heaven; therefore one should avoid flesh . . . He who during a hundred years
annually performs the horse sacrifice and he who entirely abstains from flesh,
enjoy for their virtue an equal reward . . . In eating flesh, in drinking
intoxicating liquors and in carnal intercourse there is no sin, for such
enjoyments are natural; but abstention from them produces great reward.[13]

What had led to the need for such humane clarification? The cynic might say
a young man called Gotama, who was to become known as the enlightened
one, Buddha, and the competition which his teaching generated. But the
social force which in some measure helped instigate the Buddha's quest for
knowledge could equally well have influenced the Brahmin teachers too. But
old orthodoxies take a long time to wither and die:

> most Brahmins aimed at attaining the heaven of the creator god Brahma by
> means of truthfulness, study of the Vedic teachings and either sacrifice or
> austerities. Some were saintly, but others seem to have been haughty and
> wealthy, supporting themselves by putting on large, expensive and bloody
> sacrifices, often paid for by kings.[14]

It was one of these Brahmins who, when asked why he sinned by indulging
in eating the sacred cow, dismissed such new-fangled ideas with the
remark: 'That may very well be, but I shall eat of it nevertheless if the flesh
be tender.'[15]

Population had steadily risen; more land was needed to feed more people;
kingdoms were expanding and drawing into their territory and influence
small kin-based communities; cities had risen as centres of administration,
developing trade based upon a money economy while the ideas of the
Upanishads were being taken to the people by travelling mystics and scholars
(rather like the Pythagorean students in Magna Graecia two hundred years
later), and these led to debates and discussions. It was a time of ferment,
when change was happening on all levels and society seemed fragmented,
undermined by doubt in the Vedic traditions yet boldly asking questions.
These travelling mystic teachers were called *Samanas*, and they roamed the
country; living by alms, stimulating debate and questioning. One central
topic must have been the relevance of the cow and how it became a pivotal
factor in the central tenets of Hinduism.

The humped cow, the zebu, was too valuable domestically to India's
economic and agricultural survival for it to be killed or eaten. It was more
valuable alive for its milk, calves and labour than dead for its meat, since it
was the only animal that could withstand the harshness of the Indian climate.
Camels get stuck in the mud of the monsoons, donkeys and horses consume
more grass and straw and cannot exist on leaves and rinds, while water
buffaloes are costlier to raise and maintain and have less resistance to

drought. So it could well have been these pragmatic factors which helped the cow to be apotheosised, as well as the Egyptian traditions of cow worship which stretch far back into prehistory.

Certainly Hindu theology, in reckoning the number of gods and goddesses in a cow's body at 330 million, raises apotheosis to a fine art. It takes eighty-six transmigrations for a soul to rise from devil to cow, and in one more migration the soul becomes a human form. But souls can easily slip back again, and killing a cow is such a base deed that a soul will slip back all eighty-six transmigrations and become a devil again. Cow worship and vegetarianism are both subsequent to this idea of transmigration and rebirth, the central doctrine of India's religion. With it belongs the concept of *karma*, i.e. that previous acts determine in what guise the soul will be reborn. The process of rebirth is called *samsara*; it has no beginning and no end, but is a perpetual cycle, either of eternal enslavement or of a process of purification through endless rebirths and deaths, until the *atman*, that breath or soul within the body, becomes one with the Brahman, the One God. But this can only happen if a person loses his or her attachment to worldly objects and becomes free of all cravings and desires.

One might be tempted to think that the changes in Hindu theology and teaching, one of them being vegetarianism, were shown the way partly by Buddhist thinking, but the Upanishads began to be written from 800 BC. The thirst for mystical self-revelation by a process of detachment from fleshly pursuits, a process which leads logically and inevitably to a modest vegetarian diet, appears to be in the very soil of the Indian subcontinent, sown there from the earliest times. No land has produced such a quantity and intensity of mystical literature. Early Buddhist thinking sharpened and quickened the process by which ideas gained resonance and greater acceptance and attained written form.

Hindu mystical thought is rich and complex; it is uninhibited by dogma and it has a keen perception of the stirrings of the religious mind. We have seen how Pythagoras was influenced by these ideas; it is astonishing how closely the lifetimes of Buddha and the Greek philosopher overlapped.

## Buddhism

Buddha lived between 566 and 486 BC.★ He condemned all killing, war and aggression, and banned all animal sacrifice and any trade that dealt in carcases. Until the end of his life the Buddhist scriptures were transmitted orally; after his death and after the rule of the vegetarian Emperor Asoka in India the texts proliferate.

> Since the causes of all evil lie within ourselves, we ourselves can, by our own efforts, rid ourselves of them, if we only know how to go about it. Like a

---

★The dates for Pythagoras are less specific – born perhaps in 580 or 560 BC, died in 500 or 480 BC. However, scholars now favour a later date for Buddha, 480-400 BC. So could Buddhism have been influenced by Pythagoras?

good physician the Buddha has given us a profusion of remedies for the great variety of our ailments. A man must first of all bring some morality into his daily life and he must observe the 'five precepts' which forbid killing, stealing, sexual misconduct, lying and the use of intoxicants. Next he must take care how he earns his living. Butchers, fishermen or soldiers, for instance, break the first precept all the time and little spirituality can be expected of them.[16]

It might have been Pythagoras speaking but the effect of Gotama on his homeland was far greater than the Greek in his, for Pythagoras did not have that long and rich mystical tradition concentrated behind him. (There was such a tradition but it was dispersed throughout the Middle East and Egypt.) It was in that tradition that Buddhist teaching took hold. But how did Gotama start such a world revolution?

Gotama was born in a small republic, Sakka, which was not Brahmanised. The rulers had a small council of household heads, one of them Gotama's father. This is the origin of the myth that he was a prince. His mother died the week after his birth and he was brought up by his aunt who was also his stepmother, and at sixteen he married. He was wealthy and surrounded by luxury but he became aware of the misery and poverty of the world.

The *Samana* movement of wandering teachers and mystics was flourishing. Gotama joined them, seeking out teachers to learn spiritual techniques: the 'sphere of nothingness', a mystical trance attained by yogic concentration; or 'the sphere of neither-cognition-nor-non-cognition', where consciousness is so attenuated it hardly exists. However, Gotama was still dissatisfied, so he turned to advanced asceticism, practising non-breathing meditation and reducing his food intake to a few drops of bean soup a day (no taboo against beans here). But he became so ill and physically weak that his body was in pain and torment, which jarred his spiritual tranquillity. He then tried a further meditative technique and while immersed in it was tempted by a devil figure, Mara, who urged him to abandon his quest and take up a more orthodox religious life to earn himself merit. Mara continued to tempt him with minor devils – sloth, cowardice, jealousy, fear of commitment, belittling others, obstinate insensitivity and self-praise – all of which Gotama fought and scorned. The 'conquests of Mara', celebrated in paintings in traditional accounts, set Gotama free to develop deep meditation.

One might ask how vegetarian Gotama's diet was before his enlightenment. Before his asceticism became extreme he would have eaten modestly. *Ghi* (from the Aryans) was the cooking medium, and still is today, but sesame and safflower oil were also used. Milk was boiled down and made into a porridge with added whole grains or toasted barley meal. Rice grew around the Ganges delta. 'Gourds, peas, beans and lentils were widely grown, as were sesame, sugarcane, mango, plantain and the pod-bearing tamarind, sharp-flavoured and refreshing. Essential spices such as pepper, cardamom and ginger were distributed throughout the country from the plantations and entrepots in the south.'[17]

Once the cow had become sacred and a taboo food, what might meat-eaters have eaten? The pig disappeared soon after the Aryan invasion, and sheep were uncomfortable in the climate, which left chicken or goat. On the coast, of course, there was plenty of fish and shellfish.

The very poor peasant probably ate nothing but stale boiled rice with half-cooked gourds or other vegetables, or perhaps a grain porridge★ mixed with mustard stalk, and washed down this unpalatable fare with an unidentified alkaline liquid that reputedly tasted like water from a salt mine. It may have been rice-boiling water left to ferment.†18

*Samanas* lived from alms and Gotama probably survived on a few grains and vegetables. Involuntary vegetarianism must have been the rule for all except the unscrupulous Brahmins and the very rich.

There is a vast Buddhist literature both in Sanskrit and in Chinese and Tibetan translations, covering hundreds of thousands of pages. The Pali canon,19 which is restricted to one particular sect, is eleven times longer than the Bible. It explains the first of the five precepts, 'to abstain from taking life', and was written in Ceylon in about AD 400, at the time of Buddhaghosa (a monk, author and commentator on Buddhist texts).

In the Theravada, among thirty-two discourses on caste, divine vision, enlightenment and self-mortification, there is a reasoned attack on animal sacrifice. In the 152 discourses comprising the Majjhima-Nikaya three touch on food: '. . . never touching flesh of fish or spirits or strong drink or brews of grain' (Dialogue 12; the same words are repeated in Dialogue 36). Dialogue 55 presents one Jivaka asking if it is true that Buddha approves of taking life and eating meat. Buddha shows by examples that this is false, and that a monk eats meat only if he has not seen, heard or suspected that it was specially prepared for him (known as 'the three pure elements'):

Those who talk like that are not accurately quoting words of mine, Jivaka, but are wrongfully misrepresenting me in defiance of fact. I forbid the eating of meat in three cases – if there is the evidence either of your eyes or of your ears or if there are grounds of suspicion. And in three cases I allow it – if there is no evidence either of your eyes or of your ears and if there be no grounds of suspicion.

Take the case, Jivaka, of an Almsman, supported by a village or a township, who dwells with radiant goodwill pervading one quarter of the world – a

---

★Little has changed over the centuries. Jill Tweedie some years ago told me of her experience of living for a week with an average Indian peasant family in the centre of the subcontinent. These women ate nothing but one chapatti a day. The chapatti for the men when they returned in the evening was smeared with a little oil and spices.
†Danilo Dolci, writing thirty years ago about the poverty of Naples,20 talks of teenage children being so hungry they drank the water the spaghetti was cooked in.

second – a third – and then the fourth quarter, pervading the whole length and breadth of the world – above, below, around, everywhere – with radiant goodwill all-embracing, vast, boundless, wherein no hate or malice finds a place. To this Almsman comes a householder or his son with an invitation to tomorrow's meal. If he so desires, the Almsman accepts, and next morning, when the night is over, duly robed and bowl in hand, he makes his way to the house, takes the seat set for him, and is served with an excellent meal. No thought comes to him that he could have wished his host either to desist now, or to desist in future, from furnishing so excellent a meal; he eats his food without greed or blind desire but with a full consciousness of the dangers it involves and with full knowledge that it affords no refuge. Do you think that at such a time that Almsman's thoughts are set on hurting himself, or others, or both?

No, sir.

Is not that Almsman then eating food to which no blame attaches?[21]

Buddhism, like much of Hinduism, appreciates the frailty of human desire, especially for the sensual and hungry enjoyment of food. The lengths that fervent Buddhists go to conquer these cravings are described here:

To such a pitch of asceticism have I gone that naked was I, flouting life's decencies, licking my hands after meals, never heeding when folk called to me to come or to stop, never accepting food brought to me before my rounds or cooked expressly for me, never accepting an invitation, never receiving food direct from pot or pan or within the threshold or among the faggots or pestles, never from [one only of] two people messing together, never from a pregnant woman or a nursing mother or a woman in coitu, never from gleanings [in time of famine] nor from where a dog is ready at hand or where [hungry] flies congregate, never touching flesh or fish or spirits or strong drink or brews of grain. I have visited only one house a day and there taken only one morsel; or I have visited but two or [up to not more than] seven houses a day and taken at each only two or [up to not more than] seven morsels; I have lived on a single saucer of food a day, or on two, or [up to] seven saucers; I have had but one meal a day, or one every two days, or [so on, up to] every seven days, or only once a fortnight, on a rigid scale of rationing. My sole diet has been herbs gathered green, or the grain of wild millets and paddy, or snippets of hide, or water-plants, or the red powder round rice-grains within the husk, or the discarded scum of rice on the boil, or the flour of oil-seeds, or grass, or cowdung. I have lived on wild roots and fruit, or on windfalls only. My raiment has been of hemp or of hempen mixture, of cerements, of rags from the dust-heap, of bark, of the black antelope's pelt either whole or split down the middle, of grass, of strips of bark or wood, or hair of men or animals woven into a blanket, or of owls' wings. In fulfilment of my vows, I have plucked out the hair of my head and the hair of my beard, have never quitted the upright for the sitting posture, have squatted and never risen up, moving only a-squat, have couched on thorns, have gone down to the water punctually thrice before nightfall to wash [away the evil within]. After this wise, in divers fashions, have I lived to torment and to torture my body; – to such a length in asceticism have I gone.[22]

One feels that Buddha in his infinite wisdom would not have approved of the lengths these monks went to, for there appears to be no spiritual development, only the mortification of the body as indulged in by later Christian martyrs, puritans and psychological sadists. In the following example the monk's remark about his 'knotted joints' seems to show inverted vanity:

Thought I to myself: – Come, let me proceed to cut off food altogether. Hereupon, gods came to me begging me not so to do, or else they would feed me through the pores with heavenly essences which would keep me alive. If, thought I to myself, while I profess to be dispensing with all food whatsoever, these gods should feed me all the time through the pores with heavenly essences which keep me alive, that would be imposture on my part. So I rejected their offers, peremptorily.

Thought I to myself: – Come, let me restrict myself to little tiny morsels of food at a time, namely the liquor in which beans or vetches, peas or pulse, have been boiled. I rationed myself accordingly, and my body grew emaciated in the extreme. My members, great and small, grew like the knotted joints of withered creepers . . . rotted at their roots; and all because I ate so little.[23]

Gotama was always very careful in his teaching to point out the 'Middle Way', that path which is taken between the full sensual indulgence in the pleasures of the world which always appears to have elements of self-destructive rage in it and the extremes of ascetic self-mortification, another form of self-hatred. The 'Middle Way' is in fact the same concept as the Greek 'Golden Mean': by moderation in all things a kind of harmony can be achieved. The message was that people were individuals responsible for their own moral and spiritual destiny. Early on Gotama became Buddha, the enlightened one, and turned no student away from his teaching, in sharp contrast to the Brahmins, who taught in Sanskrit, unintelligible to all except the academics, and accepted only males from the top three classes.

In the early texts is a picture of Buddha calming wild animals, as Pythagoras did, even a charging elephant that stopped and bowed its head, allowing Buddha to stroke it. His teachings urged non-violence and compassion towards all creatures and all forms of sentient life. This view springs out of the cycle of rebirth in which all life is involved. *Samsara* means 'wandering on', and the rebirths are almost infinite. On the night of his enlightenment Buddha remembered a hundred thousand of them over vast stretches of time, as animals, insects and invisible beings. These are all a lower class of rebirth, in which suffering and pain will be greater. Higher rebirths are as gods and humans. The gods become more and more refined as they escape from all mortal memories of pleasure and the world, experiencing the 'formless realm'. Lastly there is the summit of existence, the most subtle form of perfection with a huge lifespan.

But, as with those of Pythagoras, Buddha's doctrines were never written down, and when facts, including dates, are so notoriously uncertain there are always voices to question some elements of traditional Buddhism. As food is basic to our physical existence, ethical questions inevitably centre upon whether Buddha really did abstain from meat and, if not, how soon the two concepts of Buddhism and vegetarianism became so intertwined.

It is thought that a council of monks met shortly after Buddha's attainment of Nirvana, when those present recited and agreed upon their recollections of his teaching. A second such council is said to have been held a century later, an account of which is given in the Mahāvastu and includes the rules regarding the consumption of meat. The Mahāvastu grew over a number of centuries, possibly beginning in the late second century BC. If we accept the dates for Buddha's life mentioned earlier, this is, of course, still 200 years after his death. Indeed, there is perhaps a parallel with the biographies of Pythagoras written by Timaeus and others discussed in the last chapter, for, in the Mahāvastu, Gotama is seen as transcendental even before Buddhahood: no dust sticks to his feet, he is never tired, he eats out of a wish to conform with the world and to give the opportunity to others to earn merit by giving him alms-food.

In the Mahāvastu certain meats are forbidden absolutely – the flesh of elephant, horse and dog – but it is clear that the eating of meat is not generally prohibited. A basic principle was that 'No one should eat meat intended for the recipient.' The rule revolves around almsgiving: monks should not pick and choose what food was acceptable in their begging-bowls for this might deprive a donor of the opportunity of gaining merit.

This continued to be the rule. When Xuan Zang (died AD 664), the Chinese scholar, pilgrim and vegetarian, visited the Buddhist sites in India he found communities that eat 'only the three pure elements'.[24] The development of pure vegetarianism for monks was due to Mahayana groups (founded around AD 200) who had been criticised by Jain and Hindu vegetarian sects, and later influenced northern and eastern Buddhism. In the Lankāvatāra-sutra, which was translated into Chinese in AD 430, is a whole chapter on the eating of meat and why Buddhists should abstain completely. It specifically condemns the rule of 'the three pure elements'. This is thought to be the first text which equates vegetarianism with Buddhism. Further reasons for abstention from flesh, it adds, are that one may be eating relatives, it is bad for the health and it causes pain to living creatures.[25]

Within his lifetime Buddha created the *Sangha*, or 'order' of nuns and monks, and the religion began to spread slowly across India. But

Hinduism was not its only rival, and of the other religions and their teachers the most prominent was Jainism, founded by Vardhamana the Mahavira, or 'Great Hero'.

## Jainism

The founder of Jainism was a contemporary of Gotama, who also reacted against the Brahmins, their wealth, elitism and sacrificial killing of animals. Jainism assimilated some Indian deities from Vedic writings, and shared many Buddhist concepts, but it developed the idea of asceticism much further, teaching that all things have life, even rocks and stones, and that the task of living is to liberate that 'life' trapped in matter and flesh by striving towards ever greater austerities. As part of their total non-violence and vegetarianism Jains would have servants sweep the dusty path in front of them to save any unfortunate insects being trodden on, and would wear gauze over their mouth and nose so as not to swallow a midge or two.

Mahavira, the Great Hero, was born in 599 BC near Patna, which made him older than Gotama. He began his wandering ascetic life at the age of twenty-eight, enduring hardship and practising meditation until he attained enlightenment, and preached Jainism for thirty years before dying at Pava in 527 BC.

Jainism preaches universal tolerance. It never evangelises and is not competitive or critical. It is both a philosophy and a religion and still flourishes, mainly in western India; unlike Buddhism it never travelled far from its birthplace.

## Asoka

It is always helpful for a new idea or movement to have friends and converts in high places, and the spread of Buddhism over India and eventually elsewhere was boosted by the Emperor Asoka, who reigned from 265 to 238 BC. Asoka inherited the Magadhan Empire founded in 543 BC in the Ganges Valley. The empire became more and more powerful for its people were brilliant administrators: taxes were levied on land, each village had its own headman to collect them, trade with the East flourished and rich deposits of iron ore were mined. When Asoka succeeded to it the empire was almost as large as modern India. Soon after Asoka became emperor he had to subjugate the eastern coastal province of Kalinga. The resulting carnage and suffering so distressed the emperor that he became a convert to the Buddhist religion. He renounced all armed conquest from then on.

Asoka ruled for thirty-seven years, adopting the principles of 'conquest by *Dharma*', the principles of right life. In an edict after the Kalinga conquest he expressed shame and remorse and claimed he would govern to please and protect his subjects according to *Dhamma*.* He continued to issue edicts throughout his reign, engraving them on rocks and pillars, now known as

---

*Dhamma* is the Prakrit form of the Sanskrit *Dharma*.

Rock Edicts and Pillar Edicts.* The word *Dhamma* is almost impossible to translate, for it has a wealth of meanings – the universal law, the social order, piety, righteousness – and Buddhists often used *Dhamma* in connection with the teachings of Buddha. The edicts speak of non-violence, tolerance of all sects and opinions, obedience to parents, respect for the Brahmin and all religious teachers, humane treatment of servants and generosity to friends. Asoka also banned all animal sacrifice and stopped the slaughter of animals for food. The whole of the large royal household had become vegetarian. A royal banquet would begin with fruits – pomegranates, grapes, dates and mangoes – continue with sweet cakes, then boiled and scented rice with a selection of vegetables stewed with spices, followed by dishes of flavoured curds and finally a dish, sweetened with honey, of milk boiled down until it thickens and tinted with saffron.[26]

As a ruler of a huge empire Asoka must have been unique in his compassion and goodness. He said: 'All men are my children. As for my own children I desire that they may be provided with all the welfare and happiness of this world and of the next, so do I desire for all men as well.'[27] He built hospitals for men and animals, planted and encouraged the use of medicinal herbs, built roads and resthouses, arranged the planting of trees and groves and the digging of wells. More success, he is reported to have said, is attained in life by reasoning with people than by issuing commands.

His espousal of Buddhism strengthened its influence outside India. He built many monasteries and took strong measures to suppress schisms within the Buddhist religious community. He prescribed a course of scriptural studies for adherents and enthusiastically sent his son and daughter to Ceylon as missionaries.

Under this benevolent and wise ruler the empire thrived, but at Asoka's death it fell apart and declined, breaking up into separate states and kingdoms, which is how it remained for many centuries until British rule. But Buddhism was now on its way to becoming a world religion and vegetarianism, as one of its most basic tenets, had a new image – it was not simply the result of poverty but an act of piety, central to self-purification, the basis of an ethical view of life, a view it took to Tibet, China and Japan, leaving Hinduism to recover its power in India. But Hinduism now had taken on the doctrine of the transmigration of souls and, in southern India particularly, on the edge of Asoka's empire, it embraced not killing animals for food. Vegetarianism in southern India flourishes today, with a large tradition of vegetarian dishes, some of which Asoka must have eaten. Some even, in their use of sesame and mustard seed, could not be so very different from dishes eaten in the early civilisation of the Indus valley itself.

It is also notable that vegetarianism in India, whether for Hindu or Buddhist, does not seem to have been a symbolic threat to the community and the moral worth of its laws. It appears to have represented a search for piety and was respected as such.

---

*The lion capital of one of these pillars found at Samath has become India's national emblem.

# 4

# Plato to Porphyry

This chapter could be subtitled 'from ambivalence to commitment', for over the 600 years it covers, with a wealth of thought and philosophical speculation, the two philosophers who were to have the most far-reaching influence, Plato and Aristotle, were the most equivocal on the question of animal rights. Writers as great in spirit as Seneca and Plutarch were committed vegetarians but had, alas, less influence on the future.

## Plato at Table

As so many of Plato's metaphysical concepts had their roots in Pythagoreanism (seen most particularly in *Phaedo*, a defence of the soul's immortality), it is mysterious that Plato never made the logical step towards vegetarianism. Food as such does not appear as a high ethical priority in the dialogues. In Plato's *Gorgias*, Socrates dismisses cooking, saying it is 'a kind of knack gained by experience . . . a knack to producing gratification and pleasure . . .'[1] Later, Socrates stresses this notion:

> cookery, unlike medicine, is a knack, not an art, and I added that, whereas medicine studies the nature of the patient before it treats him and knows the reasons which dictate its actions and can give a rational account of both, cookery on the other hand approaches in a thoroughly unmethodical way even that pleasure which is the sole object of its ministration . . .[2]

Philosophers can perhaps dismiss food if they see it as beginning its life in the kitchen, a few inert ingredients which need only to be prepared, cooked and served. The mistake of entirely ignoring where food comes from is frequently made nowadays, because the gap between modern technological farming, the supermarket and the kitchen full of modern appliances is an ever-widening one; but one would have thought this mistake was less easily made in previous ages, when live creatures were squawking and running around in the yard and the house, and a great deal of skill, thought, care and experience went into the selection, breeding, feeding, slaughtering and butchering of an animal, all of which activities, on the ideal Platonic farm, would demand ethical decision-making.

Pythagoras not only had a horror of the slaughterhouse but found it difficult to be near either a butcher or a cook.

Though Socrates ate meat he disapproved of certain parts of the carcase, such as the udder, entrails and such offal as the brains because of their negative effects upon the temperament. Socrates' influence then and later appears to have been only in encouraging moderation: his advice was not to eat unless hungry. This view may have been born of a general indifference to food: when his wife, Xanthippe, was ashamed of a meal, he told her not to mind because reasonable guests would put up with it, while the others could be dismissed as unworthy of consideration. Do we infer from these passages in *Gorgias* that Plato wants diet to be brought within the control of a mathematically based medicine? In any case, does he include abstinence from meat in such a scheme of control? – because, unlike Pythagoras, he sees the whole animal kingdom in a light which anticipates the later Christian sense of superiority over the living world. For animals, according to Plato, can be anarchic, bursting with an irrational spirit, and therefore threatening: Socrates (or is it Plato speaking?) believed that men were happier than beasts as beasts lacked speech and could not perceive the existence of the gods. As the Platonic man has an immortal soul, he is therefore naturally superior to animals, and hence may eat them. But there is an indication that Plato is equivocal on the subject; in the second book of *The Republic*, Socrates speaks to Glaucon on the details of the ideal city:

'But let us consider the matter and not draw back. And first, let us consider what will be the manner of life of men so equipped. Will they not spend their time in the production of corn and wine and clothing and shoes? And they will build themselves houses; in summer they will generally work without their coats and shoes, but in winter they will be well clothed and shod. For food they will make meal from their barley and flour from their wheat, and kneading and baking them they will heap their noble scones and loaves on reeds or fresh leaves, and lying on couches of bryony and myrtle boughs will feast with their children, drink wine after their repast, crown their heads with garlands, and sing hymns to the gods. So they will live with one another in happiness, not begetting children above their means, and guarding against the danger of poverty or war.

Here Glaucon interrupted and said: 'Apparently you give your men dry bread to feast on.'

'You are right,' I said; 'I forgot that they would have a relish with it. They will have salt and olives and cheese, and they will have boiled dishes with onions and such vegetables as one gets in the country. And I expect we must allow them a dessert of figs, and peas and beans, and they will roast myrtle berries and acorns at the fire, and drink their wine in moderation. Leading so peaceful and healthy a life they will naturally attain to a good old age, and at death leave their children to live as they have done.'

'Why,' said Glaucon, 'if you had been founding a city of pigs, Socrates, this is just how you would have fattened them.'

'Well, Glaucon, how must they live?'

'In an ordinary decent manner,' he said. 'If they are not to be miserable, I think they must have couches to lie on and tables to eat from, and the ordinary dishes and desserts of modern life.'[3]

Socrates opposes Glaucon's suggestion, claiming that this would entail the pursuit of luxury rather than good health. And further, he argues, the pursuit of luxurious meat–eating, the need to satisfy a population's lavish needs, leads inevitably to war. As Dombrowski says: 'That the republic was to be a vegetarian city is one of the bestkept secrets in the history of philosophy.'[4]

In the *Laws* one Clinias states (obviously with Plato's approval) that vegetarianism is a widely current and highly creditable tradition.[5] In *Epinomis* Plato talks of men long ago who were wise and condemned the devouring of animals:'Plato bestows on their rule a blessing of the first order, eating barley and what is still admirable . . .'[6]

Plato may reflect very dimly Buddha's attitude in that he recommends a diet without flesh but says that it would be an unkindness to refuse a portion of meat offered as alms. There is also a feeling that he rather disapproved of food – it was necessary fuel but never a pleasure. After his visit to Sicily he wrote:

> When I came to Sicily I was in no way pleased at all with 'the blissful life' as it is there termed, replete as it is with Italian and Syracusan banqueting: for thus one's existence is spent in gorging food twice a day and never sleeping alone at night and all the practices which accompany this mode of living.[7]

## Greek Food

Perhaps these passages are best placed in context by examining the food of the Hellenic age.

The culture of classical Greece was of such magnificient power and beauty, and had such enormous influence upon western society that, up until very recently, we hardly considered what these people actually ate. In fact historians were dismissive as to the cuisine, agreeing that the Attic dinner consisted of two courses, the first a kind of porridge and the second a kind of porridge. Both were made from barley and we have already seen that this derogatory remark was far from true. Scholars had ignored all the food details in the hundreds of Attic comedies from which Athenaeus quoted.

When examining food in past cultures we tend only to look at the food of the elite, for that small minority is the one that has left records. However, we should not forget the millions who slaved and worked the soil for their diet is highly informative too. The majority of peoples in the Ancient World were farmers cultivating land which was bordered by wild forest, mountains and sea and these places teemed with life that could be caught and eaten. By the time of the Golden Age much of the forests of Attica had been cut down for ships and the heavy rains of winter now washed the top soil away. Good pasture for livestock grazing was a problem. The majority of people were poor, eating meat only perhaps twice a year at the major festivals, they depended on foods from the wild to flavour and augment their diet. From the wild they ate seeds, lupins are mentioned, nuts and bulbs, iris rhizomes were a favourite and a host of green leaves and herbs. Wild foods were a larder of myriad flavours and textures. It is these foods with their thousands of trace minerals which enriched the diet and which we lack today.

The olive tree, its fruits and oil, was central to the cuisine and agricultural economy of Greece. We cannot now imagine eating a Greek meal without its presence, it was the same then. The audience for the Attic comedies were certainly not farmers, they were all city people, not just the elite, but the tradesmen and shopkeepers, the craftsmen, potters and armourers. So the frequent food references were appreciated by an audience of all classes. They were as food obsessed as we are now.

They loved fish more than any other food. There was a great range eaten, mentioned in the literature are shellfish, tunny, pike and carp, grey mullet, blue fish, catfish, conger eel, dogfish (types of shark), skate, ray, sturgeon and swordfish. Tunny was the most important economically, its route of annual migration known to fishermen since prehistory. It would have been sliced in steaks, fried on iron skillets in olive oil and while cooking be sprinkled with aromatic herbs and cumin. To be served only with a green salad, according to Archestratus. How very contemporary they sound, and so they should; people do not change overmuch, the human condition remains the same and so do our palates, our sense of flavour and good taste. The Greeks of the Golden Age are only forty-eight generations ago; compared to the time human beings have taken to evolve that is a brief second.

Tunny was also salted and exported in jars from southern Spain, Sicily and Byzantium. Salted sturgeon was not so common, and generally eaten as an appetiser. But let us look at what a dinner might have contained for the elite – the ruling class of Athens.

It would have begun with sweet wine and appetisers. These might be small dishes of asparagus, capers, lightly poached cardoon stalks, beet leaves wrapped around little parcels of rice, herbs and spices, portions of baked baby eel wrapped with chard leaves, a dish of carrot, celery, and sesame seeds, some chopped chicory or mustard greens tossed in oil and vinegar, sliced fennel, grape hyacinth bulbs sprinkled with a salty cheese, fava beans cooked in chicken stock and flavoured with oregano, some baby leeks eaten raw, fried cicadas (the egg bearing females were much favoured), small birds spit roasted, a dish of chopped mint to accompany the sea urchins, quail eggs, pickled scallops, salted anchovies, salted or smoked mackerel sent from Byzantium and squid in its ink, dishes of crabs, lobsters and prawns, various mushrooms and truffles, a dish of spring onions and chives, some purslane, radish and rocket, a dish of poached rock samphire and a bowl of fresh watercress. To add more flavour there would have been salt, fish sauce first made by the Greeks on the coast of the Black sea, honey, roasted sesame seeds, olive oil, vinegar, silphium and long pepper. Black peppercorns arrived in the Ancient World early AD at the time of Augustus. These would all have been served with bread, the amount and variety is similar to anything served now here or in Turkey or North Africa. It is the Mediterranean experience and it has been there for many centuries. Of course this variety and amount would only occur at a huge and special banquet; generally for dining with a few friends one would have had about a half dozen of these.

Afterwards, at this dinner people might have eaten fish*. Tunny or shark steaks or a whole grey mullet, or a great mound of indiscriminate tiny fish dredged in flour and fried just as we eat whitebait. They might have had grey mullet served whole; chunks of great eels drenched in a green sauce were prized as delicacies. Shark steaks were eaten sprinkled with cumin, salt and green olive oil. Different cooking methods were recommended for different cuts. Cookery books containing hundreds of recipes were very popular. They have sadly all been lost, but Athenaeus mentioned their popularity.[8]

After the fish course there might have been hare, a favourite dish, because it was small and considered exclusive.† Archestratus wants hare to be cooked simply, grilled on the spit, then just sprinkled with chopped coriander, salt, cheese or dipped into highly flavoured sauces. The offal and blood were prepared and cooked separately in a stew with herbs, vegetables, wine and spices.

Pork was the commonest meat on Athenian menus. Pig was much valued for every part could be eaten and they were easily fed with scraps and allowed out into the forests to root for themselves. Pigs were highly economic creatures, they cost very little to raise and their return was enormous. A fact, in this century, which Chairman Mao recognised when he said every Chinese family should keep a pig. Sow's womb was thought a delicacy especially after a miscarriage. Also the pig carcass was salted and smoked for hams and bacon.

Both sheep and goats were valued for their hides, wool, milk and manure, more than their carcass meat But sheep and goat were also regularly sacrificed so people ate them then. Because the adults were so valued kid and lamb became a luxury, only slaughtered for feasts and festivals. The greatest sacrifice to the gods would have been a whole ox, because oxen were used to pull ploughs and carts and what you were killing was a valued working creature. This is why eating beef represented an unwelcome gluttony and was frowned upon.

Of the wild animals almost everything was eaten, even lions and bears, dogs and puppies. Wild boar, goat, ass, fox and deer were all hunted, skinned and roasted, though the offal was much prized and would have been cooked

---

*Large fish heads were considered a great delicacy, they were lightly poached, and for the elite, the various parts were prepared with their requisite sauces by slaves.
†Though hares were a common sight on the plains around Athens.

separately in a stew, while the marrow bones and the tongue were also treated as separate items.

The Greeks, as did the Egyptians, farmed many of the wild birds. Quail was valued because they laid so many eggs. Geese were force fed and pigeons, pheasants and mallards were all bred and kept for food. The hen reached Greece from India and Persia quite late, but certainly before 600 BC, the rooster was called the Persian Awakener. Eggs were used soft boiled in cooking, or the yolks and whites were used separately. Eggs from peahens and Egypt geese were thought to be superior to all other eggs.

Beekeeping was a highly specialised skill as honey was much valued, used in cooking and confectionery; honeycombs could be bought in the market in Athens.

In the heat of the Mediterranean milk would sour quickly, besides it was a precious commodity, much more appreciated when turned into cheese or yoghurt (pyriate). So milk was despised, was thought to be a sign of poverty as only rural people drank it, while butter eaters was also a derogatory term – a name for the Thracians.

Sheep and goat's milk cheeses which used rennet from fig were made. Cow's milk cheese was thought to be the richest. Cheese was wrapped in leaves to keep it fresh. Cheese was eaten with honey, fruits, vegetables, olives figs and bread.

Juicy fruits could also be appetisers, to refresh the palate at the start of the meal, fruits were also dried and nuts were served with the wine. In the summer the fruits of Greece were, of course, abundant, so fruits were also slightly denigrated, thought of as food for travellers or workers in the fields and the poor. Fat quinces spread north from Crete, while mainland Greece had orchards of apples, pears and plums. Watermelons and musk melons were both imported from Egypt. In the wild pomegranates grew with sloes and sour cherries. A new fruit from Greece were the cucumbers from the Himalayas eaten as an appetiser. Fig leaves were pickled as now and used as wrappers for food. Myrtle berries were chewed fresh after the meal with dried dates and dried figs. Medlars, arbutus fruits, (from the so called strawberry tree) mulberries, blackberries and winter cherry, were all made into desserts. Also, to complete the meal there were almonds, fresh or ground, walnuts, filberts, hazelnuts, sweet chestnuts and pine kernels. All of these could have been made into sweetmeats mixed with spices, eggs and flour. Mastic, that wonderful aromatic resin from the lentisk tree in Chios would be chewed.

Some vegetables were also associated with the poor and therefore thought not appetising. These vegetables were many of the wild ones, asphodel, chervil, fat hen, wild spinach, mustard greens, golden thistle, squill. Some vegetables were boiled together to form a rustic dish: alexanders, fennel, asparagus, carrot and chicory. But some vegetables must have been highly respected otherwise no cookery book would have been dedicated to them.

Certainly, the vegetables used as flavourings were highly prized. Garlic, basil, coriander leaf and seed, mustard and oregano were the most popular. Others were almonds, sesame seeds, raisins, fennel, dill, capers, onion, leek, honey, must, vinegar, olive oil, salt, egg and cheese. Also wormwood, anise, basil, cumin, hyssop, rue, sage, thyme, pennyroyal (for flavouring lentil soup), flax seed and poppy seed as an aromatic garnish on breads.

There were two aromatics not indigenous to Greece which had to be imported. Sumach, its red cluster of seeds was only prepared as a flavouring in Syria and then exported to the rest of the civilised world. Solon in the 6th century wrote a poem in its praise. And sylphium which only grew in Greek Cyrene in North Africa. This bulb which the Ancient World was addicted to is thought to be like asafoetida, for the Romans, when they could not get any more sylphium, went over to using asafoetida. The Greeks grated the bulb onto birds before roasting and also mixed it with cheese and vinegar to flavour fish, it was used extensively in sauces and marinades. (The Romans ate the whole bulb and stem sliced and preserved in vinegar.) Let us hope it has not really vanished, it is just that no one looks for it anymore. The wild plants were harvested so completely (for attempts at cultivation failed) that it died out in the first century AD.

According to Athenaeus there was a wealth of different kinds of bread, seventy-two types using different flours – barley, wheat, rice, coarse or finely ground – made with milk or oil. Bread flavoured with cumin, poppy seeds, fennel, coriander, raisins, fenugreek, nigella, marjoram, rosemary, capers, sage, cabbage leaves, garlic and onion. Bread made into all kinds of shapes: braids, crescents, animals, mushrooms. The Greeks were master-bakers and even at the time of the Roman Empire the Greeks were the bakers of Rome.

Athenaeus also gives us some fish recipes by Archestratus (*fl.* 450 BC), the gastronome, writer and cook: recipes for tuna, parrot fish, mullet and eels, which are first of all intently concerned with where the fish is caught, exhibiting a gourmet discernment and a knowledge of tides, seasons and the natural life-cycle of the fish itself. When it comes to the cooking, an Archestratus recipe would be much appreciated today. On parrot fish:

> When you have it, eat it whole; once you have smeared it with cheese and oil, place it in a very hot oven, spread crushed salt mixed with oil and cumin over it, pouring it out with your hand as though you were taking it from a fountain presided over by some deity.

Not only was there an abundance of food cooked to the highest gastronomic standards, but food also was a source of ethical discourse. The philosopher has concluded that food exists for sustenance and not pleasure; when that line is crossed anxiety begins. Socrates disapproves of the man who dines greedily; his judgement of table manners is very precise, for if a man does not take an equal amount of bread (*sitos*) as he does of other foods (*opson*) or stuffs his food into his mouth when it is too hot and has to gulp it down noisily it all reflects badly on his character. He is an *opsophagos*, a term later used to mean one politically corrupt and taking bribes.[9] Food is a dangerous area in philosophy, it is seen as a beguiling trap, too many have lost their souls to such sensual indulgence, so while it is clear that gourmet cooking of a high standard flourished in the Golden Age, philosophers tended also to pour scorn upon the pursuit and enjoyment of it. Yet the Pythagoreans seemed to have been mocked and lampooned with more gusto than others. Perhaps with such gastronomy tempting the circumspect gourmet, those that totally ignored such delights were thought a little crazy and worthy of ridicule. Nothing much has changed.

## Aristotle

The Platonic ambivalence is shared to an even greater degree by Aristotle. As he played a part in medieval Christian thinking, such ambivalence is rather to be regretted, for he was much revered and has helped shape many of our attitudes in society today. Aristotle denies the power of thought to animals, maintaining that they are capable only of sensation and appetite, and that they need the rule of humankind in order to survive. (Why or how animals flourish in the wild he appears not to have considered.) In the Aristotelian view plants and animals exist for the use of humans. In one passage he equates animals with slaves, by saying the ways we use tame animals and slaves are not very different. (This, of course, merely illuminates how the Greeks saw their slaves.) How very different from Pythagoras, who saw the immortal soul in everything, although even Aristotle admits: 'we should approach the inquiry about each animal without aversion, knowing that in all of them there is something natural and beautiful.'[10]

Aristotle also writes sympathetically of the Orphic view: 'the poems known as Orphic say that the soul borne by the winds, enters from the air into the animals when they breathe.'[11] This view of breath as akin to soul is close to the Hindu view and that of Homer, and Aristotle seems here to agree with Pythagoras that animals have souls. To be inconsistent was not a crime then, as it seems to be today – we must understand that the complexity of the world and the enthusiastic exploration of it were mirrored in such ambivalence.

We find a true vegetarian again in Theophrastus, Aristotle's pupil. Born in Lesbos in 372 BC he studied in Athens under Aristotle and became his friend, travelling back to Lesbos with him, where Aristotle established a philosophical circle in Mytilene, the capital. It was here that Aristotle first studied biology and scrutinised the natural aims of plants and animals, for in knowing their final goals he believed that he could understand their structure and development. Perhaps his pupil began work on his own *Inquiry into Plants* and *Growth of Plants*, two of his books which have survived, but his own findings and thoughts differ from his teacher's in a quite radical way. He did not think that animals existed for the sake of humans, and thought killing animals unnecessary and unjust, and that the habit of eating them must have begun when war destroyed crops. If plants and vegetable foods were abundant there was no need to eat animal flesh.

## The Stoics

After Aristotle's death Theophrastus became head of the Lyceum at Athens. His vegetarianism was a result also of his worship of the Golden Age, when libations were performed with honey, oil and wine. He believed that when animal sacrifices began, the gods became angry and humankind turned to atheism.

What effect did any of these men have on the eating habits of their contemporaries? Very little, probably, for whether to abstain or not from meat appears to have been a personal decision. Take some cynics of the fourth century BC, for example, who were often compared to Socrates: Diogenes had a Socratic dislike of gluttony which led him to a diet of vegetables, cheese and figs; another, Metrocles, dined from lupin seeds, while Crates wrote a poem in praise of a vegetarian utopia:

> There is a city, Pera, in the midst of wine-dark vapour,
> Fair, fruitful, passing squalid, owning nought,
> Into which sails nor fool nor parasite
> Nor glutton, slave of sensual appetite,
> But thyme it bears, garlic, and figs and loaves,
> For which things' sake men fight not each other,
> Nor stand to arms for money or for fame.[12]

A friend of Plato's, one Menedemus, would eat only olives as a rebuke to an extravagant host and, it is said, became sick when he learned that he had eaten meat by mistake.[13]

These isolated incidents tell us very little. It would seem that there was no vegetarian group or movement which continued after the Pythagorean school had broken up. Nor was there much help in clarifying former ambivalence from the new school of the Stoics led by Zeno (335-263 BC), who taught that plants existed for animals and animals for humans, a concept which Biblical texts promoted. Animals are irrational, Zeno claimed; therefore to extend justice towards animals would abuse the very principle of justice; hence, as they are incapable of receiving justice, we do not need to give it. Yet Zeno, we are told, lived such an ascetic life that no meat ever passed his lips anyway – he lived on bread and honey.

Such a highly limited diet was eaten by another Stoic and contemporary, Epicurus (341-270 BC) whose school of disciples in Athens studied philosophy in his garden. They lived off barley bread, water and a half-pint of wine a day, hardly what is now thought of as an Epicurean meal. During a famine Epicurus saved his students by handing out a few beans to them as a daily ration. Epicurus taught that humankind was the centre of the universe – anthropocentrism. Death is not to be feared as there is no future life for the soul, which dissolves immediately, once it has left the body, into the primordial atoms from which it was compounded. The sole criterion of good and evil is sensation; thus he declared that pleasure was the beginning and end of life. But this rather positive and celebratory view was undercut by Epicurus' qualifying definition of pleasure as the absence of pain. He said that one should avoid those foods which, though giving pleasure at the time, afterwards leave one feeling deprived. It is a subtle insight, for the source of all gluttony lies in that feeling of deprivation; the reason behind all addiction and all longing for certain foods and drinks lies in that anger, irritation and lust. So ironically the Epicureans believed that pleasure could best be achieved by practising self-restraint and avoiding desire. Epicurus aimed for a withdrawn and quiet life enriched by the company of friends – women were allowed into the garden as students, which caused comment, rumour and scandal.

These basic Epicurean subtleties Athenaeus seems to have missed, for Epicurus became a synonym for luxury and pleasure early on. He quotes Epicurus as saying: 'As for myself I cannot conceive of the Good if I exclude the pleasures derived from taste, or those derived from sexual intercourse, or those derived from entertainments to which we listen, or those derived from the motions of a figure delightful to the eye.'[14] But the essential message of Epicurus was more profound. Real peace of mind comes from rejecting all superstition and religious rites. Temperance and loyalty are stressed, while hedonism and gluttony are frowned upon. Life becomes the finest pleasure because hell and fear are vanquished with the knowledge that life does not continue after the grave, for the fewer desires and longings one has, the less the pain of unsatisfied longing.

The school of Epicurus, then, followed a meagre diet, living off vegetables and fruit. They did so to preach how little food is required for the sustenance of humans. On the killing of animals, they tended to agree that such action was dictated by taste.

Epicurus himself was Stoic to a degree upon the subject: he thought that death would hardly be a misfortune as when he was alive he could not suffer it and when dead he would be past suffering. This would be true for animals as well as humans. His atomist view, that humans and animals were mere machines, and his view that everything in the world was created for our pleasure, was taken up by the Romans. It is a view which allows untold cruelty to be inflicted on sentient beings without anxiety, while the concept of pleasure was divested of all Epicurean subtlety by the Romans and turned into something crude and unfeeling to all others. It is this which Athenaeus reflects, a kind of gustatory indulgence without end.

Epicurus was grossly misinterpreted. He wished to find a path free from desire and from fear, superstition and illusion. He was unconcerned about the soul ascending to the divine; he wanted to show humankind's self-sufficiency, to throw people back upon their own resources, independent of God. He believed that the human spirit had been crushed by the burden of religion and must be set free to work out its own solution. Epicurus was, in fact, the first humanist.[15]

## Rome

In Rome, where it was not unusual to see 2,000 gladiators killing each other and 230 wild animals billed to die in the same afternoon, while people could be condemned to be eaten by the beasts as part of public entertainment (the law was repealed eventually by Constantine in AD 326), it is perhaps astonishing that anyone became a committed vegetarian. Yet they existed. Even though the public games continued interminably with ever more ghastly cruelties, there were moments when the crowd had had enough. The elder Pliny described this scene in 55 BC, when Pompeius had arranged a grand spectacle for the populace in which a large number of elephants were forced to fight:

> When they lost the hope of escape, they sought the compassion of the crowd with an appearance that is indescribable, bewailing themselves with a sort of lamentation, so much to the pain of the populace that forgetful of the imperator and the elaborate munificence displayed for their honour, they all rose up in tears and bestowed imprecations on Pompeius, of which he soon after experienced the effect.[16]

Cicero records the same event:

> What followed for five days, was successive combats between a man and a wild beast. It was magnificent. No one disputes it. But what pleasure can it be to a person of refinement, when either a weak man is torn to pieces by a very powerful beast, or a noble animal is struck through by a hunting spear. The last day was that of the elephants, in which there was great astonishment on the part of the populace and crowd, but no enjoyment. Indeed, there followed a degree of compassion, and a certain idea that there is a sort of fellowship between that huge animal and the human race.[17]

In fact the very grossness of this cruelty towards humans and animals must have so repulsed and nauseated some that inevitably they embraced the notion of a non-violent world. At the imperial feasts we read of episodes where hundreds of different fish were served and mountainous quantities of beef wild boar, venison, ostrich and peacock were eaten; perhaps some people ate vegetables out of a feeling of nausea at such a surfeit and waste. Certainly we find a hint of this in the Stoic writer, Seneca (4 BC–AD 65), who became a vegetarian and wrote of the pagan festival that would be transmogrified into Christmas in a way that sounds horribly pertinent to us now: 'December is the month when the city most especially gives itself up to riotous living. Free licence is allowed to the public luxury. Every place resounds with the gigantic preparations for eating and gorging, just as if the whole year were not a sort of Saturnalia.'

Seneca strikes another contemporary note when he also writes:

An ox is satisfied with the pasture of an acre or two: one would suffice for several elephants. Man alone supports himself by the pillage of the whole Earth and Sea. What! Has Nature indeed given us so insatiable a stomach, while she has given us so insignificant bodies? No: it is not the hunger of our stomachs, but insatiable covetousness which costs so much.[18]

It is not surprising that he was an admirer of Epicurus and wrote that his teaching was just and holy, going on to complain that Epicurus was misunderstood, defamed and undervalued by popular writers of the Stoic school. Seneca had to forgo his vegetarianism, or pretend to, because of imperial suspicion, but continued to practise it in private life. He tutored Nero, was condemned to be killed by Caligula (but Seneca argued that his life was sure to be short anyway), was said to be a friend of St Paul, and, though part of the Stoic tradition, often criticised it. He had a Pythagorean teacher, Sotion, who would have made him sympathetic to the idea of abstention from flesh and given him the passion to denounce, unlike Plotinus, the cruelty to animals in the amphitheatre.

Seneca wrote much in defence of a moderate diet, inveighing against the indulgences of the time:

You think it a great matter that you can bring yourself to live without all the apparatus of fashionable dishes; that you do not desire wild boars of a thousand pounds' weight or the tongues of rare birds, and other portents of a luxury which now despises whole carcases, and chooses only certain parts of each victim. I shall admire you then only when you scorn not plain bread, when you have persuaded yourself that herbs exist not for other animals only, but for man also – if you shall recognise that vegetables are sufficient food for the stomach into which we now stuff valuable lives.[19]

Just after Seneca's sixtieth birthday Nero pronounced the death sentence. His wife insisted on dying with him. As he died he dictated his last thoughts, but his blood flowed slowly from the cut vein, so he took hemlock. This failed too, so he was carried into a steam bath and there suffocated.

Ovid, born in 43 BC, also came under Imperial suspicion and was exiled in AD 17 to a remote part of the Empire, Tomis (on the coast of the Black Sea, now modern Constanta, Rumania), where, in what was a provincial backwater, he died six years later.

That both Seneca and Ovid were punished by the imperial purple is no coincidence. In the city states of Greece enquiring minds with unfashionable views were tolerated if not fostered, the city states being small and flexible enough to allow a collection of disparate views to flourish without feeling overly threatened. Rome was another matter; the vast empire always in a state of growth yet at its heart always insecure, its power vulnerable to criticism, enforced conventional piety towards its gods on all its citizens. The Romans felt hostile to Greek thought which explored anti-social tendencies so the Pythagoreans were denounced or banished. Stoicism was approved of as it emphasised the conventional duties of life and virtue. Those persons of 'refinement' that Cicero refers to had to toe the line with the rest. Critical views of the ruling elite tended to be kept quiet. However, vegetarianism becomes inevitably a lifestyle which at times is impossible to keep private. Such views may seem quite harmless to the ruling classes and the whole apparatus of statecraft, yet the lifestyle is an unspoken criticism. But, more than that, vegetarianism is one of the signs of a radical thinker, the individual who criticises the status quo, who desires something better, more humane and more civilised for the whole of society. It makes meat-eaters uneasy and they often react aggressively.

Ovid is now considered by many a greater poet than Virgil. His main work, *Metamorphoses*, 'is without doubt the most witty and ingenious book that has come down to us from the ancient world'.[20] In the long, magnificent poem 'The Doctrines of Pythagoras' he gives a speech to Pythagoras himself that Charles James Fox thought 'the finest part of the whole poem'. The speech incarnates the theory which the whole of *Metamorphoses* is based upon, borrowing ironically enough not a Pythagorean idea but one from Heraclitus, that the universe is in a state of continual flux. Everything, in fact, metamorphoses itself into something else – 'nothing retains its form; new shapes from old'[21] – except the soul. Here Ovid is completely Pythagorean: 'I'll be born above the stars/Immortal.'

His poem speaks of a man, Samian by birth, who fled from Samos and became an exile. 'He was the first to ban as food for men the flesh of living things.' Then Ovid allows Pythagoras to speak:

> There are the crops,
> Apples that bend the branches with their weight,
> Grapes swelling on the vines; there are fresh herbs
> And those the tempered flame makes soft and mellow;
> Milk is ungrudged and honey from the thyme;
> Earth lavishes her wealth, gives sustenance
> Benign, spreads feasts unstained by blood and death.[22]

Then Ovid praises the beauties and peace of the Golden Age when 'no blood stained men's lips . . . until some futile brain/envied the lions' diet and gulped down/A feast of flesh to fill his greedy guts'.[23] He mourns for all the animals that have done us no wrong being killed every day, and fulminates against humankind involving the gods in this crime by using animals for sacrifice. The ox at the altar:

> Splendid with gold and garlands, stands before
> The altar, hears the prayer, watches the priest
> Sprinkle, he knows not why, between his horns
> Upon his brow the meal his toil has grown;

Then the knife strikes, crimsoned with blood, the knife
He saw perhaps reflected as it fell.[24]

He concludes:

He who can slit his calf's throat, hear its cries
Unmoved, who has the heart to kill his kid
That screams like a small child, or eat the bird
His hand has reared and fed! How far does this
Fall short of murder? Where else does it lead?
Away with traps and snares and lures and wiles!
Never again lime twigs to cheat the birds,
Nor feather ropes to drive the frightened deer,
Nor hide the hook with dainties that deceive!
Destroy what harms; destroy, but never eat;
Choose wholesome fare and never feast on meat![25]

This long poem, recording Ovid's disgust with animal slaughter while celebrating pastoral serenity and the Pythagorean creed of nonviolence, must have been a key work in influencing the young Plutarch, who was born some thirty years after Ovid's death at Tomis.

## Plutarch

We are possibly nearest to the work of this Greek writer, biographer, essayist and historian (who was born in Boeotia in AD 46 and lived until AD 120) in the historical plays of Shakespeare, who lifted great chunks of Plutarch from the translation by Sir Thomas North of the *Lives* published in 1579. His works were a major influence on a number of diverse people and events. Marcus Aurelius went into battle with a copy of the *Lives*, the Emperor Julian quoted from Plutarch and so did Rabelais, Montaigne and Bacon. Plutarch's essays also influenced Charlotte Corday, who assassinated the French revolutionary leader Jean-Paul Marat. She spent the day before reading Plutarch, knowing that she, too, would soon be part of history.

It is astonishing then that one of Plutarch's most passionate themes, a horror of killing and consuming the dead flesh of animals, has had no influence whatsoever. Future societies and individuals appear to have disregarded this element in his work. There is an excuse perhaps in that Plutarch's *Morals (Moralia)*, which includes the 'Essay on Flesh-Eating', runs to sixteen volumes. It also includes 'Rules for the Preservation of Health' and other essays which speak of the vegetarian diet in a remarkably contemporary manner. Plutarch is the first Greek writer not to link his vegetarianism with the concept of the transmigration of souls: when his two-year-old daughter died he refused to believe that she would return.

In his 'Rules for the Preservation of Health' his tone is reasonable: 'Indigestion is to be feared after flesh-eating for it very soon clogs us and leaves ill consequences behind it. It would be best to accustom oneself to eat no flesh at all, for the earth affords plenty enough of things fit not only for nourishment but for delight and enjoyment.'[26] But his thought is more precisely expressed in this passage from his *Symposiacs*:

> We can claim no great right over land animals which are nourished with the same food, inspire the same air, wash in and drink the same water that we do ourselves; and when they are slaughtered they make us ashamed of our work by their terrible cries; and then, again, by living amongst us they arrive at some degree of familiarity and intimacy with us.[27]

The essay 'Beasts are Rational' is a dialogue between Odysseus, Circe and Gryllus, one of the men that Circe turned into a pig. Odysseus pities Gryllus in this form and wants to change him back. But Gryllus argues that animals are happier: they do not lust for wealth, nor are they adulterers; the females attract the males with natural scents, nor do animals force themselves sexually upon men as men do animals. Plutarch again links overeating with disease, and points out that animals feed upon the foods which are proper to their natures, whereas humans devour all, eating flesh not of necessity but out of greed.

Pliny also thought that the plainest food is the most beneficial, going on to observe that 'from over-eating man derives most of his diseases'.[28]

In his essay on 'Flesh-eating', Plutarch impassionedly explains the reasons for Pythagoras' abstention from meat: 'How could his eyes endure the spectacle of the flayed and dismembered limb? How could his sense of smell endure the horrid effluvium? How, I ask, was his taste not sickened by contact with festering wounds, with the pollution of corrupted blood and juices?'[29]

He speculates on how meat-eating began, and imagines the globe a savage and uncultivated wilderness, whose infertility provoked early humankind to kill. But his contemporaries have no such excuse: 'What struggle for existence, what goading madness has incited you to imbrue your hands in blood?' Are you not ashamed, he asks, when you splatter the free fruits of the earth with blood? How strange it is, he reflects, that we do not kill the fiercest animals for our food, the tigers and wolves, but hunt and kill the innocent and defenceless. Many of these defenceless and shy creatures the Romans were to farm, keeping roe deer and red deer in wooded enclosures, raising hares and keeping pigeons. Thrushes, a great favourite, were kept in aviaries and fed on a special diet of millet, crushed figs and wheat flour. Snails were fed on milk until too fat to live in their shells and dormice fattened on nuts. Plutarch praises animals' charm and grace, notes how we ignore their plaintive cries and bemoans the waste of food after the feast, the uselessness of their sacrifice: 'Kill to eat if you must or will, but do not slay me, that you may feed luxuriously.'[30]

Plutarch argues that man is not naturally a flesh-eater, seeing that he is unlike all other carnivores: 'He has no curved beak, no sharp talons or claws, no pointed teeth . . . on the contrary, by the smoothness of his teeth, the small capacity of his mouth, the softness of his tongue and the sluggishness of his digestive apparatus, Nature sternly forbids him to feed on flesh.'[31] But, he says, if you still want flesh, then kill it yourself, but with natural weapons; not with axe of knife, but with hands, teeth and jaws. Then sit down and eat:

> Do not boil, roast and altogether metamorphose the meat by fire or condiments. You entirely alter and disguise the murdered animal by the use of ten thousand sweet herbs and spices that your natural taste may be deceived . . . [we] mix together oil and wine and honey and pickle and vinegar with all the spices of Syria and Arabia – for all the world as though we were embalming a human corpse.[32]

His demand that meat be eaten raw would have been particularly nauseating to his Greek and Roman readers. Archestratus[33] tells us that a great many people feel a repulsion for bloody meat, so meat was first boiled and then roasted.* Raw meat summoned up an image of the Maenads, the wild women who could tear an animal to pieces and eat the meat raw. To eat meat thus was to become beastlike, to be primitive and uncivilised.

Plutarch asserts also that it is not only by cooking that we disguise the origins of the food: we describe meat as a 'delicacy' and drown it in delicate sauces. He claims that meat-eating clouds the mind and dulls the intellect, and notes how difficult it is to convert a meat-eater: 'Now that men are saturated and penetrated, as it were, with love of pleasure, it is not an easy task to attempt to pluck out from their bodies the flesh-baited hook.'[34]

Lastly he inveighs against the cruel abuse in the methods of preparation and slaughter of animals. Two thousand years later how familiar this sounds – our methods may have changed, but the animals' suffering stays much the same.

## The Neoplatonists

This is the term we now give to the school of philosophy which flourished from the third to the sixth century AD. In one sense it was the only philosophical structure in opposition to early Christianity, though in some respects they merged, converts to one faith embracing the other. It was based, of course, on Plato's teaching (hence was imbued with Pythagorean thought), but also borrowed much from Aristotle and the Stoics. Gorman, however, argues persuasively that the Neoplatonists owed much more to Pythagoras than to Plato: 'Since Pythagoras had not revealed his secrets in

---

*Detienne sees the boiling and then roasting of meat as a symbol of civilisation, for plain spit-roasting, he claims, was primitive. I am not convinced by Detienne's argument, based on the manner by which the Titans cooked the child Dionysus. All meat sacrificed at the altar would have been first boiled and then roasted. This seems a practical way of ensuring that large haunches of meat were thoroughly cooked through to the bone.

writing they could not quote him, so that they did the very next best thing and quoted dialogues and passages from Plato in which they knew that Pythagorean mysticism was contained.'[35] The founder, Plotinus, interests us because he was also the teacher of Porphyry, whose *On Abstinence from Animal Food* is the only classic text other than Plutarch's which is devoted to the subject.

It was Iamblichus, another biographer of Pythagoras, who transformed the work of Plotinus, attempting to develop a theology encompassing the rites, myths and divinities of paganism. He displaced the purely intellectual and spiritual mysticism of Plotinus with theurgy and a magical conjuration of gods. He asserted that beyond the One of Plotinus, which identified with the Good, there was a yet higher One outside all human knowledge. Iamblichus believed in a process of purification, much as Pythagoras had, which involved complete abstinence from meat, yet among his surviving works is none on diet.

Plotinus was born in AD 205, fifty years before the birth of Iamblichus, and, inclined to be a late starter, did not decide to pursue philosophy until the age of twenty-eight. He went to Alexandria in search of a teacher, and there attended lectures by the most eminent professors but was reduced to depression by their inadequacy. Then a friend took him to hear Ammonius, and after the first lecture Plotinus announced: 'This is the man I have been looking for.' He stayed with Ammonius, who was a lapsed Christian and the teacher of Origen, for eleven years. Plotinus longed to travel to the East to learn more of the philosophies of Persia and India, so after his long sojourn as a disciple he joined the expedition of the Roman Emperor Gordian III against Persia. But Gordian was murdered, the expedition was a rout and Plotinus had to escape to Antioch and thence to Rome. There he settled and taught, gaining a reputation for wisdom and restraint, living a life of extreme asceticism. He allowed himself little sleep and for obscure reasons also refused to wash in a public bath but instead had a daily massage at home. 'Plotinus seemed ashamed of being in the body, so deeply rooted was this feeling that he could never be induced to tell of his ancestry, his parentage or his birthplace.'[36] Like Pythagoras he used the physiognomy and body movements of his pupils as a means to understand them: 'When he was speaking his intellect visibly illuminated his face . . . he radiated benignity.'[37] He also set forth the principles of Pythagoras and of Plato 'in a clearer light than anyone before him'.[38]

His diet was undoubtedly a healthy one – Rogatianus, an active member of the Roman Senate, became a disciple of Plotinus and was cured of his gout, for he ate only every second day and was punctilious in his abstinence from meat. Porphyry, in his *Life* of his teacher, tells us that his own ascetic regimen included total chastity, yet he moved with ease among patrons and disciples whose married state he took for granted. He had a fine-tuned body; as vibrant as a well-used lyre. Following the example, again, of Pythagoras he shrouded his teaching in such secrecy (he had a secret pact with the pupils of Ammonius not to divulge his teaching) that it is quite possible that he taught vegetarianism and that this has remained undiscovered by us. Porphyry, his pupil and biographer, did not include any vegetarian teachings in the writings, the *Enneads*, which he collected and published. Gorman considers them to be little more than apologies for the Roman Empire, for Plotinus never condemned the games and the barbarities at the amphitheatre as Seneca did. But in the *Enneads* there is often a fusion of flesh and spirit which is both beguiling and contemporary in its feeling. Plotinus is often haunted by spiritual longing; 'a sweet touch of the fullness of life', startlingly sensuous in its soft and gentle exuberance, frequently flooded his soul, stilling all thoughts of mere physical love.[39] Plotinus, more than any other Neoplatonist, seems to be in supreme control of his physical body and blissfully content with his asceticism. 'This is no affirmation of an excited body, but of a soul become again what she was in the time of her early joy.'[40]

As we know, Plato did not address himself to the subject of animal killing in a direct manner but only by inference in the passage on what was eaten in *The Republic*, so it is unlikely that the Neoplatonists would make vegetarianism an issue. Publicly their diet was acceptable as part of a true asceticism; thus it did not attract controversy. Plotinus was much approved of by the Emperor Gallienus, who gave him permission to build a new city based on the ideals of *The Republic*, to be called Platonopolis. Perhaps if this project had gone ahead – the Senate vetoed the idea – we might have seen an ascetic community in practice that happened also to be vegetarian.

We can argue from the *Enneads* that Plotinus was vegetarian from the evidence that he agreed with Pythagoras, first, that human souls can be reincarnated in the bodies of animals, and, second, that animals feel both pleasure and pain, unlike plants. Plotinus refused to use medicine that came from animals. Further, Pythagoreanism teaches that the earth and everything in it are somehow permeated with neutral forces; matter itself obstructs the song of the gods. Therefore the purpose of life is not to become too deeply entangled in the material world, but to remain on the edge, the outside. The Chaldean Oracles* claim that the words of Apollo himself tell humankind to avoid 'deepening the plane', for that would be to risk creating a solid, something impermeable, where the cosmic music might not be heard. Here, in essence, is the most profound argument for a meagre vegetarian diet that provides enough nutritional value to survive but no more.

An earlier Neoplatonist and Pythagorean was Apollonius of Tyana. Born in the same year as Jesus, he also could perform miracles, cast out devils, heal the sick and raise the dead. He was a strict vegetarian who travelled to Babylon and India as well as Spain, Italy and Ethiopia. His biographer, Philostratus, tells us that when travelling through Pamphylia he was horrified

---

*The Chaldean Oracles, composed in the second century AD by Julianus the Theurgist and his son, had great influence on the Neoplatonists. The work combined Plato and Pythagoras with Persian creeds, magic and mythology. The rites included Zoroastrian ideas of esoteric fire.

to see the people starving because the grain merchants, with the connivance of the magistrates, were keeping grain back to sell for a higher price elsewhere. Apollonius addressed the magistrates: 'The Earth is the common mother of all, for she is just. You are unjust, for you have made her the mother of yourselves only. If you will not cease from acting thus, I will not suffer you to remain upon her.' The magistrates were so terrified that they filled the market with grain immediately.[41] It is always more difficult for the authorities to accept penury and self-sacrifice in an individual who comes from a rich and respectable family. Such it was with Apollonius, who had long hair, wore only linen and was shod in papyrus sandals. The Romans hated such Greek philosophers and claimed that their degeneracy corrupted youth. Perhaps Apollonius' most dramatic and memorable feat was after the accession of the tyrannical Emperor Domitian. Domitian immediately began a purge of philosophers, crucifying any that were caught. Apollonius gave himself up to the tribunal, but as he was about to be sentenced he vanished, reappearing at the same time in the south of Italy. He ended his days at Ephesus, and announced the death of Domitian at the exact time it happened in Rome.

Though it was not an official doctrine, the popularity of vegetarianism among the Neoplatonists continued throughout the rise and growth of the Roman Empire, culminating in Porphyry and his work. It is not surprising that the Roman writers and philosophers condemned over-eating and opted for a meagre vegetarian diet themselves, for they lived in a society which, with the Roman expansion into world trade, was obsessed with food. Romans were addicted to Indian pepper, obtained spices from Malabar, cassia leaf and ginger from China, ostriches from Africa, crocodiles from Egypt, oysters from Britain. Apicius[42] lists the ingredients for a sauce: onion, cumin, coriander, pepper, rue, penny royal, sage, chervil, chives, cinnamon, wild celery, mint, oregano, thyme, shallots, dill, marjoram, cardamom, fennel, and juniper berries – all this and more to be ground together with oil, honey, vinegar and wine.

## Porphyry

Porphyry was born in AD 232 in Tyre, Phoenicia. His original name was Malchus, which is a Syrian name meaning King. His name was hellenised at Athens by his Greek teacher of rhetoric, hence Porphyry – purple-robed. Besides Plotinus, another of his teachers was Origen, an early Christian theologian whose extraordinary celibacy was explained by his having castrated himself. After having joined the school of Plotinus at Rome, at the age of thirty Porphyry attacked it, writing a book to refute certain doctrines. Another pupil, Amerius, replied, and after a second confrontation Porphyry recanted, confessing his errors. After that he became a loyal and enthusiastic follower.

Among forty-three different publications he wrote a treatise against the Christians, a work divided into fifteen books – unfortunately Theodosius II publicly burnt it and only fragments survived lives of Pythagoras and of Plotinus, and an Epistle to Anebo, a refutation of pagan theology which includes, as one would expect, a denunciation of animal sacrifice. He also wrote a commentary on Aristotle's *Categories* which stimulated medieval developments in logic.

*Abstinence from Animal Food* is in four books. The first is addressed to a friend, Firmus, who has stopped being a vegetarian: 'When I reflect with myself upon the cause of your change of mind, I cannot believe that it has anything to do with reasons of health and strength. You, yourself, used to assert that the fleshless diet is more consonant to healthfulness.'[43] Porphyry hopes that the change was not due to nostalgia for the gluttonous enjoyment of meat, nor to a wish to adhere to orthodox customs. Next Porphyry argues against other sects that may have influenced Firmus in his decision: the Stoics, Peripatetics and Epicureans, and one Claudius the Neapolitan who wrote a treatise against vegetarianism (it has not survived) which Porphyry summarises and then refutes. He expresses the belief, shared by Pythagoras and Plutarch, that eating meat creates a violent and aggressive personality: 'It is not from those who have lived on innocent foods that murderers, tyrants, robbers and sycophants have come, but from eaters of flesh.'[44] (In our own time the fact of Hitler's vegetarianism should by now have disabused us of this notion.)

The second book condemns animal sacrifice and explores religious symbolism, the souls of dead bodies and demons. The third book discusses justice and how we must extend it towards animals as they are endowed with high degrees of reasoning and to some degree moral perception. Animals, Porphyry argues, are proper objects of justice:

> By these arguments I have demonstrated that many species of the lower animals are rational . . . justice is due to rational beings . . . we do not extend the obligations of justice to plants, because there appears in them no indication of reason – we use corn and beans when they have fallen on the earth and are dead. But no one uses for food the flesh of dead animals, unless they have been killed by violence, so that there is in these things a radical injustice . . . to destroy living and conscious beings merely for luxury and pleasure is truly barbarous and unjust.

He concludes this passage: 'If indeed the destruction of other animals and the eating of flesh were as requisite as air and water, plants and fruits, then there could be no injustice, as they would be necessary to our nature.'[45]

Porphyry points out that, although 'crocodiles, snakes and other monsters destroy and devour men', they act savagely through want and hunger; but we do so 'from insolent wantonness and luxurious pleasure amusing ourselves as we do also in the Circus and in the murderous sports of the chase. By thus acting, a barbarous and brutal nature becomes strengthened in us, which renders men insensible to the feeling of pity and compassion.'[46]

The fourth book reviews dietary habits in the past. Porphyry speaks of the Essenes as sharing their property and goods and as being lovers of justice; though not complete abstainers from meat, they are considered by him to be almost vegetarian in practice. The view expressed by Josephus differs slightly: 'pursue the same kind of life as those whom the Greeks call Pythagoreans and live above a hundred years by means of their simplicity of diet.'[47]

Porphyry goes on to mention the historians of Syria, who allege that at an early period the people abstained from all flesh and animal sacrifice. He tells the following story of how meat-eating began:

> In the beginning no animal was sacrificed to the gods, nor was there any positive law to prevent this, for it was forbidden by the law of nature. In the time of Pygmalion [a Phoenician who reigned in Cyprus], however, an occasion occurred in which it was thought necessary to redeem life by life, and an animal was sacrificed and totally consumed by fire. Some time after the introduction of this practice, a part of the burnt offering happening to fall on the ground, the priest picked it up, and burning his hand in the action, in order to mitigate the pain, applied his fingers to his mouth. Enticed by the flavour of the flesh and unable to restrain his eager desire, he ate and gave part of the sacrifice to his wife. When Pygmalion was made acquainted with this atrocity, he caused them both to be thrown down a rock, and gave the priesthood to another; the new priest soon fell into the temptation of his predecessor and was punished in the same manner. His fate, however, did not deter imitation and that which was committed by many was soon practised with impunity by all.[48]

We see in this fable that men and women were prepared to die for a morsel of burnt offering, revealing how Porphyry must have felt the desire for meat to have been in fact so ingrained and compelling in his fellows that it had become an addiction.

Porphyry lived at a time when intellectual, religious and mystical concepts were all in great ferment. The early Christians were struggling to survive, immersed for the most part in Gnostic speculation, and an extraordinary number of monotheist sects and beliefs, many of them vegetarian, were claiming eternal truths for themselves. But paganism was also flourishing. Mithraism and the other mystery religions, as we shall see, held great sway over the peoples of the Mediterranean, and animal sacrifice continued in many pagan religions. So Porphyry's clear, unadulterated praise of a vegetarian lifestyle and its respect for all creatures must seem all the more remarkable – as we have already discussed, to refuse involvement in animal sacrifice was to set oneself apart, to question the foundation of society itself.

Porphyry died in AD 306, just before the reign of Constantine, during which Christianity was officially recognised, as a matter of expediency, in AD 313. The effect of Christianity (bringing with it the Judaic tradition) upon Neoplatonism was devastating, with its opposition to concepts like justice and non-violence towards animals and to vegetarianism itself. The Pythagorean idea that all sentient beings have equal rights with humankind would not die altogether, but Christianity, as it gained power, was determined to bury the belief, and it was suppressed for almost a thousand years. For Christianity proclaimed humankind the dominant species, a belief which is still a motivating force in the world today.

# 5

# Early Christianity

Would Christianity have become a worldwide religion if St Paul had not existed? Might Christians then have remained simply another Judaic sect rather like the Essenes? Certainly the history of the human relationship with the animal kingdom would have been radically different if Western society had not become thoroughly imbued with the Judaeo-Christian concept of human supremacy. What was it that thrust Christianity out from a small imperial colony to influence the entire Roman Empire and beyond?

## St Paul's Gospel
One of the major tenets of Christianity was the concept of salvation and immortal life through Christ so passionately believed in by Paul. In the early years there can be no doubt that it was his zeal which fired the growth and expansion of the Christian religion around the Mediterranean and into northern Europe and the Middle East. Paul, the most fiery and authoritative of the Apostles, believed that God's final day of judgement was imminent, that God was about to reveal himself and free the world of evil, that on this day too Jesus would return and deliver those who believed he was the Lord.

Paul saw his future life's work as the most zealous of missionaries, to all nations, to prepare them for the day of God's coming. His travels were energetic and persistent: from Palestine up the coast to Sidon and further north through Syria to Antioch and Tarsus, through Asia Minor and across to Ephesus, down to Rhodes and by sea to Crete, back to Greece, Corinth, Athens and the north, Philippi and across the Dardanelles to Asia again. Later, as a captive of Rome, he was shipwrecked in Malta for three months with his warders but was heard with respect by the 'first man of Malta'. Then, when Paul reaches Rome, the narrative in the Acts of the Apostles ends and we have no way of knowing what happened. Did Paul continue preaching or was he executed by the Romans? Paul, the historical personage, vanishes from history around AD 60.

The discoveries in 1945 of ancient scrolls at Nag Hammadi and in 1949, by a bedouin boy, of the Dead Sea Scrolls at Qumran have shed much new light on those years before and immediately after Christ, a light which is often murky because of scholastic squabbles or deliberate lethargy on the part of the Catholic Church to release material which might stray from the Pauline versions. As we shall see, thoughts and beliefs which became heretical in later years, that involved asceticism and non-violence towards both animals and people, had their roots in the years between 150 BC and AD 100. It is important to realise that the text of the Bible we know was not established until quite late, around AD 800, though much of it was known as early as the second century, and the Gospels were written down long after the crucifixion, which occurred between AD 30 and 36. The earliest Gospel, of Mark, was composed around AD 66, those of Matthew and Luke around AD 70 and 75, and that of John another twenty years later, around AD 95. The Gospels, because they were written in the infancy of a religious movement, had a significant purpose: to bear witness to the assured truths that the faithful *ought* to know. They were part of a proselytising force which both reflected the new faith and codified it for future generations. The Gospels are more about faith than history, and some would say more about Paul than Jesus. What we read there is Paul's version of Jesus as gathered by the Apostles from the Christian followers in those eastern Mediterranean cities. The only book in the New Testament that might be accepted as an historical account is the Acts of the Apostles, which covers the years between AD 30 and 64 or thereabouts. It was written by a Greek named Luke sometime between AD 70 and 95. Certainly the Acts is a work that testifies both to the vigour of the new religion and to the energy and piety of Paul, for it is his story and travels that the Acts recounts.

The finds from Nag Hammadi and Qumran indicate the possibility of another Jesus, quite different from the one we find in the Pauline version, a Jesus who had connections with sects which were not meat-eating. Some of the Gnostic literature pre-dates the Gospels, and the Jesus revealed there is far more psychologically subtle and in many ways nearer to Buddha. If this Jesus had been publicised, praised and believed in, the history of the relationship between humankind and animals in the last two thousand years would probably have been vastly different. Imagine a Christian religion which had colonised half the world and was basically vegetarian and akin to Buddhism. It is important then to explore how Paul's version became the acceptable one.

Inevitably in Paul's earnest missionary work and copious letters he spread customs that were inherently Jewish, including food regulations and taboos of the most complicated kind. The Jewish faith included the Mosaic dietary laws, which is what interests us. Paul was travelling as a zealous missionary and winning great numbers of converts, but if we read between the lines in Acts, we wonder whether early Christianity wanted the converts or whether they thought of themselves as Christians at all.

Paul, then Saul of Tarsus,[1] first appears at the stoning of the first martyr, Stephen, as a dedicated enemy of the early Christian Church, chosen to lead an armed posse to ferret out and arrest the Christians at Damascus. This is not the Damascus in Syria but Qumran. On the way there Saul has a mystical revelation and hears a voice asking him: 'Why are you persecuting me?' Saul is blinded but reaches Qumran, where his sight is restored. He tells the posse of soldiers to return to Jerusalem. Now Saul is converted, changes his name to Paul and joins the community, remaining there three years. He then returns to Jerusalem, where the community is suspicious of him: their leader is James (supposedly the brother of Jesus), whose diet was ascetic and who was thought to be a strict vegetarian by the early church fathers.

## The Essenes

The community at Qumran is thought to have been made up of Essenes, who were considered to be vegetarian by Pliny the Elder, Josephus and Philo of Alexandria. They were Pythagorean in their beliefs and habits and this was taken to mean a community sharing all worldly goods, a celibate male world, ascetic and meatless: and, further, a pacific community with a belief in the transmigration of souls. By the end of the nineteenth century it was accepted that the Essenes had been a group of esoteric, vegetarian, mystic Christians, but the evidence of the Dead Sea Scrolls contradicts that view and the ancient writers do not agree upon the details. Philo claims that the Essenes were against animal sacrifices, but animal bones have been found in pots buried in the ground, obviously not remains of a meal but of ritual significance.

The Greek word 'Essene' is thought to be one of many terms meaning 'a widespread movement of anti-Jerusalem, anti-Pharisaic non-conformity of the period'. It is 'from such an "Essene-type of Judaism" that Christianity is descended'.[2] The early Christians referred to themselves in the Gospels and the Acts as 'Nazorean' or 'Nazarene', the equivalent of the Hebrew 'Nozrim', which is like 'Nozrei ha-Brit', Hebrew for 'Keepers of the Covenant', a term used by the Qumran community to describe themselves. The ruling body of Qumran was based in Jerusalem. There is a theory that the Qumran community was the early Church led by James, the brother of Jesus.[3] What evidence we have also points to its members leading a dedicated ascetic life. Porphyry is impressed by them:

> They are despisers of mere riches, and the communistic principle with them is admirably carried out. Nor is it possible to find amongst them a single person distinguished by the possession of wealth, for all who enter the society are obliged by their laws to divide property for the common good. There is neither the humiliation of poverty nor the arrogance of wealth. Their managers or guardians are elected by vote, and each of them is chosen with a view to the welfare and needs of all. They have no city or town, but dwell together in separate communities . . . They do not discard their dress for a new one, before the first is really worn out by length of time. There is no buying and selling amongst them. Each gives to each according to his or her wants, and there is a free interchange between them . . . They come to their dining-hall as to some pure and undefiled temple, and when they have taken

their seats quietly, the baker sets their loaves before them in order, and the cook gives them one dish each of one sort, while their priest first recites a form of thanksgiving for their pure and refined food.[4]

Porphyry also links their frugal diet with their being able to withstand oppression, torture and death, as in this passage which anticipates so many descriptions of the persecution and brutal end of Christian heretics to come:

> And so great, indeed, is their simplicity and frugality with respect to diet, that they do not require evacuation* till the seventh day after the assumption of food, which day they spend in singing hymns to God, and in resting from labour. But from this exercise they acquire the power of such great endurance, that even when tortured and burnt, and suffering every kind of excruciating pain, they cannot be induced either to blaspheme their legislator, or to eat what they have not been accustomed to. And the truth of this was demonstrated in their war with the Romans. For then they neither flattered their tormentors, nor shed any tears, but smiled in the midst of their torments, and derided those that inflicted them, and cheerfully emitted their souls, as knowing that they should possess them again. For this opinion was firmly established among them, that their bodies were indeed corruptible, and that the matter of which they consisted was not stable, but that their souls were immortal, and would endure for ever, and that, proceeding from the most subtle ether, they were drawn by a natural flux, and complicated with bodies; but that, when they are no longer detained by the bonds of the flesh, then, as if liberated from a long slavery, they will rejoice, and ascend to the celestial regions.[5]

It would seem likely that the Essenes and the early Church, even if they were not one and the same, were almost vegetarian in practice, beginning that long tradition of asceticism which was to influence the early church fathers. But why were they not completely vegetarian and why was this message not at the heart of their ethics? Could it have been because of the Mosaic dietary laws which tend to have on this issue an oppressive and limiting influence upon Jewish and Christian thinkers? We might further ask why this semi-vegetarian lifestyle did not become part of the Christian heritage when the early Church under James had incorporated it into their doctrine. This, I suggest, is due almost certainly to their new convert, Saul of Tarsus, now Paul.

Once Paul had rejoined the disciples at Jerusalem, he offended them in some way and was exiled to his birthplace, Tarsus. There he began his

---

*The Essenes must have suffered horribly from bowel disorders if this was true, and it is most unlikely. However, Porphyry may have noticed their fastidiousness over their excrement and where the task of opening the bowels might be performed. Disciples were given trowels and told to go out into the desert to perform the act. They had a hygienic sense not common in their time.

missionary work, but was that what the controlling group in Jerusalem wanted? Were they solidly part of the Judaic tradition, keepers of the covenant, thus of the Mosaic law itself or had they begun to break away? Stephen was stoned to death because he upheld the law, and the Qumran sect were strict and rigid in their rules, having a three-year apprenticeship for all new disciples. If Paul was converting in Tarsus, he was not observing the Qumran rules, yet he was keeping to some tenets, as we shall see, of the Mosaic laws.

He also journeyed to Antioch (about AD 43), where the disciples were first called Christians. Paul stayed teaching in Antioch, where five years later some members from the leadership in Jerusalem visited and were shocked at the laxity of Paul's flock, which was not adhering to the law. The schism had begun between Paul and the new Christians and the Jerusalem leadership led by James, the brother of Jesus. The main and most profound difference between them was that in Paul's canon Jesus was deified and worshipped, while in the Jerusalem group Jesus was the teacher and the only deity was God: 'Jesus said, "If you bring forth what is within you, what you bring forth will save you. If you do not bring forth what is within you, what you do not bring forth will destroy you."'[6] We also glimpse Jesus with his companion, Mary Magdalene, in a physical loving relationship,[7] a very real human being with human desires, a far cry from the Pauline divinity.

But Paul preached something quite different, something mystical and powerful, that faith in Christ opened the believer to the sanctifying power of the Holy Spirit, for Christ had died for the sins of mankind and was now reserved in heaven as God's agent for the last day of judgement. Christ's spirit fed and nourished the soul, but what of physical food and the physical body? There is in all the Pauline teaching little about food, except the command to avoid the meat from sacrifices and not to 'sit at meat in the idol's temple' as it would encourage others to eat meat, i.e. return to paganism. 'I will eat no flesh while the world endureth, lest I offend my brother.'[8]

Perhaps Paul's view of vegetarianism is best seen in Romans.[9] In a passage which includes the exhortation 'let us not judge one another any more' he refers to vegetarians disparagingly: 'For one believeth that he may eat all things; another, who is weak, eateth herbs.' Later in the same chapter (21) Paul writes: 'It is good neither to eat flesh nor to drink wine, nor anything whereby thy brother stumbleth, or is offended, or is made weak.' We can take it that this passage, similar to the one from Corinthians quoted above, also means that pagan sacrifices must be avoided, but in mentioning weakness does he mean that the vegetable diet is to be avoided as well? Another passage[10] mentioning abstinence from meats is a direct reference to Gnostic sects in that it links a refusal to eat meat with a condemnation of marriage.

What concerned Paul was not the question of meat-eating *per se* (which was not seen by Hebraic tradition as an ethical question) but the political issues between the older Jewish traditions and the new sections of the Christian Church in Rome and Greece, as well as the significance of the pagan and Jewish sacrificial altars and the growing popularity of Gnosis itself. This preoccupation obscured entirely the nature of what was roasted upon the altars and those ethical questions the ritual involved; nor did the rights of the animal kingdom obtrude even vaguely into Paul's world. Jesus, on the contrary, cured a lunatic[11] by taking the devils out of him and putting them into a herd of two thousand pigs which then promptly jumped into the sea and drowned themselves.

The story of the Gadarene swine was not lost on Christian leaders. Augustine would argue that the welfare of animals needed no consideration and after citing the example of the drowning pigs suggested that animal suffering meant little to human beings. Paul asked: 'Does God care for oxen?' in a passage[12] that compares how man was loved and favoured by God. The image of God the Shepherd tending with love and care his human flock, first expressed in Psalm 23 and later elaborated by Jesus,[13] is double-edged. A shepherd, after all, tends his sheep only to slaughter them for their meat. Defenders of Jesus claim that his concern for animals is expressed in two brief passages, in which he says that everyone should water their ox on a Sabbath[14] and help 'a son or an ox' out of a well,[15] but these surely illustrate obvious self-interest. It can be powerfully argued that Jesus himself was within the Judaic tradition clearly stated from Genesis to Isaiah.

Because Judaic tradition was incorporated in Pauline Christianity, it imbued, too, the writings of many of the early Christian leaders – Augustine of Hippo, in particular – and it lay oppressively over the relationship between the Christian Church and the animal kingdom for almost two thousand years.

## The Dietary Laws

Everything hinges upon the dietary rules in the Old Testament. In the beginning paradise is vegetarian. Not only humans but all creatures are herbivores. Adam and Eve and all living creatures lived harmoniously together, in a Golden Age. Yet there is no question, even in this Utopia, who was the superior creature. Let man, God decreed, 'have dominion over the fish of the sea, and over the fowl of the air, and over the cattle, and over all the earth, and over every creeping thing that creepeth upon the earth'.[16]

Man has been made in the image of God, yet he cannot be God and must be shown to be less than God – hence the taboo of the fruit from one particular tree, which is denied to Adam and Eve, and which Eve understood as a 'tree to be desired to make one wise'.[17] As we have seen, Buddhist asceticism is part of a philosophy to allow each of us to become wiser and more knowledgeable, whereas in this Judaic parable the serpent defines knowledge: 'ye shall be as Gods, knowing good and evil.'[18] 'God said, behold the man is become as one of us, to know good and evil; and now, lest he put forth his hand, and take also of the tree of life, and eat and live forever.'[19] God feared competition so humankind was cast out of paradise.

The notion of the immortality of the soul did not appear in Judaism until the second century BC and it was not an indigenous concept, coming via Plato, Pythagoras and Egypt. Humanity could not live eternally as God can, nor could it be allowed to kill, for only God can give life or take it away. Hence meat-eating was an impossibility, for to get meat humans had to kill animals. The fundamental difference between humanity and God is expressed in the difference in their foods.[20]

After the Fall, Adam and Eve are in a world where thorns and thistles grow and ills and slaughter proliferate. Later, Cain and Abel, grown to manhood, both make offerings to God. Cain, a tiller of fields, brings him the fruits of the earth; Abel, a keeper of sheep, brings 'the first-born of his flock and the fat thereof'.[21] God has no respect for Cain's offering but praises Abel's.* The furious filial jealousy thus created in Cain leads to the murder of Abel. So animal sacrifice, an act which horrified and nauseated Pythagoras, is pleasing to God. God may consume living beings, even in the form of human sacrifice (the story of Abraham and Isaac being the last remnant of the practice), while human nourishment was to be edible plants. Nor was it going to be easy for humankind to survive by the cultivation of the soil: Cain is punished for murder by God, who makes the earth stony and infertile, but Abel's issue multiplies, yet so full of evil that God destroys the earth and everything in it except Noah and the Ark in the Flood.

It is the Flood which heralds the beginning of a new dietary era. After the Flood humanity was able to kill animals for food. At the time of the Flood, God had not separated animals into clean and unclean – if he had, the Flood would have been an opportunity to drown all the unclean animals. Instead, God gives directions to Noah to take on board the Ark 'everything that creepeth upon the earth'.[22] When the Flood abates God speaks the words which are the origin and the vindication of all Christian dealings with the animal kingdom: 'And the fear of you and the dread of you shall be upon every beast of the earth, and upon every fowl of the air, upon all that moveth upon the earth, and upon all the fishes of the sea; into your hand are they delivered.'[25]

Humankind had been given God's sanction to exploit and kill any other living creature for sustenance and pleasure. In fact, Noah's first action when he embarked on dry land was to kill some of the creatures he had been saving and to cook them on the altar, such cuisine being pleasing to God,

---

*The myth has a Sumerian ancestor in which the brothers are Dumuzi and Enkimdu, the former a shepherd-god as Abel was, the latter a farmer-god like Cain. Both myths represent[23] the ancient feud between the desert and the sown land, between nomad and farmer. The rejection of Cain's offering implies a failure of crops which needs a form of expiatory ritual, hence the slaying of the shepherd in the field so that his blood may fertilise the soil: 'The earth has opened her mouth to receive thy brother's blood.'[24]

The interpretation of the myth is that God has to curse the slayer but also protect him. Cain takes flight. He has to be driven out of society in order to regain his purity, hence he is protected by God as a sacred person. The mark of Cain distinguishes him as part of this sacred class. The Hebrew ritual of the Day of Atonement, when one goat is slain while another is driven out into the desert, reflects this concept.

who 'smelled a sweet savour'.[26] However, God and humankind cannot both eat meat for that makes them equal. So God goes on to say: 'But flesh with the life thereof, which is the blood thereof, shall ye not eat.'[27] To consume meat without consuming some blood is virtually impossible, but the injunction is sternly repeated throughout the Old Testament:

> And whatsoever man there be of the house of Israel or of the strangers that sojourn among you, that eateth any manner of blood: I will even set my face against that soul that eateth blood and I will cut him off from among his people . . .[28]

> Notwithstanding thou mayest kill and eat flesh in all thy gates whatsoever thy soul lusteth after . . . only ye shall not eat the blood.[29]

The difference between humankind and God is no longer signified by the eating of meat and the eating of plants, but by the eating of flesh or blood. Blood belongs to God. If the blood is let out, meat becomes permissible for humans.

The setting apart of the blood becomes a ritual. Before the animal can be eaten the priest pours its blood over the altar, separating God's share of the sacrifice from the human share, while the murder of the animal itself is redeemed by giving its essential life force, the blood, to God. The blood of the sacrificed creatures also takes the place of the guilty slayer:[30] 'For the life of the flesh is in the blood, and I have given it for you upon the altar to make atonement for your souls; for it is the blood that makes atonement by reason of the life.'[31] Killing an animal without the priestly ritual becomes murder: 'blood guilt shall be imputed to that man; he has shed blood; and that man shall be cut off from among his people.'[32]

This paradox, that the slaughter of animals is encouraged while their blood is forbidden, permeates the whole of Judaic dietary belief, as well as confusing the Christian apologists of meat-eating itself.

## Christian Expansion

The first few hundred years AD were a ferment of religious, political and philosophical dispute: the mystery religions still held popular sway. Gnosticism was gaining ground with its defiant belief in the personal knowledge of God separate from ritual, Christians were arguing among themselves. There was in these years much cross-fertilisation between the pagan and the Christian, and many adherents to Christianity later changed their minds and returned to a form of Neoplatonism. Ammonius, the teacher of both Plotinus and Origen, was one such. Tatian began as a Christian and a meat-eater, then drifted towards Gnosticism and severed his ties with the Church, beginning a strict vegetarian life and gaining converts, the Encratites (p.130). Others who were to have greater influence over the future did the opposite: Augustine of Hippo, once a strictly vegetarian

Manichean, became a convert to Christianity and a hysterical critic of the Manichean religion.

But much of these few hundred years of Christian growth, while Rome was still intact as an empire and when Christians were being persecuted, remains little known. All we do know for certain is that Christianity spread over a wide area in a relatively short space of time. Trade and travelling were a time-honoured method of getting ideas across seas and continents. Persecution also helped to scatter Christians. The Christian sects furthest from the centre of civilisation tended to be the most heretical; bishops would constantly have to visit and show the community the error of their ways. Language was also a problem: 'a traveller did not go far in the Roman Empire before he confronted the effects of Babel.'[33] For instance Celtic was spoken in the West, Iberian in Spain, Punic and a Libyan dialect in Africa, Coptic dialects in Egypt. Hence an understanding of local dialect and language was necessary to the spread of the vital message, and bilingual converts must have been treasured for their potential teaching abilities. What was taught in those early years must have been essentially Pauline – at its best, a hymn to humane values: 'There is neither Jew nor Greek, there is neither slave nor free, there is neither male nor female; for you are all one in Christ Jesus.'[34] This was a doctrinal break with Judaism, which believed in distinctions in food, sex and living. But in pragmatic terms females were certainly the second sex and Christianity has never, until very recently, examined gender inequality. As to slavery, which the whole of the Roman Empire and the known world at that time was built upon, the Jesus of the Gospels had never discussed the issue.

Jesus (or was it Paul?) had promised the inauguration of a new age, the Kingdom of God, yet life went on much as it used to, except for the cruel persecution of Christian believers; hence the concept of the Second Coming – the new age would not be fully revealed until Christ returned in glory. Whether to kill to eat meat or not seemed of little moral importance weighed against the Second Coming.

Early Christians by now were thoroughly imbued with the sanction given in Genesis, believing that meat was one of the blessings of God given to humankind for their pleasure and sustenance. Besides, the heretical sects tended to be vegetarian, so to reject meat-eating attracted suspicion. But the issue was far from black and white. Early Christians who were truly holy and pious ate very little, sometimes only water and bread or, at the most, beans, bread and a few green leaves. This, however, was not considered to be a vegetarian diet – eating less food was a method by which the soul in pursuit of God dominated the wanton desire of the flesh.

## Asceticism

An explanation given for Genesis, 9:2 – that all living creatures must now live in dread of humankind – was that it was essentially a political message. After the flight from Pharaoh's Egypt, with the Jews still influenced by

Egyptian religion and worship, it was necessary to cut free. There had to be, then, no worship of animals, no anthropomorphism, no sacred bull or golden calf. Animals had to be subdued, not venerated. The human relationship with God was not to be adulterated by an animal intermediary.

Though the ancient Jewish world had long accepted this pronouncement from God, there were some Christian leaders in these early years, when the Roman Empire was in decline, who opposed the theological tide against animals.

Tertullian (AD 160-240) fulminated against the professing Christians of his day who claimed that Christ and his Apostles had permitted meat-eating. His *On Feasting or Abstinence against the Carnal-Minded* is a fine piece of rhetoric in which he links meat-eating, in a now time-honoured manner, with ill health and disease: 'Nature herself will inform us whether before gross eating and drinking, we were not of much more powerful intellect, of much more sensitive feeling, than when the entire domicile of men's interior has been stuffed with meats, inundated with wines, and fermenting with filth in course of digestion.'[35] He praises Daniel, 'who preferred vegetable food and water',★ and interprets God's command to Aaron − 'wine and strong liquor shall ye not drink' − to mean that gluttony should be refrained from altogether: 'It is not consistent with truth that a man should sacrifice half of his stomach only to God, that he should be sober in drinking, but intemperate in eating.'[37] But he does have a difficult job interpreting Paul's indifference to meat-eating. On Romans, 14 he says: 'And even if he has handed over to you the keys of the slaughterhouse or butcher's shop in permitting you to eat all things, excepting sacrifices to idols, at least he has not made the kingdom of heaven to consist in butchery.'[38] Tertullian's dislike of Christian meat-eaters reaches its apotheosis in the following passage: 'Your belly is your god, your liver is your temple, your paunch is your altar, the cook is your priest, and the fat steam is your Holy Spirit; the seasonings and the sauces are your chrisms and your eructations are your prophesyings.'[39]

It must be said that Tertullian's dislike of the eating of flesh is due to asceticism; nowhere does he mention the right to live of the slaughtered creatures. He is, in this, a child of the Old Testament. His fervour is based on a belief that gluttony obtrudes on spiritual awareness: 'Consistently do you men of flesh reject the things of the spirit . . . we are sure that they who are in the flesh cannot please God'[40] (not meaning who are themselves of flesh, but who desire it).

Flesh is linked in Tertullian, perhaps for the first time, with lust and carnal desires:

For they that are after the flesh do mind the things of the flesh; for they that

---

★Perhaps the only good publicity in the Bible for a vegetarian diet is in Daniel, when Daniel is befriended by the prince of the eunuchs and begs for 'pulse to eat and water to drink' for him and his friends, rather than the meat and wine which Nebuchadnezzar sends them. After ten days 'their countenances appeared fairer and fatter in flesh than all the children which did eat the portion of the King's meat.'[36]

are after the spirit, the things of the spirit. For to be carnally minded is death; but to be spiritually minded is life and peace . . . so then they that are in the flesh cannot please God . . .[41]

It is surprising that Tertullian had to exhort his fellow Christians in this manner, for it was commonly believed by the church fathers after the first century AD that Christ and the Apostles, in common with the Essenes, abstained from meat-eating. St Peter described his diet to Clement of Rome: 'I live upon bread and olives only with the addition, rarely, of kitchen herbs.'[42] Clement of Alexandria tells us that 'Matthew, the apostle, lived upon seeds and hard shelled fruits and other vegetables without touching flesh.'[43] Others – Hegesippus and St Augustine – state that St James 'never ate any animal food, living on seeds and vegetables, never tasting flesh or wine'.[44]

There is, though, not a shred of evidence in the Gospels that the disciples abstained from meat. We know that they and Jesus ate fish, and the Last Supper has always been thought to contain meat as it is a Passover meal, in which meat would have been eaten; Mosaic law decrees that meat is to be roasted and eaten with unleavened bread and green and bitter herbs. The traditional *seder* plate contains horseradish, parsley, roasted egg, celery leaves, lamb shank, haroset (chopped fruit and nuts) and salt water. This, like the American Thanksgiving, commemorates a historical event, in this case the beginning of the identity of the Jewish race, the flight from Egypt and the sparing of the firstborn of the Israelites when the Lord 'smote the land of Egypt' on the eve of the Exodus. In 1300 BC all meats were roasted; there were no cooking pots and many plants were still uncultivated, hence all green leaves were wild and bitter, while bread was unleavened. Yeast represents fermentation and therefore change, which we shall see Mosaic law was overly circumspect about. And, most importantly, there is no mention in Jesus' teaching, or that of his disciples, including St Paul, and later followers, of the respect due to animals or of a refusal to kill for meat. The early Christian writers seem to have fantasised the Apostles' meatless asceticism – but why did they feel such a picture was necessary?

The answer is that Christian thinking radically altered how people approached God. In the Jewish faith sanctity or holiness rests only in God or those places where God dwells, the Ark of the Covenant and, later, in the temple at Jerusalem. To touch the Ark was to court immediate death, for humanity is profane while God is sacred. Furthermore the God of the Old Testament is a God only seen as incarnated in the nation of Israel, in its people, in its destiny, in its struggles for freedom.

In Hebrew thinking the initiative is always with God. The prophets from Moses onwards plead their spiritual inadequacy, but the 'hand of God' is upon them and they are taken and become an instrument to relay God's message to his people. To be taken by God in this manner a prophet would have to be a Jew who kept the law, and a central part of the law was the detailed precepts on diet. It is clear from as early as the wanderings in the wilderness that God is intimately related to the everyday life of his people, their food and drink, trials and triumphs, work and play. This God is easily made angry by the smallest transgression of the laws, so there would have been no question of those nearest to God breaking a dietary law and *not* eating meat.

In contrast, the New Testament sees divine holiness as being made available to humankind through grace. Sanctity becomes a distinguishing mark of the Christian faithful; it is the goal of the Christian life for all, but is attained in this life by only a very few. Christian expansion meant that Gentiles became converts, Gentiles often with a philosophical tradition of asceticism behind them derived from Pythagoreans, Stoics and Epicureans; they had no doubts that in the striving towards a knowledge of God an austere diet played its part, that fasting helped to subjugate the flesh and release the flight of the spirit.

It seemed obvious, then, to the early church fathers that the Apostles must have eaten modestly. Their nuts, bread and vegetables were a form of self-sacrifice, of mortifying the body in order to purify the soul, but this was merely a matter between them and God, owing no responsibility at all to the sentient creatures occupying the rest of the earth. St Augustine crystallised these feelings: not to kill animals, in his view, was the height of superstition and there was no need to behave towards animals as towards humans.[45]

Before Augustine the early Church was peopled with Christian thinkers who adopted the Apostles' asceticism, surviving on a frugal diet without meat, yet ignoring the issue of violence inherent in the meat-eaters' diet. An exception was Titus Flavius Clement, founder of the Alexandrian school of Christian theology, who lived at the end of the second century AD and died possibly in AD 220. He came near to a dogmatic denunciation of meat-eating in his discourse *Gnostic Memoirs upon the True Philosophy*. The work was an attempt completely to regulate all parts and functions of the body, so that it might better be put into the service of God. Clement attempted what many might think the impossible. A profound admirer of Greek philosophy, especially the Stoics and Platonic metaphysics, he wished to fuse Greek thinking with the Christian creed.* He wished to extract the best from Plato, Epicurus, Aristotle and the Stoics, the idea of moral grooming, the body and soul being in subjugation to a higher power, and to weld these together into Christian theology. A strong theme throughout his writing is a particularly Epicurean dislike of pleasure: 'some men live that they may eat, as the irrational beings "whose life is their belly and nothing else". But the

---

*In one sense early Christian thinkers thought this fusion of Greek philosophy and Hebraic thought had already been achieved. They believed that the best of Greek philosophy was derived from the Jewish sacred scriptures. Much later it was discovered that an Alexandrian Jew – Aristobulus – had deliberately forged passages in the Orphic poems and Sybilline predictions to gain respect from the Greek rulers for his own nation's Jewish scriptures. Aristobulus was counsellor to Ptolemy VI (181-145 BC).

tutor enjoins us to eat that we may live.'★ Health and strength, Clement goes on to say, consists of plain fare. Food and drink is for sustenance not pleasure

> since the body derives no advantage from extravagance in food. On the contrary, those who use the most frugal fare are the strongest and the healthiest and the noblest; as domestics are stronger and healthier than their masters and agricultural labourers than proprietors and not only more vigorous but wiser than rich men. For they have not buried the mind beneath food.[46]

He makes the point that it is unnatural for life to depend on death; it is inhuman, Clement says, to fatten ourselves on dead cattle. He asks: 'why should cooks be held in higher esteem than the tillers of the ground?' He praises the simple fare of Christ's loaves and fishes, calling it 'God–given and moderate food'. Though a lover of Pythagoras, Clement here shows no compassion for the multitude of dead fish cooked and eaten on the day of this miracle. Yet his vegetarianism appears passionate enough, as in this passage: 'We must guard against those sorts of food which persuade us to eat when we are not hungry, bewitching the appetite. For is there not, within a temperate simplicity, a wholesome variety of food – vegetables, roots, olives, herbs, milk, cheese and fruits?' Clement attacks gluttony constantly: 'But those who bend around inflammatory tables, nourishing their own diseases, are ruled by a most licentious disease which I shall venture to call the demon of the belly.' He explains the Judaic food taboos: 'altogether only a few animals were left for food. For God had prohibited those that had died, or were offered to idols or had been strangled . . . thus a frugality had been enjoined on the Jews by the Law in the most systematic manner.' He also interprets the food laws as symbols, as others were to do after him. For example, Moses forbade the children of Israel to eat the hyena because the sexual habits of the hyena were disreputable – they mounted each other frequently and often when the female was pregnant.

Clement also praises Pythagoras: 'the altar at Delos was celebrated for its purity, to which alone, as being undefiled by slaughter and death, they say that Pythagoras would permit approach.'

Clement, of course, did not believe in the transmigration of souls, so his abstention from meat is based on ascetic rationalism, on the linking of flesh-eating with the stimulation of passion which would disrupt the stability of Christian commitment: 'If any righteous man does not burden his soul by the eating of flesh, he has the advantage of a rational motive.

'Pythagoras seems to me to have derived his mildness towards irrational animals from the Law.' Clement's explanation owes everything to the commonly held theory that the Greeks owed their ideas to the Jews.

---

★The source of this idea is Socrates, according to Athenaeus: 'They live that they may eat, but he himself [i.e. Socrates] eats that he may live.'

For instance, he interdicted the employment of the young of sheep and goats and cows for some time after their birth: not even on the pretext of sacrifice allowing it, on account both of the young ones and of the mother; training men to gentleness by their conduct towards those beneath them.

Clement then quotes Pythagoras demanding that the newborn stay with their mothers for the proper time: 'For if nothing takes place without a cause and milk is produced in large quantity in parturition for the sustenance of the progeny, he who tears away the young one from the supply of the milk and the breast of the mother, dishonours Nature.'[47]

Butchering practices of the time, as well as those of tenderising or flavouring meat (many of them continuing in some form or other until the eighteenth century), may seem particularly horrendous to the modern reader but they were no less so to people like Clement. Plutarch describes these practices:

To slaughter swine they thrust red hot irons into their living bodies so that, by sucking up or diffusing the blood, they may render the flesh soft and tender. Some butchers jump upon or kick the udders of pregnant sows, that by mingling the blood and milk and matter of the embryos that have been murdered together in the very pang of parturition, they may enjoy the pleasure of feeding upon unnaturally and highly inflamed flesh. Again, it is a common practice to stitch up the eyes of cranes and swans and shut them up in dark places to fatten.[48]

Clement comments upon these vile practices:

The Law, too, expressly prohibits the slaying of such animals as are pregnant till they have brought forth . . . those too that kick the bellies of certain animals before parturition, in order to feast on flesh mixed with milk, make the womb created for the birth of the foetus its grave, though the Law expressly commands 'but neither shalt thou seethe a lamb in his mother's milk'. For the nourishment of the living animal may not be converted into sauce for that which has been deprived of life; and that which is the cause of life may not co-operate in the consumption of its flesh.[49]

## Meat and Milk

The command, 'Thou shalt not seethe a kid in his mother's milk', occurs three times in the Bible,[50] and has been a great puzzle to many commentators. It may be partly linked to the laws against incest mother and son must not be in the same pot or bed.[51] Maimonides, the medieval Jewish philosopher, claims the ban was because the boiling of a kid in its mother's milk was a ritual act in the Canaanite religion. He considered that the aim of many of the more mysterious Mosaic dietary laws was to break with heathen practices.[52] Cooking meat in milk seems odd in the first place, yet this injunction has had enormous influence on kosher cooking,★ as it was interpreted to mean that meat and dairy products should not be eaten at the same meal.

Mary Douglas[54] thinks that the separation of meat and milk honours the procreative functions, honours the Hebrew mother and her initial unity with her offspring. However, it is Jean Soler[55] who is most illuminating, not just on the fusion of meat and milk, but on all the Mosaic dietary strictures. If the Exodus and the Revelation at Sinai need to be a re-creation of the world and a new beginning for the Hebrew people, then they have to be distinct from all humankind, but how exactly? To do this, Soler posits a harking back to Genesis and an attempt to make human food the purest, the most perfect, thus reflecting pious aspirations on the Hebrews themselves. As we have seen, the food at the Creation was vegetarian, so was there historically an attempt by Mosaic law to turn the Hebrews into vegetarians? There are hints.

## The Quail Plague

Manna, the only daily nourishment given by God in the wilderness, is a vegetal substance: 'It was like coriander seed, white, and the taste of it was like wafer made with honey.'[56] The Hebrews had huge flocks of sheep which they did not slaughter and eat – strange, because they murmured much against God for not leaving them in the land of Egypt 'by the flesh pots'[57] so much, in fact, that God sent them quails and manna.[58] But the Hebrews were not satisfied: 'We remember the fish, which we did eat in Egypt freely, the cucumbers, and the melons, and the leeks and the onions and the garlic. But now our soul is dried away: there is nothing at all beside this manna, before our eyes.'[59] An ungrateful lot, God quite naturally felt, even though his people were most industrious with the manna: 'And the people went about and gathered it and ground it in mills, or beat it in a mortar and baked it in pans and made cakes of it and the taste of it was as the taste of fresh oil.'[60] They still felt the loss of meat: 'And the mixed multitude fell a-lusting and the children of Israel also wept again and said, "Who shall give us flesh to eat?"'[61] All this so angered God that he sent them another great multitude of quails but this time poisoned: 'and while the flesh was yet between their teeth, ere it was chewed, the wrath of the Lord was kindled against the people and the Lord smote the people with a very great plague.'[62]

Elsewhere (see p.48) I have mentioned Aristotle's observation: 'some fruits are unfit for us to eat, but fit for others, like the henbane and hellebore, which are poisonous to men, but good food for quails . . .' The Hebrews did not know of the antidote – eating boiled millet with the poisoned quail – which Didymus of Alexandria mentions: 'as quails feeding on hellebore are

---

★'The whole of Jewish gastronomic life is divided into meat (*flayshik*) and dairy (*muchik*). The faithful begin by dividing their kitchens down the middle. They keep separate sets of dishes and pots and pans. To help them avoid mistakes, soap for dishwashing is sold in colour-coded bars (red for meat, blue for dairy).'[53]

pernicious to the persons who eat them, causing convulsion and giddiness, you are to boil millet along with them: and if a person having eaten them be taken ill, let him drink decoction of millet . . .'[63] Numbers tells us that a wind blew in from the sea and deposited the quails round about the Hebrew camp 'two cubits high upon the face of the earth'.[64] Ever since the dawn of history along the north African coasts nets are used to catch the exhausted quails after their southward migratory flight in the autumn, across the Mediterranean sea, where little green food is available. The quail then feeds on hellebore and henbane, the seeds of which contain toxins that tend to become concentrated in the muscles of the birds owing to dehydration. Ancient writings, between the fourth century BC and the third century AD,[*] draw attention to the sometimes unfortunate consequences of eating quail. The peoples of the northern shores of the eastern Mediterranean regarded the eating of quail with great caution.

God had warned his chosen people that they would become sick of meat, 'until it comes out of your nostrils and becomes loathsome to you.'[65] Obviously it also killed a great number of them: 'There they buried the people that lusted.'[66] But despite such a dire experience Moses still allowed the eating of meat, though with two restrictions: firstly, the taboo against blood was reinforced and, secondly, certain living creatures were to be forbidden.

## Clean or Unclean

In Leviticus and Deuteronomy a formidable number of creatures are labelled either clean or unclean. There is no explanation, and both lists are identical.[67] Over sixty verses list the creatures, birds, fish, rodents and serpents, tabulating precise distinctions. The only land creatures approved of have four legs and are cloven-hoofed: cud-chewing ungulates are the model for proper food — herbivores, in fact. Anything that deviates from this pattern is unclean and forbidden: that includes four-footed creatures which fly, or creatures with two legs and two hands which go on all fours. A spurious concept of normality is constructed; for example, of the creatures that live in water, all that have fins and scales are proper food, but anything else is taboo, hence all shellfish, squid and octopuses are forbidden. Carnivorous animals have killed and eaten other animals, therefore anyone who ate them would also be unclean.

If a wild animal is to be clean it has to conform with the patterns of the domestic animals. Any deviation from the cloven hoof is considered a blemish, so the coney, the hare and all rodents are unclean. Hence, too, all sacrifices to the altar have to be scrutinised carefully for perfection, as in Ancient Egypt: 'You shall not offer to the Lord your God an ox or a sheep in which is a blemish, any defect whatever; for this is an abomination to the

---

[*]This was also true later: both Avicenna and Maimonides in the Middle Ages warn against eating quail meat.

Lord your God.'[68] Any alteration from the supposed norm also counts as a blemish. Further, substances that become changed are considered just as unclean. Fermentation alters substances, so neither leavened bread nor wine can be offered to the Lord, nor honey, as that is a secondary substance.[69] Salt was essential in sacrifice because it preserves food, rather than alters it.

All possibility of alteration or mingling was rigorously excluded: 'You shall not let your cattle breed with a different kind';[70] 'You shall not plough with an ox and an ass together';[71] 'You shall not sow your field with two kinds of seeds';[72] 'Nor shall there come upon you a garment of cloth made of two kinds of stuff.'[73] It follows too that mixed marriages are taboo, as also the children of such marriages, who may not enter the assembly of the Lord.[74] Soler suggests that Jesus was entirely unacceptable to the Hebrews as he was God-man or God become man – such a hybrid being anathema to them.

Christianity, led by the hybrid Jesus, disrupted the rigid distinctions that were so important to the Hebrews, yet at the same time it was heavily influenced by them. Peter's dream,[75] in which God unfolds a sheet containing myriad forms of animals bidding Peter to eat, is a vivid illustration of the break with the Mosaic law. Peter answers that he cannot eat as 'I have never eaten anything that is common or unclean.'[76] But three times God bids Peter to eat, which is interpreted by Peter to mean that Christianity is for all, Jew and Gentile alike, and the chapter ends with Peter baptising Cornelius after they share a meal.

In the end Christians, though inheriting the Mosaic dietary laws, did not accept them in their entirety, but many of the unclean animals remained taboo in the Christian countries, such as, by and large, the horse, camel, donkey or mule, as well as the unclean birds, the eagle, kite, raven, owl. Nevertheless, in giving such precise instructions in Leviticus and Deuteronomy, God's law required Jew and Christian alike to eat some meat as part of the holy scheme of things. Vegetarian Christians like Clement could only get away with their behaviour on the grounds of pure asceticism. The ethics of non-violence towards animals or metaphysical doctrines on animal souls were never given as reasons for a vegetarian mode of life. To eat a taboo creature was to break the Mosaic law, to sunder all ties with the one living God; hence how much more heinous a crime would it have been for an orthodox Jew to be a vegetarian and refuse to consume any meat from either list. The very act of being vegetarian suggests that Mosaic law is entirely irrelevant, that the vegetarian lives in a state of greater purity and is therefore closer to God than the orthodox Jew by representing the era before the Fall was an heretical idea. The Christian vegetarian was also breaking with these traditions, that holy sanction whereby God provides for humankind out of his munificence. For Christians, it was only acceptable to renounce meat-eating if you called it asceticism and, better still, went off into the desert to practise it.

The retreat to the Egyptian desert started by Anthony around AD 270 exerted an enormous pull on pious young men in the cities, who saw it as one method of conquering their sexuality and coming nearer to God. In caves carved from the rock beyond the tombs which were at the edge of the green oasis where the villages were, these men survived on nuts, berries and grasses and what bread they could beg for, spending their days in prayer and study and their nights in vain hopes of not having a nocturnal emission. The lack of such emissions was taken to mean that the grace of God had descended upon them, though it is of course more likely to have been due to the paucity of nourishment. Though the desert fathers were undoubtedly vegetarian it was again only because of the struggle of the early Christians for pre-eminence over their own flesh, and not out of any respect for other creatures.

One such man was John Chrysostom, whose name means 'golden voiced' as he became an orator of great power and brilliance. He was born at Antioch in AD 347 into a military family, studied law and was instructed in the art of oratory by a famous rhetorician, Libanius, who had been a friend and counsellor of the apostate Emperor Julian. Chrysostom soon gave up the law and took up theology; influenced by the Essenes, he abandoned all rights to private property and lived a life of strict asceticism, abstaining from all meats and living for two years in a cave on Mount Silpios.

Chrysostom wrote passionately and at length, 700 homilies in all and 242 letters. His style is oratorical, somewhat frantic: 'no streams of blood are among them [the asceticsl; no butchering and cutting up of flesh; no dainty cookery; no heaviness of head. Nor are there horrible smells of flesh meats among them or disagreeable fumes from the kitchen . . .' He concludes this passage: 'We follow the ways of wolves, the habits of tigers; or rather we are worse even than they. To them Nature has assigned that they should be thus fed, while God has honoured us with rational speech and a sense of equity. And yet we are become worse than the wild beasts.'[77]

Chrysostom is acutely conscious of the processes of digestion and of waste residues. His writing shows an awareness of the putrefaction in life unlike anything written before, but this is the tone all the cultures of Christendom would soon be familiar with:

> Why do you thus gorge your own body with excess? Consider what comes of food – into what it is changed. Are you not disgusted at it? The increase of luxury is but the multiplication of filth . . . Nourish the body, but do not destroy it. Food is called nourishment, to show that its purpose is not to hurt, but to support us. For this reason, perhaps, food passes into excrement that we may not be lovers of luxury.[78]

However, meat-eating for Christians was part of the fabric of their life in praise of the Lord, part of the glory of God, part of the created world, one of the delights that God had given them for their sustenance and pleasure. We must not forget too that a haunch of roasted meat also stood for wealth, affluence and social position. If you ate no meat at all it meant you were poor, not that you were vegetarian.

As we have seen, the very early Church may well have almost been vegetarian. The Essenes are unlikely to have killed animals, except for ritual slaughter, and their diet was certainly of the most moderate and ascetic kind. It was Paul the missionary who widened the Church to include Gentiles, who made no distinctions in diet – the fewer rules the better when it comes to converting people. Yet the ascetic way of life which the Essenes followed had its many disciples and it was the groups whom the early Church was offended by, who promulgated a vegetarian diet as part of their ideology, that in these years had as much power and sway over the public as the orthodox Church. For many hundreds of years it was not at all certain which religion, if any, might conquer the world. Certainly many of the unorthodox sects seemed to be more likely winners than the Church itself.

# 6

# Gnostic Sects
# and the Manicheans

In the last twenty years we have learnt more about the religious ferment and ideas immediately after the crucifixion than we ever knew, or were allowed to know, before. The Nag Hammadi texts, buried for almost 2,000 years, contained many Gospels, of Thomas, Mary, James, Philip, of Truth, the Apocryphon of John, of James, the Apocalypse of Peter, and many other writings which tell a different story, revealing more complicated and subtle truths than the revelations found in the orthodox four Gospels. Yet there is little agreement between all these texts. Divergent groups all claim to be the inheritors of Christian revelation. Asia Minor at this time appears to have been particularly fertile in divine speculation. Hundreds of rival teachers all claimed to teach the true doctrine of Christ.

## Whence Came the True Voice of God?

Christians in churches scattered from Asia Minor to Greece, Jerusalem and Rome split into factions, all claiming authenticity and arguing over church leadership.[1] In this maelstrom of passionate ideology it is impossible to pin down the reappearance in religious attitudes of the vegetarian ethic, but reappear it did and somehow not merely as Christian asceticism but as respect for life. It certainly shows itself flourishing in Mani, the founder of Manicheanism, in AD 226 when he broke away from his father's vegetarian sect, the Elchasaites. The idea, of course, was active enough in philosophical thought at the same time, as we have seen in Plutarch, Plotinus and Porphyry, but because Hebrew thought had suppressed the vegetarian ethic, the religious sects which now embraced it had in some form or another to be opposed to or critical of the Old Testament (this we find in Marcion, Mani and others).

The early Gnostic teachers too, like Valentinus, in their intense mysticism also showed a respect for life or the spirit within the material world. They taught that Jesus himself passed on secret knowledge to his disciples which could only be understood by the spiritually mature (this was initiation into the gnosis) and that the risen Christ continued to reveal himself to certain disciples. Paul, of course, says much the same,[2] when in a trance he heard 'things that cannot be told, which man may not utter' and later a 'secret wisdom' which can only be shared with those Christians he feels to be mature enough.[3] In this it might be difficult for us to distinguish between Gnostic and orthodox and it was as true then. Gnostic believers certainly worshipped in church as well as having meetings amongst themselves; for many decades, perhaps even centuries, after the crucifixion, because they had so many dogmas and concepts to choose from believers were never clear as to which ones were approved of by the bishop. This state of affairs could not continue.

The leaders of the orthodox Church had to clarify dogma and give the Church a clear leadership. One of the main tenets of Gnostic belief was that individuals drew upon their own spiritual experience, the gnosis, to reveal the truth of God. Tertullian was enraged by this: 'every one of them modifies the traditions he has received.'[4]

Valentinus taught that the real God was a source beyond all the concepts like Father, Creator, Son, and was, in fact, an incomprehensible primal principle, a God behind the images of God, a ground of being. The author of the Gospel of Philip talks of the names or titles that God has as being deceptive:

> Very deceptive, for they divert our thoughts from what is accurate to what is inaccurate. Thus one who hears the word 'God' does not perceive what is accurate, but perceives what is inaccurate. So also with 'the Father' and 'the Son', and 'the Holy Spirit', and 'life', and 'light', and 'resurrection', and 'the Church', and all the rest – people do not perceive what is accurate, but they perceive what is inaccurate . . .[5]

We know now that Christian mystics down the centuries would agree with Valentinus, for their absorption into the 'ground of being' has always been their purpose. Yet in the first two hundred years AD this religious need was seen to be too confusing and alarming, too uncontrolled for the early church fathers to administer. For efficient administration the bishop had to be all-powerful over his flock; there had to be one precisely defined God and one bishop who would rule the community as God rules heaven, as the master, king, judge and lord.

Clement of Alexandria was acutely aware of the teaching of Valentinus and of its insidious power over his flock, for Valentinus taught that the real God was this primal being behind the concepts of master, king, judge and lord. Imagine a Gnostic initiate replying to the bishop: 'You claim to represent God, but, in reality, you represent only the demiurge, whom you blindly serve and obey. I, however, have passed beyond the sphere of his authority – and so, for that matter, beyond yours!'[6] Gnosis, the orthodox knew, offered theological justification for refusing to obey the bishops and priests. This had to be heretical, for their beliefs could undermine the whole of the early Church. It was a short step to believing that such doctrines must stem from the devil.

## The Equality of Women

One of the great attractions of the Gnostic religions was that, in sharp contrast to the Hebrew tradition, it made women equal to men in their devotions. What is more, God, in many of the texts at Nag Hammadi, embraced both masculine and feminine elements. Some of the Gnostic sources stress that the secret tradition learnt from Jesus through James and Mary Magdalene was to pray to both the divine father and the mother. Though Valentinus states that God is essentially indescribable, he also suggests that the divine can be thought of as a dyad – a group of two – and he divides it into the Primal Father, representing ineffable depth, and the Mother of the All, representing Grace and Silence. Followers would pray to the Mother as the mystical eternal Silence; the cup of wine in the Mass symbolises her blood and the thought that Grace might flow into the body of all who drink.

But by AD 200 all the feminine imagery of God the Mother had been erased from the orthodox Christian tradition, except of course in a much weakened form for the worship of the Virgin Mary. Yet by the beginning of the third century the Gnostics were flourishing, partly because their ranks were filled with women. Bishop Irenaeus from the Rhone Valley is much irritated by it, complaining that the Gnostic teacher Marcus has attracted 'many foolish women' from his own congregation which included the wife of one of his deacons. Tertullian likewise finds it all infuriating: 'These heretical women – how audacious they are! They have no modesty; they are bold enough to teach, to engage in argument, to enact exorcisms, to undertake cures, and, it may be, even to baptize!'

One of the first vegetarian teachers to outrage the orthodox bishops by appointing women on an equal basis with men as priests and bishops was Marcion, who arrived in Rome in AD 130. Marcion taught a belief that owed everything to Jesus and nothing to the Old Testament, for the God depicted there, Marcion claimed, took delight in wars and was the creator of evil things. Jesus came from a source far higher than this Jehovah, and Marcion went on to reject all those parts of the New Testament which showed an approval of the Old. The only Gospel Marcion allowed was a specially edited version of Luke.

Luke is thought to have been put together by the Christians of Antioch and contains many of Jesus' most uncompromising observations: the blessed of the world were the poor, the homeless, the rootless and the oppressed, hence the message of the Second Coming for the masses was profoundly attractive. Unlike the poet Valentinus, we first see in Marcion the beginnings of dualism: 'the universe in his opinion had been brought about by a forming power far removed from the radiant tranquillity of the highest god',[7] another explanation of cruelty and oppression which would appeal to the world's poor. Yet Marcion went further and named the creative force as the God of Jewish law, which had imposed on humankind restraints that cut human beings off from one another; these distinctions – from circumcision to abhorrence of pork and shellfish – that label the Hebrews as, if not special, at least different from all others were, some might argue, the creed which spawns nationalism and spurns such concepts as the family of humankind. Marcion's version of Luke was highly selective: it omitted the birth and baptism of Christ, the temptation and all preaching from the Book of Isaiah. Marcion adored Paul, so he included ten of his epistles, but all references to the Old Testament were removed.

Because Marcion encouraged women his sect also attracted wealthy widows, who then influenced their families, so that Marcionites had a broad base in wealthy middle-class families with money in trade and shipping. Marcion himself came from a family which had made a fortune from a ship-owning business which traded between the Black Sea and Italy.

Marcionite communities thrived in the mountainous regions of Syria and Asia Minor, men and women gathered together in celibacy, alive to the human spirit. Spending their time in prayer, singing and tilling the fields, they had a fierce sense of group activity. By the fourth century there were Marcionite communities in Rome, Palestine, Arabia, Syria, Cyprus, the Thebaid (Upper Egypt) and Persia. Cyril of Jerusalem warned the faithful that they must not step into a Marcionite church by mistake.[8] It was easy, especially for pagans, to confuse a Marcionite church with an orthodox one.

Paul's statements in Corinthians that 'women should keep silent in churches' and be subordinate for it was 'shameful for women to speak in church'[9] were of course in direct contradiction to the Marcionites' encouragement of women, a policy we shall see in all the vegetarian Christian heresies from now until the thirteenth century. Marcion was simply carrying on an earlier pagan tradition in Greece and Asia Minor in which women participated with men in religious cults of the Egyptian goddess Isis and the Great Mother and in which women were also revered, as in some of the mystery religions thriving still at the time of Marcion.

Socially, too, at this time women were making themselves felt, in education, the arts and professions such as medicine.[10] Quite violent changes were occurring, reflecting many of the issues which are part of our social fabric today:

> Under the Empire, 'women were everywhere involved in business, social life, such as theatres, sports events, concerts, parties, travelling with or without their husbands. They took part in a whole range of athletics, even bore arms and went to battle . . .' and made major inroads into professional life. Women of the Jewish communities, on the other hand, were excluded from actively participating in public worship, in education, and in social and political life outside the family.[11]

Yet orthodox Christians accepted Paul's view that women were to be 'subject in everything to their husbands'. What is more, at the time of the bitterest struggle between orthodox and Gnostic at the end of the second century, churches began to adopt the custom of the synagogues and separate the women from the men. Equality of the sexes had become a sign of heresy. Tertullian summed up the orthodox view: 'It is not permitted for a woman to speak in the church, nor is it permitted for her to teach, nor to baptize, nor to offer [the eucharist], nor to claim for herself a share in any masculine function – least of all, in priestly office.'[12] Hence the great popularity of the various and flourishing sects which encouraged women's involvement. By the year AD 200, both orthodox and Gnostic Christians claimed to represent the true Church, accusing the others of being false and hypocritical. The battle lines were drawn. But the Gnostic sects themselves in these years were bewilderingly diverse.

## Gnostic Variety

In Edessa the apostle Addai claimed to have received the gospel through an exchange of letters between the King, Abgar, and Jesus himself directly before his crucifixion. Then there was Elchasaios (his name means 'hidden power'), who rejected the letters of Paul but made Jerusalem into the centre of world religious devotion. His *Book of Elchasaios* encourages an ethical way of life, observance of the Sabbath and circumcision. Christ was considered a great teacher but not divine, though he could be reborn countless times in other bodies. Many other sects diverged because of their intense asceticism.

The Encratites condemned marriage and the use of meat and wine, though they accepted the dogmas of the Church. Tatian, a Syrian rhetorician, had to rewrite various Pauline texts to make them concur with the Encratic observances, for they even substituted water or milk for wine in the Eucharist. They believed that the soul was destroyed by the sexual act.

The Montanists accused the orthodox Christians of laxity and mediocrity. The founder, Montanus, declared himself the prophet of a third Testament, a new age of the Holy Spirit. Tertullian himself was a convert, leaving the Catholic Church in disgust, for the moral rigour of the Montanists appealed over the laxity of the Catholic bishops. Times of fasting were lengthened, martyrdom was embraced and marriage was discouraged. Montanists were intensely mystical: their prophets descended into trances and spoke with the voice of spirits. They preached that the Second Coming would occur in Phrygia at a special plain between two villages. The Emperor Justinian destroyed the Montanists in his reign in the sixth century.

Novatian (AD 200-258) was a Roman Christian theologian and a leader of the Roman clergy who proclaimed a rigorous doctrine in opposition to the elected Pope. He set himself up as anti-Pope and his movement spread across the empire. In his work *Concerning Jewish Foods*, obviously bewildered by their complexity, he pointed out that the dietary laws of the Old Testament must not be taken literally, but must be understood spiritually. The

Novatians merged gradually with the Montanist sect.

The more orthodox bishops disliked extreme asceticism; where should the line be drawn? In AD 330 the Council of Gangra in northern Asia Minor condemned the teachings of Eustathius of Sebaste for their self-righteous and exaggerated asceticism, for they taught that married couples could not be saved, forbade people to eat meat, and encouraged the women to cut their hair short and dress like men. The Gangra council hated such forms of exaggeration as it led to a false view of matter, i.e. dualism, and that particular doctrine was to haunt all of the heretical sects, as it was the Christian Church itself.

All of these groups are now known as Gnostic heresies, for they all share the characteristic of claiming to be possessed of greater esoteric knowledge than the orthodox Christians. They believed that knowledge gained through personal mystical experience was of far greater significance than dogma or doctrine or faith. As we have seen, only a very few of these Gnostic sects held power and influence in real competition with the orthodox Christians, most notably Marcion. But Marcion influenced another group, who seemed in those first few hundred years to challenge the supremacy of the growing Catholic Church – the Manicheans. So feared were they and so long their shadow that for centuries the very word became a synonym for heresy. The Church felt that, though the devil reigned in all other heresies, he had raised his throne in that of the Manicheans. In celebrating a strict vegetarianism among their Elect and in keeping the flame of it alive throughout the Dark Ages, they are far more interesting and worthy of our respect than the grubby, highly slanderous picture left us by Christian saints and writers.

## Manicheanism

In this ferment of Gnostic speculation it is not surprising that one man should become inspired and lead a mission in the manner of Paul the Apostle to convert the world. Mani, the founder of Manicheanism, was not born in Asia Minor, where so much of the Gnostic fervour was generated, but further east. He came from the great kingdom of Persia, whose state religion was the dualist creed of Zoroaster. He was born in a sectarian Elchasaite village near the new Sassanian capital at Ctesiphon on the Tigris. It was this small sect, the Elchasaites (who observed the Mosaic law), which had converted Patik, the father of Mani. It was the Elchasaites among whom Mani grew up and it was they who influenced his childhood and youth. While worshipping in a temple Patik had heard a voice telling him not to eat meat, nor to drink wine, nor to marry, but he was already married and his wife gave birth to Mani in AD 216. When Mani was four years old his father sent for the child to teach him the precepts of the Elchasaites. They were vegetarians and worked in the fields; the boy would have harvested the fruit and cereals and gathered firewood. No women were allowed in the sect and the writings of St Paul were detested. They celebrated the Eucharist with unleavened bread and water and washed themselves and their food according to certain rules of purity. Visions ran in the family and Mani, at the age of twelve, had the first of many which found favour with his father's religion.

Twenty years after the four-year-old Mani joined the sect he began to criticise its main tenets. Purification by washing with water obviously perturbed him; he told the Elchasaite elders: 'There is no value in this ritual washing with which you cleanse your food ... consider how when someone purifies his food and then partakes of it after it has been ritually washed, it is apparent that from it comes blood, bile, burps and shameful excrement. . .' Mani argues that the foulness from the body is the same whether a food has been ritually purified or not: 'All defilement is from the body . . . you yourselves are clothed in it.'13 Bodily purification had no spiritual significance whatsoever; true purity came from mental knowledge. The dualist concept was very clear to Mani; the body and everything that emanates from it is evil while the mind and spirit belong to God. Surely this is Chrysostom speaking? This loathing and hatred for defilement of matter is a theme that was to run throughout Mani's life.

The elders did not much care for Mani's critical eye or his claim that he was protected by the might of angels and that the powers of holiness had been entrusted to him for his safe-keeping. One of his angels was his divine twin, an emanation of the Jesus of Light that gave him guidance. Perhaps what annoyed his fellows most was Mani's attitude to food, for he did not wish to harvest the fruit and vegetables himself, but only to accept them as alms. Later Mani was to make this into a significant part of the Manichean religion, but then it must have been construed as laziness or arrogance. Neither would Mani's reasons for his reluctance have endeared him to them. Blood, he claimed, oozed from the places where the plants had been hurt by the sickle; the vegetable world cried out with a human voice at the pain it received. When taken by force to pick dates, the tree spoke to Mani calling him a murderer. So angry were the Elchasaites that they eventually attacked Mani and almost killed him, but his father, Patik, beseeched them not to be sacrilegious. Mani travelled to the capital, Ctesiphon, after his divine twin had told him: 'Hope will be made manifest and preached by you in every clime and zone of the world and many men will receive your word.'14 There, two Elchasaites joined him, regarding him as the true prophet. Later, his father became another disciple, convinced that Mani was in touch with the divine.

Mani's teachings were influenced by Marcion, though he never admitted the debt, and by yet another heresy, Bardaisanism. From Marcion Mani borrowed a certain Pauline devotion and an antipathy to Judaism; while from Bardaisanism he borrowed some mythology, and the concept of the separate existence of darkness (not just the absence of light) as a contaminating primordial force.

In the *Manual of Discipline* found at Qumran humankind is divided up into two antithetical groups, dominated, respectively, by a Spirit of Darkness and a Spirit of Light. In the *Manual* it is the duty of the faithful to loathe and curse the alien and wicked people who were dominated by the Spirit of Darkness. Dualism had long and deep pre-Christian roots, though for the Qumran brotherhood the people of the Spirit of Darkness were possibly the Romans, their oppressors. But there can be no doubt that Manicheanism borrowed much from Qumranic ideas and literature, including Enoch, a Hebrew prophet, and his works. These were merged seamlessly into Mani's legends, the *Book of the Giants*.

There are three moments: Former Time, Present Time and Future Time. In the first only Light and Darkness exist. Light is wisdom and Darkness folly. There are no heavens or earths. In Present Time, Darkness invades Light, and there is a cosmic battle as Light tries to repel the invader. In the struggle Light enters Darkness but can only be free of its new body when the physical body wears out. In Future Time truth and falsehood return to their roots. Light once more belongs to the Great Light and Darkness returns to the Ultimate Darkness.[15] This book, one of seven canonical scriptures of the Manicheans, includes the description of a battle to explain the origin of wisdom and folly (*not*, let it be noted, good and evil).

Mani was a visionary, poet, artist and missionary. His theology has a startling originality, the creation myths forming the basis of an elaborate ecclesiastical organisation which allowed the religion to outlive all its Gnostic predecessors by many centuries.

A Chinese Manichean handbook states: 'Everyone who wishes to join the sect must know that Light and Darkness are principles, each in their own right, and that their natures are completely distinct.'[16] The book explains the beginning of creation according to Mani, how the enlightened souls of men of divine origin came to be clothed in the body of matter which is evil. In all men, therefore, there is a divine spark buried in the matter of this world, encased in the flesh of the body. We know this spark of divinity from its attributes: intelligence, knowledge, reason, thought and deliberation. These will in turn engender the five virtues: love, faith, contentment, patience and wisdom. These will enable the soul to withstand the attack of the flesh and to combat the rebellious tendencies of sin.

It is almost impossible to disentangle the refusal to eat meat (i.e. flesh) with the desire to be continent. Historians have noted the latter and tended to dismiss the former as a trivial adjunct, yet they are both part of the aspiration to be pure spirit. The sexual act was avoided so as not to propagate more matter, and meat (i.e. dead flesh) not consumed as it would weigh down the corporeal body and delay the time before it became pure spirit.

But Mani's view of the body was not as negative as the view of other Gnostic leaders. He believed that the bodies of his believers could play a part in redeeming the universe. The whole of matter, including our bodies, Mani taught, contains light particles which are imprisoned like insects in amber. The divine intelligence also embodied itself into perfect men, prophets who are seen as redeemers: first Seth,★ the third son of Adam, then Noah, Abraham, Shem, Enosh, Nikotheos and Enoch. As Manicheanism spread it diplomatically collected the founders of the great religions (though Jesus already had his role), Buddha and Zoroaster; the final and most complete manifestation of the perfect redeemer was Mani himself.

From St Paul, Mani borrowed the terms of Old and New Man. Matter is the old Adam submerging the soul in a drunken sleep while the New Man is constantly striving to come alive and dominate the body. To help the soul into its new life there were five commandments that had to be observed: not to lie, not to kill, not to eat flesh, to keep ourselves pure, and to bless and accept the state of poverty while honouring humility and kindness.

There were also three seals to be observed, that of the mouth, the hands and the thoughts. The Seal of the Mouth forbade blasphemous speech, the eating of meat and the drinking of wine. Meat contained fewer light particles than plants, because animals fed off the plants and some of the light which they had ingested escaped. Wine was thought to be the 'bile of the Prince of Darkness' because drunkenness wiped out all memory of divine origins. A Persian Manichean text lists among the sins of wine-drinking: unconsciousness, sickness, regret, contentiousness, fear of falling, strife and punishment.[17] The Seal of the Hands commands the believer not to hurt the light particles imprisoned in matter. These particles are seen as an attribute of the divine creator of the universe, but also as being within the redeemer of the suffering Jesus suspended upon the cross which is present in all plants, earth, stones and rocks. So Manicheans were forbidden to till the soil, pluck fruit or harvest any plant, nor were they to kill anything, creature or insect, no matter how small. (The similarity with Jainism is striking and it is very likely that Mani in India met with Jains as well as Buddhists. He certainly would have heard of their ideas from quite early on as the Tigris was a trading route.) The Seal of the Thoughts meant a ban on all sexual intercourse which would result in the procreation of more matter.

Such rules, of course, were entirely impractical, for they could only lead to virtual starvation and the extinction of the human race. But a select group of the more advanced disciples could, with Mani, adopt them. Thus the adherents were divided into two groups, the Elect and the Hearers (similar to the two groups around Pythagoras). The Elect, in their rigorous adoption of the rules, are the leaders of the Church.†

Food takes on a particularly significant role for, with the help of the Elect and their digestive systems, the light particles are released – the Elect in their purity are able to refine the light particles and release them through their

---

★There was yet another Gnostic sect which called themselves Sethians from this offspring of Adam.
†The Manichean ecclesiastical hierarchy is divided into the Leader, the successor to Mani, with twelve apostles, seventy-two bishops and 360 elders. Then come the Elect and the Hearers.

belches. Meals, then, were a holy tribute to God, a form of sacrament which began with a prayer by the Elect to absolve them from procuring the food. The Hearers gathered and prepared the food and attended the meal itself, which was referred to as the Eucharist. The commandments were less strict for the Hearers: they were allowed to eat fish and to marry, but procreation was frowned on – better by far to gain followers by conversion or by the gift of a child from a grateful parent who had possibly been healed. This was a common practice, the child starting at a tender age to be schooled in the precepts of the religion, as Mani had been at four. Hearers were also allowed to possess property and wealth, taking Jesus seriously when he told his disciples to make friends with the 'Mammon of Iniquity'.[18]

The only Hearer we know of was Augustine of Hippo. His experiences are dealt with later, but it is interesting to note that though procreation was frowned upon he lived with his concubine, but in thirteen years they only had one child, so perhaps he practised some form of restraint or birth control. Augustine revered the Manichean Elect. He would fast all day Sunday but prepare and bring them their special meals on other days. He would also have listened to the readings of the great cosmic myths which told of the origins of the world and explained the destiny of the soul.

From Buddhism or perhaps Pythagoras, Mani also borrowed the idea of the soul's transmigration. Though the Elect when they died returned to the Kingdom of Light, the Hearers underwent a series of reincarnations in the bodies of fruits and vegetables and eventually into the Elect themselves.

The stories of the teachings of Mani were never seen as fiction or myth, but as historical truth, given to Mani as a divine revelation. For an intellectual like Augustine, Manicheanism ultimately exposed all its weakness in this conviction, for it could easily be destroyed in public debate. However, in Mani's lifetime and for the next two hundred years the religion spread over Asia Minor and to east and west. Churches were established from Turkestan to Carthage. Mission became the driving force in the religion. Mani modelled himself upon Paul and was as much a missionary as a religious leader. In *Sabubragan*, a work written by him, Mani declares in tones both Pauline and messianic: 'My Church will go towards the West and she will go also towards the East. And they shall hear the voice of her message in all languages and shall proclaim her in all cities.'[19]

Mani's missionaries were the Elect, who travelled light. They were only permitted to possess enough food for one day and a single garment had to last a year. These Elect were souls already suffused with light, with no room for the sexual fantasies that crowded in on the Desert Fathers and St Augustine. The Christian communities came to see the Elect as something akin to the Apostles, men and women who walked the roads of Syria, moving from city to city in long missionary journeys:[20]

[They] took up the cross upon them, they went from village to village.
[They] went into the roads hungry, with no bread in their hands.

They walked in the heat thirsty, they took no water to drink.
They went in to the villages not knowing a single person.
They were welcomed for His sake.[21]

As the religion spread westwards to Egypt and north Africa, north to
Armenia and Greece, the Manicheans were helped by the fact that the
Christians had gone before and had prepared the ground, so that the people,
to a certain extent, were now sympathetic to hearing more about a new
Apostle of Christ. Whether new adherents of the religion instantly gave up
eating meat we have no way of knowing, yet it seems likely. The Hearers
were allowed to eat fish, and a fish, vegetable and grain diet would have been
more or less what new converts were eating anyway, but the Manicheans'
belief that plants and fruits contained light particles which were part of the
original Godhead must have taught a new respect and care for them.

Mani early on had made friends with Shapur, the ruler of ancient Iran's
Sassanian dynasty. Shapur had given him permission to travel, preach and
convert throughout the territory. Zoroastrianism was, however, the state
religion and a new ruler, Vahram, and a new High Priest, Kirdir, were far
from as tolerant of Mani as Shapur had been. Kirdir regarded Manicheanism
as a heresy of Zoroastrianism, a few of whose ideas and deities Mani in his
inimitable way had collected in his own theological system. Mani believed
that the new rulers could be persuaded to become friendly to
Manicheanism. He met them at court and was instantly thrown into jail
where he died soon after from torture, in AD 276.

The Sassanians continued to persecute Manichean and Christian alike.
But the religion had already moved towards the west. Soon after Mani's
death Bishop Theonas of Alexandria warned his flock against being deceived
by the 'madness of the Manicheans', and we know that the Manicheans were
powerful enough to be banned in Rome by AD 311. The rapid spread of the
religion galvanised the Christians into denouncing their practices and
doctrines. Manichean thought was compressed into three themes: dualism,
asceticism and astrology. Abstinence from meat became a sign of a heretic,
and soon orthodox churchmen saw the Manichean heresy everywhere,
including in those Christians who practised an ascetic mode of life. Timothy,
Patriarch of Alexandria from AD 380 to 385, was so alarmed by the spread of
Manicheanism that he instituted food tests among his clergy and monks;
those who refused to eat meat would then be interrogated.

The Emperor Diocletian in AD 302 warned of the potential threat of the
Manicheans; what worried him as much as anything else was that they came
originally from Persia, Rome's constant enemy and threat. It was decreed
that the leaders be burnt along with their abominable scriptures, while their
followers would be sent to the quarries, their property confiscated and added
to the imperial treasury. Soon after, Diocletian began the 'Great Persecution'
of the Christian Church, which continued until the accession of
Constantine in AD 312. The following year the Edict of Milan granted

toleration for all religions. As the persecution ended Manicheanism began to be accepted by the authorities as part of Christianity, though it was still fiercely attacked by the Christians themselves. A biography of Mani appeared in AD 340 which was hugely popular. However, it was mainly an elaborate piece of fiction designed to throw sinister light upon the founder. It became the main source of material for the early history of Manicheanism and was used in the Middle Ages as ammunition against the Albigensian heresy (see p.157). Augustine ignored the work, though attacking the Manicheans, which strongly implies how false he knew the book to be.

The Emperor Theodosius banned the Manicheans in AD 381. Christians were condemned if they 'crossed over to Judaean rites or Manichean infamy'. By then, because of adverse propaganda, Manicheanism had become associated with magical acts and obscene rites: 'In the mind of Theodosius, Christianity and citizenship were coterminous and anyone who denied Christ automatically made himself an outlaw of the Christian Roman society.'[22] Yet again, a vegetarian group was isolated, placed on the fringes of society, not because of the abstention from meat itself, but because of the ideology that led to such abstention. Reverence for Jesus was, of course, implicit in Manicheanism, but there was no concept of personal salvation through Christ, and this, with their encouragement of women as equals and the abstention from meat, was enough in the fourth century to make them heretics.

The authorities quite often got it wrong, as the Inquisition was to do later for several centuries, accusing the innocent and unable to distinguish between ideologies. Jovinian was a Christian monk who rebelled against the rigorous asceticism of his order. He left the monastery and in Rome celebrated wine and food, becoming a considerable *bon vivant*. He attacked the ascetic Christians because of their rejection of marriage and their refusal to eat meat which God had created for their use. He was tried for Manichean errors, the charge based primarily on his claim that Mary did not remain a virgin after the holy birth. That he was not a Manichean should have been obvious from his lifestyle, but the word was now beginning to be a synonym for deviation from the orthodox, for heresy itself. Another deviation was Priscillianism. Priscillian (AD 340–85), a Christian bishop, was considered a Manichean, judged guilty of sorcery and immorality, and was executed. Priscillian's crime was to aim for higher spiritual perfection through asceticism: he outlawed all sensual pleasure, marriage, and the consumption of wine and meat. Genuine writings by Priscillian discovered late last century prove that his teaching owed little to Mani, but everything to his own eccentric interpretation of Biblical text.

Both Priscillianism and Manicheanism were seen as dangerous perversions of an exalted form of Christian living, for the Desert Fathers had become a fashionable ideal. Accounts of these Christian hermits living in the desert wilderness, surviving on a few berries and roots, became popular reading, influencing women of noble birth in Rome. Women who went on fasts and looked thin, pale and sad were referred to by others as nuns or 'Manicheans'. A commentator on the Pauline Gospels makes a dig at the Manicheans' influence on these rich and titled women: 'They seek out women who always want to hear something for sheer novelty and persuade them through what they like to hear to do foul and illicit things. For the women are desirous to learn though they do not possess the power of discrimination.'[23]

In Manicheanism, for the first time, we see a new and quite different reason for the abstention from meat. Compared to the Pythagorean dogma which entails respect for another living creature because it contains a living soul, the Manichean and the dualist reason is a negative one based on fear, suspicion and distrust. Matter is bad, matter is evil, all flesh derives from the realm of darkness and the partaking of flesh will weigh the spirit down, so that it can no longer fly to God. Eat meat and you will trap the spirit in more flesh.

In the Manichean legend of creation all the innumerable species of animals were descended originally from the Kingdom of Darkness. Though their progenitors had many an adventure flirting with light, animals ended up with fewer light particles than plants so they were rated by Mani as lower in the hierarchy of values than vegetables. Animals did not rate highly in the ancient world of Asia Minor. But there is one redeeming feature in the mythology: while lightness is interpreted as wisdom, darkness is explained as folly – not sin or evil necessarily, but folly stemming from ignorance, greed, stupidity or selfishness. It is perhaps such psychological perception that helps explain Manicheanism's power for so long over the dissident faithful.

Another reason for its power is that it explained evil, the problem which has beset all religions that have a creator God of supreme goodness at their centre. The Manichean exegesis of an invasion of good by the forces of evil which then coexist explains why humans do not have complete control over their actions, however good their intentions are. Manicheans would ask Christians at public debate: 'Whence evil if it is not derived from some sort of principle? If it is God's will that man should do good why was he not created perfect and hence incapable of sinning?'

The commentators on Manicheanism simplified the mythology so that it appears more crudely dualist than it was. There is no space to give Mani's description of the creation of the universe and the battle between light and darkness, but suffice it to say that it is far more complex and appealing than has been acknowledged.* The mythology in later dualist sects, the offspring

---

*Earlier commentators and scholars would have benefited by the discovery of many new Manichean texts from Tun-huang and Turfan at the beginning of this century. This Chinese evidence, in one case completely new, is listed in Lieu, *op. cit.*, which has been invaluable in the writing of this chapter. More Manichean manuscripts were discovered in the West and Lieu's book lists six different works: (1) the letters of Mani (lost in the aftermath of the Second World War in Berlin before being properly examined); (2) the Psalm Book; (3) the Kephalaia; (4) Commentary on the Living Gospel; (5) a history of Mani and the early years of the sect; (6) the Homilies.

of Manicheanism (see Chapter 7), has a much more simplified black-and-white approach to the world and humankind. This perhaps misled later commentators to simplify Manichean doctrine: 'the eternal and alluring taint of the Manichee, with its simple and terrifying explanation of our plights, how the World was made by Satan and not by God, lulling us with the music of despair'. So wrote Graham Greene, but if he had read the texts listed below he would have discovered nothing simple, little that was terrifying and much that was spiritually illuminating.[24]

## Augustine of Hippo

Much of our black picture of the Manichean sect comes to us from St Augustine's attack in his two books, the autobiographical *Confessions* and the polemical *Concerning Heresies*. Augustine was nineteen when he joined the sect and became a Hearer. He stayed for ten years, eventually finding no intellectual satisfaction. He read many of the Neoplatonists, including Plotinus, and left to become a Christian convert. Augustine then took some pleasure in publicly debating with the Manichean Elect on doctrine.

Augustine's full loathing for Manicheanism is expressed in *Concerning Heresies*:

> their Elect are forced to consume a sort of eucharist sprinkled with human seed in order that the divine substance may be freed ... they attempt to purge a part of their god, which they really believe is held befouled just as much in human seed as it is in all celestial and terrestrial bodies and in the seeds of all things. And for this reason it follows that they are just as much obliged to purge it from human seed by eating, as they are in reference to other seed which they consume in their food. This is the reason they are also called Catharists,★ that is, Purifiers, for they are so attentive to purifying this part that they do not refrain even from such horrifying food as this.
>
> Yet they do not eat meat either, on the grounds that the divine substance has fled from the dead or slain bodies, and what little remains there is of such quality and quantity that it does not merit being purified in the stomachs of the Elect. They do not even eat eggs, claiming that they too die when they are broken and it is not fitting to feed on any dead bodies; only that portion of flesh can live which is picked up by flour to prevent its death.† Moreover, they do not use milk for food although it is drawn or milked from the live body of an animal ...
>
> They believe that the souls of the Auditors are returned to the Elect, or by a happier short-cut to the food of their Elect so that, already purged, they would then not have to transmigrate into other bodies. On the other hand,

---

★The Cathar heresy itself appeared 600 years later.
†St Augustine claims that flour was sprinkled 'beneath a couple in sexual intercourse to receive and commingle with their seed'. He is saying that any body fluids lost in the act of love were picked up with the flour and eaten. But he does also admit that this loathsome business could have been practised by another sect altogether.

they believe that other souls pass into cattle and into everything that is rooted in and supported on the earth. For they are convinced that plants and trees possess sentient life and can feel pain when injured and, therefore, that no one can pull or pluck them without torturing them. Therefore, they consider it wrong to clear a field even of thorns. Hence, in their madness they make agriculture, the most innocent of occupations, guilty of multiple murder.[25]

Augustine's attack upon the Manicheans began a long tradition of libel and rumour which was to continue for another thousand years and more. It is difficult or well-nigh impossible now to establish the truth. However, as Augustine was only a Hearer and never became an Elect, and as the Elect kept much of their ritual a secret, can Augustine be that reliable?

Manicheanism failed, according to Runciman, because it was too anti-social:

> The authorities in that hard bellicose age, with civilisation on the defensive against the barbarian invader, could not approve of a faith wherein all killing, even of animals, was forbidden, and whereof a considerable number of believers wandered about, refusing to work, refusing to notice secular regulations, living on the charity of others and exercising a vast influence on the whole community.[26]

But Manicheanism, like the many-headed Hydra, could not be killed easily; its doctrines, dualist explanation and superficial adaptations to the teaching of the orthodox Church had too much appeal. Mani was the first since Pythagoras to give an ideological structure to the refusal to eat meat, so that it became part of an explanation and description of the invisible world. His influence was for a time as strong as Christianity itself and his ideas, including vegetarianism, would continue to convert. Manicheanism survived in the Near East as late as the seventh century, while in the Far East as far as China it had a foothold well into the sixteenth century and the Manicheans were known as 'vegetarian demon worshippers' (see p.339).

From the Near East, Manicheanism with vegetarianism at its centre would reach the Balkans and from there eventually come to southern France and northern Italy. Its dogma always had a certain surrealist expansiveness, an attempt to unify Christianity and paganism; much of this aspect is exemplified by Agapius, an Arian bishop of Cyzicus in Mysia, whom Photius criticised 'in all his books of which he shows himself feigning the name that belongs to the Christians, but none is proved such an enemy of Christ by those very works'.[27] Agapius mocked the Old Testament, believed that the tree in paradise was Christ, worshipped air as a god,* and abstained from meat, wine and sexual relationships. Agapius borrowed much from Plato and

---

*See the idea of breath in Homer and Hinduism.

Pythagoras, believing in the transmigration of souls. He also worshipped the sun and the moon as gods and announced them as consubstantial with God. This maddened Photius: he described Agapius as 'altering and translating almost all the terms of piety and of the Christian religion into other meanings, either strange and abominable, or monstrous and foolish . . . teaching perversely behind the names of our dogmas quite different things'.28

It was those 'quite different things' which began to take hold of the poor and deprived, which seemed to explain more vividly and more truly the savage cruelty of their world, and which moved slowly from Armenia at the eastern end of the Black Sea around its shores to the Balkan peninsula and thence north to Bosnia and across to the Languedoc, which is the subject of the next chapter. By then all heresies were coming to be lumped together by the orthodox Church as Manichean, but all religions change as they grow and spread, as these heresies did, flourishing under different names in different countries. What we can say with certainty is that they were all dualist and for the most part completely non-violent as well as vegetarian; the latter feature most historians have not thought to be greatly significant.

# 7

# The Bogomils, the Cathars and the Orthodox Church

At the height of the Roman Empire the Balkan peninusula was one of the richest of Rome's provinces. It was studded with richly populated market towns, and from its fertile soil there came an abundance of grain, vegetables, fruit and wine. Geographically it separated East and West and in times of instability it became a main thoroughfare for invaders. When the hordes of Visigoths and Huns arrived the original peoples took refuge in the mountains, and fields lay untilled, while harvests were destroyed. But the invaders moved on: the Visigoths to Gaul and Spain, while the Huns, after Attila died, were defeated and dispersed. Early-medieval society was the result of a violent and complex confrontation between the declining Roman Empire and the constant and brutal pillaging of the barbarians.

From the east people were propelled by a desire to conquer territory in Europe for its wheat, oil, wine, timber, furs, copper and tin. But Byzantine foreign policy wished also to safeguard its frontiers, in both the east and the north. In the east the Arabs often allied themselves with some of the heretical sects* and were a constant source of trouble. The northern border was Thrace, which had become a perpetual battlefield in the struggle of the Byzantine Empire against the invaders from the north, the Avars and the Slavs. Several Byzantine emperors, believing they could kill two birds with one stone, pursued a policy of transplanting groups of heretics from Armenia in the east to Thrace in the north. This must have seemed at the time an effective way of breaking up the heretical communities, and by placing them in a region surrounded by orthodox Christians there was a chance of gaining

---

*In particular the Paulicians (see p.145), who became a threat to the Byzantine Empire in the years 668–98. Constantine III and Justinian II sent two expeditions to repress the heresy. The Paulician leader, Silvanus (named after Silas, one of Paul's companions), was stoned to death and his successor, Simeon (Titus), was burned alive.

new converts.* Instead, it is thought by Theophanes,† the heretics not only remained unconverted but also spread their own pernicious beliefs.

By this time the Slavs had spread all over the lands between the Danube and the Aegean Sea. The Slavs had no central government but they organised themselves into local democratic communities and settled happily to farm. It took another invasion for the Slavs to weld their land into a nation. A branch of the Finno-Ugric peoples, from that huge northern area stretching from Norway to Siberia and from the Carpathian Basin in central Europe to the Ukraine, invaded the peninsula. This branch, the Magyars, meeting with the Bulgar Turks, conquered the southern part of the peninsula, crossing the Danube and subjugating the Slavs. The peasants were now ruled by a military caste of Bulgar nobility and the Byzantine Empire could do little to oust them. But the alien domination that the Slavs suffered helped to organise and unify them, while at the same time intermarriage between the two peoples became common and the Bulgar language died out.

The great Roman roads, still in working order, ran from Armenia and Persia to the edge of Asia Minor and up through the Balkans to the Adriatic Sea, a perfect conduit not only for trade but for refugees and ideas. There was one idea that obsessed religious communities at that time – dualism – whether they accepted it or refuted it. That profound and perplexing question – why is the world so evil? – was an insoluble problem for those who longed to believe in a God of supreme goodness. Surely the only explanation for the sorrows and cruelties of the world must be that there were two gods, one good, the other evil, who must be battling for the soul of humankind. Yet to believe that Satan was as powerful as God was to give in ultimately to despair.

Greek Stoics and Neoplatonists recoiled from the world of matter and of flesh. Zoroaster had taught that life was a permanent struggle between spirit and matter – good and evil. Buddha taught that only by disassociating ourselves from worldly things can we come to know good. All these ideas permeated the Christian conscience as in its infancy it was striving to make the world intelligible. Gnostic thought gathered all these ideas together and joined them to Christian beliefs, and it was this amalgam which came from Asia Minor into the Balkan countries. It found among the peasants a sympathetic hearing, for Slav mythology was dualist. Chernobog and Byelbog were the gods of darkness and light. The former was thought of as

---

*Emperor Constantine V (Copronymus) twice transferred eastern populations to Thrace: in 745 a large colony of Syrian Monophysite heretics (a doctrine stemming from Aristotle and the Neoplatonists later codified by Averroës (1126-98)) and in 757 again a large number of Syrians and Armenians, to repopulate the plague-stricken districts of Thrace.

†Theophanes (752-818) was a Byzantine monk, theologian and chronicler, the main source of seventh- and eighth-century Byzantine history. In *Chronographia* he writes of the Byzantine victory over the Arab besiegers of Constantinople (674-8) and describes 'Greek fire', an explosive mixture that could be hurled great distances and enabled the Byzantines to destroy the Arab fleet.

very powerful, the cause of all calamities, and prayers were offered to him at banquets to avert misfortune.

Persecution of the heresies in the Byzantine Empire and especially under Justinian I (483–565) turned heretics into refugees. Justinian, noted for his administrative reorganisation of the imperial government and for his codification of laws in the *Codex Justinianus* (534), threatened to withdraw the right of heretics to bequeath their possessions to their children if they did not renounce their former beliefs.

> The churches of these heretics, as they are called, especially those who professed the doctrine of Arius,★ possessed unheard-of riches. Neither the whole Senate nor any other very large body in the Roman State could compete in wealth with these churches. They possessed treasures of gold and silver, and ornaments covered with precious stones, beyond description and beyond counting, houses and villages in great numbers, and many acres of land in all quarters of the world.[1]

Procopius goes on to tell us:

> A great number of people, even though they held orthodox beliefs, depended upon [the churches] at all times for their livelihood, justifying themselves on the ground that they were merely following their regular occupations. So by first of all confiscating the property of these churches the Emperor Justinian suddenly robbed them of all they possessed.[2]

But the army of officials which Justinian sent came up against fierce resistance, since what the emperor asked them to do was blasphemous. Many killed themselves or were killed by the soldiers; a great majority abandoned the land and went into exile; the Montanists of Phrygia locked themselves in their own churches and set the buildings on fire. A hundred thousand people lost their lives and some of the most fertile land in the world was left with no one to till it. 'For the owners of these acres, Christians one and all, this business had disastrous consequences; for though the land was yielding them no profit at all, they were compelled to pay to the emperor in perpetuity annual taxes on a crippling scale, since these demands were pressed relentlessly.'[3]

---

★Arius (250–336) was a Christian priest of Alexandria whose teaching gave rise to Arianism, which affirmed the created, finite nature of Christ. He integrated Neoplatonism with a literal and rationalist approach to the New Testament texts. His major work was *Thalia*, 'Banquet', which was in verse and popular enough to be widely spread in song by travellers and labourers. The Council of Nicea declared Arius a heretic in 325 after he refused to sign a statement that declared Christ to be divine. Arianism is considered to be an early form of Unitarianism. Arius is regarded by the Jehovah's Witnesses as a forerunner of Charles Taze Russell, the founder of their movement. The Arian movement, like most of the popular heresies, was ascetic, meat and wine being considered indulgences of the flesh.

## The Paulicians

Among the heretics who had been transposed to Thrace were groups of Paulicians, among them some Armenian architects. A stepping-stone between Manicheanism and the Bogomils, the Paulicians took their name – though there is some dispute about this – from the Apostle Paul. Influenced by Marcion they rejected the Old Testament completely and some of the New; they honoured the Gospel According to Luke and the letters of St Paul. They were dualist, but believed that an evil God created the world and all living matter, while a good God created the world to come. They did not revere the Virgin Mary as they did not believe Jesus could have taken on flesh, as flesh was evil. Jesus had been created in Heaven and merely passed through Mary as if through a canal. Mary then had other children by Joseph. The real Mother of God to be adored was Heavenly Jerusalem. Nor should the body and blood of Christ be taken, for the real sacrament was his Word. They saw no value in the Cross, but rather despised it as a symbol of murder and cruelty. They also rejected the sacraments of baptism and marriage and the whole hierarchy of priests, bishops and Church; instead they had ministers and notaries and an upper class of initiates who were rechristened with Pauline names. In their dislike of consecrated churches (any abode could be a meeting-house for prayer) they also rejected all images, icons and relics.

Ironically the Paulicians called themselves Christians, as we shall see the Bogomils did also, and contemporary writers were certain that they followed a reformed and simplified version of Manicheanism, though some later commentators question this.[4] Both the Paulicians and the Manicheans raised dualism to a metaphysical doctrine. They saw the visible material world as the very creation of an evil force outside the jurisdiction of God. The deity of goodness might only be experienced after death and the disintegration of self. There are important differences, however, between the two sects. The Manichean ideal was to lead a life of contemplation and reclusive monasticism, while the Paulician was to lead a life of action, and even war. Nor is there any evidence that the Paulicians abstained from meat, wine or sex, or practised any other form of asceticism.

## The Massalians

In a letter to Peter, Tsar of Bulgaria, written some time between 940 and 950, Theophylact, the Patriarch of Constantinople, described 'an ancient and newly appeared heresy . . . Manicheanism mixed with Paulicianism'. The doctrines he lists are all true of Paulicianism except for abstention from sexual intercourse and a refusal to eat meat and drink wine. He writes that the heretics reject lawful marriage and maintain that the reproduction of the human species is a law of the demon. Manicheanism was unknown in Bulgaria, and Theophylact was in fact describing another dualist sect, the Massalians, who had existed in Bulgaria for probably more than a century.

The Massalians spread over a large part of Asia Minor in the fourth and fifth centuries from Cappadocia and Lycaonia to Pamphylia and Lycia. They were close to the Christian Encratite sects who condemned marriage and the consumption of meat and wine. In most respects their doctrine was similar to that of the Paulicians, but they held that prayer was the most essential occupation (the name Massalians, or Messalians, derives from a Syriac word meaning 'those that pray') and vital for salvation, for it was only through prayer that the demon (which could not be expelled by baptism) could be vanquished. Continual prayer could achieve a state of pure spirit, in which the soul became possessed of a sacred delirium that showed itself in jumping, dancing and symbolically trampling under foot the expelled demon. Once this state of purity was achieved sin was no longer possible and all discipline and restriction became superfluous. Massalians could therefore then indulge in all the worldly delights of sexual pleasure, wine and food. Hence they were renowned not only for extreme asceticism but for their extreme immorality as well.

What Theophylact most feared in this heresy was the possible combination of Paulician militancy and aggression with Massalian sexual licence and immorality. For Theophylact their growing presence must have conjured up a vision of impending Satanism. But it was some twenty years later that a new heresy emerged that was to pose so many problems for the orthodox Church over the next few centuries. It was named after the priest who preached its message – Bogomil.

## The Bogomils

It came to pass that in the reign of the orthodox Tsar Peter of Bulgaria, there appeared a priest by the name of 'Bogomil' (Beloved of God), but in reality 'Bogunemil' (not beloved of God). He was the first who began to preach in Bulgaria a heresy, of which I shall relate below. As I commence to condemn the teachings and the deeds of the Bogomils, it seems to me that the air is polluted by their deeds and preachings. But for the sake of the pious I shall expose the deceitful teachings of these in order that no one, after knowing them, shall fall into their snares, but keep afar from them, because, as God says, 'Each tree is known by its own fruit.'

The heretics in appearance are lamb-like, gentle, modest and quiet, and their pallor is to show their hypocritical fastings. They do not talk idly, nor laugh loudly, nor do they manifest any curiosity. They keep themselves away from immodest sights, and outwardly they do everything so as not to be distinguished from the Orthodox Christians, but inwardly they are ravening wolves. The people, on seeing their great humility think that they are Orthodox, and able to show them the path of salvation; they approach and ask them how to save their souls. Like a wolf that wants to seize a lamb, they pretend at first to sigh; they speak with humility, preach, and act as if they were themselves in heaven. Whenever they meet any ignorant and uneducated man, they preach to him the tares of their teachings, blaspheming the traditions and orders of the Holy Church.[5]

The Bogomils were a growing and popular movement when Cosmas preached his long, detailed sermon against them. Later, in 990, he published a book against the heresy, fulminating against the clergy for allowing it to flourish. The number of Bogomils was now considerable. Their popularity was increased because they represented a form of passive resistance by the Slav peasants to their Bulgar or Graecised overlords (Bogomils did not believe in violence to animals or fellow creatures[6]). We have to wait another two hundred years before we can find a written account of Bogomil dogma, by which time the main heresy had split into various friendly sects and colonised further lands. The Dragovitsa sect in the south was nearer to the Paulicians (who were still flourishing in this region) in their beliefs, and were also influenced by the Massalians, who began to revive at this time. By the end of the eleventh century they were in Macedonia with the original Paulicians, and along the coasts of Asia Minor; to the north the Bogomils had begun to colonise Serbia and Bosnia, and thence Croatia and Dalmatia.

Byzantium was in a state of religious ferment; religious leaders preached an amalgam of pagan and Christian ideas, Pythagorean metempsychosis, Neoplatonism and Marcionite contempt for the Old Testament. None of them was as successful as the charismatic Basil, a renegade monk from Macedonia who had arrived in Constantinople to spread the Bogomil heresy. Soon he had collected a vast congregation, and the Emperor Alexius I, anxious at this new heretical influence on his countrymen, summoned Basil to the palace, falsely claiming that he desired to be converted to the Bogomil faith. Basil fell into the trap. He extolled the virtues and piety of the Bogomils and confessed the sect's dogma to the enquiring emperor. But imperial dignitaries had been eavesdropping and had recorded Basil's heresies. He was imprisoned and resisted even Alexius' efforts to convert him. In the end the Holy Synod, perhaps recalling St Augustine's harshness towards sinners, urged that Basil should be burnt. The rest of the Bogomil leaders were now arrested and only those who chose to be burnt at a cross rather than at an unadorned stake were spared. All the rest were burnt, going to their deaths with great serenity.

But this was far from the end of the Bogomil faith. By the reign of the Emperor Manuel I, it was back. One synod denounced two Christian bishops and another sentenced a Bogomil monk, Niphon, the leader of the Bogomil heretics, to be confined in his monastery at Peribleptos. But the very next Patriarch, Cosmas Atticus, was sympathetic. To the horror of the orthodox he let Niphon free and even offered him the hospitality of the patriarchal palace. Later rumours also implicated the Emperor Manuel. From this position of power this very other-worldly faith began to influence the West.

But what was this faith? Its dogma and myths show its clear roots in Manicheanism and Paulicianism. Cosmas tells us that the Bogomils desired a complete renunciation of the world, so they drank no wine, ate no meat and disapproved of marriage. This view was deduced from their dualism: the visible world was the creation of the evil one, and to escape from that domination and to be united with God all contact with matter and the flesh had to be avoided, these being the devil's best instruments for gaining mastery over human souls. Cosmas writes: 'They say that the Devil has ordered men to take wives, to eat meat and to drink wine.' He goes on to say that the heretics avoid marriage, meat and wine not from pious abstinence as ascetic Christians do but because the heretics 'consider them abominable'.[7] Cosmas was forced to discriminate thus, as in heterodox monastic circles in the Eastern Church the monastic rule prohibited the eating of meat, in the belief that it incited lust. As in both Mani's and Marcion's mythologies, the Old Testament was utterly rejected, the Virgin Mary was not revered – it was thought that Jesus entered the Virgin through her ear, took flesh there and emerged by the same orifice – the sacraments were thought useless, icons and feast days were ignored, and the Cross was utterly detested.

Zigabenus, the scribe to Emperor Alexius who had taken down the words of the duped Basil, gives more detail on Bogomil mythology. Satan, like Christ, was the Son of the Father, but he revolted out of pride (as Isaiah describes[8]) and was cast out with his rebellious angels. Thence he created the world so that he might reign alone and be supreme. The problem with all dualist mythology is the inverse of the Christian dilemma: if Satan created the world and all that is in it, how did the divine spark, the longing for God, enter humankind? Various explanations are to be found throughout Gnostic literature. The version told by Zigabenus from Basil's description is that once Satan created man from earth and water, the water, symbolising life, kept on trickling out. So Satan asked his father to breathe life into man, which God duly did. As God is timeless he must have realised what an unholy mess this contradiction of divinity encased in Satanic flesh would become. Nevertheless, not content with Adam, he created Eve in the same manner. This myth, one might infer, also tells us how all other sentient creatures upon the planet had no divinity in them but were completely manufactured by Satan. One might wonder then why the Bogomils avoided slaughtering these devilish animals. The answer lies in quite other factors which help to explain why Bogomilism flourished at the time it did.

Bogomils revered the Book of Revelation as well as the four Gospels and the Acts of the Apostles, but they considered Moses to be a dupe of Satan. The sect was divided into those that were baptised, called the Elect, and those waiting for baptism. These candidates had to spend much time in prayer, self-expurgation and confession. Women were equal with men, as they were in all the heretical sects (another reason, one suspects, for their popularity★), and once the initiate was baptised (not with water but by having St John's Gospel placed on his or her head), the Holy Ghost invoked and the Pater Noster repeated, further time was set aside for living soberly, in continual prayer and learning. When all this could be proved to have been done a further ceremony took place and another Elect was admitted. Women Elect deserved the title of the Mother of God, because the Holy Spirit resided in them and they could give birth to the Word.

The Bogomil heresy, Runciman tells us, was born amidst peasants whose physical misery made them conscious of the wickedness of things.[9] Their daily life was vulnerable not only to the rigours of the weather upon their crops but to the constant threat of invasion, plague or famine, or the exploitation by landlords, the Church or the crown. The orthodox Church quickly grew to be unpopular with the peasants: the rich ornateness of vestments and church interiors were an affront, nor did the growing power of the monasteries hold the peasants in thrall, for the monks exacted tribute from neighbouring villages and lands; the monastic excesses that began now and were to later flourish in the Middle Ages must have alienated the poor even more, while they could have had little respect for the deception practised by abbots and monks on fast days – not only was fish allowed but rabbits were bred, as they had been by the Romans, for their fully developed foetuses which were classified as 'not meat'.[10]

The Bogomils preached a crusade against the great and the powerful of this world, the rich, the elders, the boyars, the Tsar himself. Their teaching gathered strength from the social oppression, the ruinous wars, the economic decline and the restlessness of the people under the oppression of Byzantium. Thus the Bogomils appealed directly to the peasant masses who regarded them as liberators.

What Moore said of the vegetarianism of the Cathars was as true for the Bogomils:

> I think another thing about not eating meat which gave it a social power as a spiritual message, and it was a message which was preached not only by Cathars but by other religions which opposed Catholic orthodoxy in this period, was that meat was the food of the hunters, of the dominators, of the people who rode horses, the people who exploited the cultivators of the land, most of whose life was singularly meatless.[11]

Idealism, of whatever kind, is always embraced more enthusiastically when it is both practical and easily attainable. Abstention from meat would have been

---

★The role of women in Hebrew culture, which Christianity took on board, was, of course, humiliating, shameful and inhumane. The rules and rites attending the days of menstruation, when women were told they were unclean, must have been an intolerable burden on the feminine psyche. It is to the lasting credit of all the Christian heresies that women were regarded as equal with men and that many of the heretical leaders were women.

no hardship at all for ninth-century Bulgarian peasants because their diet in any case would have been mainly vegetable, unless they lived near the coast where fish and shellfish would have been plentiful. Whether fish was eaten or not we do not know for certain. The Elect were strictly ascetic, as the Manicheans were, and kept to a pure vegetable diet, but until the initiate had passed through the two baptisms there would, I suspect, have been no strictures against the eating of fish. Obolensky believes that, though evidence is lacking, it is probable that the tenth-century Bogomils were divided into two distinct groups: the ordinary 'believers', who were not bound to rigorous asceticism with regard either to sexual intercourse or to food, and the Elect, who were.[12]

Most of the peasants lived inland and their diet would have been little different from that in Ancient Greece a thousand years before: new wine to drink, plenty of bread made from barley, wheat and rye flours, cheese and a few eggs (see Zigabenus on Basil below), and for vegetables – turnips, radishes, onions, leeks, cabbage, spinach and cress, root tops and sprouting nettles and thistles.[13] Yoghurt would have been made from milk and a porridge made from the grains; many of the vegetables would have been pickled for the winter. The peasants may or may not have trapped the odd hare, rabbit or game bird to augment this diet, but the farmer who reared cattle would have sold his beasts at market for the table of the landowner or local nobility. Even without the Bogomil faith the farmer would have been unlikely to eat a haunch of beef. Cattle were primarily raised for other reasons than to provide meat: oxen were draught animals, cows were for milk, sheep for wool and milk. Males, if not used for stud or labour, are the animals most likely to have been used for meat and, therefore, sold for subsistence.

The Byzantine Bogomils under Basil were more ascetic than their Bulgarian predecessors; Zigabenus tells us that they forbade marriage and eating of meat, cheese, eggs and 'other things of their kind'.* They also had a novel way of interpreting the text of the Bible – John the Baptist's diet, as described in Matthew,[14] of locusts and wild honey is explained thus: the locusts were the commands of Mosaic law while the wild honey was the Gospel, which seems like honey to those that receive it and wild to those that do not. Later a priest, Jeremiah, disapproved of by the orthodox, wrote works popular with the Bogomils. Jeremiah rewrote Biblical text in order for it to fit into heretical belief; thus the locusts of John's diet are altered to vegetarian dishes (not particularly appealing but perhaps suitable for an

---

*It is possible that milk and the dairy products made from it were thought to have a close connection with blood as they were later. In the *Haven of Health* (Thomas Cogan, 1584) we read: 'Milke is made of blood twice concocted; . . . for until it come to the pap or udder, it is plain blood, but afterward by the proper nature of the paps it is turned into milk.' If this connection existed there was a double horror from blood being spilt as in murder and blood being drunk as in the sacrament.

ascetic) of cane, roots and wood shavings. The last obviously refers to tree bark, which wild deer are partial to.★

But heresies change in time, as does the orthodox Church, and there is no rigid dogma, belief or practice that remains absolute and true of all the Bogomils from the ninth century to the fourteenth. For example, the two false bishops of the diocese of Tyana excommunicated in 1143 preached a rather more modified form of asceticism, namely that after abstaining for three years from sexual intercourse, meat, milk and wine a man can indulge in all of them without sin. They were obviously Massalian and could have been two of the Dragovitsa Bogomils, but by the tenth century Massalian beliefs (with their equivocal feelings on asceticism) had permeated the Bogomils in Bulgaria. Here they lost their reputation for asceticism completely. Sexual excess or dubious orgiastic practices were a major sin levelled at most of the heretical sects (but not at the Bogomil Elect). It is often difficult to extract the possible truth from such accusations unless we can examine the dogma itself, as we do later when looking at the Cathars. Anna Comnena wrote in 1148:

> For two very evil and worthless doctrines which had been known in former times, now coalesced; the impiety, as it might be called, of the Manicheans, which we also call the Paulician heresy, and the shamelessness of the Massalians. This was the doctrine of the Bogomils compounded of the Massalians and the Manicheans.[15]

Certainly sexual indulgence and impiety were linked to the Cathars from, as we shall see, the very moment they appeared, and much of this they may have inherited from the Bogomils. With these orgiastic sagas in the background, what must have particularly irritated and appalled all orthodox clergy was how the Bogomils appeared to be, and were accepted for long periods as, Christians. But sexual excess was only one small fragment of the story. What must also have galled the orthodox was to see the opposition behaving in a more exemplary and ascetic manner. The refusal of the Bogomil Elect to eat meat or to drink wine, and their celibate life, were in striking contrast to the majority of churchmen, who, as Cosmas declaims, were lazy and indulgent, giving no guidance or teaching to their flock.

## Royal Converts

Inevitably the Bogomils spread further into Europe. To the west, in Serbia, they forgot their principles of passive resistance, fought, lost and were soon

---

★The locusts were very likely to have been the fruits of the carob or locust tree (*Ceratonia siliqua*) which grows all over the Mediterranean countries and which were eaten both green and dry. They also might have been the fruits of the African locust (*Parkia africana*), another nutritional legume. Either way, Jeremiah need not have created his vegetarian dish.

crushed, while their leaders were driven into exile. However, they exerted their influence more successfully further west, in the great province of Bosnia, where eventually in 1199 the monarchy and court became converted to the Bogomil faith. Apart from the whole royal family, ten thousand of their subjects were also converted and Bogomilism became the state religion of Bosnia. The King, titled Ban in Bosnia, was one Kulin, who by this action infuriated Pope Innocent III, who wrote to neighbouring monarchs to ask them to depose Kulin by force. The Bogomils destroyed the cathedral at Kveshevo and kept the bishopric vacant for thirty-five years, but with a Hungarian army about to invade, Kulin gave in and abjured the heresy in front of the papal legate. Rome now demanded the abandonment of heretical practices: the sexes now had to be kept apart in monasteries, while altars and crosses were restored for the observation of feast and fast days. Rome did not demand that meat be eaten again – though we do not know whether the court were actually vegetarian during their years as converts to Bogomilism, or even whether their conversion was due to piety and a desire for asceticism or to pragmatic diplomacy, for Kulin's conversion back to Rome did not halt the popularity of the Bogomil faith in Bosnia itself. Another king returned to the faith and another pope sent envoys to plead with the heretics, but Bosnia was obdurate. By 1250 Pope Innocent IV lamented that Bosnia had fallen totally into heresy. It was still a papal torment in 1360, when Pope Urban V called Bosnia 'a cesspool of heresy of all parts of the world'.

It might be argued that the vegetarian tradition was not kept alive in these heretical sects in any pure and compassionate form, that the dogma was born of a negative source – the refusal to ingest more matter – or as a refinement of asceticism. The idea that meat equals flesh and that flesh is loathsome and somehow prejudicial to the exercise of the spirit takes no account of the rights of those creatures we share the planet with. It is a doctrine that expresses fear of humanity more than a love of God. With such ideas, animals too became easily associated with the devil and his evil minions; hence the domestic cat came to be seen as the witch's familiar.

But the Turks were about to vanquish Bogomilism for ever. They were encroaching over the Balkan peninsula and by 1463 had at last invaded Bosnia. The Sultan ordered that the nobles who embraced Islam could keep their estates. Within a year the Bogomil faith had begun to die. By the end of that century Bosnia was a Mohammedan province.

What is left of these beliefs and sacred legends? Their symbols appear in Tarot cards, in which the devil directs the affairs of the world and Pope Joan is the High Priest, the Mother Elect, the source of gnosis. Some of the beliefs may have been used in the secret rituals of the Templars, which are partly based on dualist traditions. In Eastern Europe traces of the beliefs can be seen in popular legends and fairy tales.[16] While later extraordinary sects in Russia appear to owe their beginnings to Bogomilism (see p.269), the immediate heritage of the Bogomils had already appeared on the other side of the Adriatic. Long before the Turkish invasion the faith had spread to northern Italy and southern France, though there is dispute among scholars over whether or not the heresy existed in the Languedoc area even earlier. We do not know for certain whether Bogomil missionaries brought their heresy to France or whether they added to similar concepts which were already flourishing there. The latter is more likely as the Gnostic tradition flourished in those areas that were distant from the early Christian Church authorities.

## Growing Heresies

Medieval Europe was still searching for its Christian identity, only given to it late in the thirteenth century by St Thomas Aquinas who codified Christian ethics into palpable dogma. But Gnostic and Manichean ideas could, until then, be held by orthodox clergy; in 991 Gerbert of Aurillac as Archbishop-Elect of Reims made a declaration of faith which showed Gnostic tendencies and a rejection of the Old Testament.[17] The first reference we have to Manicheans in France is in the chronicle of Adhémar of Chabannes, written in Angoulême, who notes that in 1018 'Manicheans appeared in Aquitaine, leading the people astray. They denied baptism, the cross, and all sound doctrine. They did not eat meat, as though they were monks, and pretended to be celibate, but among themselves they enjoyed every indulgence. They were messengers of Antichrist and caused many to wander from the faith.'[18]

A few years later, in 1022, ten canons of Orleans, who had impressed everyone by their piety, turned out to be Manichean. They had all been converted by a peasant who carried with him a dust made from dead children which immediately made everyone a Manichean. Some Manicheans were discovered and destroyed at Toulouse, and messengers of Antichrist appeared in various parts of the West, concealing themselves in hide-outs and corrupting men and women whenever they could. The ten canons were deprived of priestly orders, expelled from the Church and finally burned. Adhémar tells us that they did not fear the fire: 'They promised to emerge unharmed from the flames, and laughed as they were bound in the centre of the pyre, but almost at once they were reduced to ashes so completely that no trace of their bones could be found.'[19] Another account of this same incident, which was the first case of burning for heresy in the medieval West, by Paul of St Père de Chartres, describes the heretics' devilish, ritual orgies. Such accounts of ritual orgies crop up countless times in the descriptions of these heretics and are very similar to tales told about early Christians. (Contemporary tales of sexual abuse and satanism are not dissimilar.)

## Pure and Vegetarian

In 1030, at Monteforte in northern Italy, we find for the first time an organised heretic community called Cathars. The name derives from the

Greek word for 'pure' and was given by the heretics to their Elect. Augustine also used it for the Manichean Elect, so it might have been in heretical use from the beginning.

Archbishop Aribert, travelling around Italy visiting his suffragan bishops of the diocese of Milan, reached Turin and heard of a new heresy in the castle of Monteforte. He asked that one of the heretics, Gerard, be brought to him and asked for an account of their beliefs:

> Whatever [the] motive in asking about the faith of myself and my brothers, I will answer. We value virginity above everything. We have wives, and while those who are virgins preserve their virginity, those who are already corrupt are given permission by our elders to retain their chastity perpetually. We do not sleep with our wives, we love them as we would mothers and sisters. We never eat meat. We keep up continuous fasts and unceasing prayer; our elders pray in turn by day and by night, so that no hour lacks its prayer. We hold all our possessions in common with all men.[20]

Gerard blithely and innocently went on in his explanations of the faith, so astounding the archbishop and all the listeners that he sent soldiers to the castle and arrested them all, including the countess, and took them to Milan, where they were all burnt, some leaping into the flames gladly.[21]

At Goslar, in 1052, heretics were brought before the Emperor Henry III by Godfrey of Upper Lorraine. 'Among other wicked Manichean doctrines they condemned all eating of animals, and with the agreement of everybody present he ordered them to be hanged.'[22] (Note how not eating meat in itself was considered wicked.)

Anselm refers to another group discovered between 1043 and 1048 by Bishop Roger II of Châlons-sur-Marne who wrote to him for advice because some peasants were following the perverse teachings of the Manicheans: 'They abhor marriage, shun the eating of meat, and believe it profane to kill animals.'[23] Anselm replied in a restrained manner and told Roger that they must not act hastily, as had happened when Priscillian, the first heretic, had been executed in AD 385 (then the commissioners had thought they could recognise his followers by the paleness of their faces, a certain sign of abstention from meat):

> Given this, when such clear arguments and biblical authority cannot be fairly or reasonably contradicted, anyone can see how reprehensibly they behaved at Goslar, when some members of this sect were captured. They were rightly excommunicated, after much discussion of their beliefs, for their stubbornness in heresy, but they were sentenced to be hanged as well. I have most diligently tried to find out what passed at this discussion, and can discover no justification for the sentence except that the heretics refused to obey the order of the bishop to kill a chicken. I cannot refrain from pointing out that if Wazo had been there he would not have consented to this

sentence: he would have followed the example of St Martin, who interceded for the Priscillianists condemned by edict of the Emperor Maximus after they had been wickedly misrepresented by a council of fawning priests, courageously preferring to risk damage to himself than not to urge that the heretics should be saved. I say this not because I want to conceal the errors of the heretics, but because it can be shown that such a decree nowhere receives the approval of the divine law.[24]

Mercy such as Anselm's was to grow rare and in a very short time vanished entirely.

It would be wrong to give the impression that all heretics at this time were inspired by Manichean notions and adopted an ascetic way of life. Some were quite the reverse. Tanchelm early in the tenth century wore gold robes, had gold entwined in his hair, was preceded by insignia and banners like a king and 'won over the goodwill of his hearers with lavish festivity as well as persuasive words'. Henry of Lausanne, or Henry the monk, seemed to be an early Rasputin:

His reputation for unusual holiness and learning rested not on the merit of his character but on falsehood, not on his morals or piety, but on rumour. Women and young boys – for he used both sexes in his lechery – who associated with him openly flaunted their excesses, and added to them by caressing the soles of his feet and his buttocks and groin with tender fingers. They became so excited by the lasciviousness of the man, and by the grossness of their own sins, that they testified publicly to his extraordinary virility, and said that his eloquence could move a heart of stone to remorse, and that all monks, hermits and canons regular ought to imitate his pious and celibate life.[25]

Henry was eventually exposed as an ignorant vagabond who enjoyed preaching because he had a mighty voice. He left France only to cause more trouble in Italy.

It was not difficult to turn the people against the Church. Whatever form they took, all the heresies criticised the Church, which had become degenerate, luxurious and wealthy, in direct contrast to the lives of Christ and the Apostles. The Church owned land and had accumulated material wealth, and with its liturgy, pomp and grandeur it acted in ways quite irreconcilable with the Gospels. Priests were openly lecherous, often living with women and producing families; they took bribes and often got drunk, ignoring entirely their holy offices. Adding to this ground-swell of disgust at the orthodox pastors of the flock was the fact that the closed medieval world was constantly being shaken out of any absolute beliefs by changing events and new ideas. The start of the Crusades drew East and West closer together, so that eastern ideas became more understandable and attractive than before, though trade between Asia Minor and Western Europe had always ensured a constant flow of ideas and information.

As we have seen, by the beginning of the tenth century there was a sudden growth in Manichean ideas in France. Pope Calixtus II held a council in Toulouse in 1119 to curse (or, as the Church put it, 'to anathematise') the heretics who denied the sacraments, baptism and marriage and rejected the hierarchy of the Church. But this could not stop the heresy either. In 1126 a heretic, Peter de Bruys, was burnt at the stake, and in 1147 Pope Eugenius III found a great number of heretics centred on Albi and asked St Bernard of Clairvaux to root out the pervading and growing rebellion from the true Church.

Everinus of Steinland in the Rhineland had already written to St Bernard telling him of the heretics in Cologne who had been put into the fire and burnt. Everinus says: 'what was most wonderful, they entered then bore the torment of the fire not only with patience, but with joy and gladness.'[26] Everinus is both perplexed and impressed, repeating to Bernard the heretical words: 'We the poor of Christ, who have no certain abode, fleeing from one city to another, like sheep in the midst of wolves, do endure persecution with the apostles and martyrs: notwithstanding that we lead a holy and strict life in fasting and abstinence . . .'[27] He goes on to tell Bernard: 'in their diet they forbid all manner of milk and whatsoever is made of it, and all that is procreated by copulation.'[28] Like Basil of Byzantium, these heretics are obviously what we now call vegan.

Early in the twelfth century, at Périgueux, a group called the Apostolics, led by Pons, claimed they were living as the Disciples had: they were ascetic, wholly vegetarian, almost teetotal and owed no money. They won many converts, including some from the clergy. A peasant, Clementius from Bucy, near Soissons, also had a group of followers thought to be without doubt the Manicheans described by St Augustine. Clementius encouraged homosexuality for both men and women as well as the occasional orgy, and believed, it is said, that if babies were conceived at such a time, at birth they would be cooked and eaten.* Clementius was imprisoned for life. Other peasants led other groups — all of the leaders came from the peasant class and were illiterate. Their heresies all showed some resemblance to the Gnostic lore described above, so they must have learnt it from an oral tradition, possibly from itinerant preachers or weavers. It was the latter who brought the heresy to Flanders, in 1144. Thirteen years later Archbishop Samson of Reims complained that the weavers condemned marriage and encouraged

---

*We will hear this accusation again and again. It seems unlikely that the only meat a vegetarian sect would consume would be that of a human baby, though cannibalism in the Dark and Middle Ages at time of famine was commonplace. If the meat was eaten at a religious ritual it may have had a symbolic aspect: partaking of the food destined for God, thus giving beneficial holy power to the worshipper. But it seems highly doubtful and smacks of a propaganda horror story — infanticide, cannibalism and black magic all rolled into one.

sexual promiscuity. In 1160 they were in England; a council at Oxford sentenced them to be branded on the forehead and driven from the city.

## Cathar Doctrine

The first details of the doctrines behind the Cathar heresy are given us by Eckbert of Schönau in his sermon against the Cathars (there were thirteen doctrines in all) written in the years 1163-7. It is detailed and informative, composed over a considerable period spent among the heretical groups in the Rhineland. Eckbert details ten heresies:

> The second heresy: avoiding meat. Those who have become full members of their sect avoid all meat. This is not for the same reason as monks and other followers of the spiritual life abstain from it: they say that meat must be avoided because all flesh is born of coition, and therefore they think it unclean.
>
> The third heresy: the creation of flesh. That is the reason they give in public. Privately they have an even worse one, that all flesh is made by the devil, and must therefore not be eaten even in the direst necessity.[29]

Eckbert describes in detail the ninth heresy – the humanity of the Saviour. He tells us that the Cathars celebrate with a festival the death of the heresiarch, Mani, and traces the origins of the Cathar sect back to Mani and his followers. Here for the first time we read a simplified interpretation of Mani's teaching that was to be the accepted one for centuries within the Christian world: 'Everything of flesh which lives on the earth, whether man or animal, originates from the prince of darkness, the devil, and is founded in his evil nature; this is why, as I have said, they avoid eating meat.'[30]

The heretics' refusal to eat meat evidently looms large before the eyes of the orthodox. As has already been pointed out (see pp.112-114), Mosaic dietary code urges the eating of the approved meats as an integral part of the path of holiness, a theme stressed by the early church fathers again and again. The Epistle of Barnabas, in particular, liked to interpret the dietary laws as metaphors for how we behave with others. These homilies had huge influence over people's minds, Barnabas being one of the most popular writers of the Apocrypha, although his advice is hardly what we would think of as Christian now:

> The meaning of his allusion to swine is this: what he is really saying is, 'you are not to consort with the class of people who are like swine, inasmuch as they forget all about the Lord while they are living in affluence, but remember Him when they are in want – just as a swine, so long as it is eating, ignores its master, but starts to squeal the moment it feels hungry, and then falls silent again when it is given food'.
>
> Next, you shall eat neither eagle nor hawk, kite nor crow. This means that

you are not to frequent the company nor imitate the habits of those who have no idea of earning their own bread by toil and sweat, but in total disregard of all law swoop down on the possessions of other people; going about with every appearance of innocence, but keeping a sharp lookout and darting glances in every direction to see whom their rapacity can prey upon next. In the same way, the birds he speaks of are the only ones that do not provide their own food; sitting indolently on their perches, they watch for an opportunity to devour the flesh of other creatures, and make themselves thoroughgoing pests by their graceless ways.

When he says, you are not to eat of the lamprey, the polypus, or the cuttlefish, his meaning is that you are not to consort with or imitate the kind of people who have rejected God altogether, and are already living under sentence of death; just as it is those fish, and no others, which are doomed to swim far down in the lowest depths of ocean, never breaking surface like the rest, but making their homes underground at the bottom of the sea.[31]

The Cathars must have seemed like peoples 'making their homes underground', in being both aloof and ascetic; to the orthodox their ideas must have been alarming and full of treachery to the believers in church indulgences such as the remission of sins.

The Cathars continued to flourish in the south of France. The first Cathar heretics appeared in Limousin, between 1012 and 1020. They were protected first by William IX, Duke of Aquitaine, and soon by the rest of the southern nobility. In 1119 the Council of Toulouse ordered the secular powers to assist the ecclesiastical authorities in quelling the heresy, but Catharism had become a mass movement and continued to grow for another hundred years, until Pope Innocent III organised the Albigensian★ crusade against the heretics. The Pope had called his bishops of Narbonne 'dumb dogs, unable to bark', meaning they were ignorant pastors and teachers, whose knowledge and experience could not deal with congregations on the verge of heresy. The missions to the Languedoc that St Bernard and Henry of Clairvaux had undertaken to offer examples of Christian life and teaching; the founding of the two mendicant orders, the Franciscans in 1210 and the Dominicans in 1216; the open debates between the heretics and the Catholics; the offers of complete absolution to heretics and their followers – all were of no avail in halting the tidal flood of feeling against the true Church. Even Pope Innocent III's decretal *Cum ex officii nostri*, in 1207, had little effect.

---

★The term derives from the town of Albi but the heretic centre was around Toulouse.

## The Albigensian Crusade

The northern nobility of France saw the subjugation of the southern provinces as an attractive aspect of this Holy Crusade, in which minor nobles with grand pretensions, like Simon de Montfort, might carve out some territory for themselves.

Thirty thousand knights and foot soldiers descended upon the Languedoc and ravaged the whole countryside, crops were trampled on and burnt, towns and cities destroyed and whole populations slaughtered. In Béziers fifteen thousand men, women and children were stabbed and hacked to pieces in the streets and in their homes by these good Christian knights from northern France. When a commander asked the papal legate how they were to distinguish heretic from Catholic, the reply, it is said, was: 'Kill them all. God will recognise his own.' He then wrote to Pope Innocent III and said: 'neither age, nor sex, nor status was spared.'[32] All the cities of the Languedoc were conquered and destroyed, Perpignan, Narbonne, Carcassonne and Toulouse. The rewards for this crusade were the same as if the army had travelled to the Holy Land: remission of all sins, an expiation of penances, an assured place in paradise, and all the booty and land a man could steal. The power of the southern nobility so sympathetic to the thought and belief of the Cathars was broken. The Church itself possibly quoted St Jerome: 'Cut off the decayed flesh, expel the mangy sheep from the fold, lest the whole house, the whole body, the whole flock, burn, perish, rot, die.'[33] It is clear that religious zeal merely disguised nationalist expansion on the part of the French king and the northern nobility, but as always the murder and cruelty only intensified the victims' sense of independence. At the end of every siege the Cathar Elect were rounded up and burnt. After the siege of Minerve, in 1210, 140 of the Elect died in the flames; in Casses, in 1211, sixty of the Elect were burnt. The women were not spared either, but if anything, provoked in the Crusaders deeper outrage and fury. Girande of Lavour, admired for the saintly life she led as a Cathar, was captured by the Crusaders, cast into a pit and stoned. Then 400 of the Elect from Lavour were burnt.

The war ended in the treaty of Paris and out of it came the Inquisition (1233), entrusted to the Dominican order. It is their meticulous records which have given us a picture of the heresy. Rainier Sacconi, an inquisitor, tells us that the Cathars believed carnal marriage to be a mortal sin and likewise that it was a mortal sin to eat flesh, eggs or cheese. But it is difficult to understand the exact qualification Sacconi is making in the following passage: 'Also, it is a common opinion of all the Cathars that whosoever kills a bird, from the least to the greatest, or quadrupeds, from the weasel to the elephant, commits a great sin; but they do not extend this to other animals.'[34] Does he mean apes, fish, reptiles . . . ? A little later in Lombardy, in the years 1267 and 1278-9, an inquisitor called Anselm of Alessandria writes of Cathar abstinence:

There is a common rule of abstinence among them, according to which all Cathars, of every sect, fast for three days each week, on Monday, Wednesday and Friday. They tell people that they fast on bread and water, but this is not true, for they abstain from wine, oil, fish and shellfish, and eat all the other things that they usually eat on ordinary days.

All the Cathars observe three fasts of forty days. The first begins at the same time as our Lent, and lasts until Easter; the second is from the first Monday after Whitsun to St Peter's [1 August]; the third from the first Monday after Martinmas to Christmas. In the first there are two weeks which are especially strict, the first and the last, when they do not drink wine, or eat oil or vegetable. They do not eat fish or shellfish at all during the three fasts, unless they are seriously ill. In the second and third fasts they have only one strict week, the first in each.[35]

Because now the Cathars went underground, the Inquisition flourished in southern France. The Dominicans went to work with a persuasive thoroughness which modern interrogation merely emulates. The inquisitors answered to the Pope and could only be called to account by Rome, so their power was enormous. In any town or district which the Papal Inquisition visited everyone was under suspicion, for mere contact with a Cathar was a punishable offence. Heretics who refused to recant were handed over to the secular powers for burning. The Cathars fled the towns and hid in small rural communities, fleeing to the forests themselves at the approach of strangers. As they were considered 'good Christians' by the people, they were befriended and helped, while the inquisitors were hated and often attacked. Evidence that you were a meat-eater and happily married with a family was now felt to be proof of orthodoxy. 'I am not an heretic,' an accused claimed in a court at Toulouse, 'I have a wife whom I love, I have children, I eat meat, I lie and I take oaths, I am a good Christian. Do not believe the Dominicans who claim that I have false beliefs. They will accuse you of the same . . . they want to drive out all the honourable citizens and seize the town from the Count.'[36]

The heretical fervour of this time had induced the Church to redefine its own dogma. At the Fourth Lateran Council in 1215 Pope Innocent summoned the patriarchs of Jerusalem and Constantinople, 29 archbishops, 412 bishops, and 800 abbots and priors to clarify once and for all the dispute over whether the wine and wafer became in reality the blood and body of Christ. It was agreed that transubstantiation did indeed take place, that the communicant was consuming the blood and flesh of Christ – not a symbol but the actuality. The Fourth Lateran Council thereby defined itself in even more direct opposition to the large numbers of vegetarian heretics.

Sexual pleasure and procreation were another area where Christian and heretic deeply diverged. The Cathar had a horror of flesh itself, from the eating of meat to the act of creating new beings. The Elect especially feared procreation, for to create another being would be to ensnare yet another angelic soul in matter, yet sexual activity appears to have been encouraged in others. 'So long as it did not lead to the conception of children they positively seemed to encourage sexual intercourse, or at least not discourage it – a complete reversal of the Catholic view.[37] Indeed, the accounts of the Inquisition reveal Cathars admitting to homosexual acts, which they did not consider a sin. If you could not be celibate, they reasoned, better by far to commit a sexual act which was not creative.*

Cathars at worship were given a 'heavenly food' and told that they would see angelic visions, which makes it seem likely that the Cathars, known to be herbalists, used hallucinogenic plants or even, as Pythagoras did, the opium poppy. Such 'heavenly food' was said to allow them, at other times, to traverse time and space, but sometimes a demon would appear in the form of an animal, the lights would be extinguished and an orgy would take place.

The more one examines Cathar beliefs the more it is understandable why the orthodox Church became ever more deeply outraged. Here was a society of meditative, learned and peaceful people who did not believe in hell, purgatory or damnation. Like the Pythagoreans, they believed souls continued to be reborn as animals or humans until they escaped from the earth entirely. There was the divine potential in all souls eventually to escape altogether from this endless cycle; no one would be damned for all eternity. After the last Cathar fortress stronghold, Montsegur, was destroyed and two hundred of the Elect were burnt without trial, Cathar power was effectively broken. The Inquisition continued to discover nests of heretics, which they destroyed, but by 1296 a general sympathy for the Cathars drove out the Inquisition from Carcassonne and there was a short recrudescence when Cathar bishops returned from Lombardy and held assemblies again in Languedoc. But the French king, the zealous Philip IV, persecuted all shades of heresy at the beginning of the fourteenth century, and the last Cathar Elect was burnt in 1330.

What legacy did this most famous of Christian heresies leave us? Cathars were tolerant of other religions. Their territory in France was a safe haven for Jews when anti-semitism in Europe was beginning; in southern France a fusion of Cathar and Jewish thought produced the Cabbala, the tradition of Jewish mysticism. The Cathars also encouraged music, poetry and painting. The art of the troubadours began in the Cathar areas, marked by intense bawdy sensuality, and their lyrics and songs influenced European poetry and music. The Cathar belief that it was possible for each individual to attain a mystical union with goodness itself – gnosis – unaided by church dogma and ritual would resurface again and again in every sect critical of Catholicism, to Luther and beyond. Yet in few of these later sects was there respect for

---

*How frequent homosexual acts among the Cathars were is hard to say. But, for what it is worth, the word for Cathar in several European languages came to be the word for homosexual: in German, *Ketzer*; in Italian, *gazarro*; and in French, *erite*. We also derive our word 'bugger' from Bulgarian, as do the Italians and French, *bulgaro* and *bougre*.

animals or a distaste for flesh-eating; for these we will have to look eventually
not to religion but to humanism.

## Two Christian Saints

That the Christian Church felt equivocal on the subject of animal rights is
clearly shown in the life of St Francis and the sermon given by St Anthony
to the fish. But this equivocation is also seen in medieval sculpture and
illuminated manuscripts where the closely observed forms of myriad animals
entwine themselves around pillars and objects. Nowhere else is the medieval
sense of fun, caricature and simple pleasure in animal life so evident. In Wells
Cathedral two hares crouch at the foot of Bishop Harewell. There are the
popular bestiaries, used as both education and entertainment, collections of
prose and verse about familiar birds, quadrupeds, reptiles and fish mixed up
with fantastic animals and travellers' tall tales. There was a strong sense of the
marvellous in the medieval mind, a delight in the grotesque, from giants and
midgets to imaginary animals such as the unicorn, the griffin and dragon, or
those animals that appear in Charlemagne's dream in the *Chanson de Roland*.
There is no doubt this society took profound delight in the animal kingdom
and celebrated it in song, verse, sculpture and paintings. In medieval
hagiography there are countless tales, some of how the saints rather in the
manner of Pythagoras could tame the beast. The blind St Hervaeus is led by
his wolf, St Kentigern of Glasgow manages to persuade a wolf to pull a
plough after he has killed the ox; another wolf carries the luggage of St
Froilanus; St Pachomius summons crocodiles to ferry him across a river;
while St Cainnic has an obliging stag who holds the holy book between his
antlers so that the saint can more easily read it. When a monk stepped on a
lizard, it is said that St Philip of Neri rebuked him with the words: 'What has
the poor creature done to you?'[38]

Yet the Christian attitude towards animals is none the less ambivalent. St
Francis, the archetypal Christian animal-lover, though he preached to the
birds – his 'Canticle of the Sun' exhorts the birds to glorify God – still ate
them. Though he addressed other animals as Brother and Sister, apparently
bestowing equality with the friars themselves upon them, meat was
prohibited only on fast days or for purely ascetic reasons. His thinking was
at first considered heretical and it was only in 1210 that he received verbal
approval, having then to wait another thirteen years before Pope Innocent
III confirmed the rules in writing, though with many changes. Itinerant
preaching was too reminiscent of the heretics and the order had to have a
hierarchical structure.

St Anthony of Padua (1195–1231), a Franciscan friar and the most famous
follower of St Francis, taught theology at Bologna. He had a reputation for
miracle-working, so his sermon to the fishes would have been one of many
which reflected his powers:

St Antony, being at one time at Rimini, where there were a great number of heretics, and wishing to lead them by the light of faith into the way of truth, preached to them, for several days, and reasoned with them on the faith of Christ and on the holy scriptures. They not only resisted his words, but were hardened and obstinate, and refused to listen to him. At last St Antony, inspired by God, went down to the seashore, where the river runs into the sea, and, having placed himself on a bank between the river and the sea, he began to speak to the fishes as if the Lord had sent him to preach to them, and said, 'Listen to the word of God, O you fishes of the sea and river, as the faithless heretics refuse to do so.'

No sooner had he spoken these words than suddenly a great multitude of fishes, both small and great, approached the bank on which he stood, and never before had so many been seen in the sea or in the river; all kept their heads out of the water and seemed to be attentively looking on St Antony's face; all were arranged in perfect order and most peacefully, the smaller ones in front near the bank, after them came those a little bigger, and last of all, where the water was deeper, the large ones.

When they had placed themselves in this order, St Antony began to preach to them most solemnly, saying: 'My brothers the fishes, you are bound as much as it is in your power to return thanks to your Creator, who has given you such a noble element for your dwelling; for you have at your choice sweet water and salt water; you have many places of refuge from the tempest; you have likewise a pure and transparent element for your nourishment. God, your bountiful and kind Creator, when he made you, ordered you to increase and multiply, and gave you his blessing. In the universal deluge all other creatures perished; you alone did God preserve from all harm. He has given you fins to enable you to go where you will. To you was it granted, according to the commandment of God, to keep the prophet Jonas, and after three days to throw him safe and sound on dry land. You it was who gave the tribute-money to our Savior Jesus Christ when, through his poverty, he had nothing to pay. By a singular mystery you were the nourishment of the eternal King, Jesus Christ, before and after his resurrection. Because of all these things you are bound to praise and bless the Lord who has given you so many and so much greater blessings than to other creatures.'

At these words the fishes began to open their mouths and bow their heads, and endeavoured, as much as was in their power, to express their reverence and show forth their praise. St Antony, seeing the reverence of the fishes towards their Creator, rejoiced greatly in spirit, and said, with a loud voice, 'Blessed be eternal God, for the fishes of the sea honor him more than men without faith, and animals without reason listen to his word with greater attention than sinful heretics.' And whilst St Antony was preaching the number of the fishes increased, and none of them left the place he had chosen.

And the people of the city, hearing of the miracle, made haste to go and witness it. With them came the heretics of whom we have spoken above, who, seeing such a wonderful and manifest miracle, were touched in their hearts, and all threw themselves at the feet of St Antony to hear his words.

The saint then began to expound to them the Catholic faith. He preached
so eloquently that all those heretics were converted and returned to the true
faith of Christ; the faithful were filled with joy and greatly comforted and
strengthened in the faith. After this St Antony sent away the fishes with the
blessing of God; and they all departed rejoicing as they went, and the people
returned to the city. St Antony remained at Rimini for several days, preaching
and reaping much spiritual fruit in the souls of his hearers.[39]

After giving this sermon to the admiring fish, St Anthony probably went
back home and grilled a few of them for supper. Or if not, the fact that fish
was an integral part of their diet, a necessity on fast days, was never
questioned by either St Francis or St Anthony, nor by the people who were
told this story. The fish might well have listened with greater attention than
'sinful heretics' but they could still be killed and eaten. The medieval mind
saw the animal kingdom in a deeply complex and contradictory way. For
example, if a swordfish had speared St Anthony's toe, it could have been
caught and put on trial for assault and criminal damage.

## The Criminal Prosecution of Animals

Nowhere is this ambivalence towards animals illustrated more colourfully
than in the criminal prosecution and punishment of animals, both wild and
domestic, a custom which began in Ancient Greece and continued to flourish
through the Dark and Middle Ages. If a domestic creature, a horse, cow, dog
or pig, happened to kill a person accidentally, often a secular tribunal would
be held and the offending animal would be tried, convicted and sentenced to
death. There were also ecclesiastical courts against rats, mice, locusts, weevils
and other vermin to prevent them from devouring crops. Animals in the
service of humans could be arrested, tried, convicted and executed; before
trial these animals were taken into custody and locked up.[40] Insects and
rodents which could not be caught and imprisoned by the civil authorities
came under the jurisdiction of the Church, whose supernatural powers were
to be used to compel the creatures to go away and not inflict such damage
again. Often a few examples of the loathsome creatures, a couple of rats
perhaps, would be brought to court and solemnly killed after curses had been
pronounced upon their kind. There was even a case in Rome, in AD 880, of
setting a price upon the heads of a troublesome plague of locusts, but to no
avail – recourse was made to exorcisms and holy water.

The Church's explanation of these noisome phenomena was like its
approach to animals themselves, divided. Sometimes they were called Satan's
creatures, sent to torment the faithful; but at other times they became agents
of God to punish sinful humankind. In the latter case it became difficult,
theologically, to exterminate them at all, but in the former people were free
to use any method that was expedient. Christ's example with the swine was
much followed and all sorts of plagues and scourges were driven into the sea.
The sea was a useful image for the unwanted effluents of the spirit.

The parable of the Gadarene swine was also useful for the domestic animal that had become homicidal – the creature was obviously inhabited by a devil or demons and not to punish it would be to allow the devil full rein to do its ghastly work and infect others. Even the site where the murder had occurred could be occupied by demons if the murder went unpunished. This concept, of course, runs deep in folklore and many a ghost story has stemmed from it, for it was thought that even a house or dwelling built on the site would be infested with demons, and those people living in it would be vulnerable to demonic possession, as well as their domestic animals, even the hens in the barnyard; what is more such infestation could continue for centuries. The rooting out of crime (particularly murder) and its punishment were vital in the battle against Satan and his demonic hordes.

Medieval law thus made animals responsible for their crime. Even though they were inhabited by the devil and must in some way have allowed the devil in, yet Christian dogma stated quite clearly that animals had no soul and could not be saved by God.

## Articles of Faith

St Thomas Aquinas (1225-74), the Dominican theologian who codified Christian thinking, interpreted Genesis, 1:28, in which God gave dominion over the animals to Adam, to mean absolute, unconstrained authority: 'it matters not how man behaves to animals because God has subjected all things to man's power . . .'[41] Aquinas considered that animals were without rational souls, were therefore imperfect and could not be immortal; they might therefore be killed and eaten. In fact, it was part of God's plan that this should occur. Aquinas goes on: 'things like plants which merely have life are all alike for animals, and all animals are for man. Wherefore, it is not unlawful if men use plants for the good of animals and animals for the good of man . . .'[42] Aquinas then points out: 'This cannot be done unless these [animals] be deprived of life . . . this is in keeping with the commandment of God himself'[43] (Genesis, 1:29, 30 and Genesis, 9:3). Only the perfect could kill for food, so animals that killed human beings and ate them were, of course, not part of the divine plan.

As Aquinas divides sin into three – sins against God, against oneself, against one's neighbour – it is more or less impossible to commit any sin against animals. So Aquinas also agreed that humans owed no kindness or charity towards animals: first, 'they were not competent, properly speaking, to possess good, this being proper to rational creatures'; second, we have no fellow feeling with them; third, charity is defined as something 'based on the fellowship of everlasting happiness to which irrational creatures cannot attain . . .'[44] The only point of being kind towards animals, Aquinas thought, was a kind of training in charity: 'if a man practises a pitiable affection for animals, he is all the more disposed to take pity on his fellow men.'[45] Animals must honour God, rather as the birds sang as St Francis desired, moved by the glory of God. In such a situation one could feel moved, but there would be no sin in killing the birds after hearing their song, then plucking and cooking them.

Aquinas was much influenced by the writings of St Augustine and of Aristotle. He redefined and Christianised the thought of Aristotle but often borrowed terms, so Roman Catholicism became imbued with the philosophical conjectures of Neoplatonism overlaid with Christian supernatural solutions. He coined the term 'Articles of Faith' to define those beliefs which the Church considered were obligatory to the faith, thus giving the Church, in some people's view, an iron straitjacket. With philosophically defined dogma and doctrine the Church now had the theory to battle with heresy, so the influence of the Dominican Inquisition grew ever more powerful, and insidious and its brief ever more sweeping.

## Medieval Fasting

Rules of fasting and abstinence in religious orders can be dated back to the first half of the fifth century AD. A statute recorded by St Hieronimus Eusebius includes 144 articles of which twenty-nine refer to diet and other ways of mortifying the body. The concept of the fast itself derives from the forty-day fast of Christ in the desert, a way of praising God while punishing the body. Lent is, of course, its yearly celebration, the other main fast being Advent, the thirty days before Christmas. Another form of fasting was to abstain from certain foods on certain days, usually meat and animal fats, which it became obligatory to forgo on Wednesdays and Fridays. Sometimes eggs and dairy produce were allowed on the meatless days, otherwise fish, either fresh, cured or salted. Instead of eggs and dairy produce, fish roe, vegetable oil and almond milk could be taken.

> Especially should you fast, so that your youth may acquire strength, and pray, for the reason that fasting subdues the vigour of the flesh and prayer raises the soul to God. It should be known, however, that some, while they indiscriminately carry out the fast, do not receive the benefits of fasting; for whatever they deny themselves one day, the next they gorge on at will. And so it is that one day of fasting serves for the following day . . .[46]

The problem for the founders of the religious communities was to get the dietary balance right. There should be enough food to satisfy hunger, enough to enable the monks to work hard in the fields and gardens, but not enough to encourage sensuality.

Up to the ninth century the day's food consisted of two meals, a soup of vegetables and a purée of pulses with oil and flour or cheese. St Benedict of Nursia (480-547) added a third dish of raw vegetables with salt, oil and vinegar.[47] St Benedict was the founder of monastic rule and was obviously a man of taste as well as a dietician. The fasting diet was limited to one meal a day and quite often not even that, sometimes only bread and water.

There were 190–200 fast days in the year. Some bread was allowed though never made from white wheat flour; those loaves were kept for guests and the sick. Bread was made from rye, barley, oats, pulses or a mixture of some or all.

Because of the pressure of hard work on the brethren as more land was accumulated by abbeys and monasteries, the amount of food allowed on each day was raised. A synod at Aix-la-Chapelle in 816 allowed the number of dishes for each meal to be increased to three cooked and one raw. Meat was allowed to be eaten on more days than just feast days. The sick were allowed to eat meat and this rule invited intrigue. Monks would feign illness so as to eat meat.

No doubt many felt such rules were oppressive yet were content to accept them as their duty towards God. What occurred in the religious houses was reflected in society. The same fast days were observed, though the rich could interpret the diet rather more comfortably and with greater ingenuity than the poor:

Almond milk was an expensive substitute for cow's milk, and on occasion it was curdled, pressed, drained, and presented as a substitute for cream cheese. Imitations were a feature of medieval cooking, and it pleased both cook and diner to pretend to break the fast, with 'eggs' fabricated from fish roe or curdled almond milk, or with the grandest hoax, a 'ham' or 'bacon' slices made with salmon for the pink meat and pike for the fat. Recipes for such imitations were still being published in France in the eighteenth century.[48]

There was one season which affected everyone, inflicting on them abstinence from fresh meat – winter. From November to April there was no pasture, the little hay that could be cut had to be saved for the oxen, the war horses and the breeding stock. The slaughter of hogs began in September, while cattle were killed on the Feast of St Martin, 11 November, Martinmas. On this day, as it could not be preserved, the offal was cooked and eaten, so chitterlings, tripe, black puddings, pasties of liver and dishes of kidneys were all consumed with great gusto, in the knowledge that such dishes in such profusion would not be available for another year. ★

Meat was the prime food which was always sacrificed throughout fast days, the next being animal fats and wine. Abstention from meat became further established as the key to the path of virtue and salvation in the extremely devious ways by which members of the Church avoided the rigours of this sacrifice. Not only were rabbits specifically bred for their embryos but the father of dogma himself, St Thomas Aquinas, stated firmly that chicken was of aquatic origin, therefore counted as fish and could be

---

★The feast and annual slaughter was called Yule. The Church managed to move the date towards Christmas and unite the two.

eaten on fast days. The saint's corpulence suggests that Aquinas did not care at all for fast days. The Church later ruled that chicken was too good for fasting and upgraded it again, taking away its fishy origins.

Fasting in the Church and medieval society emphasised the importance of meat and kept it at the centre of public awareness, thereby, of course, making the decision not to eat meat as significant as it had always been.

# 8

# The Renaissance

Meat-eating had now become solidly entrenched in the mores of society. It was not only a matter of customs and manners, but was rooted deep in the psychology of behaviour backed by powerful sacral concepts. These latter may have been partly secularised at every meal; the food could be enjoyed only after grace was solemnly announced, only after deference was shown to God the provider and sustainer of life itself.

From prehistory we know that the carcase of a hunted animal was shared among the group, unlike gathered vegetable and plant foods. This, we might infer, means that eating meat from a slaughtered animal was a social event, allowing all people to share and congregate together. It was the food which unified the social group beyond the ties of family kinship. Meat which was shared became a token of the group itself of its identity, unity and power. Meat from the earliest times became a symbol of many things, and these symbols, far from disappearing, went on growing in power and complexity. Meat still performs this very first ritual role of unifying a family and being the focal point of a feast or celebration.

Meat, also in very early times, became the essential means by which humans communicated with the gods. The smoke and aromas of the spices were the food of the gods and they were given it before people were allowed to eat the meat itself. The ritual of the animal sacrifice, the blood spilt, the method of slaughter, was all carefully kept to. When Christianity finally halted this practice it had already invested its own rituals with much of the same symbolism: in the Mass it is the body and blood of Christ which are consumed by the celebrant, the smoke of the censer having already wafted to heaven.

From the earliest times, too, meat was a visible sign of wealth and power, whether it was the number of cattle and livestock owned or the number of joints of meat and variety of creatures served up at a banquet. Not only had meat acquired a sacred image as a god-given, god-blessed substance, like the mythical manna, but it was surrounded, too, by the aura of mammon, of wealth and temporal power.

Yet in Christian society those monks and saints who had chosen to turn away from the world could give up not only the affluence associated with meat but its sacred aspects as well. For they, as we have seen from the days of Pythagoras, were consuming a diet nearer to that of the gods, an austere diet which, in subduing the flesh, would incite closer affinity to God. Such asceticism was never considered by society to be vegetarianism. No Christian mystic or monk was ever called a follower of the Pythagorean diet, as heretics were, even though the actual ingredients of the diet might be exactly the same.

For a vegetarian philosophy to exist (see p.37), it needs an ethical system of greater power and significance than the prevailing code in society.

## Riches and Famine

Christianity, with its sanction in Genesis (see p.114) and its belief in human dominance, was far too powerful for the Gnostic heresies to defeat. But in the early Renaissance the Church was beginning very slowly to lose its power. The discovery and reappraisal of the great pagan philosophers brought astonishing ideas into the open. But, except for a few rare spirits, meat-eating remained the cornerstone of society; for anyone, except a Christian mystic, to abstain from it was rare.

We may have an exaggerated view of the daily diet of the rich in the Middle Ages as it is only the menus of the great feasts which have come down to us. Dorothy Hartley[1] quotes one as beginning with brain in sharp sauce, then head of boar, young swans, capon, pheasant, heron, sturgeon, venison, suckling pigs, peacocks, cranes, rabbit and chickens. There was a host of other smaller birds eaten as well: curlews, egrets, quails, snipe and larks. But you did not have to be royal or one of the great families of the land, for even the tables of the medieval minor noblemen were full of meat and fish:* beef, mutton, pork, veal, game and venison, and carp, pike, eels and lampreys.[2] They ate bread made from white wheat flour, drank red and white French and German wine, ale, beer and cider. The household expenses of the Bishop of Hereford, Richard de Swinfield, for the years 1289-90 include fresh and salted meats, game, venison and wildfowl, salted and pickled vegetables as well as fresh onions, leeks and garlic. In the menu accounts of feasts hardly any reference is made to fresh vegetables or fruits. It is possible that they were thought of as the food of the poor and therefore not suitable for inclusion in a royal or noble banquet. Certainly the poor, and especially the rural poor, sustained themselves on a diet of grains, vegetables and what was known as 'white meat', which meant dairy produce. Peasants seldom ate meat unless they were successful at poaching (but the Royal Forest laws were harsh and rigorous) or the lord of the manor gave a feast to celebrate the bringing in of the harvest. The food given out to the peasants in return for their labour tended to be barley, oatmeal, wheat, herrings (usually dried and salted,

---

*The medieval feast was structured on three separate meat courses, followed by three separate fish courses. Each of these courses was brought to a close by a dish of pastry, a sweetmeat or a jelly, often elaborately devised and decorated, known as a 'subtlety'.

occasionally smoked) and ale or beer. Such a diet was augmented by any vegetables grown or picked in the wild: cabbages, onions, leeks and garlic, the last used to flavour the cereals, but beans were also ground and a flour made out of them. The accounts of the Abbot of Battle show that the workers got two meals a day: bread, ale and cheese, and at vespers, bread, ale, pottage, herrings and cheese. The pottage was a gruel without meat, made with peas and beans.

At the end of the thirteenth century one of the small Ice Ages★ began and Europe got appreciably colder. The Baltic Sea froze over twice, in 1303 and 1306, so the agricultural growing season became much shorter. Population increases in the century before had reached a delicate balance with the agricultural techniques of the time. Crop yields could not be raised, or poor soils made more productive. The poor of Europe were probably undernourished before, but the failure of crops, heavy rains, likened to the Biblical Flood, and long icy winters now produced famine and diseases.†

Peasants live close to the seasons. Autumn meant the end of all green food from woods and commons. The last wild fruit was finished, the corn gathered, the fowls which had eaten the fallen grain had also been eaten (if you were lucky enough to have acquired one). In winter there were grain, root vegetables and some pickles, but little else. If you were fortunate and had a cow or a pig, they were kept to breed from in the spring. But if you were on the point of starvation, they were killed and eaten and your future had been consumed too.

The majority of Christian Europe had to survive on a vegetable diet but not from choice or ideology. The writers of the ancient world that were extolled and who became influential were Aristotle and to a lesser degree Plato (none of the Pre-Socratics, with their view of the spirit within all things), and if later writers like Ovid and Seneca were admired, their opinions on animals and flesh-eating were ignored.

The fast days of the Church after the Norman Conquest grew more numerous than before, but these meatless days were merely seen as a mortification of the flesh and aimed to reduce carnal lusts, for meat was thought to stimulate the passions. Fish, on the other hand, were thought conducive to piety: 'All manner of fish is cold of nature and doth ingender phlegm; it doth little nourish.'[3] There was the whole of Lent in which to have your phlegm engendered, every Wednesday, Friday and Saturday, too much by far for this fifteenth-century schoolboy who wrote: 'Thou wilt not believe how weary I am of fish, and how much I desire that flesh were come in again, for I have ate none other but salt fish this Lent, and it hath engendered so much phlegm within me that it stoppeth my pipes that I can

---

★The Little Ice Age, caused by an advance of polar and alpine glaciers, lasted until about 1700.
†France suffered more than England. Forty-eight famine years were recorded in the eleventh century and in the twelfth century it was estimated that people died of hunger on average one year in four. In England the serious famine years were from 1315 to 1321, in the reign of Edward II.

neither speak or breathe.'[4] Poor lad, one imagines that a vegetable diet without fish would not have occurred to him nor stimulated much excitement either. There is no doubt that the emphasis on meat-eating as not only desirable and pleasurable but also necessary to health intensified in our national consciousness throughout this time. The converse would also be true, that a hatred of fish-eating (astonishing for a small island community) and of the vegetable diet (equally astonishing as our soil is more fertile and productive than that of many of our European neighbours) was also imprinted in us. For both fish and vegetable consumption are still linked with inadequacy or poverty, and punishment.

Fish days had greater significance in the second half of the sixteenth century, for two major reasons: to encourage ship-building and train mariners, and to relieve the demand for meat, which had grown rare and expensive. A 1595 proclamation declares that if one fish day a week was observed, 135,000 head of beef could be spared each year.

But it is the type of fuel that also determines what and how you eat. Tannahill[5] points out that a roaring fire is far less desirable around the Mediterranean than it is in northern Europe; besides, the forests of southern Europe were being used for charcoal for the metal-workers. Simple enclosed charcoal stoves were used in the south, with flat heating plates above which could be used for quick dishes cooked very briefly. In the north there was plenty of wood and thousands of miles of forests; cooking tended to be done on spits or from one pot or cauldron hanging over the fire. The Mediterranean method favoured fish and vegetable cooking and unleavened bread or doughs like pizza that could be cooked flat outside the heat and not baked in the oven. In the north the fuel favoured the barbecuing of great hunks of flesh while the cauldron could boil smaller cuts of meat with vegetables. The poor made their meals from the cauldron too, though the flavouring might come only from meat bones without flesh on them. The cauldrons were rarely emptied, except at Lent, and Tannahill thinks the taste of the winter salt pork and cabbage would have lingered on long after the pork was eaten. But all the cooking of Christendom, from whatever region, was designed around the consumption of animals.

We might think, looking back, that the close proximity in which humans and livestock lived would engender feelings of compassion, but the reverse was the case. We shall see later that the vegetarian movement grew in strength and popularity with the rise of urban communities. The closeness of human and animal in the medieval and Renaissance world is an aspect of life hidden to all but traditional farmers, but it is very important to the way animals were considered as creatures. Pigs and hens ran in the streets of towns and cities, cocks crowed at dawn on the steps of old St Paul's, animals slept with their owners or just beneath them on the muddy ground floors of houses where their droppings lay. Strong-smelling herbs would be sprinkled over the straw and ground to help disperse the pervasive and constant smell of ordure.

Milk, and its products, was an essential part of the diet but must also have contributed to infectious diseases because cows were milked in unhygienic conditions. Much of the milk was made into cheese and great quantities of whey were drunk: 'by reason of the affinitie whiche it hath with mylke, it is convertible into blood and flesh . . .'[6]

For most people who kept a sow and a few chickens and were able to buy bread and milk, the main source of protein would have been from cheese, whey and eggs. They would have slaughtered their animals to sell in order to buy more flour, salt and vegetables. The bacon they would have cured themselves from their own pigs, so the few animals they had in their care meant to them their own family's survival. They were vitally important, representing sustenance and life, and as such the animals would have been nurtured and cared for, and fed with choice scraps to make them plump enough for slaughter. Prayers were said to particular saints to ensure that the animals thrived and prospered until then. Both chickens and pigs not only lived off scraps but helped clear some of the muck thrown into the streets from the houses. Livestock, to the majority of people, were not sentient creatures with independent lives, but were part of the extended family, the foundation of their existence, and an animal's death was a necessity no one could deny. As we have seen in other ages, to have questioned such killing would have been to threaten the structure of society itself, something only the mad or those touched by Satan would do. Yet a few distinguished voices did write with compassion in the early Renaissance – though they may have been rather lonely voices, their works sometimes unpublished until after their deaths – feeling sorrow and unease at a creature's death agonies, questioning why food should be hunted and slaughtered.

## Dissident Voices

The voices are first heard at the beginning of the Renaissance. The works of the ancient writers were being newly discovered and their ideas were having influence. In 1439 Cosimo de Medici began sending his agents all over the world in a quest for ancient manuscripts. In 1444 he founded the Library of San Marco, the first public library, which began to collect works influenced by Pythagoras, Neoplatonism and Gnostic thought, and these began to be translated for the first time. They were in direct contrast to the collections of books the Church approved of. When Cosimo created an academy of Pythagorean and Platonic studies, Renaissance philosophy began to explore concepts from the Classical world with new energy.

Erasmus (1466-1536), the Dutch humanist, scholar, and friend of Thomas More, in his *Praise of Folly* satirises the huntsman and the ritual kill. Erasmus placed the genius of Folly itself in the pulpit, the main reason the book could not be published in his lifetime. In this passage he observes the hunt and its killing:

When they, the sportsmen, have run down their victims, what strange pleasure they have in cutting them up! Cows and sheep may be slaughtered by common butchers, but those animals that are killed in hunting must be mangled by none under a gentleman, who will fall down on his knees, and drawing out a slashing dagger (for a common knife is not good enough) after several ceremonies shall dissect all the joints as artistically as the best skilled anatomist, while all who stand round shall look very intently and seem to be mightily surprised with the novelty, though they have seen the same thing a hundred times before; and he that can but dip his finger and taste of the blood shall think his own bettered by it.[7]

Sir Thomas More, in 1516, published his *Utopia*, in which the Utopians also condemn hunting and the slaughtering of these wild creatures:

But if the hope of slaughter and the expectation of tearing the victim in pieces pleases you, you should rather be moved with pity to see an innocent hare murdered by a dog – the weak by the strong, the fearful by the fierce, the innocent by the cruel and pitiless. Therefore this exercise of hunting, as a thing unworthy to be used of free men, the Utopians have rejected . . . ★

For they count hunting the lowest, the vilest, and most abject part of butchery; and the other parts of it more profitable and more honest as bringing much more commodity, in that they, the butchers, kill their victims from necessity, whereas the hunter seeks nothing but pleasure of the innocent and woeful animal's slaughter and murder.[8]

The Utopian religion, More wrote, insisted that 'no living animal should be killed in sacrifice for God has no delight in blood and slaughter, for He has given life to animals to the intent that they should live'.[9]

More was also one of the first observers to point out that huge amounts of land are needed for livestock rearing. This piece of invective could easily serve today as a diatribe against the blight of mass farming:

They [the oxen and sheep] consume, destroy, and devour whole fields, houses, and cities. For look in what parts of the realm doth grow the finest and therefore the dearest wool. There noblemen and gentlemen, yea, and certain abbots, holy men no doubt, not contenting themselves with the yearly revenues and profits that were wont to grow to their forefathers and predecessors of their lands, nor being content that they live in rest and pleasure nothing profiting, yea, much annoying, the public weal, leave no land for tillage – they enclose all into pasture, they throw down houses, they pluck down towns and leave nothing standing, but only the church to be made a

---

★These criticisms of hunting are all the more astonishing when one realises that much of the food, the bulk of it, on the banqueting table would have derived from the hunt. It is, we should surmise, a criticism of privilege, of surplus, of waste as well as needless cruelty and the triumph of the strong over the weak.

sheep house; and, as though you lost no small quantity of ground by forests, chases, lands, and parks, those good holy men turn dwelling-places and all glebe land into wilderness and desolation . . . For one shepherd or herdsman is enough to eat up that ground with cattle, to the occupying whereof about husbandry many hands would be requisite. And this is also the cause why victuals be now in many places dearer; yea, besides this, the price of wool is so risen that poor folks, which were wont to work it and make cloth thereof, be now able to buy none at all, and by this means very many be forced to forsake work and to give themselves to idleness. For after that so much land was enclosed for pasture, an infinite multitude of sheep died of the rot, such vengeance God took of their inordinate and insatiable covetousness, sending among the sheep that pestiferous murrain which much more justly should have fallen on the sheep-masters' own heads; and though the number of sheep increase never so fast, yet the price falleth not one mite, because there be so few sellers.[10]*

At around this time, too, an essay was written by a priest and friend of the Pope which had to wait a hundred years, until 1648, for publication. It was written by Jerome Ronarius and entitled 'That the irrational animals often make use of reason better than men'. The treatise, according to a later reader, was distinguished 'by its severe and serious tone and by the assiduous emphasising of just such traits of the lower animals as are most generally denied to them, as being products of the higher faculties of the soul. With their virtues the vices of men are set in sharp contrast.'[11] The title and the arguments reveal that Plutarch's essay (see p.98) was the original inspiration. The Renaissance, of course, owes much of its stimulus to the rediscovery of the Classical arts, and writers previously unexamined were now read with a sense of discovery, ideas long buried resurfaced again. One of those ideas, there can be no doubt, is that animals were sensitive to pain and that humans, therefore, owed them consideration and concern. Yet acceptance of this central idea, so obvious and so simple, was delayed by almost three hundred years, for it was buried beneath scientific enquiries, as we shall see, into whether animals had souls or not. Another factor contributing to this delay may have been the lack of commitment to the cause on the part of such writers as Erasmus and Sir Thomas More, for though they wrote movingly on the plight of animals, neither gave up eating meat. Nor did the French essayist Montaigne, who had seemed equally moved by pain and suffering:

---

*Upon this passage Howard Williams, the nineteenth-century reformer and author of *The Ethics of Diet*, commented: 'these sagacious and just reflections upon the evil social consequences of carnivorousness may be fitly commended to the earnest attention of our public writers and speakers to-day. The periodical cattle plagues and foot-and-mouth diseases, which, in theological language, are vaguely assigned to national sins, might be more ingenuously and truthfully attributed to the one sufficient cause – to the general indulgence of selfish instincts, which closes the ear to all the promptings at once of humanity and of reason, and is, in truth, a national sin of the most serious character.'

For my part I have never been able to see, without displeasure, an innocent and defenceless animal, from whom we receive no offence or harm, pursued and slaughtered. And when a deer, as commonly happens, finding herself without breath and strength, without other resource, throws herself down and surrenders, as it were, to her pursuers, begging for mercy by her tears, this has always appeared to me a very displeasing spectacle. I seldom, or never, take an animal alive whom I do not restore to the fields. Pythagoras was in the habit of buying their victims from the fowlers and fishermen for the same purpose.[12]

Montaigne believes cruelty to animals will lead inevitably to cruelty to fellow creatures, and the view that the murder of humans began because the murder of animals was commonplace was yet another idea to resurface from the Classical past:

Dispositions sanguinary in regard to other animals testify a natural inclination to cruelty towards their own kind. After they had accustomed themselves at Rome to the spectacle of the murders of other animals, they proceeded to those of men and gladiators. Nature has, I fear, herself attached some instinct of inhumanity to man's disposition.[13]

His last reflection is almost dualist, but in using the word 'nature' instead of 'God' he avoids the taint of heresy. He adds that surely theology enjoins us to have some sympathy with animals (but, unfortunately, does not quote chapter and verse — it would have been interesting to know his source) and concludes the passage with a thought new to his age but familiar enough from Plutarch and others: 'Considering that one and the same Master has lodged us in this palatial world for his service, and that they are, as we, members of His family, it is right that it should enjoin some respect and affection towards them.'[14]

Montaigne then, splendidly passionate, attacks the supposed supremacy of man:

Let him shew me, by the most skilful argument, upon what foundations he has built these excessive prerogatives which he supposes himself to have over other existences. Who has persuaded him that that admirable impulse of the celestial vault, the eternal brightness of those Lights rolling so majestically over our heads, the tremendous motions of that infinite sea of Globes, were established and have continued so many ages for his advantage and for his service. Is it possible to imagine anything so ridiculous as that this pitiful, miserable creature, who is not even master of himself, exposed to injuries of every kind, should call itself master and lord of the universe, of which, so far from being lord of it, he knows but the smallest part? Who has given him this sealed charter? Let him shew us the 'letters patent' of this grand commission. Have they been issued in favour of the wise only? They affect but the few in that case. The fools and the wicked – are they worthy of so extraordinary a favour, and being the worst part of the world, do they deserve to be preferred to all the rest? Shall we believe all this?

Presumption is our natural and original disease. The most calamitous and fragile of all creatures is man, and yet the most arrogant. It is through the vanity of this same imagination that he equals himself to a god, that he attributes to himself divine conditions, that he picks himself out and separates himself from the crowd of other creatures, curtails the just shares of other animals his brethren and companions, and assigns to them such portions of faculties and forces as seems to him good. How does he know, by the effort of his intelligence, the interior and secret movements and impulses of other animals? By what comparison between them and us does he infer the stupidity which he attributes to them?[15]

Lastly he recollects Plato's picture of the Golden Age and how humankind had an advantage then because they could communicate with animals and learn from them: 'by which they acquired a very perfect knowledge and intelligence and thus made their lives more happy than we can make ours. Is a better test needed by which to judge of human folly in regard to other species?'[16] It is interesting that Montaigne selects the Golden Age for his example, but not the time in Eden before the Fall; it is as if he was so soaked in the Classicism of the Greeks that the Hebrew allegory, exactly similar, did not occur to him. Yet Montaigne does not take the logical step of denouncing the slaughter of animals for the consumption of meat; he seems to play with the idea without taking it to its natural conclusion – 'Who doubts that a child, arrived at the necessary strength for feeding itself, could find its own nourishment? The earth produces and offers to him enough for his needs without artificial labour'[17] – a failure all the more surprising in the light of his final observation, one as true now as it has ever been: 'Nature has furnished us with every plant we need, to shew us, as it seems, how superior she is to all our artificiality; while the extravagance of our appetite outruns all the inventions by which we seek to satisfy it.'[18]

## Renaissance Man Himself

But before Montaigne and roughly contemporary with both Erasmus and More one giant among men passionately denounced the slaughter of animals and loathed meat-eating: Leonardo da Vinci (1452–1519), Renaissance man himself, possibly the greatest draughtsman ever to have lived, possessed of an infinite curiosity which drove him on in an unstinting examination of life's myriad phenomena. Yet in the sixty or so biographies in the London Library on his life and work, only one book bothers to discuss his vegetarianism.

Freud wrote a work[19] analysing Leonardo, seeing in him a man in conflict between pity and aggression. As symbols of the former, Freud cites Leonardo's vegetarianism and his habit of freeing wild caged birds at the market;* as for the latter, Freud thought that his military inventions, his participation in Cesare Borgia's campaigns, and his practice of accompanying condemned criminals to execution in order to draw their facial expressions showed suppressed sadism.

Leonardo's inventions or near-discoveries would have made him remarkable enough without the paintings or drawings. He designed the first armoured vehicles, several types of aircraft and helicopters, anticipated the submarine and almost discovered the circulation of the blood. He dissected corpses and made anatomical drawings hundreds of years ahead of his time. Around and among all these drawings and sketches he wrote copiously. His views on vegetarianism and his pity for animals were no secret – a letter from India, written by Andrea Corsali in 1515, to Giuliano de Medici (Leonardo's patron) tells us: 'Certain infidels called Guzzerati do not feed upon anything that contains blood, nor do they permit among them that any injury be done to any living thing, like our Leonardo da Vinci.'

There is throughout Leonardo's scattered notes a rising disgust with man himself, as here: 'King of animals – as thou hast described him – I should rather say King of the beasts, though being the greatest – because thou doest only help them, in order that they may give thee their children for the benefit of the gullet, of which thou hast attempted to make a sepulchre for all animals.'[20] Eissler, who wrote a psychological study of Leonardo[21] criticising Freud's work, does agree with Freud that phrases in which, for example, Leonardo refers to the mouth as 'a sepulchre for all animals' denote a man at the edge of depression. Vegetarians, of course, might disagree. Leonardo writes: 'Now does not nature produce enough simple vegetarian food for thee to satisfy thyself? And if thou art not content with such, canst thou not by the mixture of them make infinite compounds, as Platina describes and other writers on food?'[22] Leonardo was clearly aware of vegetarian cuisine. Bartolommeo Sacchi, called Il Platina, wrote the first Italian cookery book since Apicius. He belonged to a club, the Academy, which was for lovers of classical antiquity. They used Greek names and studied the philosophy and thought of the ancient world. Such pursuits were considered pagan and could bring charges of heresy. A vivid idea of the cooking of the Renaissance can be gathered from Platina's collection of recipes (see p.180).

Eissler considers that Leonardo, when dissecting his corpses, had to unconsciously fight off cannibalistic impulses. Again, this is a bizarre thought to vegetarians, who have a natural horror of eating flesh, whether from animal or human.† Perhaps Eissler and Freud would argue that such a horror

---

*A common superstition in Paris at the time was that, if you freed a wild bird, it became a magic sacrifice which promised success in love and business.
†Eissler also suggests: 'It is worthwhile deliberating whether it was specifically the conflict about cannibalism that caused the inhibition in Leonardo's contemporaries against going ahead with anatomical studies.' This conjecture is also unrealistic. In Rome at that time there were no food shortages – they were to come later, in the second half of the sixteenth century when the population tripled. Anatomists came from the professional class, hence were fairly well fed, and corpses that deteriorate fast are not the most appealing of dinners.

is merely a defence against the desire. But Eissler sees Leonardo's revulsion for humankind as part of an oral-sadistic impulse, as in this passage which likens man to a lavatory: 'Some there are who are nothing else than a passage for food and augmentors of excrement and fillers of privies, because through them no other things in the world, nor any good effects, are produced, since nothing but full privies results from them.'[23]

It is clear that Leonardo's learning, his intellectual speculation and his knowledge allowed him to make observations on the rest of humanity with a degree of detachment. 'We make our life by the death of others' is a comment which would not be appreciated by the normal meat-eater. 'In dead matter there remains insensate life, which on being united to the stomachs of living things, resumes a life of the senses and the intellect.'[24] Eissler thinks such passages must show 'an acute aversion against food, at least in the form of flesh'.[25]

To offset his revulsion for humans, he does express great pity for exploited animals, sheep, cows, goats and the like: 'From countless numbers will be taken away their little children and the throats of these shall be cut, and they shall be quartered most barbarously.'[26] Of the cruelty inflicted on animals Leonardo writes:

> Of asses which are beaten, O indifferent nature, wherefore art thou so partial, being to some of thy children a tender and benignant mother, and to others a most cruel and pitiless stepmother? I see thy children given into slavery to others, without any sort of advantage, and instead of remuneration for the services they have done, they are repaid by the severest suffering, and they spend their whole life in benefiting their oppressor.[27]

Even the most cursory glance at the landscapes in Leonardo's great paintings, or the studies of rocks and water, shows that Leonardo perceived enormous and vigorous life not only in the effects of nature clouds, torrents, shadows and light – but in matter itself, in the very stones and pebbles, making us recall those Pre-Socratic philosophers who saw the spirit in everything. It is as if Leonardo has dissected nature itself, and drawn back an outer skin to show us the circulation of sap or spirit beneath the rocks. It is this oneness with all life, felt so intensely, which makes Leonardo so astonishing as a man and an artist.

In Leonardo's work the Church is not praised or worshipped, but stands only as a representation of the spirit of God made visible in bricks, mortar and church laws. He is devoted to it only in its role as patron. His heart and soul are turned in another direction, to humankind itself, alone with nature, part of the living universe. Leonardo is the first great humanitarian. In Leonardo, Montaigne, More and Erasmus, the knowledge of their own humanity and what they feel for the plight of others in their suffering engulf notions of Christian ideology. It cannot sweep the ideology away, for the whole social structure is built upon this Christian foundation, and these philosophers and artists are unable to escape fully from the demands of their time. But in their humanity are the beginnings of an ideological structure to compete with Christianity. We will see, through the next few hundred years, that structure being strengthened and added to.

## Food as Secular Ritual

In the meantime the cooking of Renaissance Rome reached an apex of sophistication, art and gluttony. Leonardo would have been only too aware of the endless lavish feasts given by the great families of Rome, Florence and Milan. The Bentivoglio family at Bologna, the Sforzas at Milan, the Medici at Florence all vied with each other in magnificence, both at table and in secular 'triumphs', based on the grateful rejoicing of Classical Rome when one of its generals returned victorious.[28]

Platina's book *On Lawful Pleasure* (*De Honesta Voluptate*) claims interest at the beginning only in a moderate diet. The book is divided into eight sections: fruit and seasonings, nuts and herbs, salads and meats, poultry, prepared dishes, sweets, eggs and frying. It became a great success, going into many reprints. Dining had already become an art, and a highly complicated one. Montaigne reports a conversation with the steward of a papal diplomat, Cardinal Carafa, the brother of Pope Paul IV:

> He spelled out to me the differences in appetites: the one we have before eating, the one we have after the second and third course; the means, now of simply gratifying it, now of arousing and stimulating it; the organisation of his sauces, first in general, and then particularizing the qualities of the ingredients and their effects; the differences in salads according to the season, which one should be warmed up and which served cold, the way of adorning and embellishing them to make them also pleasant to the sight. After that he entered upon the order of serving, full of beautiful and important considerations.[29]

Drama and scenic tableau began to be intertwined with the feast itself. Catherine de Medici of France became a mistress of the feast as theatre, her festivals taking place out doors and in. Her daughter, Marguerite de Valois, remembers a picnic given by her mother when boats were disguised as whales, hiding the musicians who played inside where once Jonah had been, and horses were dressed as elephants. The feast was served by girls dressed as shepherdesses and afterwards nymphs danced in candlelight.

Some idea of the magnificence of the food and its display in the high Renaissance is given us by Vincenzo Servio in his description of the wedding of the Duke of Mantua in 1581:

> The first service from the Sideboard were large salads decked out with various fantasies such as animals made of citron, castles of turnips, high walls of lemons; and variegated with slices of ham, mullet roes, herrings, tunny,

anchovies, capers, olives, caviar, together with candied flowers and other preserves. Then there were venison patties in the shape of gilded lions, pies in the form of upright black eagles, pasties of pheasant, which seemed alive, white peacocks adorned and re-clothed with their fanned-out tails, and decked with silken ribbons of gold and divers colours, as well as long gilded confections which hung everywhere about the peacocks, which were stood erect as in life, with a perfume emanating from the kindled wad in their beaks and an amorous epigram placed beneath their legs. There were also three large statues in marzipan, each four hands high. One was the Horse of Campidoglio to the life, the second Hercules with the Lion, and the third a Unicorn with its horn in the Dragon's mouth. The table was filled with many other things – jellies, blancmanges in half relief, spiced hard-bake, royal wafers, Milanese biscuits, pine kernels, minced meat, cakes of pistachio nuts, sweet almond twists, flaky pastries, pasta with meat sauce a la Romana, salami, olives, salted tongues, Indian turkey hens stuffed and roasted on the spit, marinated pullets, fresh grapes, strawberries strewn with sugar, wild cherries, and asparagus cooked with butter in various ways.[30]

No wonder Cornaro, a long-lived dietitian from Venice, wrote: 'O wretched and unhappy Italy can you not see that gluttony murders every year more of your inhabitants than you could lose by the most cruel plague or by fire and sword in many battles?'[31] Cornaro wrote several books (he was in his long life a contemporary of Leonardo, born in 1465 and dying in 1566) with such titles as *A Treatise on a Sober Life* and *An Earnest Exhortation to a Sober and Regular Life*, the last published in the ninety-third year of his age. He was a convert to the most moderate form of eating after a youth of indulgence. Born in Venice and belonging to one of the foremost families, he had, he tells us, so impaired his digestion that by the age of thirty-five his days and nights were spent in continual suffering. All the remedies were tried and medicines consumed and then a new medical adviser suggested a change of diet. Cornaro found the new diet unbearable, but every time he lapsed his old ills resurfaced, so unwillingly he kept to a strict regimen of vegetables and water and after one year found himself entirely well. On this diet he became a centenarian and remained in the best of health until the end. He was, however, a dietitian rather than a thinker and humanist, and though he eschewed meat he did not consider the plight of the animals themselves.

## Rediscoveries

The Italian Renaissance marks a time when independent thinking was accompanied by a rejection of ecclesiastical authority. This opposition to the Church was linked with the rediscovery of antiquity, the realisation that people were concerned with ethical ideas, with an analysis of the meaning of life and the realities of good and evil, long before the existence of Christ and the supremacy of the Christian Church. This came as a huge blast of fresh air into the dusty catacombs of Catholicism. The Renaissance still revered authority, but now it tended to be the authority of the ancient scholars and philosophers.

It was not an age renowned for morals. Guicciardini, the historian, wrote in 1529: 'no man is more disgusted than I am with the ambition, the avarice, and the profligacy of the priests, not only because each of these vices is hateful in itself, but because each and all of them are most unbecoming in those who declare themselves to be men in special relations with God.'[32] Humanism, however, was encouraged. Nicholas V (1447–55) gave papal offices to scholars whose learning he respected. His apostolic secretary, Lorenzo Valla, was an Epicurean and accused St Augustine of heresy. Russell points out[33] that the Renaissance broke down the rigid scholastic system which had become an intellectual straitjacket and revived the study of Plato, promoting independent thought as scholars had to choose between him and Aristotle, giving them first-hand knowledge free from the comments of Neoplatonists and Arabic thinkers. The activity of the mind in itself had become a delightful social adventure, in complete contrast to cloistered meditation which had to be kept always within the confines of orthodoxy. Plato had an extraordinary popularity in a world used to Aristotle. The Socratic dialogues were read aloud and debated; Cosimo de Medici died listening to one of the dialogues; but, as we have seen, Plato could not enlighten Renaissance scholars on the rights of animals, for his works avoided the issue.

The observation of the natural world was much strengthened by the popularity of a group of texts attributed to Hermes Trismegistos, translated by a Florentine scholar (Marsilio Ficino) in 1460, which as we shall see were considered to be the source of Greek philosophy. Again the mistaken assumption was made (see p.118) that Greek philosophy, especially the ideas of Plato, stemmed from earlier Jewish thought, as these Hermetic texts (as they were called), which were strongly Gnostic, had many Christian echoes. They were a mixture of the occult, philosophy and theology ascribed to the Egyptian god Thoth, or in Greek, Hermes Trismegistos, meaning Hermes the Thrice-Greatest. He was believed to be the inventor of writing and the patron of all the arts dependent on writing. The texts date from the middle of the first century AD to the end of the third and take the form of the Platonic dialogue, which partly accounted for their popularity. However, what the texts communicated was an amalgam of religion, science and natural history, a view of the world as a web of affinities. They taught that all matter was impregnated with an active spirit through which God worked. The Hermetic writings were, in fact, quite heretical, for they returned to the idea of the celestial trapped within all matter, as Mani's light particles were in flesh. The Hermetic writings stressed that those hidden powers could be tapped, captured and controlled. Humans were conceived of as natural magicians, for they were the key link in the chain of being between matter and spirit. Thus the Hermetic texts taught that through magic and alchemy humans could control the powers of the universe. By studying the Hermetic texts, the lost wisdom of Hermes, the hidden connections between material things, animals and plants could be understood. Giordano Bruno was one man whose thought was much affected by these works.

## Explorations

Giordano Bruno (1548-1600), philosopher, astronomer, mathematician and occultist whose theories anticipated modern science, in his dialogues *Cause, Principle* and *Unity* taught that the world was All in the One, we are all World-Soul, God is both transcendent and manifest in the world and nature. He rejected the traditional geocentric (earth-centred) astronomy, suggesting that the universe was infinite, constituted of innumerable worlds similar to those of the solar system. He went on to add that the Bible should be followed for its moral teaching but not for its astronomical implications. He considered that religion had its uses as a method of governing ignorant people, while philosophy was a discipline of the elect by which they behaved themselves and governed others. He revived the atomism of Epicurus, deriving a doctrine of monads (animate atoms). He was accused of heresy and tried. He defended himself by admitting minor theological errors and tried to emphasise the philosophical character of his beliefs. The trial continued for seven years, ending with Bruno refusing to retract. Pope Clement VIII ordered that he be sentenced as an impenitent and pertinacious heretic. He was brought to the Campo di Fiori, his tongue in a gag, and burned alive – for insisting that humans were worth no more than ants. In the Renaissance his views were anathema to the authorities, but they gained in influence and were eventually to flower in the eighteenth century. Though his emphasis on the magical and the occult are today criticised, many nowadays would find his holistic (as we might call it) views of the universe quite acceptable.

The Hermetic texts seemed to be inspired by ancient wisdom, and for the first time since Porphyry philosophers had to pause and look at animals not as creatures of potential food value, but as entities that could contain fragments of the secrets of the universe. For the first time in a thousand years animals were observed for the life within them, their nature and habits scrutinised not as if they were aliens but as possible fellow inhabitants of the world with potential spiritual values. This was a huge step forward, for the idea seeped into the consciousness of men, and created a Prospero who could conjure spirits from the air, a sorcerer who had power over everything living in his small kingdom. Hermetic writings also revered Pythagoras, but more for his emphasis on numbers as the basis of all truth in nature than for his regard for the sanctity of animals; the Renaissance took up the belief in fundamental mathematical harmonies, which laid a basis for the astronomical work of Copernicus and Kepler.

In such a world we find Paracelsus, the German physician and alchemist: 'Man is a star. Even as he imagines himself to be, such he is. He is what he

imagines . . . Man is a sun and a moon and a heaven filled with stars . . .
Imagination is Creative Power . . .'34

Another German who had tremendous influence on religious and
vegetarian thought was Jacob Behmen (1575-1624). (The name can be spelt
Böhme or Boehme.) His works spawned the movement called Behmenism,
a forerunner of the Theosophists. Behmen was a philosophical mystic who
influenced Idealism and Romanticism. His most famous work, *The Great
Mystery* (1623), attempts to unite Biblical doctrine with Renaissance nature
mysticism. In his last five years he wrote copiously: from 1619 to 1624 he
produced thirty works. He lived through a ferment of ideas: Lutheran
passions, Anabaptism, Paracelsian occultism and humanist ideas, with the
discovery too of Pythagoras and Plutarch and their compassion for animals.
Between 1644 and 1662 all his writings were translated into English. He is
almost impossible to read today, being turgid, deeply obscure and often quite
batty. But Behmen preserved important elements of the Hermetic traditions,
regarding astrology as at least a partial road to the truth.35 He taught that the
fundamental human kinship with the universe was the basis for mystical
union with God. This is the heart of Behmen's non-violence. To kill is to
break and sunder the mystical union. To slaughter animals for food is to build
barriers between the soul and God.

Renaissance technology also paved the way for the age of science. The
invention of printing, gunpowder and the compass radically changed the
world in a way no medieval scholar could have dreamt of. Printing spread
knowledge and ideas far beyond the limited medieval circles of university
and Church. The compass made it possible to discover new territories and
gunpowder to conquer them. The exploration of the world revealed, among
many other bizarre and varied discoveries, animals, birds and fish of
astonishing beauty and originality – new creatures to kill and eat, yet they
were also, simply because of their newness, studied with some awe as an even
more remarkable aspect of the magical world. It is interesting to note that
the first discoveries were named after the birds, those brightly coloured
feathered creatures fluttering amongst dense foliage, chattering and
shrieking, or circling about the small ships in silent majesty: not only the
Canary Islands, but the Azores (from the Portuguese *açôres* – hawks), while
Brazil's nickname was 'parrotland'.

When Christopher Columbus' expedition began to explore and discover
other civilisations, some customs impressed them. The Aztecs kept vast
storehouses of grain saved for the years of bad harvest, when corn could be
distributed to the hungry. In Peru, too, there were no beggars – everyone
worked and everyone ate. In Europe starvation was a fact of life, the winter
a season of cold, illness and death, while the years of famine had not much
eased since the Middle Ages.

Did the relationship between animal and native American influence the
Europeans? They prayed for the spirit of the animal before hunting and
killing it; the spirits of the dead wandered in animal disguises; the animals

were gods themselves,★ or were thought to be equal to humans, and human flesh was eaten more readily than that of the animals themselves. This simplifies the beliefs and practices of diverse tribes and civilisations, but something of these attitudes was present throughout the continent, north and south, a feeling that the native Americans *shared* their world with other creatures rather than just subjugating them. This must have struck the Europeans as merely one more alien facet of the New World, a curiosity and nothing more.

Though the writers of antiquity had been rediscovered, the discoveries in the Americas were now to prove that some of the most distinguished were wrong or plainly inadequate. Pliny's *Natural History* comprised thirty-seven books but none mentioned the llama. Aristotle had said that the equator was so hot life could not possibly survive there. Joseph de Acosta, in 1570, crossed directly under the sun on his way to America and wrote: 'what else could I do then but laugh at Aristotle's Meteors and his philosophy . . .?'[36] The explorers brought a new world of discoveries back to Europe which contradicted not only the pagan thinkers of antiquity but Genesis itself. How, for example, could Noah have saved the llama from the Flood when he did not know of its existence? If Eden and Mount Ararat were both in Asia, how could the Americas be crammed with people and animals? It was all very bewildering.

Nor did it seem to the invaders that their staple food, meat, was eaten much at all. There were few large mammals which could be slaughtered, so instead the natives ate insects, which much revolted the Europeans: 'Large fat spiders, white worms that breed in rotten wood and other decayed objects.'[37] They also found that a large haunch roasting over a fire was likely to be part of a human being, for the Carib Indians ate their enemies after they had been killed in battle. The Caribs were as skilled in their butchering as any master butcher in a European city: 'guts and limbs [were] eaten, and the rest salted and dried like our hams.'[38] When the Spanish conquered Mexico they found that the Aztec civilisation rested on ceremonial cannibalism'[39] which horrified and nauseated them – nothing to the Europeans could have seemed more godless and diabolic, and the practice made their own habit of eating meat just from selected animals even more virtuous. To the Europeans, their choice of meat was the very definition of civilisation; hence the native Americans' choice was its very opposite.

Gunpowder was the technical means of subjugation and would hasten the oppression of those native people, whose ideas on meat-eating and the

---

★Examples are too numerous and too diverse to list in detail. The Kwakintl tribe believed that it was possible to identify with a particular beast, bird or fish and to be that creature in human disguise, shedding the human form at night and becoming the creature, or after death returning as a human with that creature's secrets, wisdom and power. This is, of course, another form of metempsychosis. It did not entail, here, an ideology of non-violence to those creatures. They could be killed and eaten in accordance with ritual.

animal kingdom were so different. Countless thousands of natives died from European diseases, for more than just food and seeds were transplanted from the Old World to the New. Gunpowder was not the only scientific discovery taken to the Americas. That hermetic world which believed the spirit or celestial soul to be locked up in matter would soon be subjected to the scrutiny of science. For during the Renaissance germinated the first seeds of that new scientific age which would delay in an unexpectedly cruel fashion the recognition of the rights of the animal kingdom. Copernican theory was published in 1543 though not much noticed until Kepler and Galileo improved on it in the following century, but the first intimation that science might be valued and fostered by militant regimes, who would disregard the lives of people and animals, was to be found in the government employment of Leonardo and later Galileo. Their work on war machines and the art of fortification would begin the long journey of scientists in government bondage.

# 9

# The Clockwork Universe

At the beginning of the seventeenth century science began to incorporate within it new ideas of the importance of humankind. There was a growing belief in the enormous capacity of human ingenuity to understand and investigate the natural world. It was felt that humankind was capable of achieving dominion over the forces of nature and that the study of God's world was somehow complementary to the study of the Bible. The Christian religion in no way took a secondary role, but became a partner with science in fostering the belief that an understanding of nature was crucial to human destiny.

## Cartesianism

One of the great debates was whether animals were possessed of souls or not. Descartes, the father of modern philosophy, nailed his wife's pet dog by its four paws to a board and dissected the creature while it was alive. This became common practice at, for example, the Royal Society in London, where all manner of live creatures were pinned down, flayed and dissected. Students examined the workings of the organs and the circulation of the blood, while the creature struggled to survive. Pepys wrote: 'and we to Gresham College, where we saw some experiments upon a hen, a dog and a cat ...'[1]* These flayed bodies seemed to the vivisectionists and to Descartes, whose theory it was, to be like the mechanism of a watch or clock with wheels, ratchets, springs, gears and weights, greater by far in intricacy of design and invention than anything humans could ever dream up, for these bodies were made by the hand of God.

As Descartes was dissecting a calf he is said to have pointed and remarked: 'Here is my library.'[2] If animals had souls, where were they? Indeed, where was the human soul and how did it combine with the body? Descartes considered that body and soul were both separate and interactive; each had its particular attributes but there must also be a site where both soul and body united to influence one another. Descartes decided the pineal gland was where the soul animated the body. The pineal is an endocrine gland found in vertebrate animals. Its apparent function, it is now understood, is to

---

*The animals were given a decoction of tobacco to see whether it produced paralysis.

be a light receptor and to control the hormone melatonin, which produces brown or black skins. Descartes saw it in a positively lyrical light for it danced and jigged like a balloon captive above a fire,[3] yet it was capable in humans – but not in animals – of observations and perceptions which were consistent with wisdom. The functions of the soul were, Descartes claimed, volition, cognition and reason, while the body was simply a highly complex machine. This doctrine of beast equals machine took hold. Animals were not only inferior according to the Bible but now they had been proved to be inferior by science too.

Descartes's explanations were based upon vivisection. But he was ingenious when he came to explain the volition of animals (they were, of course, without cognition and reason). He suggested the idea of 'animal spirits' which drove the animal machine, gases which flowed through the nerves and moved the muscles.

Descartes maintained that animals, even the highest, had nothing at all in common with humankind. He based his argument on the faculty of speech, citing the fact that, though some animals could imitate human sounds, none could use sounds as a symbol to communicate thought. This does not merely prove that animals have less intelligence than human beings, he argued, but that they have none at all, marvellously contrived automatons though they are. Nevertheless, Descartes's work, which described a mechanical view of nature – the clockwork universe – was a rational attack upon the Renaissance Hermetic view and eventually swept it almost entirely away. Descartes claimed that reality is composed of two substances: matter, characterised by its spatial extension, and spirit, a substance characterised by its thinking powers. Animals were without the latter, so they were purely mechanical things, no different from a clock with its wheels and weights. Although clocks are able to keep time accurately, this is strictly a mechanical function and not a sign of intelligence. So too do animals have their capabilities, but so too are they mechanical and not intelligent.

By far the wittiest reaction to Descartes was that of Fontenelle,★ who pointed out that when the male dog machine mounted the female dog machine the result would be a third little machine, something that two watches fail to achieve. Fontenelle's Countess comments on this new universe:

'I perceive', said the Countess, 'Philosophy is now become very Mechanical.' 'So mechanical', said I, 'that I fear we shall quickly be asham'd of it; they will have the World to be in great, what a watch is in little; which is very regular, and depends only upon the just disposing of the several parts of the movement. But pray tell me, Madam, had you not formerly a more sublime idea of the Universe?'[4]

---

★Bernard le Bovier, sieur de Fontenelle (1657–1757), writer and scientist. In his *History of the Oracles* (1687) he subjected pagan religions to criticisms that the reader would inevitably see as applicable to Christianity.

Isaac Newton's theories on universal gravitation did nothing to weaken the concept of the mechanical universe. Quite the opposite: it seemed that Newton's authority was squarely behind the view of the cosmos as a vast mathematical system whose regular motions accorded with mechanical principles on which human beings were puny and almost irrelevant spectators: 'In Newton, the Cartesian metaphysics . . . finally overthrew Aristotelianism and became the predominant world-view.'[5]

The mechanistic view was challenged by Gassendi (1592–1655), who attacked Descartes in his *Meditations*. The book says little about the relationship between humankind and animals, but Gassendi showed that physical functions and reactions in animals are closely bound up with their emotions. He ridiculed the use of speech as a criterion for determining an animal's intelligence, saying that animals have their own ways of communicating with each other. In a letter to a friend, Van Helmont, who argued that humans were formed expressly as carnivores, Gassendi counters with the argument that, on the evidence of their teeth, they must have been herbivores:

> That from the conformation of our teeth we do not appear to be adapted by Nature to the use of a flesh diet, since all animals (I spoke of terrestrials) which Nature has formed to feed on flesh have their teeth long, conical, sharp, uneven, and with intervals between them – of which kind are lions, tigers, wolves, dogs, cats, and others. But those who are made to subsist only on herbs and fruits have their teeth short, broad, blunt, close to one another, and distributed in even rows. Of this sort are horses, cows, deer, sheep, goats, and some others. And further – that men have received from Nature teeth which are unlike those of the first class, and resemble those of the second. It is therefore probable, since men are land animals, that Nature intended them to follow, in the selection of their food, not the carnivorous tribes, but those races of animals which are contented with the simple productions of the earth . . . Wherefore, I here repeat that from the primaeval institution of our nature, the teeth were destined to the mastication, not of flesh, but of fruits.[6]

Gassendi goes on to quote Plutarch (see p.98) on why humans do not kill their prey with their own teeth and claws and ends by saying that we are not furnished for hunting, much less for eating other animals:

> In one word, we seem to be admirably admonished by Cicero that man was destined for other things than for seizing and cutting the throats of other animals. If you answer that 'that may be said to be an industry ordered by Nature, by which such weapons are invented', then, behold! it is by the very same artificial instrument that men make weapons for mutual slaughter. Do they do this at the instigation of Nature? Can a use so noxious be called natural? Faculty is given by Nature, but it is our own fault that we make a perverse use of it.[7]

In *Ethics* he sums up his thoughts upon the subject:

> There is no pretence for saying that any right has been granted us by law to
> kill any of those animals which are not destructive or pernicious to the
> human race, for there is no reason why the innocent species should be
> allowed to increase to so great a number as to be inconvenient to us. They
> may be restrained within that number which would be harmless, and useful
> to ourselves.[8]

Gassendi was not alone in his dislike of the Cartesian view. Spinoza found it
too chilling, and though he conceded that animals do not have the same
nature as us, he had no doubt that they have emotions. Their feelings are, of
course, different, Spinoza declares, but nevertheless they are feelings.

## More Dissidents

In England the vegetarian ethic seemed to have suddenly flowered and it
was to continue to grow until the present day. The seventeenth century was
a time for radical ideas. Religious faith was an area for dispute and sects
began to proliferate: the Ranters, Judaists, and later the Southcottians and
Swedenborgians. They all abstained from animal food. There was a general
change in how people thought of animals. Moral objections began to
appear as people found they had a distaste for the subjugation and
exploitation of animals: 'as the threat from wild beasts receded, so man's
right to eliminate wild creatures from whom he had nothing to fear was
increasingly disputed.'[9]

As the New World had been discovered and Western societies learned of
other alien native cultures, it was gradually understood that the savage might
be human too, if once converted to Christianity. The savage became, though
somehow still inferior, undeniably part of the human race. Pocahontas, an
American Indian princess, married an Englishman, bore a son and died at
Gravesend in 1617. Fifty years later the phrase 'noble savage' first appeared,
in a play by Dryden, *The Conquest of Granada*.

> 'Obeyed as sovereign by thy subjects be,
> But know, that I alone am king of me.
> I am as free as nature first made man,
> 'Ere the base laws of servitude began,
> When wild in woods the noble savage ran.'

It was not such a huge leap for Christian Europe to go from considering the
savage to considering the beast. In their natural state, it was thought, there
was little difference between them, so if a savage could be noble it stood to
reason that a beast could be too. But once you admitted that this potential
existed, it was inevitable that you must treat the animal with kindness and
concern. How then could you kill it for its meat?

Before and during the English Civil War there was a revival of the 'free spirit', last seen in medieval Europe. Its adherents showed the same self-exaltation and self-deification, a dislike of private property and the desire to abolish it, and that curious mixture of asceticism and sexuality that one finds in some of the early Gnostic sects and continuing throughout all the heresies. Called Ranters after their habit of spouting non-stop all the time, they mixed piety and blasphemy, according to George Fox, the founder of the Quakers, who visited some in prison in Coventry in 1649. At least one of them, John Robins, together with his disciples, made it his practice to abstain from meat and drink, while another, Jacob Bottomley, wrote: 'I see God is in all creatures, man and beast, fish and fowl and every green thing from the highest cedar to the ivy on the wall; and that God is the life and being of them all.'[10] This, in fact, was the Neoplatonic pantheism of the free spirit. Another Ranter, Aliezor Coppe, wrote of God that he is 'in Heaven, Earth, Sea, Hell . . . filleth all things, all places . . . is All in All'.[11] It is difficult to find among the Ranters any consistent teaching against the eating of meat. Some refused for the reasons we have now become familiar with, that God lived in those creatures as vividly as he did in ourselves, while others ate meat and drank ale and wine as part of a sensual celebration of life itself. Coppe was one of the Ranters that Fox met in prison and he was certainly one of the Ranters who brought the movement into disrepute. How could such a man gather so many followers, asked one of them, Richard Baxter, 'men and women professing the zealous fear of God', brought near to God by 'revelling, roaring, drinking, whoring, open full-mouthed swearing ordinarily by the wounds and blood of God, and the fearfullest cursing that hath been heard'?[12]

## Thomas Tryon

The most pure and ardent vegetarian of this time was Thomas Tryon (1634–1703). Thomas Tryon's life straddles a curiously vital part of British history, and much of what occurred within his life span is pertinent to the way our society works today. He was born in 1634, a few years after Charles I dissolved Parliament. The dissolution sprang out of the monarch's belief in his Divine Right. Tryon died in 1703, one year after Queen Anne had ascended the throne and fifteen years after the 1688 Glorious Revolution, which allowed a Parliament to be formed independent of the monarch. So Tryon's formative adolescent years were spent in a republic, ruled by rigorous ascetic beliefs, while he was twenty-six when the Restoration occurred, a period notorious for its amorality and licentiousness.

The seventeenth century is crucial to the understanding of our own century, and Thomas Tryon seems to me important because he is not only a product of it, but also a severe critic of much of the emerging characteristics which identify that century. Tryon remains the only voluble ascetic, celebrating the foods of asceticism, in a long tradition which links the ancient world with our own contemporary concerns. Yet Tryon is also very much a product of Cromwell's Republic: he is self-educated, rising from the rural working class to become an author of fifteen books, many of them going into second and third editions in his lifetime; these works influenced luminaries of succeeding centuries like Benjamin Franklin, Joseph Ritson and Shelley. Indeed, he influenced his own contemporaries too, like Aphra Benn the playwright, and her circle.

He was born in a small village, Bilbury, near Cirencester. His father, William, was a tiler and he was sent to the village school, but he barely learnt to read when his father in 1643 put him to work spinning and carding. As this was the time of the Civil War and the Puritans were at that time losing the struggle, it must have seemed a time of great uncertainty; no doubt his father found the boy the first job he could get which earnt two shillings a week. The war ended in 1646 with the Puritans victorious. Thomas was eleven and he became a shepherd tending a small flock of sheep. But he longed to travel, so in 1652 having sold his three sheep for the sum of three pounds he trudged to London and became apprenticed to a hatter in Bridewell Dock, Fleet Street. Soon after, following his master's example, he became an Anabaptist, working overtime in order to buy books. Through endless reading he educated himself, studying in particular astrology and medicine. In 1657, influenced by the mystical works of Behmen, he broke with the Anabaptists and became a Pythagorean – he was twenty-three. In becoming a Behmen he was joining a lively, radical but intensely pious tradition which in its unorthodoxy shocked and frightened the majority. But Tryon joined this faith just a few years before the Restoration; such faiths were not only already unpopular they were now heartily detested.

The seventeenth century saw the change from a largely agricultural society, where both men and women were labourers, to a mercantile society where feudalism finely died and the *petit-bourgeoisie* grew in its stead. Tryon starts off as a shepherd and ends up as a member of the bourgeoisie. He has become part of this brave new world where the market ruled, for it 'depended on the spread of a new personality type, one able to control animal urges and to delay the satisfaction of present wants for future gains one governed by internal constraints . . .'[13] It was a society where the parvenu first appeared in any appreciable number* and made a huge splash within society, where fortunes were made by speculation on the soaring markets of the East Indian trade. Like Sir Josiah Child who rose from a merchant's apprentice to the management of the East India Company's Stock and was worth, according to John Evelyn, £200,000. Evelyn wrote of visiting his gardens constructed in a barren spot in Epping Forest where planting walnut trees and making fishponds many miles in circuit had cost a prodigious amount.[14]

But the less successful members of society knew now that there was also

---

*Continuing to appear in ever greater numbers throughout the next three centuries until they became commonplace.

a faint possibility of them becoming rich beyond their wildest dreams. This new society of middle-class people redefined the gender roles and that of the family itself. They put a high premium upon self-discipline, hard work and frugality, ('I betook myself to water only for drink, and forbore eating any kind of flesh, confining myself to an abstemious self-denying life. My drink was only water, and food only bread and some fruit.'15) for class, for the first time, was now fluid and by these means a person could rise in the world, as Tryon was doing to positions of power, wealth and authority. And if not quite that, at least to owning a handsome new house and being able to commission a portrait of the family to adorn it.

Men went out into the world to trade and make their fortunes, while the women stayed at home and became the living symbol of the husband's wealth and position. The end of the seventeenth century saw the first stirrings in the birth of capitalism which turned the male into a competitive animal. Also, a copulating one within the confines of marriage.* The burgeoning population tended to be crowded into urban centres which grew into a seething morass of human hunger and desire, in Defoe's phrase, 'the miserable that really pinch and suffer want.'16 It is a century of extremes, of science, reasoning and new discoveries, the beginning of agricultural technology and the growth of cities and the first official fire engines, an age where the first English settlement in India began and the new Cathedral of St Paul's was built, an age which saw the Societies for the Reformation of Manners, which wanted to banish prostitutes from the streets and make it illegal for a man to eat a mutton pie on the Sabbath, where Congreve's *Double Dealer* and Farquhar's *Beaux' Stratagem* were staged and Jeremy Collier's *Short View of the Immorality and Profaneness of the English Stage* was eagerly read. It is an age which created the Bank of England and the coffee house, where tea and chocolate were also first drunk, where Hawkesmoor built elegant churches and Queen Mary collected blue and white Delft china. In the year of the Restoration one of the first Ice Houses was built in St James Park where summer drinks were kept and sold from a stall.

There was a new emphasis on sexuality within the marriage, which Puritanism had spawned. It came particularly from Calvin who said that sexual expression between man and wife need not only be for procreation, it could also be part of the love which bound the marriage. This was revolutionary, before sex for pleasure had tended to occur outside the marriage. But the age of marriage was still late, around 28 for men and 26 for women between the years 1600 and 1850. Tryon married Susannah, 'a sober young woman' whom he did not succeed in converting to his 'innocent way of living'17 in 1661 when he was twenty-seven. The celibacy

---

*There is an astonishing rise in the population of England from 4.9 million in 1680 to 11.5 million in 1820. Between 1791 and 1831 (the core years of the Industrial Revolution) it grew 72% from 7.7 million to 13.28 million, the fastest rate of increase anywhere in Western Europe. Life expectancy at birth increased by 6 years from about 32 in the 1670's to 39 in the 1810's. Fertility rose 2.5 times greater than mortality.

rate declined from 25% in 1641 to 10% in 1690. The beginnings of the Industrial Revolution meant a little more money for the lower classes, which meant savings could be put aside and commitment to marriage made.

The end of the seventeenth century also marks the beginnings of a new social obsession which would become a great driving force in the commerce of the new Industrial age about to dawn in the following century – that of social emulation. Or keeping up with the Joneses. With the onset of the new *petit-bourgeoisie* eager to rise we have a social structure which is all eyes upon everybody else, ever watchful for new styles and modes, for the details of public display. By the eighteenth century everyone had a money income and was prepared to spend it on the details of social emulation. 'Social imitation and emulating spending penetrating deeper than ever before through the closely packed ranks of eighteenth century society.'[18] A huge increase in small rural factories which produced non-essential goods ocurred at this time, toys, pins, lace, glasses, cards, puppets and toothpicks. The class that bought were neither the poor or the rich, they were the middle-income market, the artisans, tradesmen, the engineers and clerks; exactly Tryon's social stratum when he was an apprentice and newly married. The textile industries began to flourish, turning out cottons, woollens, linens and silks. Crockery in new designs poured out of Staffordshire potteries. Birmingham factories produced buckles, buttons and brooches. All this to bedeck the female who was in search of a partner and the resulting family. This fusion between sexual needs and the beginnings of capitalism marks the age in a most striking manner. But what placed an idealistic gloss upon the biological need was also completely new. Publishers were booming, women's journals, stories and novels were being read and they all had one theme – romantic love.

It had now become fashionable to marry for love. Before marriages had been planned by the parents and the suitability of partners was worked out strategically, for land, property and class. And though these issues still had great power to persuade and occupy the concerns of parents, the younger generations themselves were obsessed with the concept of 'falling in love'. So we must accept that Tom Tryon and Susannah married for love and settled down in the London of the Restoration, Charles II had returned the year before and almost at once the Republic that had moulded the young shepherd vanished into the shadows of society and became a butt for jokes and caricatures in the new drama. How this new society must have dazzled Tryon where lewdness was flouted as flagrantly as the new money that stemmed from trade. One can well understand his vision of a hard-working, restrained and dedicated society, fuelled by self-sacrifice, becoming strengthened by the excesses of the Restoration.

Yet undoubtedly, Tryon was caught up into it too, for the relationship between sex and capitalism had a spin-off, and it was the connection between consumerism and the family.* All the new goods and clothes were

---

*He was a Hatter after all and dealt in beaver skins. In his mind he must have known that he made a living out of the slaughter of that animal.

bought, worn and used, firstly, to beguile and attract sexually, the end result being marriage and a family. Because secondly, society placed enormous significance upon the family as an effective system which consumed. Hume wrote in order to govern men they must be fuelled and animated 'with the spirit of avarice.' And later, 'people work harder to consume more.'[19] More clothes and objects were used to raise the status of the family, to emphasize its attraction and place in society. Consumerism was the new machine which activated the whole of society, Bernard de Mandeville (1670-1733) in his *The Fable of the Bees* argued that if pride and luxury were banished, goodly numbers of artisans would starve within half a year. 'The idea of man as a consuming animal with boundless appetites, capable of driving the economy to new levels of prosperity, arrived with the economic literature of the 1690's.'[20]

But what of food and man's appetite for that, was this boundless too? If we look at a writer like Gervase Markham (whose book *The English Housewife,* though he died in 1637, went on being printed after his death) one gets a picture of what was thought to be a suitable meal for the middle classes, who were furiously emulating their gentry. Markham refers to a 'humble feast' of thirty-two dishes which 'is as much as can conveniently stand on one table.' There are sixteen items of meat, a brawn with mustard, three boiled capons, boiled beef, a chine of roasted beef, a neat's* tongue, a roast pig, goose, swan and turkey, a haunch of venison, a venison pasty and a kid with a pudding in its belly. There were also side dishes, an olive pie, a custard, salads and fricasses. A simple fricasses contained fried eggs, collops of bacon, ling†, beef and young pork. While a compound fricasses described as 'Things of Request and Estimation in France, Spain, Italy and the most Curious Nations,' contained all that as well as Tansies, scrambled egg made with cream and the juices of wheat blades, violet and strawberry leaves, spinach and walnut tree buds, with grated bread, cinnamon, nutmeg and salt, sprinkled with sugar. The meal finished with a marrow-bone pie, made by alternating layers of jerusalem artichokes, currants, dates, sliced sweet potato, candied eringo roots and marrow, spiced with sugar.

Young Tryon could never have eaten such a meal, it was far out of his class, but he must have read the book (Markham was a well-known and famous author) for he was soon to write cookery books himself. What would have struck him most forcefully, I believe, was a sense of staggering waste. Though all of the uneaten food left at table was eaten by the servants and any over would then have been given to the beggars waiting around the kitchens outside. For in the one hundred years up to Tryon's birth the price of food rose by 120% without any corresponding increase in wages. As an infant and growing lad, food must have been scarce and because of the Civil War, possibly infrequent, for the only meat usually eaten by farm labourers

*A cow, ox or calf.
†*Molva Molva,*a long fish rarely distinguished from cod, and like cod generally salted.

– poultry – became expensive and sought after as a luxury food. Pepys writes in 1661 that, 'At night my wife and I had a good supper by ourselves of a pullet which pleased me much to see my condition come to allow a dish like that.' His condition then was £600 a year. In 1665 Pepys gave a dinner for nine friends to celebrate the anniversary of 'being cut for the stone'* in which he served a fricassee of rabbits and chickens, a leg of boiled mutton. three carps in a dish, a side of lamb, a dish of roasted pigeons, four lobsters, three tarts and a lamprey pie.

London was a frenetic centre of trade and commerce, with animals being driven through the streets to supply the carcasses for such feasts. Every time Tryon walked out of his door he would have passed the butchers and the slaughtering premises at the back of the shops, heard the cries of frightened animals and smelt the spilt blood. He would also have passed the Cook Shops where 'four spits, one over another, carry round each five or six pieces of Butcher's Meat, Beef, Mutton, Veal, Pork and Lamb; you have what quantity you please cut off, fat, lean, much or little done; with this, a little Salt and Mustard upon the Side of a plate, a bottle of beer and a Roll; and there is your whole feast.' So reported a French visitor.[21]

Tryon could not be aware of the great events of the day or not hear the details of such things as the royal banquets. In 1679 the corporation of Edinburgh welcomed the King's brother, James, the Duke of York with a feast which among the usual amounts of beef, mutton, ducks, hens and rabbits, included large decorated pies. A large gilded turkey pie the colour of rubies. A lamb's pie 'à la mode' also gilded with a gold fringe, a shrimp pie in vermilion colour and three gilded trotter pies. It is not surprising, considering the amount people ate that in most cookery books there were recipes for Surfeit water, concocted especially for the digestion. One contained aniseed water, poppy flowers, 'lickorices' saffron, figs, raisins and a handful of marigold flowers.

People felt equivocal about vegetables. They did not appear in the royal banquets, except as an ingredient in a meat dish or as a flavouring in a soup or sauce; they were thought to be food for the poor as country people grew them. Yet as towns grew so did market gardens sited just outside, every large town had its belt of gardens which supplied the markets with vegetables and fruit. Tryon would have seen and noted with satisfaction that the towns now had a supply of vegetables, which when he was a boy would only have been available in the country. London had market gardens at Lewisham, Blackheath, Wanstead and Ilford.† But the standard of cooking vegetables was no better than when Castelvetro had written about the subject some eighty years before. The same French visitor complained that when they boiled beef

---

*Pepys was operated on to extract a gallstone on March 26th, 1658 and he kept the day as a festival each year where his stone was passed around at dinner. Stones were a common affliction, possibly caused by a high incidence of calcium and a deficiency of Vitamin A in the diet.
†A vegetable market at Liverpool grew up because of an influx of French Canadians who wanted cheap vegetables for their soups.

they 'besieged it with five or six heaps of cabbage, carrots, turnips or some herbs or roots well salted and swimming in butter.' The English he thought were not 'delicately served.'[22]

Given all this one is not surprised to find Tryon rather gloomily having to accept that society cannot be converted to a vegetable diet. Yet constantly in all his books he recommends it as the only healthy manner of eating. He was born in the country, he knew the farm labouring poor intimately for they were his family which he had left behind him. So what did they eat? Certainly not the prodigious amounts of meat consumed by the rich. It was only at the end of the century that farmers began to experiment with feeding their cattle throughout the winter with root vegetables and cakes made out of rape seed after the oil had been pressed for domestic lighting. In the winter the wealthy ate game, including much venison. The poor made do with powdered beef, meat preserved by powdering with dry salt, which was described as 'tough, hard, heavy and of ill nourishment, requiring rather the stomach of another Hercules (who is said to have fed chiefly of Bulls flesh) then of any ordinary and common ploughman.'[23] The poor ate bread, fish, beans, cheese, a little bacon and what they could trap or snare. 'Husbandmen and such as labour can eat fat bacon, salt gross meat, hard cheese . . . coarse bread at all times, go to bed and labour upon a full stomach, which to some idle persons would be present death.'[24]

Tryon knew that the cottage gardens were a source of a supply of vegetables to these hungry people. He had learnt as a boy to value them as good food, seeing his mother prepare and cook with them. But he also knew that once people moved away from the soil they immediately affected a snobbism. English maids when they went to France stuck their noses up at eating the vegetables which all the French maids loved. So Sir Ralph Verney writes in his Memoirs.[25] Tryon must also have been aware that once those self-same farm labourers enlisted in the army or navy their diet would be notable for a complete abstinence of vegetables. Though they would be fed with beef, bacon, fish, butter, cheese, vinegar, bread and beer and have pepper, sugar, nutmeg and ginger to flavour their food, their diet would be totally deficient, we now know, in Vitamin C.

Hardly surprising then that Gideon Harvey, physician to Charles II, called scurvy the Disease of London.[26] Gerard had graphically described the symptoms some fifty years before. The gums are loose, swollen and ulcerous, the mouth stinking, thighs and legs full of blue spots, the feet swollen and the face pale. Gerard recommended garden cresses as being good against the disease. William Cockburn, physician to the Fleet at the end of the century, believed scurvy was caused by an over indulgence in salt foods. There is a terrible story of some ships in 1695 being moored in Torbay for a month, during which time the men had not been allowed to land. Cockburn urged the Commander, Lord Berkeley, to put the sick men ashore, but Berkeley claimed that if he did they would all desert. But the men became so ill that they were finally numbering a hundred gaunt skeletons, scarcely able to move. These men were rowed to land where they were able to get carrots and turnips and 'other Green Trade'. Within a week they were crawling about and soon all but two or three were fit to return to duty.[27]

Scurvy was almost unknown in France, an outbreak in Paris in 1699 caused much concern, which shows the protection the French maids were acquiring in eating up their green salads. It was not that the antidote to scurvy was not known, for when a person succumbed they were given either oranges, lemons, scurvy grass★, parsley, chervil, lettuce, rocket or strawberries. They were simply not thought of as part of a necessary preventive diet, though all were thought to cure loose teeth and heal spongy foul gums. There were infusions of barley and lemon rind or scurvy grass ale. This last was made up of one pint of the juice of scurvy grass, watercress and succory (chicory) mixed with one gallon of ale. It was mostly drunk in the early spring when the symptoms of scurvy would have been at their worst.

So when Tryon first started to write in his 48th year his books were full of advice for healthy eating.[28] He recommended a vegetable diet and abstinence from tobacco and alcohol. He also wrote on the benefits of clean sweet beds, the cure of bed bugs, and toothache, on the excellency of herbs, how to make all people rich, he pleaded for the humane treatment of black slaves and a new method of how to educate children. Even a tract upon the evils of war, and in particular, religious war, a dialogue which one writer thought was 'worthy of the most trenchant of the humanitarian writers of the next century.'[29] All this was interspersed with much mystical philosophy. He described his objects in writing as 'to recommend to the world temperance, cleanness and innocency of living . . . to give his readers Wisdom's Bill of Fare . . . and at the same time to write down several mysteries concerning God and his government.'[30]

Though a Pythagorean from the age of twenty-three, his wife, as we have seen, refused to be converted and so meals at home must still have had meat in them for the rest of the family. There is something definitely testy often in his remarks, an asperity that creeps in not unlike George Bernard Shaw. 'Though I have before shown the inconveniences of the feeding upon flesh (so commonly and in such excess as is nowadays practised) and rather recommended the lovers of wisdom and health to more innocent use of grains, fruits and herbs, yet since there is no stemming the tide of popular opinion and custom, and people will still gorge themselves with the flesh of their fellow animals, I have thought fit here to give a particular account of each sort of flesh, that at least you may choose that which is most proper for your constitution and least prejudicial to your health.'[31] He goes on to give advice on various meats and the best way of cooking them. For example: 'There are various sorts of fowls, most of which men eat, some

---

★*Cochlearia officinalis*, part of the *Cruciferae* family, abundant on the shores of Scotland. A small, low-growing plant with thick, fleshy, glabrous, egg-shaped leaves. (Hence other name – spoonwort.)

wild, others tame, of the two the wild are the more wholesome for food, their nature is more airy and cleaner and of a dryer substance, affording a better and firmer nourishment.'[32]

Much of his advice has a contemporary ring to it. 'All kind of melted butter and fried food, be they what they will, are hurtful to the health of all people.' Butter was only eaten by the poor, but the rich cooked in great amounts of it. 'Fatness is very comely in Men and Women when it doth not exceed the medium, nor proceed from Idleness and intemperance in Meats and Drinks . . .'[33] It would be another thirty years before obesity reached a zenith in society.

Tryon is against sugary foods and thinks they are especially bad for children. Though advocating temperance he also writes a book on the *New Art of Brewing Beer, Ale and other sorts of Liquors* which went into three editions in the same year – 1691. The Wine Act of 1688 had imposed a heavy tax on wines from France giving a stimulus to home brewing. A crop of books and pamphlets appeared at that time with instructions on how to make wine from vinegar, clary juice, pippin cider and blackberry water. Tryon's more reliable work must have seemed a blessing.

Tryon in advocating ascetism and self-discipline in diet and life was only in fact reflecting the hard-work ethic which had imbued the new mercantile middle-class, but he took it one or two steps further into forms of dietary self-abstinence which they would find it hard to countenance. What is also interesting is that Tryon was not in the least hidebound by the zealous forms of Christianity which he must have immersed in as a child. He would eulogise the milder manners of the followers of Pythagoras or of the Hindus* and condemn the violence of Christians. '. . . far greater advantages would come to pass amongst Christians, if they would cease from contention, oppression, and (what tends and disposes them thereunto) the killing of other animals, and eating their flesh and blood . . .'

Tryon's main contribution to the history of food was to revive the metaphysical concepts of the pre-Socratics, that all living matter contains the divine spirit; then to apply it to daily life, though ironically his own business contradicted such a personal belief – an inconsistency which endears itself to me. Yet his proseltysing for the vegetable diet was an astonishingly brave commitment to make within his age. He made his mark and was to influence not only those writers mentioned above but also Lewis Gompertz, the founder of the RSPCA. What Tryon did was to keep the Pythagorean ethic alive in a society alienated by it.

Tryon's influence extended in the next century to Joseph Ritson in 1802, in his essay on 'Abstinence from Animal Food', and thence to Shelley. Tryon

---

*They were rapidly becoming a popular example among philosophers. Voltaire was to praise them in the following century both in essays and novels.

wrote copiously, publishing many books,* some of them useful manuals for the house; like many a radical vegetarian before him he valued women: 'the whole preservation of men's health and strength does chiefly reside in the wisdom and temperance of women.'[34] His range was wide: *Friendly Advice to Gentlemen Planters of East and West Indies* is an enlightened plea for more humane treatment of negro slaves. He also wrote recipe books: *Bill of Fare of Seventy-Five Noble Dishes of Excellent Food*, published in 1691, has to be one of the very first vegetarian cookery books. He wrote on education, on economics, a handbook on how to save money – showing how a man may live plentifully on two pence a day – and a guide to the true worship of God. Beneath all this industry was a fund of solid good sense: 'Most men will, in words, confess that there is no blessing this world affords comparable to health. Yet rarely do any of them value it as they ought to do till they feel the want of it.'[35] How contemporary this seems. 'Now, the sorts of foods and drinks that breed the best blood and finest spirits are herbs, fruits and various kinds of grains . . . so likewise oil is an excellent thing of nature, more sublime and pure than butter . . .'[36]

Tryon's strong distaste for meat is illustrated in this passage:

It is a grand mistake of people in this age to say or suppose: That Flesh affords not only a stronger nourishment, but also more and better than Herbs, Grains, etc.; for the truth is, it does yield more stimulation, but not of so firm a substance, nor so good as that which proceeds from the other food; for flesh has more matter for corruption, and nothing so soon turns to putrefaction. Now, 'tis certain, such sorts of food as are subject to putrify before they are eaten, are also liable to the same afterwards. Besides, Flesh is of soft, moist, gross, phlegmy quality, and generates a nourishment of a like nature; thirdly, Flesh heats the body, and causeth a drought; fourthly, Flesh does breed great store of noxious humours; fifthly, it must be considered that 'beasts' and other living creatures are subject to diseases and many other inconveniences, and uncleannesses, Surfeits, over-driving, abuses of cruel butchers, etc., which renders their flesh still more unwholesome. But on the contrary, all sorts of dry foods, as Bread, Cheese, Herbs, and many preparations of Milk, Pulses, Grains, and Fruits; as their original is more clean, so, being of a sound firm nature, they afford a more excellent nourishment, and more easy of concoction; so that if a man should exceed in quantity, the Health will not, thereby, be brought into such danger as by the superfluous eating of flesh.

What an ill and ungrateful sight is it to behold dead carcasses and pieces of bloody, raw flesh! It would undoubtedly appear dreadful and no man but

---

*Books by Thomas Tryon which relate to food and diet and advocate vegetarianism are: *Health's Grand Preservative* (1682); *A Treatise of Cleanness in Meats and Drinks* (1682); *The Way to Health, Long Life and Happiness* (1683, 1691, 1697); *The Way to Make All People Rich* (1685); *Miscellania* (1696); *Monthly Observations* (1688); *Wisdom's Dictates* (1691); *The Good House-Wife Made a Doctor* (n.d., 1692); *The Way to Save Wealth or Notable Things* (n.d., 1697); *The Way to Get Wealth* (1702, 1706).

would abhor to think of putting it in his mouth, had not Use and Custom from generation to generation familiarised it to us, which is so prevalent, that we read in some countries the mode is to eat the bodies of their dead parents and friends, thinking they can no way afford them a more noble sepulchre than their own bowells. And because it is usual, they do it with as little regret or nauseousness as others have when they devour the leg of a Rabbit or the wing of a Lark.[37]

## Soul Searching

However, the spirit of the age was against Tryon and others. Physicians and biologists were fired with new enthusiasm to investigate the natural world, no longer content to collate what Plutarch or Aristotle had said. They were led by the work of Marcello Malpighi (1628-94), an Italian physician and biologist who founded the science of microscopic anatomy. Through the microscope he described the major types of plant and animal structures, marking out for future generations of biologists the major areas to be researched in botany, embryology, human anatomy and pathology. His work was a revelation. A complex world was revealed by the microscope which had been totally unimagined before. Though Malpighi had his enemies, the new discoveries were too exciting to be ignored and scholars and teachers taught their students to discover for themselves. Dissection of animals became part of the academic syllabus, while new discoveries continued to be made.

Jan Swammerdam (1637-80), a Dutch naturalist, published *The Bible of Nature*, a collection of microscopic observations of insect life, which was the first to contain information on insect brains and nervous systems. He demonstrated the presence of butterfly wings in caterpillars about to undergo pupation, previously thought to have been a mysterious metamorphosis. One of his experiments showed that muscles alter in shape but not in size during contraction; before, people had believed Galen's theory that a fluid passed through the nerves causing the movement. He discovered that there was blood in the capillaries and that blood did not change into flesh at the periphery of the circulation system, which is what the ancients believed. In such matters and in countless others the seventeenth century was untying the knots which had kept the medieval age so closely entwined with the Classical world. Also, the insights into the minutiae of living matter appeared to make any differences between human beings and animals entirely disappear. Beneath the skin we all appeared the same.

But what of the soul, that fine distinction between humans and the brute beast below? In all this dissection, in the discovery of the heart pumping the blood around the tissues, and that greyish sponge contained within the skull, where was an organ that had the functions of a soul? Descartes's naming of the pineal gland as the site of the soul remained unconvincing. Leibniz's answer satisfied some who craved a reasonable theory based upon science. Everything corporeal, according to Leibniz, consists of small units called monads, and each monad has a soul; all matter is composed of monads, hence everything is possessed of soul, including, of course, animals. Yet animals' souls are not as complete as human ones. Leibniz taught that in nature a strict hierarchy existed of states of consciousness. At the very bottom existed the quiescent soul of inert matter doomed to an eternal sleep, then came the passive, defenceless being of the plants and above that the dreaming souls of the lower animals; a little further up there existed the more wakeful consciousness of the higher organisms and at the top the most active and perfect kind of self-consciousness, exhibited by humankind.

Somehow this theory made animals more respectable. They could be numbered among God's creatures, acceptable to God and not just relegated to fodder for humans. Yet Leibniz's theory was merely a variation on Descartes's thinking; the concept of monads merely added another mechanical detail to the picture. The aesthetics of the mechanism were beginning to be admired. There were craftsmen who turned from the making of clocks to construct mechanical animals; Jacques de Vaucanson made a duck which picked up grain, digested it and expelled it.

These ideas were taken further by the French physician La Mettrie (1709–51) who in his *Natural History of the Soul* cast doubt upon its existence. The book was burned by the public hangman and La Mettrie had to flee France. His next work, *Man the Machine*, reversed all the Cartesian ideas and argued that if animals were machines, human beings were too. Though human speech was a distinguishing characteristic between people and animals, La Mettrie pointed out that we had not always had this faculty. If human beings could learn to talk, why not animals? He recommended that experiments should be done with apes so that they might be taught to speak. Many of his experiments were designed to secure proof that humans and animals react in the same fashion. He found that even in death there were exact similarities. The body does not die all at once, as would have to be assumed, La Mettrie argued, if the soul left the body at a definite moment in time. However, he also had to admit that the lower life forms have a greater tenacity for clinging to life: the flesh of cold-blooded animals, such as turtles, lizards and snakes, quivers longer after death than that of the warm-blooded animals. A frog's heart, he noted, continues to beat for an hour after removal from its body. Yet these were differences of degree; compared with the animals – ordinary clocks, as it were – human beings were more ingenious timepieces.

## To Eat Meat or Not?

Amongst all this biological speculation, Tryon was not utterly alone in his espousal of the vegetarian ethic. The problem of whether humans should kill and eat animals was debated and written about by scores of people, some of whom were renowned in their particular fields. John Ray (1627–1705), a Fellow of the Royal Society and a leading naturalist and botanist, who worked on distinguishing species in plants and animals, defined the concept of 'species' as the smallest unit below the genus, making it possible to distinguish between several thousand animals. This work preceded Linnaeus★ and his own lasting and massive *Botanical Philosophy*. Ray enumerated 18,625 species in his *Historia Plantarum*. He also did much zoological work, forgotten now for he made a few basic errors (whales were numbered as fish), and wrote monographs on four-footed animals, snakes, birds, fish and insects while also writing a piece which his friend, John Evelyn, quoted with admiration.

The use of plants is all our life long of that universal importance and concern that we can neither live or subsist with any decency and convenience, or be said, indeed, to live at all without them. Whatsoever food is necessary to sustain us, whatsoever contributes to delight and refresh us, is supplied and brought forth out of that plentiful and abundant store. And ah! (he exclaims) how much more innocent, sweet, and healthful is a table covered with those than with all the reeking flesh of butchered and slaughtered animals. Certainly man by nature was never made to be a carnivorous animal, nor is he armed at all for prey and rapine, with jagged and pointed teeth and crooked claws sharpened to rend and tear, but with gentle hands to gather fruit and vegetables, and with teeth to chew and eat them.[38]

Almost an exact contemporary of Ray's and Tyron's, Evelyn (1620-1706) wrote over thirty books on fine art, forestry and religion as well as his diary. He travelled abroad at the time of the Civil War but at the Restoration became a civil servant working on a commission for wounded mariners, prisoners of war, street lighting, the Royal Mint and the repair of old St Paul's. He was concerned at the dwindling supply of timber and advised on the planting of trees; in his *Sylva, or a Discourse of Forest-trees and the Propagation of Timber* he described various types of trees, their cultivation and use; this study had gone through ten editions by 1825. His *Acetaria, a Discourse of Sallets*, can still be used as a gardening and cooking manual today; in it Evelyn reveals his enthusiasm for the health, long life and wholesomeness of the 'Herby-Diet'.

Another writer who paused to consider the ethics of slaughtering animals in order to eat them was Margaret Cavendish, the Duchess of Newcastle, a copious writer of poems, plays, letters, orations and philosophical discourses. Her poem, 'The Hunting of the Hare', is written with much genuine feeling. Here are the last twenty lines:

★Linnaeus (1707-78) was extremely concise when it came to his observations on diet; of fruits and beans he says: 'this species of food is that which is most suited to man, as is proved by the series of quadrupeds analogy, wild men, apes, the structure of the mouth, of the stomach, of the hands.' He is not noted, though, for keeping to the diet he recommends.

But Man doth think that Exercise and Toile,
To keep their Health, is best, which makes most spoile.
Thinking that Food, and Nourishment so good,
And appetite, that feeds on Flesh, and Blood.
When they do Lions, Wolves, Beares, Tigers see,
To kill poore Sheep, strait say, they cruell be.
But for themselves all Creatures think too few,
For Luxury, wish God would make them new.
As if that God made Creatures for Mans meat,
To give them Life, and Sense, for Man to eat;
Or else for Sport, or Recreations sake,
Destroy those Lifes that God saw good to make:
Making their Stomacks, Graves, which full they fill
With Muther'd Bodies, that in sport they kill.
Yet Man doth think himselfe so gentle, mild,
When he of Creatures is most cruell wild.
And is so Proud, thinks onely he shall live,
That God a God-like Nature did him give.
And that all Creatures for his sake alone,
Was made for him, to Tyrannize upon.[39]

However, such sentiments did not stop us from becoming a nation of meat-eaters. Henry More in 1653 even considered that cattle and sheep were only given life in the first place so that their meat could be kept fresh 'till we shall have need to eat them'.[40] More (1614–87) is as good an example as any of the spiritual and ethical ambivalence of many idealistic minds over the issues of animal rights and meat-eating. More spoke of 'that exceeding hail and entire sense of God which nature herself had planted deeply in me'.[41] Furthermore he declared that his mind 'was enlightened with a sense of the noblest theories in the morning of his days'.[42] He also tells us that his very body gave forth a flower-like fragrance.[43] More was a Cambridge Platonist and the most mystical of this group. He was brought up as a Calvinist, became a Cartesian and corresponded with Descartes. His beliefs were tied in with the ordered mechanical concept of the universe and this, perhaps, explains his idea of sheep and cows being created in order to keep their meat fresh. Nor did More have anxieties about the punishment of animals: 'when animals grew troublesome, then man had the right to curb them, for there is no question but we are worth more than they.'[44]

Growing affluence permeating down into the middle classes induced the habit of meat-eating to grow to what must seem to us today to be alarming proportions. Seven or eight meat dishes were quite normal for a two-course meal; three-quarters of the meal would be composed of meat, and the rest would be soups, puddings and sweet dishes. This section of the population was, of course, grossly overweight. It is known from Rowlandson's cartoons that eighteenth-century gentlemen were not only obese but riddled with gout and all the ills attendant on obesity. Sydney Smith wrote to his friend, Lord Murray, and told him he had consumed forty-four horse wagon loads of meat and drink throughout his life. He also worked out that this meant he had starved to death 'fully a hundred persons'. George Cheyne, an influential physician, at one point in his life weighed 32 stone.[45] Except for the poor, who never ate meat at all, it has been estimated that on average 147½ pounds of meat were consumed per annum per head.* England had become the most carnivorous country in Europe and Europe led the world in meat consumption.

Beef had become the most popular meat of all. In the middle of the seventeenth century the Government refused to tax the drovers who brought down cattle from Scotland. Graziers in Yorkshire had petitioned Parliament saying that the cattle were 'fed, maintained and fatted with far less charge than can possibly be done in England',[46] thus underselling their own breeds, but Scottish beef was prized as it is today and any duty imposed would have been too controversial.

Methods of making meat more tasty or tender were no less barbarian than they had been since antiquity. Such habits and rituals of tenderisation seem to have become fixed into a tradition, part of the folklore of the kitchen:

> Poultry, in order to put on flesh after its long journey from the farms, was sewn up by the gut – a practice which, according to Tobias Smollett, rendered the flesh rotten; turkeys were bled to death by hanging them upside down with a small incision in the vein of the mouth; geese were nailed to the floor; salmon and carp were hacked into collops while living to make their flesh firmer; eels were skinned alive, coiled round skewers and fixed through the eye so they could not move. 'I know nothing more shocking or horrid,' said Pope, 'than the prospect of kitchens covered with blood and filled with the cries of creatures expiring in tortures.' But expire in tortures they did. The flesh of the bull, it was believed, was indigestible and unwholesome if the animal was killed without being baited. Butchers were liable to prosecution if the brutal preliminaries were omitted. Calves and pigs were whipped to death with knotted ropes to make the meat more tender, rather than our modern practice of beating the flesh when dead. 'Take a red cock that is not too old and beat him to death,' begins one of Doctor William Kitchiner's recipes.[47]

Factory farming was flourishing:

> The Elizabethan method of 'brawning' or fattening pigs was 'to keep them in so close a room that they cannot turn themselves round about . . . whereby they are forced always to lie on their bellies'. 'They feed in pain,' said a

---

*This figure is as much as contemporary consumption in the USA.

contemporary, 'lie in pain and sleep in pain.' Poultry and game-birds were often fattened in darkness and confinement, sometimes being blinded as well. 'The cock being gelded,' it was explained, 'he is called a capon and is crammed in a coop.' Geese were thought to put on weight if the webs of their feet were nailed to the floor, and it was the custom of some seventeenth-century housewives to cut the legs off living fowl in the belief that it made their flesh more tender. In 1686 Sir Robert Southwell announced a new invention of 'an oxhouse, where the cattle are to eat and drink in the same crib and not to stir until they be fitted for the slaughter'. Dorset lambs were specially reared for the Christmas tables of the gentry by being imprisoned in little dark cabins.[48]

Nor over the centuries had the methods of slaughter changed or become in any way more considerate to the beast about to be killed:

> Methods of slaughter were coldly rational. As Dr Johnson remarked, the butchers 'have no view to the ease of the animals but only to make them quiet for their own safety and convenience'. Cattle were poleaxed before being killed, but pigs, calves and poultry died more slowly. In order to make their meat white, calves and sometimes lambs were struck in the neck so that the blood would run out. Then the wound was stopped and the animal allowed to linger on for another day. As Thomas Hardy's Arabella explained to Jude, pigs should not be slaughtered quickly. 'The meat must be well bled and to do that he must die slow. I was brought up to it and I know. Every good butcher keeps them bleeding long. He ought to be up till eight or ten minutes dying at least.'[49]

Though God's sanction in Genesis was held up still as a reason for natural human dominance, seventeenth-century farming practices were by now causing comment, even if only amongst a minority. The perennial concept of the Golden Age, that paradise before the Fall, was appearing in works of the imagination. In Milton's *Paradise Lost* the angel Raphael makes a prophecy that the human race will be nourished by fruit only:

> time may come when men
> With angels may participate, and find
> No inconvenient diet, nor too light fare.
> And from those corporal nutriments perhaps
> Your bodies may at last turn all to spirit,
> Improved by tract of time, and winged ascend
> Ethereal as we;[50]

Nor would it be true to say that all churchmen accepted the literal Genesis sanction. Milton's French contemporary Bossuet, popular Parisian preacher and Bishop of Meaux, tutor to the Dauphin, wrote:

Before the time of the Deluge the nourishment which without violence men derived from the fruits which fell from the trees of themselves, and from the herbs which also ripened with equal ease, was, without doubt, some relic of the first innocence and of the gentleness for which we were formed. Now to get food we have to shed blood in spite of the horror which it naturally inspires in us; and all the refinements of which we avail ourselves, in covering our tables, hardly suffice to disguise for us the bloody corpses which we have to devour to support life. But this is but the savage violences which are introduced into the life of the human species. Man, whom in the first ages we have seen spare the life of other animals, is accustomed henceforward to spare the life not even of his fellow-men. It is in vain that God forbade, immediately after the Deluge, the shedding of human blood; in vain, in order to save some vestiges of the first mildness of our nature, while permitting the feeding on flesh did he prohibit consumption of the blood. Human murders multiplied beyond all calculation.[51]

Bossuet's linking of the killing of animals with warlike aggression was, of course, not new, nor was he the only one to voice such opinions. David Hartley, the English physician and philosopher, said that 'Taking away the lives of animals in order to convert them into food' did 'great violence to the principles of benevolence and compassion'. 'This appears,' he added, 'from the frequent hard-heartedness and cruelty found amongst those persons whose occupations engage them in destroying animal life, as well as from the uneasiness which others feel in beholding the butchery of animals.'[52]

The association of meat-eating with war seemed logical enough when people contemplated the world of suffering after the Fall. The idea that meat-eating, because it occurred after the Fall, was a sign of moral degeneration was slowly gaining some credence. This idea was bolstered by scientists discovering from evidence in human teeth and intestines that human beings were originally not meat-eaters. But abstention from meat as a health issue was also coming to the fore. The gargantuan Dr Cheyne was, surprisingly, an authority on diet. Though his first publication in 1705 was entitled *Philosophical Principles of Religion*, his vast weight and obesity were soon causing such physical disabilities – apoplectic giddiness, violent headaches and depression – that it became a case of 'physician, heal thyself'. His life appears to have been a struggle against giving up meat altogether. On first retiring from his Bath practice, expecting that his end was near, he reflected on the follies and vices of the modern diet and he decided to eat mainly fruit, vegetables and milk with a little meat once a day. Around the year 1712, when he was forty-two, feeling a great deal better in himself he tended to relax his moderate diet and published a highly successful volume entitled *An Essay on the Gout and Bath Waters*. His fame spread, but so did his waistline until he grew to the frightening weight of 32 stone and could not get in or out of his carriage to visit his patients without assistance. He went back to a strict diet of milk and vegetables and within two years all his maladies had disappeared.

Dr Cheyne had influence and powerful friends: he converted John Wesley, so he says in his journals; he was a friend of Sir Hans Sloane and of the novelist Samuel Richardson; he even made Dr Johnson give up drinking wine and take tea with Mrs Thrale instead. Cheyne went on writing books until the end of his life and never slipped back on his vegetable diet, though the tone of the last books was less successful with the public. His *Essay on Regimen: together with Five Discourses Medical, Moral and Philosophical* may well have been too austere:

> The question I design to treat of here is, whether animal or vegetable food was, in the original design of the Creator, intended for the food of animals, and particularly of the human race. And I am almost convinced it never was intended, but only permitted as a curse or punishment . . . At what time animal food [flesh] came first in use is not certainly known. He was a bold man who made the first experiment. To see the convulsions, agonies and tortures of a poor fellow-creature, whom they cannot restore nor recompense, dying to gratify luxury, and tickle callous and rank organs, must require a rocky heart, and a great degree of cruelty and ferocity. I cannot find any great difference, on the foot of natural reason and equity only, between feeding on human flesh and feeding on brute animal flesh, except custom and example.[53]

At around sixty years he gives us a picture of his own diet in his 'Author's Case', after being a vegetarian without a lapse for sixteen years:

> My regimen, at present, is milk, with tea, coffee, bread and butter, mild cheese, salads, fruits and seeds of all kinds, with tender roots (as potatoes, turnips, carrots), and, in short, everything that has not life, dressed or not, as I like it, in which there is as much variety than in animal foods, so that the stomach need never be cloyed. I drink no wine nor any fermented liquors, and am rarely dry, most of my food being liquid, moist, or juicy. Only after dinner I drink either coffee or green tea, but seldom both in the same day, and sometimes a glass of soft, small cider. The thinner my diet, the easier, more cheerful and lightsome I find myself; My sleep is also the sounder, though perhaps somewhat shorter than formerly under my full animal diet; but then I am more alive than ever I was. As soon as I wake I get up. I rise commonly at six, and go to bed at ten.[54]

It was David Hartley who attended his friend Dr Cheyne in his last illness and it was he who emphasised the possibility of a kinship with the animal world. We have heard him on the unease that people feel when observing the slaughter of animals; he goes on to say:

> It is most evident, in respect to the larger animals and those with whom we have a familiar intercourse – such as Oxen, Sheep, and domestic Fowls, etc.

...They resemble us greatly in the make of the body in general, and in that of the particular organs of circulation, respiration, digestion, etc; also in the formation of their intellects, memories, and passions, and in the signs of distress, fear, pain, and death. They often, likewise, win our affections by the marks of peculiar sagacity, by their instincts, helplessness, innocence, nascent benevolence, etc etc, and if there be any glimmering of hope of an hereafter for them – if they should prove to be our brethren and sisters in this higher sense, in immortality as well as mortality – in the permanent principle of our minds as well as in the frail dust of our bodies – this ought to be still further reason for tenderness for them.

This, therefore, seems to be nothing else than an argument to stop us in our career, to make us sparing and tender in this article of diet, and put us upon consulting experience more faithfully and impartially in order to determine what is most suitable for the purposes of life and health, our compassion being made, by the foregoing considerations in some measure, a balance to our impetuous bodily appetites.[55]

## Two Poets

John Gay (168-1732), most renowned now as the author of *The Beggar's Opera*, was another concerned with the ethics of violence, animal slaughter and meat-eating, his views expressed in his *Fables* of 1727. Animal slaughter drew from Gay some terse lines: 'Against an elm a sheep was tied: / The butcher's knife in blood was dyed – / The patient flock, in silent fright, / From far beheld the horrid sight.'[56] From another we read the couplet: 'All animals before him ran, / To shun the hateful sight of man.'[57] But perhaps Gay's sympathies are most graphically shown in the following extract. Pythagoras walks in contemplation through the fragrance of the day and comes by chance to a farm where the farmer has nailed a kite to the barn wall with its wings displayed, as its kind has been killing his hens:

'Friend,' says the Sage, 'the doom is wise –
For public good the murderer dies.
But if these tyrants of the air
Demand a sentence so severe,
Think how the glutton, man, devours;
What bloody feasts regale his hours!
O impudence of Power and Might!
Thus to condemn a hawk or kite,
When thou, perhaps, carnivorous sinner,
Had'st pullets yesterday for dinner.'[58]

Another poet, a friend of Gay's, much exercised too over the horrors of animal slaughter and meat-eating was Alexander Pope (1688-1744). It is clear that the human domination of all other creatures fills him with unease.

It is humankind that 'destroys all creatures for their sport or gust'.[68] 'I cannot think it extravagant,' he writes:

> to imagine that mankind are no less, in proportion, accountable for the ill use of their dominion over the lower ranks of beings, than for the exercise of tyranny over their own species. The more entirely the inferior creation is submitted to our power, the more answerable we must be for our mismanagement of them; and the rather, as the very condition of Nature renders them incapable of receiving any recompense in another life for ill-treatment in this.[60]

A close friend of Pope's was Dr John Arbuthnot (1667–1735), physician and wit who attended to members of the royal family, including Queen Anne. Arbuthnot is famous for his *History of John Bull*, but he also wrote an *Essay Concerning Ailments* (published 1730) which recommends the vegetable diet as a preventive and cure to certain diseases.

Despite these humanitarian notions, this anxiety over the ethics of meat-eating, the clockwork universe moved inexorably onwards. Science with an energy born of itself edged the boundaries of knowledge further outwards and to do so had to commit endless cruelties on defenceless animals. Because of theological disapproval at the use of human corpses for dissection,* animals took their place; Malpighi's work on respiration was based on experiments with dogs, frogs and turtles, and he first discovered red blood corpuscles in a hedgehog. Dogs were used for the first blood transfusions in the belief that their familiarity with man must count in their favour, before the introduction of sheep's blood into human veins. Vivisection became a scientific obsession and endless experiments were made: limbs were cut off to see if they would regenerate, bowels drawn out, skins pulled off living creatures, organs removed, blindness induced and senses blocked. In time all this work began to be known more widely and a sense of outrage began to grow. Did human beings have the right to inflict this new agony and suffering upon animals? Voltaire was one of the fiercest critics of vivisection:

> There are barbarians who seize this dog, who so prodigiously surpasses man in friendship, and nail him down to a table, and dissect him alive to shew you the mezaraic veins. You discover in him all the same organs of feeling as in yourself. Answer me, Machinist, has Nature really arranged all the springs of feeling in this animal to the end that he might not feel? Has he nerves that he may be incapable of suffering? Do not suppose that impertinent contradiction in Nature.[61]

---

*Dissection of the human corpse in fact has a long history, as far back as Ancient Egypt, but according to Celsus, the Roman physician and medical writer (*fl.* first century AD), experimenters also used live criminals, 'procured out of prison and dissecting them alive, contemplated, while they were yet breathing, what nature had before concealed'.

## Pierre Bayle

It was Voltaire, of course, who most notably encouraged and promoted a spirit of freedom and scepticism within his age, but we shall turn to him in the next chapter. He had one great precursor, whom Voltaire himself saluted 'as one of the greatest men that France has produced . . . more learned than Plato or Epicurus', while his writings were described as 'the library of Nations'. He was Pierre Bayle (1647-1706), born in a tiny town at the foot of the Pyrenees in the Comté de Foix. This was Cathar country but Bayle was born into the heresy of his time – Protestantism. He was more or less self-educated and became a solitary and erudite man. He expressed the germ of the ideas which would reach their fulfilment in the eighteenth century. In his own age he became caught up in Louis XIV's persecution of the Protestant Huguenots. He fled to the Hague and never saw his family again. When his younger brother was imprisoned in Paris, and died there, unable to reach Bayle at the Hague, Bayle was filled with guilt and anguish, seeing clearly the great evil that religious faiths can inflict. In his attack on faith (and much else) he helped to bring forth what is known as the Age of Reason and to lay some of those foundation stones necessary for the vegetarian movement which spread a hundred years after his death:

> [Bayle] starts from the axiom that all written history is unreliable, being composed from a subjective point of view and influenced, in the pernicious form of flattery or satire, by personal affections or prejudices. He attacks superstition in all its many varieties. He points out that every sect has its own favourite miracles and denies the validity of those miracles which are believed in by other sects. Superstition, he argues, is a purely subjective emotion. He suggests that the bones of a dog would prove as efficacious as the relics of a martyr, provided that the worshippers were subjectively convinced of their magic. He attacked priestcraft and the *odium theologicum*, and even allowed himself to be ironical about Saint Augustine. He contended that, whatever the Church might teach, there did exist such a person as the good pagan, and the good unbeliever, taking Atticus as an example as well as Spinoza. He advocated 'natural religion', by which he meant the 'ethics of a man of reason'. His moral was that 'every action committed against the light of conscience is essentially evil'.[62]

His most famous work was the *Dictionnaire* – which elicited attack, censure and discontent – the bulk of which consists of quotations, anecdotes, commentaries and erudite annotations that attack orthodoxy. Bayle was convinced that philosophical reasoning led to universal scepticism but human nature compelled blind faith, a perceptive observation in a world where the Christian Church of whatever persuasion was the most powerful force in society. However, the dictionary's influence was huge and those who read it with a sense of revelation and gratitude numbered the great of the world. Frederick II of Prussia commissioned two abridgements, while Benjamin

Franklin and Thomas Jefferson both recommended it to their friends. It is also interesting to note how sympathetic the dictionary entries on the Manicheans and the Paulicians are. It was Bayle who gave such oppressed minorities dignity by respecting their ideas and analysing them seriously. His work paved the way for the new liberalism and humanitarianism which would appear after his death. Bayle encouraged the exercise of reason, analysis and scepticism; and new ideas had to replace blind faith, ideas powerful enough to keep superstition in its place. The seventeenth century was too rich in speculative ideas for them to be absorbed quickly. Newton had first taught that existing myths may not be in accord with scientific fact, while Locke had taught that ideas were not innate★ but derived from experience. In order for humans to allow natural rights to animals they had first to find them for themselves. In the eighteenth century people were able to speak up for their rights for the first time in the Christian world.

Now ideas were about to emerge based upon humankind rather than God, or, it might be said, based on the idea of God within humankind. These would take another two centuries to grow, but would provide an ethical structure powerful enough to compete with orthodox religion.

---

★The latest work in genetics on identical twins separated at birth gives striking evidence that more behaviour is innate than Locke had taught. Also, some diseases and afflictions in the mature adult have now been discovered to be inherent within the growing embryo.

# 10

# The Rise of Humanism

The idea that people in themselves had natural rights by their very existence was one which had a difficult and long infancy. This movement which contained ideas of justice, freedom, constitutional rights and a humanitarian belief in the brotherhood of humankind we now know as the Age of Enlightenment, and its ideas received wide assent among European intellectuals. The birth of humanism was reckoned to lie in Socrates, Plato and Epicurus. These philosophers had found a regularity in nature by the sheer exercise of their reason, and reason as exemplified in Socrates was valued as the path to human happiness. Epicurus was dangerous for he was considered an atheist, but Stoicism itself might be revived and writers were impressed by reading the Stoic Emperor Marcus Aurelius:

> Think on this doctrine: that reasoning beings are created for one another's sake; that to be patient is a branch of justice; and that men sin without intending it. All that is harmony for thee, O Universe, is in harmony with me as well. Nothing that comes at the right time for thee is too early or too late for me. You will find rest from vain fancies if you do every act in life as if it were your last.[1]

Such thoughts seemed in their wisdom to be almost religious.

A scholarly Dutch jurist, Hugo Grotius, as early as 1625 published a work which invoked the idea of a natural law as a rule governing international relations. What was more, this natural law was quite independent of Christian theology. Grotius was an optimist. The moral power of the natural law derived from humans' innate nature, which was inherently good – to harm others was to harm oneself. But these ideas hardly affected the turmoil of the Thirty Years War (1618-48).

## The Reforming Spirit

How animals were treated hinged upon whether humankind was innately good or not and that in turn depended upon the doctrine of original sin. Locke by his teaching had demolished not only the concept of innate ideas but also that of innate depravity: babies could not be born stained with original sin because they were born as innocent and blank as a piece of white paper which their environment would write upon. Therefore, the manner by which you improved the individuals was to improve their environment. This gave reason and significance to the improvement of the human lot on earth, in direct contrast to the Middle Ages, when iniquitous poverty and hardship would be endured, in the knowledge that faith would bring reward in paradise. Now there was not only a humanitarian zeal to reform living conditions, but the conviction that, in so doing, the inner person would also be improved.

Doing good came down to reason and its powers of deduction. To know what was right was to commit oneself to the action of doing right. The law of nature, impossible to define adequately, was firmly based upon the belief that people were born virtuous, but were degraded by false education, corrupt institutions and bad laws. This natural law no longer stated what was, but what ought to be, so though somewhat ill defined, natural law did become a movement that was critical and reformist.

Prisons were one of the greatest blights of eighteenth-century life vicious and corrupt, the prisoners disease-ridden and almost starved. The penal reformer John Howard was a committed vegetarian, but he knew that the quality of the vegetable ingredients offered to prisoners was poor. What prisoners needed was food, any type of food that he could persuade the authorities to allow into the prisons:

> Those who drink only water, and have no nutritious liquor, ought to have at least a pound and a half of bread every day. The bread should be one day old and then honestly weighed to them. If once a week (suppose on Sunday) some of the coarser pieces of beef were boiled in the copper, and half a pound of the meat without bone given to each prisoner, with a quart of the broth, this Sunday dinner might be made an encouragement to peaceable and orderly behaviour . . .[2]

Locke broke with the Cartesian mechanistic view of the universe. He believed in direct observation and this showed quite clearly that animals had feelings, and communicated with each other and with human beings. Differences between ourselves and animals were differences of kind. Locke was convinced that the way people treated animals anticipated how they treated each other. People who are indifferent to the animals in their charge will be indifferent towards their fellows. A healthy programme of education must include teaching children to be considerate to animals:

> One thing I have frequently observed in Children, that when they have got possession of any poor Creature, they are apt to use it ill: They often torment, and treat very roughly, young Birds, Butterflies, and such other poor Animals, which fall into their Hands, and that with a seeming kind of Pleasure. This I think should be watched in them . . . and if they incline to any such Cruelty,

they should be taught the contrary Usage. For the Custom of Tormenting and Killing of Beasts, will, by Degrees, harden their Minds even towards Men; and they who delight in the Suffering and Destruction of Inferiour Creatures, will not be apt to be very compassionate, or benign to those of their own kind . . .[3]

Today it is hard to imagine how bizarre this notion must have seemed. If our children are unkind to animals, we are shocked and they are reprimanded or punished. But 250 years ago, animals were there for human use, for food, profit or entertainment. What did it matter what you did to them as long as their value was not impaired?

## Belief and Scepticism

Today we might also be tempted to think that only a few intellectuals expressed this scepticism of Biblical lore, this belief in natural rights and laws, but from other writers we learn how irreligious England was. Montesquieu, in 1728, said: 'there is no religion and the subject, if mentioned in society, evokes nothing but laughter.'[4] Bishop Butler, in his preface to the *Analogy of Religion* in 1736, wrote that most men had ceased to look on Christianity even as a subject of enquiry, 'its fictitious nature being so obvious';[5] while Bishop Watson considered 'that there never was an age since the death of Christ, never one since the commencement of this history of the world, in which atheism and infidelity have been more generally confessed'.[6]

One might think that such a thoroughly irreligious society would no longer accept the idea that God created all the beasts upon the earth, fowls in the air and fishes of the sea for the pleasure and sustenance of humankind. But ideas so embedded in the human psyche as the relationship between humankind and God expounded in Genesis could not vanish overnight. The Doctor Pangloss vision of the world, soon to be demolished by Voltaire, was alive and well. Richard Bentley observed in 1692 that 'all things were created principally for the benefit and pleasure of man'.[7] The natural obedience of animals was illustrated so often that Jeremiah Burroughes noted: 'you may see a little child driving before him a hundred oxen or kine this way or that way as he pleaseth; it showeth that God hath preserved somewhat of man's dominion over the creatures.'[8] Even wild creatures outside the limits of domestication knew their place in this perfectly ordered world, so Philip Doddridge in 1763 expounded in a course of lectures. The instinct which brought fish in shoals to the seashore 'seems an intimation that they are intended for human use'.[9] How well God had conceived this world, even down to matching animals to climate and human needs. Camels lived in Arabia where there was little water and savage beasts had been sent to deserts where they could do little harm. There was no confusion over whether animals had rights, either. Lancelot Andrewes, in 1650, was quite certain that animals 'could not own land, for God had given the Earth to men, not to sheep or deer',[10] while he rejected the Manichean doctrine that man had no right to kill creatures, for the sixth commandment against murder did not apply to non-humans.

Yet the climate of the age was against solid piety and church devotions in the traditional manner. Clergymen could hold several livings at once and often left their parishioners to the ministrations of an uneducated curate. Laziness and worldliness, as we know from the novels of the period, had greater attractions than church duties. In such times when the established Church is in disrepute, new sects are inclined to spring up. The Jansenists in France were the Calvinists of Roman Catholicism; the Anabaptists in Germany preached a form of Christian socialism; the Moravians were a Saxon sect who claimed to have revived the Hussite doctrine, and they, in turn, influenced John Wesley (1703-91). It was Wesley's creation, the Methodist movement, which was to sweep England. In 1770 there were over 29,000 members and 121 preachers; twenty years later the numbers had swollen to over 71,000, with 48,600 in America. Wesley eschewed all meat-eating, but did not make it an ideological issue. Considering the might of Methodism, the history of the vegetarian movement would have been radically different, somewhat akin to Hinduism, if Wesley had explored the ethics of violence in society. But Wesley saw his personal stand merely as one of pious asceticism, firmly placed within the Christian tradition. Asceticism was also a habit. At the age of eleven he was admitted to Charterhouse with its public school system of fagging, well known for its brutality and bullying. This often amounted to the older boys depriving the juniors of their meat ration. Wesley managed to rise above it all by living entirely on bread and water, and seems to have been content to do so. Afterwards he would assert that this was the secret of his strong constitution. At Oxford he formed with his brother, Charles, a Holy Club which practised fasting on two days every week. This seems to have become a habit for his lifetime. Certainly in his journals Wesley claims that he practised complete abstinence from 'gross foods'. He muses in his journals on a letter written to a clergyman in 1744: 'if there are two dishes set before you, by the rule of self-denial, you ought to eat of that which you like the least. And this rule I desire to observe myself always to choose what is least pleasing and cheapest; therefore I feed much upon milk. It is pleasant enough and nothing I can find is so cheap.'[11]

That abstention from meat did not become an ideological issue is hardly surprising, for though almost the last letter Wesley wrote was to Wilberforce and the anti-slavery campaigners, he never criticised the condition of the prisons (as Howard and others did) or the barbarity of the penal laws, the convict hulks or the use of child labour and the conditions in the factories. On schools he is reported to have said that they exist 'to break the will of the child'.[12]

## Voltaire

In contrast, Voltaire, whose life (1694-1778) covers much the same period, had an acute sense of the values of society and its cruel inhumanity. Voltaire's influence too was vast, and in no other figure do we see the idealism of the age illustrated as finely. He was a great humanitarian and crusader against injustice (he was also penny pinching and amassed a fortune from dubious sources), a great wit, satirist and critic, a writer of drama, poetry, essays and tales, the most famous of which, *Candide*, was written after the trauma of the Lisbon earthquake on All Saints Day, 1 November 1755. This event was crucial. The report which first reached Voltaire was that 15,000 men, women and children had been killed within the space of six minutes, crushed beneath the bells and towers of the churches of Lisbon. Out of a population of 275,000 between 10,000 and 15,000 lost their lives. The whole of Christian Europe was profoundly perplexed. How could the all-loving God have murdered so cruelly those pious Christians at their devotions? The puritans could claim that it was an act of divine vengeance upon the sinfulness of the world. Yet many priests, nuns, sacred relics and paintings by Titian, Correggio and Rubens were destroyed, leaving some obvious sinners and heretics to walk free. Everyone battled to answer the great enigma:

> The Jansenist, Etienne Rondet, wrote a whole book to prove that the disaster was a divine comment on the iniquity of the Inquisition and the Jesuits. The Protestants of London argued that it must be ascribed to God's disapproval of the Portuguese, in particular for their addiction to abominable papal practices and their avowed worship of the Mother of God. It was even suggested that the Saints had begged God to choose their own particular festival as the date for his demonstration.[13]

Voltaire was deeply disturbed. The comfortable complacency of his beliefs, especially in the theodicy of Leibniz and the doctrine that all is best in the best possible of worlds, was shattered irrevocably. He first wrote a poem on 'The Disaster of Lisbon', then wrote *Candide*, which attacks the whole optimistic school of thought and the idea that God is love and compassion:

> After the Lisbon earthquake Voltaire ceased to be so certain about his deism, so confident in the great geometrician, and lapsed into a vague form of agnosticism arguing that, since we could never expect in this world to understand the purposes of Providence, we must avoid abstract speculation, content ourselves with our daily tasks, and cling to hope. 'Why do we exist?' he wrote, 'why is anything anything?'[14]

Yet afterwards his passion for human rights and his campaign against individual injustice seemed to be, if anything, more intense and more consistent. His hatred of cruelty to both men and animals runs through his work. Of Isaac Newton, Voltaire comments, in a book published in 1741:

> He thought it a very frightful inconsistency to believe that animals feel and at the same time to cause them to suffer. On this point his morality was in

accord with his philosophy. He yielded but with repugnance to the barbarous custom of supporting ourselves upon the blood and flesh of beings like ourselves, whom we caress, and he never permitted in his own house the putting them to death by slow and exquisite modes of killing for the sake of making the food more delicious. This compassion, which he felt for other animals, culminated in true charity for men. In truth, without humanity, a virtue which comprehends all virtues, the name of philosopher would be little deserved.[15]

Voltaire had great admiration for the Hindus:

> The Hindus, in embracing the doctrine of Metempsychosis, had one restraint the more. The dread of killing a father or mother, in killing men and other animals, inspired in them a terror of murder and every other violence which became with them a second nature. The Christian religion, which the Quakers alone follow out to the letter, is as great an enemy to bloodshed as the Pythagorean. But the Christian peoples have never practised their religion, and the ancient Hindu castes have always practised theirs.[16]

In his romances, such as *The Princess of Babylon*, Voltaire's horror of meat-eating is apparent:

> A dining-hall, whose walls were covered with orange-wood. The under-shepherds and shepherdesses, in long white dresses girded with golden bands, served her in a hundred baskets of simple porcelain, with a hundred delicious meats, among which was seen no disguised corpse. The feast was of rice, of sago, of semolina, of vermicelli, of maccaroni, of omelets, of eggs in milk, of cream-cheese, of pastries of every kind, of vegetables, of fruits of perfume and taste of which one has no idea in other climates, and a profusion of refreshing drinks superior to the best wines.[17]

In the same story the hero visits Rome and describes the feasts there:

> The dining-hall was grand, convenient, and richly ornamented. Gold and silver shone upon the sideboards. Gaiety and wit animated the guests. But, meantime, in the kitchens blood and fat were streaming in one horrible mass; skins of quadrupeds, feathers of birds and their entrails, piled up pell-mell, oppressed the heart, and spread the infection of fevers.[18]

A writer and professor of medicine, Antonio Cocchi (1695–1758) wrote a key work read and admired by Voltaire, *The Pythagorean Diet*, published in 1743 but not translated into French until 1762. In it Cocchi defends and praises Pythagoras and the vegetable diet. He explains:

> I wished to show that Pythagoras, the first founder of the vegetable

regimen, was at once a very great physicist and a very great physician; that there has been no one of a more cultured and discriminating humanity; that he was a man of wisdom and of experience; that his motive in commending and introducing the new mode of living was derived not from any extravagant superstition, but from the desire to improve the health and the manners of men.

## Paine

There was one man, above all, who expressed the ideals of the Enlightenment in a practical and energetic way: Thomas Paine (1737–1809), the son of a Quaker born at Thetford in Norfolk. With his books *Common Sense* and *The Rights of Man* he influenced world events: 'It would be difficult to name any human composition which has had an effect, at once so instant, so extended and lasting. *Common Sense* turned thousands to independence who before could not endure the thought.'[19] So Sir George Trevelyan wrote of Paine's book, published immediately before the War of Independence in the American colonies. It was Paine who coined the term 'the United States' and the idea of human natural rights that must be struggled and fought for, which apply to all individuals, of whatever class, colour or creed was his. Paine's ideas are still profoundly relevant today. Without acceptance of the ideas of universal suffrage, civil rights, freedom of thought and speech in a conceived ideal of the equality of human rights, human beings could not begin to allow the concept of animal rights room to seed itself, much less grow.

The Rights of Man caused a huge uproar after it was published in 1791 as it attacked organised religion. Paine maintained he was a deist but the Church claimed he was an atheist. Between 1795 and 1799 fifty hostile responses to the book were published, and Paine's many critics could state that the connection between atheism and republicanism was close. Although Paine was called 'Apostle of Beelzebub' and 'Agent of Lucifer', the book was widely circulated among the working classes. In America it sold eight editions in 1794, seven the following year and two in 1796.[20] In Philadelphia thousands of copies were sold at auctions for a mere cent and a half each, whereby children, servants and the lowest people had been tempted to buy. An American Presbyterian prophesied a fate worse than Sodom and Gomorrah if unbelief prevailed; he defended the Mosaic account of the Creation as 'so natural and even necessary that I cannot conceive how it could have been otherwise'.[21] But there were plenty of Paine's readers who could well imagine it otherwise.

## Paley

The difficulty that Christian theologians were in at this time is best seen in William Paley (1743–1805), priest, utilitarian philosopher and author, whose work *View of the Evidence of Christianity* (1794) was required reading for entrance to Cambridge University up to the beginning of the 20th century.

He considered that the art of life consisted in establishing the right habits. On whether man should eat flesh or not, Paley dithers:

> A right to the flesh of animals. This is a very different claim from the former ['a right to the fruits or vegetable produce of the earth']. Some excuse seems necessary for the pain and loss which we occasion to (other) animals by restraining them of their liberty, mutilating their bodies, and, at last, putting an end to their lives for our pleasure or convenience.[22]

When it comes to Genesis itself, Paley continues to write with almost nervous equivocation:

> To Adam and his posterity had been granted, at the creation, 'every green herb for meat', and nothing more. In the last clause of the passage now produced the old grant is recited and extended to the flesh of animals – 'even as the green herb, have I given you all things'. But this was not until after the Flood. The inhabitants of the antediluvian world had therefore no such permission that we know of. Whether they actually refrained from the flesh of animals is another question. Abel, we read, was a keeper of sheep, and for what purpose he kept them, except for food, is difficult to say (unless it were sacrifice).[23]

Paley was also exercised over what is still a very contemporary concern. Here he argues that rearing livestock on pasture needed for cereals is an inefficient way of feeding people:

> Many ranks of people whose ordinary diet was, in the last century, prepared almost entirely from milk, roots, and vegetables, now require every day a considerable portion of the flesh of animals. Hence a great part of the richest lands of the country are converted to pasturage. Much also of the bread–corn, which went directly to the nourishment of human bodies, now only contributes to it by fattening the flesh of sheep and oxen. The mass and volume of provisions are hereby diminished, and what is gained in the amelioration of the soil is lost in the quality of the produce.[24]

That Paley, still a meat–eater, argued these points shows that such issues were controversial at the time.

## Franklin

The ethical questions stemming from meat-eating also worried Benjamin Franklin (1706-90). It was due to him that Thomas Paine first went to America,[*] but it was a book by Thomas Tryon (see p.200), *The Way to*

---

[*]They met in London in 1774 and Franklin urged Paine to seek a new life across the Atlantic and gave him a letter to his son-in-law, Bache, describing Paine as 'an ingenious and worthy young man.

*Health, Long Life and Happiness, Or a Discourse of Temperance*, which converted Franklin, at the age of sixteen, to vegetarianism. He wrote in his autobiography that he was delighted with the diet for he saved money and in eating separately he found more time to study. He kept to the diet when he moved to Philadelphia and worked for a printer, Samuel Keimer, whom he persuaded to go on a similar diet. Keimer soon lapsed from the diet; nor was Franklin to keep to his ideals for much longer either. On a sea trip Franklin's fellow-passengers fished when their boat was stranded off Block Island. Franklin noticed that inside the large codfish was another smaller fish swallowed whole. Here Franklin found what appeared to him a natural law – that favourite explanation of the age – by which every living thing flourished because of the death of another. Hence human beings were justified in killing and eating lesser creatures. Franklin returned to eating fish, fowl and meat and never again in his long life had second thoughts about it.

Adam Smith was also a meat-eater but he nevertheless observed:

> It may, indeed, be doubted whether butcher's meat is anywhere a necessity of life. Grain and other vegetables, with the help of milk, cheese and butter, or oil (where butter is not to be had) it is known from experience, can, without any butcher's meat, afford the most plentiful, the most wholesome, the most nourishing and the most invigorating diet.[25]

## Ritson and the Cry of Nature

However, one who had no doubts and who influenced many who came after him was Joseph Ritson (1752-1803), who was born in Stockton-on-Tees. He claimed descent from a family that held land, though his father was a servant in the employ of a Stockton tobacconist. Ritson worked hard and became an antiquarian and critic who in the first part of his life published commentaries on Shakespeare and an anthology of songs from Henry III to the Revolution. In 1772 he read Mandeville's *Fable of the Bees*,★ which made him forswear all animal food and subsist solely on milk and vegetables. His fame and importance lie in his *Moral Essay upon Abstinence* (1802), which begins, like so much in this book, with a brief history of the ancient philosophers and their opinions, going on to claim how unnatural flesh-eating is to human physiognomy and how such a diet of blood will engender ferocity in those that consume it:

---

★Bernard Mandeville (1670-1733), Anglo-Dutch moral philosopher, born at Rotterdam. He published *The Fable of the Bees*, a long poem, between 1714 and 1728, an allegory about a hive where the bees all prospered because vice, greed and treachery all flourished among them. When Jove made all the bees become virtuous their state declined into ruin. Mandeville's theory was that 'private vices increase public benefits'. His work was admired by Johnson, Voltaire and Coleridge, for he first suggested that vice was a necessary evil and that 'no society can be raised into a rich and mighty Kingdom without the vice of Man'.

That the use of animal food disposes man to cruel and ferocious actions is a fact to which the experience of ages gives ample testimony. The Scythians, from drinking the blood of their cattle, proceeded to drink that of their enemies. The fierce and cruel disposition of the wild Arabs is supposed chiefly, if not solely, to arise from their feeding upon the flesh of camels: and as the gentle disposition of the natives of Hindustan is probably owing, in great degree, to temperance and abstinence from animal food.

Ritson also connects the English blood sports with meat-eating:

The barbarous and unfeeling sports (as they are called) of the English – their horse-racing, hunting, shooting, bull and bear baiting, cock-fighting, prize-fighting, and the like, all proceed from their immoderate addiction to animal food. Their natural temper is thereby corrupted, and they are in the habitual and hourly commission of crimes against nature, justice, and humanity, from which a feeling and reflective mind, unaccustomed to such a diet, would revolt, but in which they profess to take delight.[26]

Ritson considers the slave trade, 'that abominable violation of the rights of Nature',[27] is due to the same cause. He believes altar sacrifice to have been the ritual which first gave human beings a taste for meat, quoting Porphyry in evidence, who in turn cites earlier writers. However, he was at pains to make clear that he was not a believer in metempsychosis, reacting to the accusation as if it was libel: 'It was probably said by ignorant people who cannot distinguish justice or humanity from an absurd and impossible system.'[28]

Here Ritson plainly establishes abstinence from meat-eating and the slaughter of animals as being unconnected with supernatural idealism or any religious structure; here it is a product of humanitarianism, the rights of human beings extended to include for the first time the rights of animals.

The *Essay* also includes a whole section on human disease and suffering with references to eminent physicians who believed the cure was in temperance and abstention from meat. Ritson was a radical – he styled himself Citizen Ritson – and an atheist. His views were not popular with the majority, who considered him dangerous. A contemporary, Robert Surtees, commented equivocally: 'to follow his plan of abstinence were absurd, and nearly impossible; yet it is surely a disagreeable necessity which drives us to form part of a system where the powerful exist by preying on the weak.'[29] Ritson, at this time, spoke for a group of like-minded people; they were all radical, followers of Paine, believers in a new form of justice for society throughout the world. They came from different classes, a variety of professions and beliefs – writers, printers, dietitians – but there is no doubt that they represented the roots of what would become the vegetarian movement itself, though that was another form of radicalism altogether.

One work, *Cry of Nature*,[30] had an enormous following. Ritson mentions the author glowingly – John Oswald (1730-93), born in Edinburgh, who enlisted in the English army as a private soldier, then was posted to the East Indies. Friends obtained for him an officer's commission as he had distinguished himself with his bravery, but he bought himself out and travelled through Hindustan to learn about the Brahman and Buddhist religions. When he returned to England he still wore Indian dress. He then embraced the causes of the French Revolution and went to Paris. There he introduced some military reforms, but died fighting with his sons in La Vendée.

Oswald writes in a style burdened with sentiment and agony. Of animals he writes:

> alas, when they are plucked from the tree of Life, suddenly the withered blossoms of their beauty shrink to the chilly hand of Death. Quenched in his cold grasp expires the lamp of their loveliness, and struck by the livid blast of loathed putrefaction, their comely limbs are involved in ghastly horror. Shall we leave the living herbs to seek, in the den of death, an obscene aliment? Insensible to the blooming beauties of Pomona – unallured by the fragrant odours that exhale from her groves of golden fruits – unmoved by the nectar of Nature, by the ambrosia of innocence – shall the voracious vultures of our impure appetites speed along those lovely scenes and alight in the loathsome sink of putrefaction to devour the remains of other creatures, to load with cadaverous rottenness a wretched stomach?[31]

When not laden down with his own prose Oswald argues well. Here he makes a point on meat-eaters which Shelley was to endorse later:

> They feed on the carcass without remorse, because the dying struggles of the butchered victim are secluded from their sight – because his cries pierce not their ears – because his agonising shrieks sink not into their souls. But were they forced, with their own hands, to assassinate the beings whom they devour, who is there among us who would not throw down the knife with detestation, and, rather than embrue his hands in the murder of the lamb, consent for ever to forgo the accustomed repast.[32]

Vivisectionists are also lambasted:

> You, the sons of modern science, who court not Wisdom in her walks of silent meditation in the grove, who behold her not in the living loveliness of her works, but expect to meet her in the midst of obscenity and corruption – you, who dig for knowledge in the depths of the dunghill, and who expect to discover Wisdom enthroned amid the fragments of mortality and the abhorrence of the senses – you, that with cruel violence interrogate trembling Nature, who plunge into her maternal bosom the butcher-knife, and, in quest of your nefarious science, delight to scrutinise the fibres of agonising beings, you dare also to violate the human form, and holding up

the entrails of men, you exclaim, 'Behold, the bowels of a carnivorous animal!' Barbarians! to these very bowels I appeal against your cruel dogmas – to these bowels which Nature hath sanctified to the sentiments of pity and of gratitude, to the yearnings of kindred, to the melting tenderness of love.[33]

A writer and printer, George Nicholson (1760-1825), was another powerful influence on those eager to listen. His book *The Primeval Diet of Man*[34] was published in 1801, its title page bearing a quote from Rousseau: 'Humans, be humane! It is your first duty. What wisdom is there for you without humanity?' A later edition in 1803 had an added section of recipes: 'One hundred perfectly palatable and nutritious substances, which may easily be procured at an expense much below the price of the limbs of our fellow animals . . .'[35]

Nicholson had a pragmatic mind, as concerned with the poor as he was with animals. He attempted in his book to answer the most common criticism, though with little hope of winning the battle. His preface sets the tone of pervading gloom:

The difficulties of removing deep-rooted prejudices, and the inefficiency of reason and arguments, when opposed to habitual opinions established on general approbation, are fully apprehended. Hence the cause of humanity, however zealously pleaded, will not be materially promoted. Unflattered by the hope of exciting an impression on the public mind, the following compilation is dedicated to the sympathismg and generous Few, whose opinions have not been founded on implicit belief and common acceptation: whose habits are not fixed by the influence of false and pernicious maxims or corrupt examples: who are neither deaf to the cries of misery, pitiless to suffering innocence, nor unmoved at recitals of violence, tyranny, and murder.[36]

However, like others, Nicholson is full of righteous anger:

Mankind affect to revolt at murders, at the shedding of blood, and yet eagerly, and without remorse, feed on the corpse after it has undergone the culinary process. What mental blindness pervades the human race, when they do not perceive that every feast of blood is a tacit encouragement and licence to the very crime their pretended delicacy abhors.[37]

He attempts to answer the most common accusations:

Opposers of compassion urge: 'If we should live on vegetable food, what shall we do with our cattle? What would become of them? They would grow so numerous they would be prejudicial to us – they would eat us up if we did not kill and eat them.' But there is abundance of animals in the world whom men do not kill and eat; and yet we hear not of their injuring mankind, and sufficient room is found for their abode. Horses are not usually killed to be eaten, and yet we have not heard of any country overstocked with them. The raven and redbreast are seldom killed, and yet they do not become too numerous.[38]

It was not only the humanists that had some influence but also the dietitians. William Lambe (1765–1847) was to influence John Newton and thence Shelley and was renowned in the first half of his life for noticing the quality of the waters at the village of Leamington and turning it into a spa. Like Doctor Cheyne and Cornaro before him, he was brought to the vegetable diet by ill health and ailments, which he had suffered from ever since his eighteenth year. Writing in the third person in his *Additional Reports* he tells the story:

> He resolved, therefore, finally to execute what he had been contemplating for some time – to abandon animal food altogether, and everything analogous to it, and to confine himself wholly to vegetable food. This determination he put in execution the second week of February, 1806, and he has adhered to it with perfect regularity to the present time. His only subject to repentance with regard to it has been that it had not been adopted much earlier in life. He never found the smallest real ill consequence from this change. He sank neither in strength, flesh, nor in spirits. He was at all times of a very thin and slender habit, and so he has continued to be, but upon the whole he has rather gained than lost flesh. He has experienced neither indigestion nor flatulence even from the sort of vegetables which are commonly thought to produce flatulence, nor has the stomach suffered from any vegetable matter, though unchanged by culinary art or uncorrected by condiments. The only unpleasant consequence of the change was a sense of emptiness of stomach, which continued many months. In about a year, however, he became fully reconciled to the new habit, and felt as well satisfied with his vegetable meal as he had been formerly with his dinner of flesh.[39]

From then on Lambe never changed (unlike both Cheyne and Cornaro who occasionally slipped). He began to use his diet as a cure for patients ill with cancer. We have an account from John Abernethy, the renowned surgeon of St Bartholomew's Hospital:

> Very recently Dr Lambe has proposed a method of treating cancerous diseases, which is wholly dietetic. He recommends the adoption of a strict vegetable regimen, to avoid the use of fermented liquors, and to substitute water purified by distillation in the place of common water as a beverage, and in all parts of diet in which common water is used, as tea, soups, etc. The grounds upon which he founds his opinion of the propriety of this advice, and the prospects of benefit which it holds out, may be seen in his Reports on Cancer, to which I refer my readers.

My own experience on the effects of this regimen is of course very limited. Nor does it authorise me to speak decidedly on the subject. But I think it right to observe that, in one case of cancerous ulceration in which it was used, the symptoms of the disease, were in my opinion, rendered more mild, the erysipelatous inflammation surrounding the ulcer was removed, and the life of the patient was, in my judgement, considerably prolonged. The more minute details of the facts constitute the sixth case of Dr Lambe's Reports. It seems to me very proper and desirable that the powers of the regimen recommended by Dr Lambe should be fairly tried, for the following reasons:-

Because I know some persons who, whilst confined to such diet, have enjoyed very good health; and further, I have known several persons, who did try the effects of such a regimen, declare that it was productive of considerable benefit. They were not, indeed, afflicted with cancer, but they were induced to adopt a change of diet to allay a state of nervous irritation and correct disorder of the digestive organs, upon which medicine had but little influence.

Because it appears certain, in general, that the body can be perfectly nourished by vegetables.

Because all great changes of the constitution are more likely to be effected by alterations of diet and modes of life than by medicine.

Because it holds out a source of hope and consolation to the patient in a disease in which medicine is known to be unavailing and in which surgery affords no more than a temporary relief.[40]

Lambe had a great belief in distilled water and the children of the Newton family were praised for their beauty: 'I am well acquainted with a family of young children who have scarcely ever touched animal food, and who now for three years have drunk only distilled water. For clearness and beauty of complexion, muscular strength, fulness of habit free from grossness, hardiness, healthiness, and ripeness of intellect these children are unparalleled.'[41]

A colleague and friend, Dr Lyford, wrote of him when he was seventy-two:

I found him to be very gentlemanly in manners and venerable in appearance. He is rather taller than the middle height. His hair is perfectly white, for he is now seventy-two years of age. He told me he had been on the vegetable diet thirty-one years, and that his health was better now than at forty, when he commenced his present system of living. He considers himself as likely to live thirty years longer as to have lived to his present age . . . Although he is seventy-two years of age he walks into town, a distance of three miles from his residence, every morning and back at night. Dr Lambe, I am told, has spent large sums of money in making experiments and publishing their results to the world.[42]

All the arguments which were to sustain modern vegetarianism were in circulation:

> not only did the slaughter of animals have a brutalizing effect upon the human character, but the consumption of meat was bad for health; it was physiologically unnatural; it made men cruel and ferocious; and it inflicted untold suffering upon man's fellow-creatures. By the end of the century these arguments had been supplemented by an economic one: stock-breeding was a wasteful form of agriculture compared with arable farming, which produced far more food per acre.[43]

## The Agricultural Revolution

By the end of the century the upsurge in humanitarian feelings had given the concept of animal rights greater propulsion and dynamism. Yet there was another more pragmatic reason for the growing vociferousness of the movement. The vegetarian campaign now had some hope of expanding because for the first time in modern history enough vegetables and cereals were available* – nothing resembling the surfeit we have now, but vegetables existed in amounts which would have astonished Samuel Pepys and possibly even have changed the character of his dinners.

The eighteenth century and to a certain extent the last quarter of the previous century are marked by the slow but steady rise of the market garden. As towns grew, so did the market gardens, sited some way outside. Every large town had its belt of gardens which supplied the markets with vegetables and fruit. London had gardens at Lewisham, Blackheath, Wanstead and Ilford. A vegetable market at Liverpool grew up because of an influx of French Canadians who wanted cheap vegetables for their soups. The Irish grew potatoes for English markets – not that the potato became popular very easily, for it was related in people's minds already with distress, famine and war. It had been primarily used since its discovery in the New World as food for pigs, but potatoes eventually became a staple food for the poor in the north of England. Cabbages, carrots, turnips and sprouts were eaten in the south. Boiled beef and carrots was a popular dish at the beginning of the century.

Cabbages, cauliflowers, turnips, carrots, parsnips, peas, beans and celery were all grown, but little else. The great range of herbs and vegetables (especially salads) which Evelyn a century before had been so enthusiastic about still stayed within the walled gardens of the aristocracy, for their use

---

*The diet menu for the Foundling Hospital in London for 1747 comprises meat (mutton, pork, beef), rice puddings, milk, bread and cheese, but no vegetables. These were added in 1762 – greens, potatoes and parsnips. Another indication of the rise in the consumption of green vegetables is the decline in scorbutic conditions. Drummond and Wilbraham[44] note that this was so between 1720 and 1760 but after the Enclosures Act they returned. Menus and recipes of the period gradually change so that by the end of the century vegetables are often included either as a dish in themselves or as flavouring cooked with the meat.

only. The quality of vegetables was generally poor. One would think that though poor-quality vegetables were available in the towns, at least their freshness would have been unimpaired in the country and so some of the vegetarian campaigners might have had a rich and varied diet. Each man was entitled to a one-acre strip on common land and there the people grew their produce and pastured their few livestock, while from the forests and heaths they gathered their winter kindling. All this common land was being taken away from them by the rich landowners. While George III was on the throne three million acres were filched from the people. There was a scientific reason behind this expropriation of common land, summed up in the Norfolk four-course system, which was created at the end of the seventeenth century, a system whereby wheat was grown in the first year, turnips in the second, then barley with clover and rye-grass undersown in the third. In the fourth year the clover and rye-grass were either cut or grazed on, and the animals further enriched the fields because their diet was better. A farmer could not grow these fodder crops in the open fields as the people used them to graze their own few livestock. Hence the idea of enclosures which would pen livestock into hedged fields, while alternative fields were used for the four-course system. All the landowner had to do was to submit a petition for enclosure on the particular stretch of land he had his eye on, then it automatically became the subject of a Bill. Though villagers could appeal they were helpless.

Such inhumanities fuelled the anger of people like Paine and Ritson but the tide was against them. Agriculture as a science had come to make itself felt. Eminent voices like the first President of the Board of Agriculture, Sir John Sinclair, were loud in claiming that common land was a form of barbarism and could not lead to efficient cultivation. Arthur Young, who travelled England to survey the land,[45] thought that the small inefficient farmer should be eliminated. And so they were, leaving the villages to come to the towns.

Drummond, though deploring the injustice, considers such changes were in the end beneficial to English agriculture:

> It was true that, apart from often being unable to afford to make changes, the villagers and small farmers were backward in their outlook and reluctant to adopt the new agricultural methods which were coming into use. The majority of the big landowners, on the other hand, were progressively minded and anxious to get better yields of crops and improved breeds of cattle.[46]

Yet what were these changes and could these have fired the indignation of the vegetarian campaigners? It was an astonishing time which radically changed the landscape of England and the efficiency by which the food was sown, cultivated and harvested. Up to this time England was still farming with implements little better than those used in the Middle Ages, but now hardly a year passed without the discovery of some useful invention. Jethro

Tull devised the first horse-drawn hoe and a practical field drill allowing less seed to be wasted and more grain harvested. Farm tools were made in cast iron and became mass-produced; the Rotherham plough was invented, a design little changed today; the first threshing machine appeared before 1800, and other machines could prepare animal feed, chop turnips and cut chaff. The most significant change was winter fodder for livestock, which enabled cattle not to be slaughtered in November. Now for the first time there was a reasonable chance of keeping a valuable animal without it degenerating into a physical wreck, and breeding from it in the spring. The idea of feeding cattle on something other than straw was learnt from Holland. William Ellis (d. 1758), a farmer and writer on agriculture, speaks of 'raw turnips, chopt or whole . . . rape-seed cakes and grain given to the cows . . . by this means they give much milk.'[47] Rape-seed was crushed to provide oil for lamps and Dutch farmers discovered that cattle loved the residue left after the crushing. As well as turnips, swedes, mangold-wurzels, potatoes, clover and cabbage were all grown to feed cattle in the winter. Animal-lovers must have been aware that farmers were considering animals in a new light, as creatures that could exist longer than a year if cared for. In fact some animals treasured for improving the breed began to be sold at auction for enormous prices. The size of the animals increased, improving the carcase meat; milk yields improved in cows, finer quality fleece was obtained from sheep and pigs grew bigger. Horses were very carefully bred for strength as they were so vital for transport and farm labour. The animals may in the end still have been slaughtered for meat, but certainly in their lives their status had risen considerably. It was just as well that greater efficiency in food production occurred for during the century the population doubled from five to ten million.

Because of the enclosures, the food of country people declined; no longer did they have a small patch of land to grow vegetables or anywhere to keep hens, a pig, or even a cow as in the old days. In the north of England the potato had at last been accepted by the last quarter of the century. In the south wheat-growing had taken over the land to provide white bread which was all the rage. A farm labourer living at Streatly in Berkshire with a wife and four children earned £46 per year.[48] The cost of their food amounted to £52 a year; they ate per week 8 half-peck loaves,* 2 lb of cheese, 2 lb of butter, 2 lb of sugar, 2 oz of tea, 1/2 lb of boiled bacon and 2 pints of milk. The diet could barely sustain anyone. The records of the farm labourer's family do not mention vegetables at all. If they existed they were root vegetables, turnips and swedes, the fodder for the cattle, and to admit to eating such food was too humiliating. Jonas Hanway, the reformer, said of the poor in Stevenage in 1767: 'The food of the poor is good bread, cheese, pease, and turnips in winter, with a little pork or other meat, when they can afford it; but from the high price of meat, it has not lately been within their reach. As to milk, they have hardly sufficient for their use.'[49]

---

*8 half-peck loaves are equivalent to a bushel of flour, which equals 8 gallons of dry weight.

The country gentleman, in contrast, lived excessively well. In Parson Woodforde's diaries and in Sydney Smith's letters the accounts of meals are heavy with meat, game, fowl, with cold tongue and ham, with roasted sweetbreads, giblet soup, pigeons, veal and marrow sauce. A dinner of bread, vegetables and cheese would have seemed to these gourmands an affront, on a cultural and aesthetic level. It certainly would have been a complete mystery to them why vegetarian campaigners, for the most part men with the education and means of gentlemen, and atheists, would have deprived themselves of so much pleasure. By the middle of the century a few vegetables were cooked with the meat – 'calf's head with cabbage' or 'bacon with sprouts'. But to eat these alone, unseasoned by meat juices or gravy, was not to be considered in the normal household.

Reformers who were not vegetarian themselves, like Jonas Hanway, urged that the poor use many more vegetables to eke out a small amount of meat. Drummond quotes one of his recipes for a beef and vegetable soup which required, to 1 lb lean beef, 1 pint of split peas, 12 oz of potatoes, 3 oz of ground rice, 3 large leeks, 2 heads of celery, salt and 9 pints of water.[50] This would have given a copious amount of weak stock, though the split peas, ground rice and potato would have thickened it slightly. In fact, the recipe could have been enriched by many more vegetables – onions, turnips, garlic, carrots. It shows the caution over vegetables that even intelligent and well-intentioned people like Hanway must have felt.

The amount of soup was intended for five stout men, and would have allowed them only 1100 calories, a great deal less than they needed. But Hanway made another greater error, as so many reformers did, in thinking that the problems of poverty could be solved by a bowl of nourishing soup, a sentiment which was to continue throughout the nineteenth century and well into our own. The poor subsisted on bread and cheese, largely because they had no fuel to cook a hot meal; the long, slow cooking needed for beef and vegetable soup was well nigh impossible for most of them.

For the middle and upper classes the eighteenth century was a time of gluttony and corpulence, and of all the diseases stemming from obesity. Ideas about a strict vegetable diet in this context became almost fashionable. The works of Cornaro were widely read, more by people, one surmises, wishing they had the willpower to go on such a diet than by people who actually had abstained from meat and were happily subsisting on plain vegetables.

If the eighteenth century marks a peak of meat consumption, it also marks a time when the nature of the meat began to alter. The diet of cattle had begun to change, and change in a way which has only recently been appreciated. 'The natural foodstuff of the ancestor of our domestic cattle was soft, bushy, leafy material, the lower branches of trees, sedges, herbs and grasses.'[51] Once the cattle were enclosed they could not always get at the vegetation they needed; the cattle tended to eat the hedgerows which had been planted to keep them in, so leafy bushes were replanted with thorns. 'Enclosing an animal in a field meant simply that man now decided what the animal should eat.'[52] The enclosures were the beginning of the artificial conditions under which livestock would be ever after fed and kept. They might get bigger faster but much of that bulk would be fat; worse, the fat was to become saturated fat, the kind injurious to health and not the polyunsaturated fat of wild beasts.

## Shelley

One of the most enthusiastic supporters of the vegetable diet was a patient of Dr Lambe's, John Newton, who, it was thought, converted Shelley. We have a picture of what the Newtons ate from Jefferson Hogg★ who was part of the select group of friends who dined with Shelley at the Newtons' home:

> Certainly their vegetable dinners were delightful, elegant, and excellent repasts; flesh, fowl, fish, and 'game' never appeared – nor eggs nor butter bodily, but the two latter were admitted into cookery, but as sparingly as possible, and under protest, as not approved of and soon to be dispensed with. We had soups in great variety, that seemed the more delicate from the absence of flesh-meat.
>
> There were vegetables of every kind, plainly stewed or scientifically disguised. Puddings, tarts, confections and sweets abounded. Cheese was excluded. Milk and cream might not be taken unreservedly, but they were allowed in puddings, and sparingly in tea. Fruits of every kind were welcomed. We luxuriated in tea and coffee, and sought variety occasionally in cocoa and chocolate. Bread and butter, and buttered toast were eschewed; but bread, cakes, and plain seed-cakes were liberally divided among the faithful.[53]

Shelley himself wrote:

> The pleasure of taste to be derived from a dinner of potatoes, beans, peas, turnips, lettuce, with a dessert of apples, gooseberries, strawberries, currants, raspberries, and in winter, oranges, apples, and pears is far greater than is supposed. Those who wait until they can eat this plain fare, with the sauce of appetite, will scarcely join with the hypocritical sensualist at a lord mayor's feast who declaims against the pleasures of the table.[54]

Like Cornaro and Cheyne, Dr Newton (who was a Zoroastrian) became converted to the diet because of ill health. He published a book, *Return to Nature*, which begins by saying that he, his wife and four children under nine

---

★Thomas Jefferson Hogg met Shelley first at University College, Oxford, and they immediately became close friends. It was he who began the myth that Newton had converted Shelley in 1813, but this was at a time when Hogg was not seeing the Shelleys. Shelley's inclination towards a non-meat diet was established a good year and a half before he met Newton on fireworks day, 1812.

years had been on the non-flesh diet for two years and their apothecary's bill in this time had amounted to the sum of sixpence. Newton is an energetic proselytiser, especially on the health-giving qualities of the diet for children. He says:

> They will become not only more robust but more beautiful; that their carriage will be erect, their step firm; that their development at a critical period of youth, the prematurity of which has been considered an evil, will be retarded; that, above all, the danger of being deprived of them will in every way diminish; while by these light repasts their hilarity will be augmented, and their intellects cleared in a degree which shall astonishingly illustrate the delightful effects of this regimen . . .[55]

Shelley (1792-1822) was a prodigious reader and was more likely to have been converted to vegetarianism by other writers on the subject. Hogg tells of an incident in Oxford when Shelley seized a baby out of its mother's arms while crossing Magdalen Bridge and started to question it about the character of its former lives, all this to prove a point about metempsychosis. Hogg, a law student from Durham, introduced Shelley to the works of David Hume, Voltaire, Paine, Franklin, Rousseau and Adam Smith. Later he read Buffon and Erasmus Darwin, the grandfather of Charles and the author of *Zoonomia* (1796), in which an early theory of evolution was propounded. A fellow student described Shelley as representing 'one of the enthusiastic and animated materialists of the French School, whom revolutionary violence lately intercepted at an early age in his philosophical career'.[56] Charles Kilpatrick Sharpe (an MA of Christ Church) wrote more generously: 'the author is a great genius, and if he be not clapped in Bedlam or hanged, will certainly prove one of the sweetest swans on the tuneful margin of the Cherwell'.[57]

Before embracing a non-flesh diet Shelley had already shocked and outraged his parents, as well as his Oxford college. A proclaimed atheist, he eloped with Harriet Westbrook, who was to become his wife. She was sixteen, he nineteen. Harriet, even at this age, expressed her horror at his godlessness: 'I was truly petrified, I wondered how he could live a moment professing such principles.'[58] Holmes says: 'Atheism implied immorality, social inferiority and unpatriotic behaviour . . . during a time of war against the revolutionary forces in Europe, it also implied treachery, revolutionism and foreign degeneracy.'[59] Not content with this, Shelley also claimed early on, in a letter to Leigh Hunt, that he believed in the secret international Jacobin society, dedicated to militant egalitarianism, destruction of private property, of religion and of superstitious social forms such as marriage.

Shelley died just before his thirtieth birthday. In his short life he produced a great quantity of work. He was a poet, essayist, dramatist, pamphleteer, translator, reviewer and correspondent. He attacked the main political and spiritual problems of his age and society. He wrote long poems and poetic dramas and accompanied these with essays on more practical aspects of the same problems. His vegetarianism was one facet of his radical character. The conversion can be dated to March 1812. Shelley and Harriet were living in Dublin at the time, where they had gone with Harriet's elder sister, Eliza, to print a collection of poems and Shelley's *Address to the Irish People*, a tract of some 12,000 words with ideas drawn from Hume and Paine. Shelley was a fervent admirer of Paine and wanted Eliza to edit a selection of Tom Paine's works to help educate the Dublin working classes. Talk of revolution made people nervous, even the reformers, in the aftermath of the French Revolution. Mob rule, it was thought, led to barbarism and injustice, and Shelley's intemperate outpourings were watched by government officials who would report to Lord Sidmouth's Home Office in Whitehall: 'a young boy, delivered a speech of considerable length and replete with much elegant language'.[60] The elegant language expressed beliefs and sentiments one might hear throughout the nineteenth century:

> It is horrible that the lower classes must waste their lives and liberty to furnish means for their oppressors to oppress them yet more terribly. It is horrible that the poor must give in taxes what would save them and their families from hunger and cold; it is still more horrible that they should do this to furnish further means of their own abjectness and misery.[61]

But Ireland, as for so many politicians and reformers, was too much for Shelley. His message was too crude, the problem too complex. He wrote in a letter dated 8 March:

> I had no conception of the depth of human misery until now. – The Poor of Dublin are assuredly the meanest and most miserable of all. In their narrow streets thousands seem huddled together – one mass of animated filth! . . . These were the persons to whom in my fancy I had addressed myself; how quickly were my views on this subject changed![62]

Four days later his wife wrote: 'we have forsworn meat and adopted the Pythagorean system. About a fortnight has elapsed since the change – we are delighted with it.'[63] It was hardly a promising moment to forswear meat, fowl and fish. Vegetables were notoriously hard to find in Ireland except for the potato. Arthur Young in his tour of Ireland in 1776 describes a family of six who ate 18 stone of potatoes and 40 lb of oatmeal in a week with milk and the occasional salted herring.

We know from the *Essays* and Note 17 in *Queen Mab* that Shelley was fervent in his renunciation of flesh. How consistent was he when it came to sitting at table? On 15 March Harriet writes a note to an Irish friend, Mrs Nugent, inviting her to dinner: 'expects the pleasure of her company to dinner, 5 o'clock, as a murdered chicken has been prepared for her repast'.[64] Did Mrs Nugent eat the chicken alone while the Shelleys sat down to a dish of potatoes? It is not difficult to believe that such was the scene, with Percy lecturing Mrs Nugent, rehearsing one of his pamphlets, on all the reasons why they should not kill a defenceless creature in order to survive.

On 4 April they left Dublin harbour and sailed for Holyhead. It took them thirty-six hours on a rough sea, and when at last they reached an inn, Shelley surprised Harriet by ordering a large meal including meat. 'You will think this very extraordinary,' Harriet wrote to Mrs Nugent.[65] We might also think it very extraordinary. But knowing the volatile nature of Shelley, knowing that his vegetarian conversion was barely a month old, and appreciating the rigours of a long rough voyage with nothing on board to eat at all, we may understand how the famished Shelley must have needed to fill his belly first and think of principles last.

With Dan, their Irish servant, they travelled south along the north Devon coast and discovered Lynmouth where they stayed that summer, Shelley writing political pamphlets, sending them off in hot air balloons and small boats, and using Dan to travel by foot around the neighbourhood sticking them to barn doors until he was arrested and imprisoned. In that summer Shelley worked, when not indignantly furious over Luddite suppression, on his first long poem, Queen Mab. He read copiously and much of the information he gleaned would go into the Notes. He worked during the summer weeks on the beach in the daytime and in the cottage in the evening: 'It was politics conducted by propaganda; polemics, visions, prophecies and philosophical disquisitions. Because it was also politics parading as poetry, Shelley hoped it might find a weak spot in the government's armour.'[66] Shelley also had an idea for a book of essays. Throughout his life he wrote on religious belief, free love, marriage and vegetarianism, but the essays remained uncollected and remain still the least known of his work. Yet some of the essays of that summer became Notes to Queen Mab. Shelley wrote to Hookham, his bookseller and publisher, in January 1813: 'The notes to QM will be long and philosophical. I shall take the opportunity which I judge to be a safe one of propagating my principles, which I decline to do syllogistically in a poem. A poem very didactic is I think very stupid.'[67]

Because of Dan's arrest and government harassment they had fled Lynmouth and found a house on the coast of Wales with a vegetable garden. Harriet was now pregnant, which might explain her diet. Shelley wrote to his friend Hogg: 'I continue vegetable. Harriet means to be slightly animal until the arrival of spring. – My health is much improved by it, tho' partly perhaps by my removal from your nerve racking and spirit quelling metropolis.'[68] But they fled Wales too after a particularly frightening shooting incident. Back in London for the private publication of Queen Mab, Harriet writes to Mrs Nugent, she who ate the murdered chicken: '. . . tho' it must not be published under pain of death, because it is too much against every existing establishment. It is to be privately distributed to his friends, and some copies sent over to America. Do you [know] any one that would wish for so dangerous a gift?'[69]

The Shelleys were now the friends of the Newtons. It was quite by accident that they met, for on 5 November, seeing a great display of fireworks in the air, Shelley rushed out into the street with the young William Godwin and traced the flashes and detonations to Dr Newton's house, where they were made welcome. From then on they spent many evenings together when the Shelleys were in London and it is then that Hogg recalled their suppers:

> Queen Mab is essentially subversive in intent, vigorously polemic in attack, and revolutionary in content and implication. Its main targets, constantly expressed in abstract categories, are, in order of importance: established religion; political tyranny; the destructive forces of war and commerce; and the perversion of human love caused by such chains and barriers as the marriage institution and prostitution. Secondary themes carry a strong puritan undercurrent, involving temperance and vegetarianism, republican austerity, and righteous moral independence of judgement. For all its irreligion, which is in many places extremely violent, the poem and the 'Notes' are fundamentally missionary in their manner of address with many overtones of sectarian tract writing.[70]

Eleven of the Notes to *Queen Mab* are brief; others are developed essays, on the labour theory of value, on free love, atheism, Christian doctrine and vegetarianism. Stanza 8 of the poem deals with flesh-eating:

> Immortal upon earth: no longer now
> He slays the lamb that looks him in the face,
> And horribly devours his mangled flesh,
> Which, still avenging Nature's broken law,
> Kindled, all putrid humours in his frame,
> All evil passions, and all vain belief;
> Hatred, despair, and loathing in his mind,
> The germs of misery, death, disease, and crime.
> No longer now the winged habitants,
> That in the woods their sweet lives sing away,
> Flee from the form of man; but gather round,
> And prune their sunny feathers on the hands
> Which little children stretch in friendly sport
> Towards these dreadless partners of their play.[71]

Note 17, which deals with vegetarianism, is yet another of Shelley's attempts to define the nature and cause of evil. Surely, he says, in man's unnatural diet there lies one cause for all the ills of the world. Yet the Note is not particularly original, repeating points we have seen already made by others. He speaks of good health: 'Seventeen persons of all ages . . . have lived for seven years on this diet, without a death and almost without the slightest illness';[72] of raw flesh being edible only when disguised: 'It is only by softening and disguising dead flesh by culinary preparation that it is rendered susceptible of mastication or digestion, and that the sight of its bloody juices and raw horror does not excite intolerable loathing and disgust';[73] and of the inefficiency of meat-eating: 'The quantity of nutritious vegetable matter consumed in fattening the carcase of an ox would afford ten times the sustenance, undepraving indeed and incapable of generating disease, if gathered immediately from the bosom of the earth.'[74]

This work, though privately printed, was to have enormous influence throughout the century. It became the most widely read, the most notorious and the most influential of all Shelley's works.

The poem and its Notes were far too radical in tone for the aristocracy; nor was it read for its literary and poetic qualities. It was middle-class and working-class radicals who bought the poem in cheap pirate editions. Because the poem was advertised in all the radical papers, it soon became a basic text in working-class culture. From these roots the early trade union movement of the 1820s, and the Chartism of the 1830s and 1840s, were to spring. Bernard Shaw was told by an old Chartist that 'Queen Mab was known as the Chartists' Bible.'[75]

The poem was to follow Shelley to the end. In his first major work he had captured something of the spirit of the coming age. His passionate message of non-violence continued throughout his works – 'I wish no living thing to suffer pain'[76] – and influenced many. His poem Revolt of Islam finally set George Bernard Shaw in his convictions (see p.261), but it was probably Gandhi who was most inspired by the Shelleyan doctrine of non-violence, feeling that 'it was infinitely superior to violence, forgiveness is more manly than punishment.'[77]

It is impossible to pin down with any accuracy the influence that Shelley's explicitly vegetarian message had on the century. As we shall see, by the 1840s the vegetarian movement had begun and was beginning to collect a growing membership. It is doubtful whether political extremism would have appealed to those members and it is certain that they would have been affronted by atheism. But the fame of the Romantic poet who wrote 'To a Skylark' and 'The Cloud' was immense, and orthodox vegetarians are likely to have taken a vegetarian Shelley to their hearts, while dismissing the political agitator and *enfant terrible*.

That Shelley continued to practise what he preached at this time is clear from a letter by Thomas Love Peacock, who visited the Shelleys when they were staying at a house at Bracknell where a Mrs Boinville, the wife of a French revolutionary émigré, lived. Here they discussed vegetarianism, atheism, naturism and French politics. 'At Bracknell,' Peacock recalled, 'Shelley was surrounded by a numerous society, all in great measure of his own opinions in relation to religion and politics, and the larger portion of them in relation to vegetable diet . . .'[78]

Late in 1813 the Shelleys took rooms in Edinburgh. Peacock (who was amused by almost everything) thought it extremely funny to find Shelley translating two of Plutarch's essays on vegetarianism, and also working on his second essay on the 'Vegetable System of Diet'. Holmes suggests that Shelley's increasing interest in vegetarianism was 'as much prompted by misplaced medical considerations as by ideological ones'.[79] Parts of this essay, Holmes thinks, suggest the beginning of a constant worry about his own health, his stomach aches, nervousness and anxiety. When he wrote on vegetarianism his original mind saw aspects of a socialist Utopia in a world turned to complete abstinence from meat, and he argues that vegetarianism could bring national independence and self-sufficiency, an end to trade, competition and the evils of commerce, while reducing the gap between the classes through the general levelling of lifestyles and the reduction of senseless luxuries.

*Queen Mab* became historically important to vegetarianism because it presented a visionary reconstruction of society, the returned dream of the Golden Age.

It is not known whether Shelley knew of the existence of the Reverend William Cowherd or of the establishment of a vegetarian coalition in Manchester in 1809, when members of the Bible Christian Church pledged themselves to abstain from flesh foods and alcohol. (Shelley seems to have avoided Manchester on his endless travels and he certainly could not have approved of a church – besides, he was only seventeen in 1809.) But it was from this coalition, led by Cowherd, that the nineteenth-century movement towards vegetarianism began and not directly from *Queen Mab* or from the great surge of radical humanism of which Shelley's poem was the last great advocate.

# 11

# Docks and Dandelions

The Pythagorean diet officially changed its title to vegetarianism⋆ in 1847, when a meeting was held at Northwood Villa, Ramsgate, a hydropathic infirmary run by William Horsell, from which emerged the Vegetarian Society. Horsell, who edited a magazine called the *Truth Tester*, responded to a letter from a vegetarian reader suggesting that a society should be formed. He convened a meeting of sympathetic friends and colleagues. Horsell had been much influenced, stimulated and reassured by the work of Justus Liebig† (1803-73), a German chemist who became famous for his research into protein in which he concluded that plants are the primary source of protein and there is no difference between plant and animal protein. This appeared to provide for the first time scientific validity for vegetarianism. Liebig was wrong – we now divide proteins into complete (animal) proteins, with a full complement of twenty amino acids, and incomplete (plant) proteins, meaning some amino acids are missing. But what Liebig wrote was exactly what the vegetarians needed to hear:

> Vegetable fibrine and animal fibrine, vegetable albumen and animal albumen, differ at the most in form. If these principles in nourishment fail, the nourishment of the animal will be cut off; if they obtain them, then the grass-feeding animal gets the same principles in his food as those upon which the flesh-eater entirely depends. Vegetables produce in their organism the blood of all beings. So that when the flesh-eaters consume the blood and flesh of the vegetable-eaters, they take to themselves exactly and simply the vegetable principles . . . the only difference between them is the action of the peculiar elements of each food upon the brain and nervous system. A Bear, who was kept in a zoological garden, displayed, so long as he had bread exclusively for

---

⋆The term 'vegetarian' was current in the 1840s but became official at the birth of the society. Later, a future President of the society, Professor Mayor, was to say the name derived from the Latin *vegetus*, meaning vigorous and lively. This etymological explanation has never seemed very convincing. From the earliest times a vegetarian seemed to signify someone passive and serene, though such figures as Tolstoy and Shaw were hardly characteristic of this public perception.
†Liebig's greatest contribution to our food supply must have been his research into artificially fertilising soil. By 1855 scores of various kinds of phosphates were being produced for farming.

nourishment, quite a mild disposition. Two days of feeding with flesh made him vicious, aggressive, and even dangerous to his attendant.[1]

Stimulated by Liebig's findings the main personalities from the Alcott House Concordium, as the educational set-up became known, and from the Bible Christian movement founded the Vegetarian Society. It was this latter branch of Christian fundamentalism which was also to organise the vegetarian movement in America and Germany.

## Swedenborg's Disciples

The Bible Christians (sometimes called Cowherdites) were inspired by the life and works of Emanuel Swedenborg (1688-1772), the Swedish scientist, Christian mystic, philosopher and theologian, who in the last thirty years of his life produced a book a year, all in Latin, all of which had an enormous following. His last work, *True Christian Religion*, sums up much of what went before. He hoped that his works would spawn a new form of Christian church, ritual and religion. Swedenborg began as a follower of the philosophy of Descartes and Leibniz, then decided to create an alternative philosophy which would be closer to a religious faith. He had little to say about the human relationship with animals, but what he did say on meat-eating was highly significant. He saw meat-eating as the most vivid symbol of our fall from grace and the source of all evil.

In 1773 the Reverend John Clowes, rector of St John's, Manchester, became a disciple of Swedenborg, yet contrived to remain within the Church of England. At the same time, various Swedenborg societies began to form and in the 1780s a Church of the New Jerusalem based on Swedenborg's ideas was founded in London. Some of the members of Clowes's congregation broke away and formed themselves into the New Jerusalem Temple, in 1793, and they invited his ex-curate, William Cowherd, to be their first minister. After seven years, in 1800, Cowherd quarrelled with his congregation and started his own chapel at nearby Salford, though still within the Swedenborgian New Church. A difference in style and interpretation developed between Cowherd and the congregation, breaking out into various controversies which would continue for the next nine years.

The appeal of Swedenborg was that through the earlier German mystic, Behmen (see p.184), his thought preserved the mystic and Hermetic traditions which Descartes and the passion for the clockwork universe had destroyed. Behmen taught that the material realm is all one of effect, whose causes are spiritual and whose purpose is divine. It is a convenient message for the poor and the deprived, for those condemned to drudgery and menial work, for all those with little hope. The path of mysticism, individual vision and revelation at least appeals as something inherently your own. However sparse the rewards of this life, no one can take God away from you. Swedenborg's mysticism was founded on the old doctrines of microcosm and macrocosm (William Blake was perhaps the most prominent

Swedenborgian, though he was never a member of one of his churches), teaching that the secret key to the great enigma and mystery of life lay in intuition and spiritual revelation. It was a view which Immanuel Kant attacked when he enquired into the spiritual claims of Swedenborg in an investigation into the world of spirits. Swedenborg's faith also revived an old heresy, Sabellianism,* the belief that God is one deity which incorporates all three facets of the Trinity. Hence God is Father, Son and Spirit; Christ was born of a woman and is not divine. Because all things have an outward and an inner form, God is manifest within all people and his kinship with nature relies on our recognition that he reflects all the laws of nature within himself. The belief emphasises the concepts of natural laws and natural rights, and human independence and individuality. The belief is also a reaction against the Age of Reason, against scientific empiricism and religious scepticism. Swedenborgianism drew on various alchemic and astrological ideas, possessed concepts of spiritual and mental healing and ideas of physical health. Theosophy and Christian Science would emerge from the same root later in the nineteenth century. The beliefs are a rebirth of Gnostic revelation. At any time before the eighteenth century the Church would have condemned them as heretical.

Yet it was not the orthodox Church which ousted the Swedenborg disciples; it was they who left the Church. In 1809 Cowherd preached on his new beliefs, as revealed to him, of vegetarianism and total abstinence and the New Church congregation this time walked out on him. Not disheartened, Cowherd built a new chapel with his own money at King Street, Salford, and coined the term Bible Christian. The Bible Christians soon attracted a large following of working-class people, partly one assumes because Cowherd offered hot vegetable soup, medical help (Cowherd was often termed 'Doctor' and was believed to be a healer) and a free burial ground.

Harvests had been bad and in 1812 the country was brought to near famine. The following year saw a huge surplus of wheat and the price came down. Then in 1814, another good harvest provoked the farmers into protests that the price of corn would be so low they would be ruined. The Corn Law of 1815 kept the price of wheat artificially high. The poor got poorer and many started to emigrate to Australia. Unemployment rose and the urban centres of industry where all the New Church chapels were sited (there was one at Hulme and one at Ancoats) became centres of caring and concern within an indifferent and bleak society. At Hulme the Reverend James Gaskill ran special classes for the education of the working people and established the Hulme Philosophical Society.

William Cobbett was horrified at the plight of the rural poor. In 1821 he wrote:

---

*Sabellius (a presbyter in the second century AD in Rome) propounded a more developed form of Monarchianism.

The labourers seem miserably poor. Their dwellings are little better than pig-beds, and their looks indicate that their food is not nearly equal to that of a pig. Their wretched hovels are stuck upon little bits of ground on the road side, where the space has been wider than the road demanded. In many places they have not two rods to a hovel . . . Yesterday morning was a sharp frost; and this had set the poor creatures to digging up their little plots of potatoes. In my whole life I never saw human wretchedness equal to this: no, not even amongst the free negroes in America.[2]

Out of the bleak prospects of the countryside, poor families moved to find work in the factories. But what they found was, if anything, worse:

A witness before Michael Sadler's Committee on Factory Children's Labour of 1831 said that he was seven when he started work: 'the hours of labour were 5 a.m. to 8 p.m. with half an hour allowed at noon. There was no time for rest or refreshment in the afternoon; we had to eat our meals as we could, standing or otherwise. I had 14½ hours' actual labour when seven years of age: the wage I then received was two shillings and ninepence per week.' This witness explained that the dust in the atmosphere often got into the food and spoiled it. 'You cannot take food out of your basket or handkerchief but what it is covered with dust directly . . . The children are frequently sick because of the dust and dirt they eat with their meal.' This was probably the extreme case. At 'good' mills there was an hour for dinner at noon, half an hour for breakfast, and another half-hour for 'drinking' in a day starting at 6 a.m. and ending at 8 p.m., but in a great many factories up to half the total mealtimes might be taken up in cleaning the spindles. The child snatches its meal in a hurried manner in the midst of work, and in a place of dust − in a foul atmosphere and in a temperature equal to a hothouse.[3]

Apprenticed pauper children that worked for the mill owners suffered most of all. The pigs kept at the mill fared slightly better and were fed first. Sometimes the children tried to steal food from the pigs, but they used to start such a noise of snorts and grunts the swineherd would run out with a whip. The children were fed on a porridge seasoned with the brine that the salted pork or beef had been cured in, a mixture that was so repulsive that even the starving could gag on it.

In 1819 the Nottinghamshire frame-knitters presented a petition to the Lord Lieutenant of the County:

From the various and low prices given by our employers, we have not, after working from sixteen to eighteen hours per day, been able to earn more than from four to seven shillings per week to maintain our wives and families upon, to pay taxes, house rent, etc. . . . and though we have substituted meal and water, or potatoes and salt for that more wholesome food an Englishman's table used to abound with, we have repeatedly retired after a hard day's labour, and been under the necessity of putting our children supperless to bed to stifle their cries of hunger; nor think that we give this picture too high a colouring when we can most solemnly declare that for the last eighteen months we have scarcely known what it is to be free from the pangs of hunger.[4]

Skilled factory workers earned a little more than those at the poverty line, £1 per week and upwards. The best-selling cookery book of the time, *System of Practical Domestic Economy* by Mrs Rundell, gave two suggested budgets, for incomes of 33 shillings and 21 shillings a week; both were planned for parents and three children. On 21 shillings the family is supposed to dispense with tea and make do with cheap cuts of meat. The diet is bread, potatoes and milk, a small amount of cheese and 6 lbs of meat a week.

The factory worker on a comparable wage, according to Dr James Kay,[*] received little or no fresh meat. Describing the daily life of a Manchester operative in 1832, Kay says that he rose at five o'clock in the morning, worked at the mill from six till eight, and then returned home for half an hour or forty minutes to breakfast. This consisted of tea or coffee with a little bread. He then went back until noon. At dinner-time, the meal for the inferior workmen consisted of boiled potatoes, with melted lard or butter poured over them and sometimes a few pieces of fried fat bacon. Those with higher earnings could afford a greater proportion of animal food, though the quantity was still small. Work then resumed from one o'clock until seven or later, and the last meal of the day was tea and bread, sometimes mingled with spirits.[5]

Meat, because of its cost, was probably a rarity in Cowherd's congregation so it cannot have been a great hardship to sacrifice it. Engels, in his *Condition of the Working Class in England in 1844*, sums up the part meat-eating plays as a symbol of how well off a family was:

The better-paid workers, especially those in whose families every member is able to earn something, have good food as long as this state of things lasts; meat daily, and bacon and cheese for supper. Where wages are less, meat is used only two or three times a week, and the proportion of bread and potatoes increases. Descending gradually, we find the animal food reduced to a small piece of bacon cut up with the potatoes; lower still, even this disappears, and there remains only bread, cheese, porridge and potatoes until, on the lowest round of the ladder, among the Irish, potatoes form the sole food.[6]

---

[*]James Phillips Kay was author of *The Moral and Physical Condition of the Working Classes Employed in the Cotton Manufacture in Manchester.*

Half the children born in towns died before they were five, while a great number of the rest were malnourished and suffered from rickets.

Cowherd's popularity was due as much to his oneness with the people, their suffering and their injustices. Bible Christians, in the aftermath of Peterloo, opened their doors to those pupils who wore green ribbons,* whereas other Sunday schools had expelled them.

Jonathan Wright, who led the vegetarian Swedenborgians in Keighley in a march, held a banner symbol of the death of the King and 'his oppressive laws'. The government expressed interest in Wright and he was forced to escape to America, where he joined his brother-in-law, William Metcalfe, in Philadelphia. The ties between the American vegetarian movement and that movement in England were very close and continued to be throughout the century.

Cowherd chose to ignore the doctrine of original sin, Pauline salvation and the importance of the crucifixion. Instead of a conversion which would wash away the sinful life in one golden moment there would be a slow growth of spiritual and moral regeneration, in which temperance and vegetarianism played their part. Cowherd cited 'the medical arguments of Dr Cheyne and the humanitarian sentiments of St-Pierre'† as influencing his conclusions on diet. Scripture was to be read for its hidden meaning, not its literal one. Though this was within the Hermetic tradition, the approach was not, but was rationalist and intellectual with value placed upon scientific enquiry. Hence not only medicine was valued, but education as well. Cowherd had as part of his Chapel an Academy of Sciences, in which William Metcalfe studied and taught Classics and finally was ordained by Cowherd. It was Metcalfe, in 1817, who took a section of his congregation at Addingham, Yorkshire – twenty adults and nineteen children – and emigrated to America. In 1850 he founded the American Vegetarian Society.

Cowherd based his vegetarianism on Swedenborg's vision of meat-eating as symbol of the Fall, like Mani, the Cathars and many others before him. Meat-eating blocked the spirit's aspirations, stopped individuals experiencing the full power of their vision. John Wright recalled Cowherd preaching:

> partaking of flesh was a result of the Fall of man; and consequently was incompatible with that state of resurrection from sensual to spiritual existence . . . flesh tended to inflame the passions and to sensualise the many and consequently to impede the reception in the soul of heavenly love and wisdom.[7]

---

*Worn in memory of those massacred at St Peter's Fields, 16 August 1819.

†Author of *Paul et Virginie*, which had a phenomenal success after it was published in 1787, being translated into English, Italian, German, Dutch, Polish, Russian and Spanish. It is a rich evocation of exotic nature in the tropical setting of Mauritius; nature is presented as only innocent and good, a pastoral Utopia. It is full of vegetarian propaganda: 'Inasmuch as the non-flesh diet introduces many virtues and excludes none, it will be well to bring up the young upon it, since it has so happy an influence upon the beauty of the body and upon the tranquillity of the mind. This regimen prolongs childhood, and, by consequence, human life.'[8]

Cowherd died in March 1816. He was just over fifty and his relatively early death was bad publicity for the efficacy of the diet itself.

But the Bible Christians were not the only element in founding the Vegetarian Society. There was another branch at the meeting of 1847 at Ramsgate, those who had attended the Alcott House Concordium.

## Concordium

In the 1838 prospectus of Alcott House, Ham Common, Richmond, the Concordium was described as an 'Industrial, Harmonic Educational College for the benefit of such parties as were ready to leave the ignorant selfish strife of the antagonistic world'. The Principal, James Pierrepoint Greaves, had been much influenced by Robert Owen and Johann Pestalozzi, both renowned educational reformers. Pestalozzi had based his own curriculum on Rousseau's plan in *Emile*, which emphasised group recitation and activities like drawing, writing, singing, exercise, model- and map-making, and field trips. He made allowances for individual differences, grouping children by ability rather than age, and advocated educating the poor and strengthening students' own talents. Robert Owen believed that an individual's character was formed by its earliest influences. If these could be improved, people would become more civilised. His success at New Lanark with his mill community and schools, opened in 1816, became known world-wide. Both Owen and Pestalozzi were great humanists. Owen went on to demand a trade union movement and new self-sufficient communities. Vegetarianism was a part of Owen's plans. Greaves added elements of self-denial and mysticism to these ideas of educational reform.

Another influence on vegetarians at this time was the French writer Antoine Gleizes (1773-1843), who began by studying medicine and stopped when he could not endure vivisection. He became a vegetarian at the age of twenty-five and thereafter ate, alone, food prepared by himself. He could not endure the sight or smell of flesh. His wife remained a meat-eater. His *Christianity Explained: or the True Spirit of that Religion Misinterpreted up to the Present Day* sought to prove that Christ's mission had for its end the abolition of the murder of animals. This was splendid grist to the mill of the Bible Christians and the Concordium, for any interpretation of the Gospels which included love and respect for animals counted as a form of spiritual revelation, therefore divine truth.

His three-volume work *Thalysie: the New Existence* was published in 1842. It is in the form of twelve discourses, with the third volume, entitled *Moral Proofs*, a résumé of the history and ethics of the subject. Its pompous, exalted style makes it almost impossible to read today but it was enormously popular among vegetarians throughout the century. The *Vegetarian Messenger* said of Gleizes in 1873: 'in contradiction to the hollow phrases of optimism and the depressing contemplation of pessimism, Gleizes restores the peace of our mind and bestows on us the hope for a future reign of Wisdom and Love.'

Alcott House aimed to put Greaves's ideas into practice. The moral growth of the children was the educational ideal, 'with a view to their becoming integral men and women',[9] for only these would change society and bring that future reign of wisdom and love to a reality. Men and women followed a simple, austere regime, beginning the day at 5 a.m. with a cold bath and exercise. Emphasis was placed on fresh air and unconstrained clothing (no wool was allowed, only cotton or linen), on raw food and celibacy. Married people were refused entry to the inner circle. Breakfast was brown bread, porridge, figs and raw vegetables. In the morning they worked and then the children ate dinner at noon while the adults ate at 1 p.m. For dinner they ate potatoes, cabbage, beet, parsnips or whatever vegetables were in season, followed by fruit and rice. In the afternoon they worked and for supper at 6 p.m. they ate brown bread, biscuits, figs, raisins or fruits and vegetables in season. At nine they went to bed. They drank water, as milk and all dairy products were forbidden. Greaves disliked institutionalised religion, rejecting churches, ritual and doctrine. Instead he propounded an overall concept of love which would conquer and solve all problems and differences. His favourite phrase was 'most loveful'. The aim of the community was to produce the 'most loveful, intelligent and efficient conditions for divine progress in humanity'.[10]

Bronson Alcott,* an educational reformer, philosopher and vegetarian, had visited the Concordium in 1842. This was after Greaves had died, but so delighted and honoured were they by the visit that the house was named after him. They gave a gala in the garden at which he spoke: 'Our trust is in purity not vengeance. Together with pure beings will come pure habits. A better body shall be built up from the orchard and the garden . . . flesh and blood we will reject as the accursed thing. A pure mind has no faith in them.'[11]

At the Alcott House Academy they had a large fruit and vegetable garden which the students laboured in. They ate and baked Graham† bread made with wholemeal flour and dried fruit as part of their vegan diet every day.

There can be no doubt that the Concordium was a fringe group well outside the perimeters of what society in general would have thought acceptable. Greaves's teachers were H.S. Clubb (later ordained) and William Oldham. Clubb had arrived there aged sixteen to teach shorthand and remained a believer and a vegetarian all his life, rising in distinction and prominence. But the life of the school was a short one (it survived ten years, ending in 1848). The public perception of such educational experiments which included a radical new diet could not have been helped by a cookery book by Mrs Joseph Brotherton but published anonymously. Published in 1821, it was entitled *A New System of Vegetable Cookery* with an Introduction recommending abstinence from animal food and intoxicating liquors. Mrs

---

*Father of Louisa May, the author of *Little Women*.

†Named after Sylvester Graham, who lectured on temperance in America (see p.256). Biscuits and flour are still named after him.

Brotherton was a member of the society of Bible Christians. Vegetarian fundamentalist Christians wrestled with the problem of New Testament text. Why, they asked, did Christ not make it clear that killing animals for meat was a sin? In the New Testament it never actually says that Christ eats meat, but he does eat fish. So Mrs Brotherton with great ingenuity reinterpreted the text: the word fish, she claims, really means water melon or lotus plant. This obviously shed new light on the miracle of the loaves and fishes. The book also made suggestions such as: 'a roasted onion applied to the top of the head will frequently relieve the most violent pain'; or 'a small bag of saffron worn at the stomach prevents sea sickness'; while for dysentery the advice is 'take a sheet of writing paper, cut it into slips, boil it in a pint and a half of milk to a pint, take it twice.'

Both Clubb and Oldham were prominent at the first conference in Ramsgate in 1847, though Clubb travelled to America in 1853 to join Metcalfe and eventually became President of the recently formed Vegetarian Society.

## Ramsgate and After

Joseph Brotherton was Member of Parliament for Salford and one of the original members of Cowherd's congregation. He chaired the Ramsgate conference while James Simpson (1812-59) was elected President of the newly formed Vegetarian Society, William Oldham of the Concordium was made Treasurer and William Horsell, of the Northwood Villa infirmary, the Secretary; 140 were at the conference, coming from all over England. The founding and the immediate future of the Society were assured because of the generosity of its President, the son of a wealthy calico printer who was educated privately in London and Berlin. His mother had trained him to avoid all food obtained by pain. He became a vegetarian from an early age, as well as an advocate of temperance. He was a Bible Christian, an admirer of Swedenborg and a member of the Anti-Corn Law League. 'The splendid banquets which were associated with the earlier annual meetings of the Vegetarian Society and which were provided at a vast expenditure of time and money were due to his liberality.'[12]

Brotherton (1783-1857) was the son of an exciseman who became a mill owner, then the Pastor to the Salford Bible Christians in 1817. After the Reform Bill (1832), which allowed parliamentary representation to those large industrial centres around Birmingham and Manchester, Brotherton became Salford's first Member of Parliament and he quickly showed his radical idealism by fighting for changes in the working hours for children in factories, the repeal of the Corn Laws and free trade. He was the very first MP in the House of Commons to speak against capital punishment.

The first conference at Ramsgate rehearsed all the arguments for vegetarianism that have been explored in these pages: it was the natural diet and the one God intended, hence meat was injurious to health while vegetables were life-giving. The ancient authors were quoted: Porphyry,

Plutarch and others. Meat production wasted land and resources; 'five acres of ground, only producing flesh for one man, per year, where 12½ men could subsist from the same amount of land producing wheat and 77½* from other vegetable food'.[13] Doctors Newton and Lambe were quoted and other proselytising authors. One of the most widely held beliefs was that slaughtering brutalised people, therefore all butchers were brutes, and that meat-eating provoked aggression. We have seen that this belief has its source in antiquity – both Pythagoras and Socrates comment on it.

Arguing around the Genesis sanction was a problem, but Brotherton emphasised the directive from God that 'flesh, with the life thereof which is the blood thereof ye shall not eat', which caused shouts of 'hear, hear' from his audience. Brotherton went on to add 'thou shalt not kill, nor shall ye eat fat nor blood in any of your dwellings.' God, it was argued, 'would not give a law which was contrary to health and to the well-being of men'.[14] Brotherton knew, he confessed, that Biblical text might sanction meat-eating, instead of those principles that strengthen men. But the idea that every moving thing was meat for you could *not* be true, for, Brotherton ends triumphantly, every moving thing is *not* fit to be meat for you.

The whole tone of the meeting was passionately ideological. Each person was morally bound to aid the progress of the human race. There was not, it was believed, an individual who could not benefit from such progress. Brotherton, concluding the meeting, was cheered when he said that 'no man could persuade him that flesh meat was necessary to health and strength, when he saw around him those who had enjoyed thirty-eight years of healthy existence without it.'[15]

The health and long life of vegetarians constantly cropped up in their publications. It was widely thought by the general public that vegetarianism and teetotalism were dangerous experiments which would threaten health. Ale and wine, after all, had been a vital part of the daily diet ever since people could remember. It was also thought that meat was essential; beef tea, for example, would be regularly prescribed by doctors for any illness. In the *Vegetarian Messenger* an account of the first annual meeting of the Society held at Hayward's Hotel, Manchester, in July 1848, records the years of abstention from meat for each person in attendance. We learn that thirty-one people had abstained from 'flesh-food' for the whole of their lives, while twelve others had abstained for from thirty-seven to forty years. At this banquet they ate savoury omelette, macaroni omelette, rice fritters, onion and sage fritters, savoury pie, bread and parsley fritters, forcemeat fritters, plum pudding, moulded rice and flummery. *Punch* had a field day and would continue to poke fun at the Society and institutions like Alcott House for the rest of the century:

---

*The Victorian concept of calories necessary for adult workmen to subsist seems hazy. The figure of 77½ people living off 5 acres of vegetables for a year could possibly be achieved on a diet of potatoes, but not much else.

We see by the papers that there is a Society in Manchester that devotes its entire energies to the eating of vegetables, and the members meet occasionally for the purpose of masticating mashed potatoes and munching cabbage leaves. 'Sweets to the sweet', is a popular maxim, and 'greens to the green' may fairly be applied to the Vegetarians. At one of their recent banquets a party of 232 sat down to a couple of courses, in which sage and onion, beetroot, mushrooms and parsley, were the principal luxuries. Jos. Brotherton, Esquire, M.P. (the gentleman who is always wanting to get the House of Commons to bed by 12 o'clock), was in the chair, and proposed a series of toasts, which were drunk in plain cold water, and as usual odd fish were present, they no doubt felt themselves quite in their element. We do not quite understand the principle upon which these gentlemen object to animal food, but if health is their object, we do not think that that will be promoted by the mixture of messes they sat down to the other day at Manchester.

In addition to their sage and onions, they disposed of several dishes of plum pudding – in itself as heavy as plumbago – as well as almonds, raisins, gooseberries, cheesecakes, custards, sago, figs and flummery. There is something very infantile in the pretended simplicity of this fare, for none but a parcel of overgrown children would sit down seriously to make a meal upon sweetstuff. We look upon the Vegetarian humbug as a mere pretext for indulging a juvenile appetite for something nice, and we are really ashamed of these old boys who continue, at their time of life, to display such a puerile taste for pies and puddings.[16]

No doubt interest from other vegetarians in London led them to set up a branch of the Society there. It was centred on a Mr Turley and his home, Arora Villa, Hampstead. One of the first members was George Dornbusch, a recent convert, who had adopted vegetarianism in 1843. He also abstained from tea, coffee, alcohol, tobacco and drugs of every kind. He took two meals a day, the first between eight and nine in the morning and the second between six and twelve, and all his food was eaten quite cold and without salt and condiments. Dornbusch is characteristic of a general feeling among the majority of members (though this was not an official line of the Society) that all flavourings, including salt, were stimulants and as bad as alcohol. This led to vegetarian food being enormously bland. To meat-eaters, especially the gourmets, it must have seemed tedious beyond belief.

Much of the image of vegetarianism formed at this time surrounds it still. At this time too vegetarian food became irradiated with moral earnestness, do-gooding and the higher grounds of purity and moral rectitude. Vegetarian food, in order to be pure, i.e. active in doing good to the body and spirit, had to be unaltered by flavourings. This concept clearly stems from Jewish dietary laws in which to alter is to blemish. Mr Dornbusch went one step further in banning salt from the table for in Judaic lore salt was treasured as a preservative. The vegetarians' emphasis upon purity in their food also had its practical side. They lived in a society where the most flagrant and appalling adulteration of food occurred, much of it in the industrial and commercial processing of the ingredients. This was first researched by Frederic Accum, in 1820, in a comprehensive work★ whose cover bore the Biblical quotation: 'There is Death in the Pot.'[17]

> Accum's researches disclosed that almost all the foods and drinks of his day were more or less heavily adulterated, and he fearlessly exposed the methods used and the names of convicted persons. His Treatise dealt in detail with the frauds practised on some two dozen articles in common use, ranging from bread, beer, and tea to wines and spirits, condiments and confectionery. In baking their bread, he found that the London bakers invariably used alum as an adulterant for whitening the inferior grades of flour known as 'seconds': 'without this salt it is impossible to make bread from the kind of flour usually employed by the London bakers as white as that which is commonly sold'. The finest white flour went to the confectioners and pastry-cooks, and the 'baker's flour is very often made of the worst kinds of damaged foreign wheat, and other cereal grains mixed with it . . . Common garden beans and pease, are frequently ground up among the London bread flour.' By the addition of a small quantity of alum (about 4 oz to the sack of 240 lb was the usual amount in Accum's day), the baker was able to pass off a cheap loaf as being made from the more expensive 'firsts' flour, and, of course, to charge for it at the higher price. He also occasionally added potatoes for cheapness, and subcarbonate of ammonia to produce a light loaf from spoiled or 'sour' flour.[18]

His book was comprehensive, especially on what was added to beer:

> In the single year of 1819 there were nearly a hundred convictions of brewers and brewers' druggists under the Excise laws for using *cocculus indicus* (a dangerous poison containing picrotoxin), multum, capsicum, copperas, quassia, mixed drugs, harts-horn shavings, orange powder, caraway seeds, ginger and coriander: these were all employed as cheap substitutes for malt or hops, allowing beer to be diluted by giving it a false appearance of 'strength' and flavour.[19]

There was little, in fact, that could be eaten and drunk which was not adulterated. Pickles were coloured green from copper, pepper had sweepings from factory floors in it, wine contained bitter almonds or spoiled cider, Gloucester cheese was coloured with red lead. By the middle of the century an excessive degree of competition between bakers, publicans and grocers led them to make greater cost cuts by even more ingenious methods of adulterating the food.

---

★*Treatise on the Adulterations of Food and Culinary Poisons*. He was vilified and attacked.

'A Treatise on the Falsifications of Food', written in 1848, leaves no doubt that adulteration had greatly increased since Accum's day, and had now reached terrifying proportions. Public institutions bore the brunt of the worst excesses of adulteration – hospitals, prisons, workhouses, barracks, schools were all supplied by tender, and the lowest was invariably accepted.

> The large number of deaths at Drouitt's Institution for pauper children in 1850 was ascribed by Dr Wakley, the coroner, to the adulteration of the oatmeal with barleymeal; the latter was less nutritious and more aperient, and diarrhoea and vomiting had been prominent symptoms of the outbreak . . .
> . . . In the 1850s Dr Hassall compiled a list of more than thirty injurious substances which he had discovered in foods and drinks . . . Several of these were deadly poisons if taken in sufficient quantity, and numerous cases are on record of death caused by cocculus indicus in rum, paralysis due to lead in cayenne pepper and snuff, and the poisoning of children by mineral dyes in sugar confectionery . . . Much more often the quantity of poisons used was not sufficient to produce immediate symptoms, but many of them were cumulative, and would leave trace elements of lead, copper, mercury, and arsenic to build up in the system over the course of time. Here again, we may well have a cause of the chronic gastritis which was one of the commonest diseases of urban populations in the early nineteenth century.[20]

No wonder, then, that once the vegetarian message was heard it was adopted and the movement in the first ten years of its existence began to grow,* helped by the fact that the diet had the obvious advantage of being cheap. Many factory operatives from the cities and towns of the north joined the Society – the diet was reported to be calming and to build up the mind and body to combat the stress of factory life.

Meat was considered to increase fever and choler. Like alcohol it stimulated the body in an unnatural and debilitating way. Victorian moral tales showed families reduced to poverty and walking the streets. The drunken father was a stock character of penny dreadfuls, of songs and ballads. No wonder vegetarianism went hand in hand with temperance; the body stimulated by alcohol was out of control, an instrument of destruction. Meat was seen as a generator of lust.

Man, the product of the industrial society, allied with man, the representative of the British Empire, was a dynamic force and British beef was part and parcel of the British man. To claim that this substance was debilitating, exhausting and disturbing was absurd, which is why society as a whole tended to relegate the vegetarian movement to the pages of *Punch*. Although vegetarianism represented hope and a means by which the poor might change their lives Samuel Smiles, author and social reformer, said of

---

*The Society doubled its membership from 478 in 1850 to 889 in 1853 – over half of these were tradesmen, mechanics and labourers.

Joseph Brotherton: 'the factory boy rose from the humble station . . . to an eminent position of usefulness, by the simple exercise of homely honesty, industry, punctuality and self-denial'[21] – meat-eating was central to society, and especially for the middle classes, as a sign of social affluence. As Engels observed, the higher you rose in society, or the richer you were, the more meat was eaten. The vegetarian could hardly even begin to erase this symbol of power and wealth.

Early in the Society's history it suffered from the death of two of its founding figures. In 1857 Joseph Brotherton died. This was a serious blow to the Society for they lost an MP who was a champion of human rights. Brotherton was also a link with their beginnings, with Cowherd, Newton and Lambe. His wife, who had collected vegetarian recipes which were first published in 1812 as *Vegetarian Cookery – by a Lady* and later published other works, remained a life-long vegetarian. Brotherton, who died aged seventy-four, is buried in an ornate grave in the Gothic style at Eccles's New Road cemetery. His monument is engraved with his favourite motto: 'my riches consist not in the extent of my possessions but in the fewness of my wants', a sentiment endorsed with enthusiasm by members of the Society.

Brotherton's death was followed by the shock of the death, two years later, in 1859, of their generous President, James Simpson, at the age of forty-eight. This was not only bad news financially – he had given to the Society five thousand pounds in the last five years of his life, and although another five thousand was left as a bequest it was never paid – but the early death was appalling publicity for the vegetarian way of life. The *Manchester City News* described Simpson as 'of a weakly and delicate constitution at his best, physically speaking, but a poor specimen of humanity'.[22] Though Simpson in his last illness had insisted: 'Let there be no mistake as to the cause of my illness, my diet has nothing to do with it, it arises from incessant overwork of the mind',[23] this did nothing to mollify the impression that the diet had everything to do with it. Beef tea, it was widely thought, might well have saved him. It is possible to conclude that Simpson was poisoned by his environment and his own factory. H.S. Clubb for a time was Simpson's secretary and he remembered the house at Foxhill Bank:

> The bleachery was very close to the driveway leading up to the residence and there was usually a large escape of sulphuric acid which was often sufficient to make breathing exceedingly difficult to persons passing up the driveway. I had frequently seen Mrs James Simpson stop and pant for breath on her way past . . . I well remember that soot from the neighbouring chimneys so blackened the fruit in the garden that it was impossible to gather it without blackening the fingers.[24]

## The Indian Mutiny

At this time the Vegetarian Society reaped unexpected support from a disaster in the British Empire. The fact that the Indian Mutiny of 1857 was caused by British insensitivity to the issue of Hindu vegetarianism was entirely lost on the British public, too horrified at the time by the Mutiny and the slaughter and confirmed in their deep belief that all Indians were savages. The Mutiny was provoked by an act of sheer foolishness on the part of the British army. The Minié rifle had been introduced into India and the cartridge paper had to be greased. Instead of using vegetable oil, the army used lard for this purpose, and the sepoys and troops of the Indian army considered themselves to be contaminated by having to bite the cartridge:

> If the issuing of these obnoxious implements of war was not the immediate cause, it is universally admitted to have been, at all events, the pretext, of revolt; and although it has been the fashion to deny that greased cartridges could or did cause the Mutiny, we incline to the opinion that, if they had not been issued to the troops, although there might have been disaffection arising from other causes, there would have been no open revolt.[25]

The mutineers themselves had already named the greased cartridges as the cause:

> Be it known, say the Sepoys of Delhi and Meerut, to all the Hindoos and Mahommedans . . . that the Europeans are united on this point first, to deprive the army of their religion and then by the force of strong measures to Christianize all the subjects. In fact, it is the absolute order of the Governor-General to serve out cartridges made up with swine and beef-fat. For this reason we have, merely for the sake of faith, concerted with all the subjects, and have not left one infidel of this place alive.[26]

Around this time the Society had been particularly pleased with the instructions issued by Sir Colin Campbell, Commander-in-Chief of the Indian army. He begins:

> Experience proves that the same amount of animal food is not required in a hot climate to preserve health and strength as in the cold one. A large amount of animal food, instead of giving strength, heats the blood, renders the system feverish, and consequently weakens the whole body. The Rajputs of Rajputana, and the Sikhs of the Punjaub, are physically as strong as Europeans, and they are capable of enduring more fatigue, and withstanding better the vicissitudes of the climate of India. This is due partly to race, but chiefly to the nature of their food, of which the staple is wheaten flour made into 'chapatis'. They eat but twice a day; and, although they partake of animal food, they do so in a very much less proportion than is the habit in Europe. The best food for a soldier is that which the country freely produces, and which is nutritious and digestible, and at the same time palatable.[27]

He then attacks the feeding habits of pigs and states that this filthy diet is transferred to humans, thus gradually poisoning the blood. Not only pork but beef is attacked in this proclamation, which must have seemed to the British soldier rather astonishing!

## Animal Slaughter

The vegetarian movement, small in numbers, could not have existed without a general change in public sensitivity over the slaughter and preparation of animals for meat. The Victorian age was no different from our own – meat was enjoyed, but no one wanted to see the transition of live animal to carcase. As early as 1756 Gilbert White planted four lime trees at Selborne between his house and the butcher's yard opposite 'to hide the sight of blood and filth'.[28] By the middle of the nineteenth century moves were being made to hide the slaughterhouses or shift them away from the centre of the town for the sake of the gentry and their sensibilities. In the great industrial centres they were often built opposite public houses and schools, which outraged vegetarians, who believed that the very sight and smell of them brutalised people.

Sometimes the sight of a slaughterhouse had the opposite effect. Richard Phillips (1767–1840) wrote: 'at twelve years of age I was struck with such horror in accidently seeing the barbarities of a London slaughterhouse, that since that hour I have never eaten anything but vegetables.'[29] J.L. Emary wrote an account of his childhood in 1921 and painted a vivid picture of the slaughterhouse in 1850 in Half Moon Passage, in Cheapside:

> The whole process of killing and the dressing of the carcases could be easily seen by passers-by. The sheep were kept in a pen within sight of the tragedy in which they would soon have to take a part. In the centre stood a large box having bars on the top, and this formed the altar of sacrifice. The sheep were taken one at a time and laid upon the top of the box, their hind legs being forcibly held apart by a stick to prevent kicking and struggling. The butcher's knife was driven right thro' the animal's neck, and was turned round and round to enlarge the wound and to sever the main blood vessels, the poor animal retaining consciousness for some time. As soon as death had taken place the body was slung up to a hook head downwards, and was then ripped open, the bowels falling out to be caught by the slaughterman. When all the viscera had been removed the carcase was stripped of its skin, and was then carried above while still warm and limp to hang for sale in the market.[30]

The French poet Alphonse de Lamartine (1790–1869), whom vegetarians learn to love and admire, had an early experience of slaughterhouses:

> I had a lamb, whom a peasant of Milly had given me, and whom I had trained to follow me everywhere, like the most attached and faithful dog. We loved each other with that first love which children and young animals naturally have for each other. One day the cook said to my mother in my presence,

'Madame, the lamb is fat, and the butcher has come for it, must I give it him?' I screamed and threw myself on the lamb, asking what the butcher would do with it, and what was a butcher? The cook replied that he was a man who gained his living by killing lambs, sheep, calves and cows. I could not believe it. I besought my mother, and readily obtained mercy for my favourite. A few days afterwards my mother took me with her to the town and led me, as by chance, through the Shambles. There I saw men with blood-stained arms felling a bullock. Others were killing calves and sheep and cutting off their still palpitating limbs. Streams of blood smoked here and there upon the pavement. I was seized with a profound pity, mingled with horror, and asked to be taken away. The idea of these horrible and repulsive scenes, the necessary preliminaries of the dinner I saw served at table, made me hold animal food in disgust, and butchers in horror.[31]

Earlier in the same book Lamartine had told how his childhood was influenced by Rousseau's *Emile* and Pythagoras. Lamartine confessed, however, to eating meat in public because of the 'necessity of conforming to the customs of society'.[32]

One sometimes feels that vegetarians gathered stories to prove their thesis of the brutalising effects of the butchers' trade with a gruesome glee. Two especially macabre incidents were reprinted in the *Vegetarian Review*. The first is particularly interesting for its strong belief in pre-natal influences:

There is confined in prison, at Boston, Mass., United States, a boy eighteen years old. His crime was killing a girl ten years old. His confession contains some startling statements. He had once before killed a boy; and he told the examiner, to whom he confessed, that the only reason for doing it was because 'he could not help it.' Now comes the point. Why could he not help it? On asking his mother relative to his case, she states that while pregnant with this child, she worked in a butchering establishment, assisting in the various duties there. The boy, born soon after, she declares has ever had a fondness for sticking knives and forks into flesh; has often bound his playmates and stuck pins into them, and treated them as a butcher would do. He was not sensual, but loved to kill. The mother had marked him in the blood. He had killed two children before being caught at it. Does not this boy's confession that he 'could not help it', and his mother's statement that she was a butcher when the child was being formed in her womb, give us a hint? How many murderers may have received a similar taint, not, perhaps, from the mother, but from the father?[33]

The second is a vivid instance of the vegetarians' belief in teaching by example:

A French Canadian had killed several pigs, and his little children had looked on in approving wonder at the process. Soon after the parents went to church, and on their return were met at the door by their oldest child, Gustave, an eight-year-old boy, who exclaimed in childish glee, 'I have killed little piggy; come and see.' He was covered with blood. What they saw may be inferred from the confession of the boy as to what had taken place. When the parents had gone to church, Gustave proposed to his little brother, Adolph, that they should play killing pig. In this request, it is supposed the unfortunate little fellow acquiesced. The youngest was to be the pig, the eldest the butcher. Gustave eagerly assisted his brother to undress for the tragedy, and, taking a small rope, tied him down securely to a rough lounge that stood in the room; he then procured the butcher knife that his father had used in slaughtering the pigs the day before, and plunged it into the throat of his passive and helpless brother. The wound was a mortal one, and it is supposed that death immediately resulted. After the child had bled his little life away, the unnatural brother, with the most incredible heartlessness, took the cord which confined the body to the lounge, and tying one end around the feet of the corpse, threw the other over the beam, and, lending his weight and strength, hoisted the body to the position in which it was found; then, not satisfied with the programme thus far carried out, the little butcher must needs disembowel his dead brother almost in the exact manner in which his father had the pigs the day before.[34]

Countless other stories of various degrees of horror were printed in the vegetarian magazines. These may have helped sales, as the Victorian reading public had a lust for horror as great as our own.

## The United States

Much of the enthusiasm for vegetarianism, socialism, new concepts in education and the Swedenborgian New Church was paralleled across the Atlantic. Cowherd's protégé the Reverend William Metcalfe and the Reverend James Clark had sailed for America with twenty adults and nineteen children, reaching America on 15 June 1817. It took them eleven weeks and the crossing was rough; the hardships they suffered 'were such that several of them quite lost sight of the purpose of their journey and only eleven of the adults remained faithful to their principles when they reached Philadelphia'.[35] The group then scattered far and wide in the search for work. It was difficult in a new country to keep to the diet, when they were poor and hungry: 'Isolated from one another, in a strange country, and among a people who had no sympathy with their habits, it is perhaps not surprising that they relaxed their interest in vegetarian principles.'[36] However, James Clark came up trumps. He managed to purchase some land in Lycoming county, Pennsylvania, and moved there with his family. Metcalfe stayed in Philadelphia to support himself by school teaching. Yellow fever struck in the autumn of 1818 and he had to close his school for several weeks. The fever kept on reappearing during the next two years and he was reduced to poverty. Friends offered financial help if he would renounce his principles of vegetarianism and temperance. Metcalfe refused. Why, one wonders, did Metcalfe's principles so distress his rich friends? After all, the movement was growing. Generally it could not then have been quite so eccentric, even in Philadelphia at the beginning of the century.

But Metcalfe was attacked by the religious press who united to denounce him. He was called 'infidel' and 'sceptic'. These insults he ignored, writing in the papers on the principles of moral dietetics. In 1821 he published an essay on *Abstinence from the Flesh of Animals* which was freely and extensively circulated. Meanwhile his wife opened a school in a northern suburb and in 1823 they managed to buy a frame building, which was opened by Metcalfe late that year as the Bible Christian vegetarian centre.

For several years Metcalfe and his church were isolated and divided, but his *essay* eventually gained them two important converts: in 1830 Sylvester Graham, a temperance lecturer who had made a study of human physiology, and Bronson Alcott. They were both impressed and completely won over by Metcalfe's message. Five years later they published the *Moral Reformer*, a monthly periodical which soon afterwards changed its title to the *Library of Health*. Metcalfe was an indefatigable publisher of tracts and papers, pouring into their publication all the funds and private monies he had. The *Independent Democrat*, *Morning Star* and the *Temperance Advocate* all lost money but helped spread the message. Nevertheless, the star of the movement in the first half of the century was undoubtedly Sylvester Graham (1794-1851), who was an earnest advocate of the health regimen (similar to the Alcott House routine) of temperance and vegetarianism. He was a major force of the times. He was ordained a minister in 1826 and lectured widely on his subjects with particular emphasis on the use of wholemeal wheat flour in bread and baking.

His health plan was Spartan – hard mattresses and cold showers and a vegetarian diet with home-baked bread. Graham was a believer in consuming as great a proportion of 'raw' food as possible. His theory was that we should eat what Adam and Eve ate before the Fall. Great emphasis, therefore, was placed on berries, nuts, seeds and fruit. He maintained that to give the best health food should be uncooked, undressed, unprocessed and unrefined. It is astonishing that Graham's imprint in wholemeal flours and breads is so clearly seen still today in bakers' and health food shops throughout the country. *

Both Greaves and Alcott met Graham in the 1830s and were influenced by him. He was attacked once by a mob of bakers and butchers worried about the popularity of his views and the effect on their trade. Temperance boarding houses following his principles appeared in New York and Boston and, in tune with the experiments of the time, commune living to Graham principles began at Brook Farm, near Boston. Graham also influenced many Shaker communities into becoming vegetarian.

---

*And that in the USA wholemeal flour is referred to still as Graham flour.

Another pioneer vegetarian community near Harvard was Fruitlands, started by Alcott on his return from England and two members of the Concordium, Henry Gardiner Wright and Charles Lane. There were always close ties with England. A kind of world brotherhood among vegetarians existed.

After the Vegetarian Society was founded in England, Metcalfe immediately suggested a like society should be formed in the United States. He wrote to Graham, Alcott and others and finally an American Vegetarian Convention assembled in New York in May 1850.* He became its President after Alcott in 1859, dying aged seventy-five in 1862.

## London and Reform

After the deaths of Simpson, Brotherton and finally their American colleague Alcott, vegetarianism went into a sudden decline. During the 1860s and 1870s membership figures dwindled (there were only 125 members in 1870), yet in the early 1880s the picture changed once again and membership rose until it reached 2,070. Membership in no way gives an exact picture of the number of vegetarians throughout the country.

A small part of this upsurge was no doubt due to the new confidence which Francis Newman gave to the Society in Manchester after he joined in 1868. He was the brother of Cardinal Newman and a professor of Latin at University College, London; possibly members felt they had a voice now in the Establishment and that Newman gave them respectability in the eyes of society. Certainly the *Vegetarian Messenger* greeted his adoption of the diet with this accolade:

> The adhesion of such a gentleman is no ordinary event. Professor Newman is a man of noble intellectual endowments, and of vast and varied culture, an author of no mean repute, a deep and clear thinker, a writer whose style is lucid, penetrating and vigorous, and whose moral instincts and aspirations are of the purest and noblest character and tendency.[37]

He became President in 1873, retiring ten years later. His successor as President was yet another professor of Latin, at Cambridge: J.E.B. Mayor.

The vegetarian movement had its adherents in London too. From the forties various London vegetarians had formed themselves into groups with such titles as the London Dietetic Reform Society, which was affiliated with the Manchester Vegetarian Society. Vegetarian groups helped to found one of the first London vegetarian restaurants, with a Mr McDougall of the People's Café Company at 1, Farringdon Road. On 22 May 1876 seven members sat down to an experimental dinner of vegetable soup, brown bread, vegetarian

---

*In 1867 Eduard Baltzer helped to found the German Vegetarian Society which kept close ties with America and England.

pie, potatoes and cauliflower with white sauce, stewed gooseberries, rice, stewed rhubarb and sago pudding. The three courses cost 1s. 4d. per head.★

The rise in popularity of the vegetarian restaurant after what must seem to us a rather dire meal is truly astonishing. By 1897 in the City of London there were 7 vegetarian restaurants. There was one in Amen Court next to St Paul's Cathedral. Another in King Street around the corner from St Mary Aldermary. One in Cheapside, nearly opposite the Bank. And one called The Apple Tree on the corner of London Wall and Moorgate Street. There were two called The Garden off Aldgate High Street in Minories and the other off the Barbican in Jewin Street. In the whole of London there were thirty-two restaurants altogether, many of them occupying important sites: the Alpha in Oxford Street, the St George in St Martin's Lane, the Ideal in Tottenham Court Road. So these restaurants were not hidden away down side streets but prominent in some of London's main thoroughfares. The restaurant in Cheapside was so popular that it had four floors open and a smoking room.

Who went to all these restaurants then? For two thousand dedicated vegetarians could not have filled 32 restaurants every day. It was the new lower middle classes, dressmakers and shopkeepers' assistants, women from genteel families who had to scrape along on a very small income, for the restaurants were safe places for women to go alone or in couples; indeed at the St George in St Martin's Lane there was a Ladies Chess Club. For up to very recently only women with loose morals were seen eating out in public. A magazine called *The Dietetic Reformer* of June 1890 remarks on this clientele that they were 'some of the more thoughtful members of the artisan class and large numbers of these- both men and women – who are engaged in warehouses and offices.'[38]

The emergence of the new educated lower middle classs (we've seen them in the novels of Mrs Gaskell, H.G. Wells and Arnold Bennett) fuelled by the ideals of socialism, the idea of the simple life, the return of the myth of the pastoral within this greater urbanisation, the Fabian movement and finally the world figure of Tolstoy lifted the image of the movement from provincial eccentricity to lofty idealism.

Relations between London and Manchester became somewhat strained in the 1880s. London wanted to be a vigorous nationwide reforming society, while Manchester felt it had been that for some time and London should merely be a branch of the central society at Manchester. In 1888 the London group sundered all ties with the original society and the London Vegetarian Society was founded.

By 1874 a new form of membership was introduced: the associate member, someone who was sympathetic but felt they could not give their complete commitment. Newman wanted to extend the associate group into

---

★It is not only the amount of food that even the vegetarians – who were all slim – seemed to consume that astonishes us, but the amount of carbohydrate and absence of fat (no olive or vegetable oil) which made this meal so unbalanced nutritionally.

grades, for those perhaps that still ate fish or chicken. He was alive to the fact that 'the number of dogmatic prohibitions against everything that makes food palatable will soon ruin our society if not firmly resisted'.[39] Between 1875 and 1896 membership reached 2,159 and associate membership 1,785. Yet some members felt that Newman was too lax.

He criticised in 1877 a book by a German, Gustav Schlickeysen, *Fruit and Bread*, as it condemned the eating of beans, lentils, fat, sugar, honey, tea and all cooked food – which made him a 'pernicious foe to our society by caricaturing our excellent arguments and running into doctrine which ninety nine out of every hundred will pronounce fanatical'.[40] Newman was opposed to any narrowing down of vegetarian doctrine, and he objected to the disuse of salt and flavourings. It is a pity that Newman did not cite as an example St Benedict of Nursia (see p.166) with his advice to eat with the meal on fast days a raw salad dressed with salt, oil and vinegar. Abstinence from the three Fs – fish, flesh and fowl – was all the Society, Newman maintained, should advocate. It is still the stand today, but Newman's dislike of Schlickeysen's strictures (very much on the same lines as Graham's in America) has not changed the view of society generally: that vegetarianism means bland, unflavoured food, dogma and puritanism.

In the winter of 1878-9 Mr Gibson Ward, who first taught at the Concordium and was now a Vice-President of the Society, wrote a series of letters to *The Times*. This letter illustrates the type of cooking which must have been characteristic of vegetarian cuisine at the time:

*A vegetarian on cheap soup. To the Editor of The Times.*

Sirs – The cheapest and best soup, pleasant, nutritious and wholesome, needs only two articles – water and lentils, well cooked. The Egyptian lentils are preferable to Italian ones, and others. They have only to be washed, soaked and boiled furiously three or four hours to make the best soup possible. Put before an epicure, without remark or information, it would be eaten as a fine gravy soup. No condiments are required to flavour it. The natural flavour is agreeable to all palates. No vegetables are required to thicken it; but there is no reason why onions, carrots, or celery should not be added if easily accessible. Indeed, the last-named – celery – is a very useful addition, not only for its nutrition, but for the alkalis it gives to purify the blood and ease the sufferings of rheumatic victims.[41]

As a result of this unpromising recipe, hundreds of letters reached both the London Food Reform Society and the Vegetarian Society asking for information and membership. A *Times* journalist, Russell, attended one of the Reform dinners and wrote a leader 'in a somewhat bantering spirit' which prompted more interest from readers intrigued about both the economic and the nutritional aspects of the diet.

The diet was frequently attacked by doctors as being deleterious to health. Some of these criticisms became accepted generally. In 1878 a paragraph appeared in the *British Medical Journal*:

> Professor Gubler, in his recent researches as to the causes of cretaceous
> degeneration of the arteries, has made the very interesting discovery that a
> principal cause lies in a vegetable diet, and thus explains the frequency of
> cretaceous arteries among the French rural population at the early age of
> forty. This is more important because it is well understood that 'a man is as
> old as his arteries,' and that chalky degeneration of the arteries is the most
> fatal kind of premature aging. Further proof he finds in the fact that the
> Trappists, who live exclusively on vegetable food, very soon show arterial
> degeneration. In districts where chalky soils load the drinking water with
> earthy salts, a vegetable diet acts more rapidly in affecting the arteries than in
> regions of siliceous formation.[42]

Newman thought it great nonsense and a Dr Nichols thought it an absurd
joke: 'The horse is a Vegetarian. Has he any chalk in his arteries? The
elephant is a Vegetarian. Does he suffer from cretaceous degeneration? The
monkeys, do they age prematurely of chalky degeneration of the arteries?
. . . Why are the Professor Gublers constantly writing such silly statements,
and stupid medical journals repeating them?'[43]

However, somehow the idea stuck that minerals within the soil were
passed on in vegetables and, once eaten, lodged in human tissue. This was one
reason why refined flours and breads were to be preferred. Another was the
idea that white bread equals gentility. The working classes had switched over
to white flour and breads at the beginning of the century, even though it was
more expensive, thus depriving themselves of some essential nutrients. But
in 1865 roller milling was invented which brought the finest white bread
within reach of the poorest.

The London members of the Vegetarian Society tended to be younger
than the original Manchester Society and were more radical. They decided
to rename themselves once more, becoming the National Food Reform
Society, further antagonising the original Vegetarian Society. Their London
chairman, Arnold Hills (1857-1927) owner of the Thames Iron Works, was
a great enthusiast for raw food (influenced by Sylvester Graham perhaps)
and he published a book, *Vital Food* (1892), which argued that raw food has
certain living qualities which are conducive to health and well-being. This
was an idea which would gather strength over the years.* As Hills had been

---

*It is still strong today (the works of Leslie Kenton). The life of raw food is seen in sprouting
seeds, onions, potatoes. This is killed either by cooking or by irradiation. They were termed
'biogenic foods' by Edmond Szekely, who studied the Essenes and claimed that he put their
ideas into a health centre at La Puerta, California, in the 1930s. Biogenic foods are seeds,
wholegrains and pulses, foods which have the biochemical capacity when germinated to
generate new life. Nutritionally, biogenic foods have the highest complement of vitamins,
minerals, essential fatty acids, easily assimilated protein, fibre and carbohydrate packed together
in all of nature. They are nutritionally perfectly balanced to boost the production of new life.

an athlete he and others were very concerned to break the image the public had that meat was essential for muscular energy. The Vegetarian Cycling Club was founded in the early eighties, some of whose members held world records. Such sporting successes were much heralded in the vegetarian magazines. Dr Allinson (who gave his name to wholemeal flour and bread) was prominent in the Reform Society, and wrote dietary recommendations on the best food for athletes. Allinson believed that vegetarianism was the best diet for endurance sports.

As the gulf between Disraeli's two nations became ever wider, one of the strongest ideas to galvanise the National Food Reform Society was that they possessed the secret by which the poor might be fed adequately. Branwell Booth, the Salvation Army leader, and his wife had become vegetarians with the belief that meat stimulated the consumption of alcoholic drinks. They 'treated' the inebriate homeless with vegetarian food, claiming that it worked as a cure.

The London vegetarians gave a series of dinners and conferences to discuss the problem of poverty. Numerous pamphlets were written on the subject.* In 1884 a dinner was held for forty cabmen and their wives. No longer were there many working-class voices, as in the forties, testifying to the economic advantages of the diet. Vegetarianism tended now to be middle-class, promoting the cause among the less fortunate.

What perhaps is not generally realised is that out of the Food Reform Society sprang a new political movement, calling itself the Fabian Society, after a Roman general, Fabius Cunctator, whose patient and elusive tactics in avoiding pitched battles secured his ultimate victory over stronger forces. The birth of the Fabian Society happened in stages.

First, Podmore, a member of the Reform Society, with others, founded yet another group, Fellowship of the New Life, in 1883 to discuss politics, social issues and agnosticism. They were mainly lower-middle-class journalists, writers and clerks searching to make sense of the world and their experience. Podmore with two friends then broke away from this group, as the Fellowship seemed more interested in forms of transcendental philosophy, and formed the Fabian Society. Shaw put it memorably: 'one to sit among the dandelions and the other to organise the docks'. The split was amicable and there was a certain overlap in membership. The Fellowship was keen to emphasise the importance of spiritual values in socialism and the virtues of the simple life, while the Fabians had to wait a few months to gather their distinctive political character and the Webbs' theory of state collectivism. Both groups were almost solely vegetarian though it was not, by far, their most significant feature.

By 1894 Beatrice Webb had joined her husband Sidney at the Fabian Society, though she did not much publicise her diet. Her choice was more a

---

*For example: *The Advantages of a Vegetarian Diet in Workhouses and Prisons*; *Cheap Dinners for School Children*; *The Dietary of the Troops*; *The Best Diet for the Working Man*.

part of her austere lifestyle, rather like an ascetic mystic, than a commitment to the plight of animals. For the Webbs the plight of the working classes and the scourge of poverty came first.

## George Bernard Shaw

Shaw was a fervent publicist of himself, his views and his lifestyle for the whole of his long life. He was a steadfast vegetarian, who had converted in 1881 after reading Shelley in the Reading Room of the British Museum. In explanation of his conversion Shaw quoted the lines from 'The Revolt of Islam':

> Never again may blood of bird or beast
> Stain with its venomous stream a human feast,
> To the pure skies in accusation steaming.[44]

When Shaw first came to London he, in his own words, cultivated literature, not on a little oatmeal but on beef and mutton. 'But I grew tired of beef and mutton, the steam and grease, the waiter looking as though he had been caught in a shower of gravy and not properly dried, the beer, the prevailing redness of nose, and the reek of the slaughterhouse that convicted us all of being beasts of prey. I fled to the purer air of the vegetarian restaurant.'[45]

However, the monotony of the vegetarian meal at that time appalled him. Was he aware that it was the earlier fear that spices and condiments were all stimulants to indulgence in alcohol and lust which gave to such vegetarian dishes as 'macaroni, rice pudding and waterlogged cabbage' a funereal gloom, and that consuming such unappealing food emphasised the moral earnestness? As if the act of eating it proved how serious and committed you were. Perhaps not, for Shaw was no gastronome; in fact he did not care for any food particularly, only really liking 'the stoneground bread which his mother had occasionally buttered for him'.[46] He said of himself: 'I am no gourmet, eating is not a pleasure to me, only a troublesome necessity, like dressing or undressing.'[47]

Yet in his typical, dogmatic manner he did not hesitate to lay down the law on the new diet:

> Do not expect to like porridge and lentils in their naked simplicity. Boil oatmeal porridge for twenty minutes; and if you think the result mere oatmeal and water, try boiling it for two hours. If you still think it as unpalatable as dry bread, treat it as you treat the bread; stir up a bounteous lump of butter in it, and do not forget the salt. In eating wheatmeal porridge, remember that there's nothing so becomes a man as moderation and an admixture of stewed fruit. If you want fancy dishes make them for yourself out of plainly cooked vegetables, with the help of rice and the cruet stand.[48]

This is hardly going to stimulate our salivary glands and is not much of an improvement on the meals at the vegetarian restaurants. But we can all agree with Shaw when he inveighs against simulated 'meat' dishes:

> do not be seduced by messy pies, entrees, or such weak concessions to the enemy as 'vegetable rabbit', 'vegetable sausage', and the like. 'Vegetable goose' is, however, to be commended when in season. It is simply a vegetable marrow with sage stuffing and apple sauce. Remember that brown bread is a good familiar creature, and worth more than its weight in flesh. Don't attribute every qualm you feel to a breakdown of your constitution for want of meat.[49]

He was delighted with the economy of vegetarianism. He saved money on his lunches by eating in those vegetarian restaurants, and believed that vegetarianism would be a benefit to world economy (see Chapter 13). He was also certain that the excreta of meat-eaters stank, certain of this until the last days of his life: 'If I were to eat meat, my evacuations would stink and I should give myself up for dead.'[50]★ Shaw thought that frightened animals, terrified by smelling blood and seeing other animals killed, stank and conveyed their stink of fear and blind terror to the carnivore. Such food must, he felt sure, abuse the human digestion. Shaw, thriving in a post-Darwinian age, and pleased to accept *Homo sapiens'* links with primates, thought that meat-eating was a form of 'restricted cannibalism' or 'cannibalism with its heroic dish omitted'.[51]

Shaw's polemics on behalf of vegetarianism must, at times, have seemed to the vegetarian societies a mixed blessing. He described the claims of some vegetarians to be free of such common ailments as tooth decay, rheumatism and even cancer as a 'blazing lie' and went on to say: 'I know of no disease from which vegetarians are exempt.'[52]† But he delighted in scotching the macho myths of meat-eating by pointing out that both the bull and the elephant were herbivores.

There was a private and a public Shaw in the matter of vegetarianism as in everything else. The private Shaw wrote: 'I am a vegetarian purely on humanitarian and mystical grounds; and I have never killed a flea or a mouse vindictively or without remorse.'[53] But because he felt that most people were vulgar, he made G.B.S. into the most 'unsympathetic' of vegetarians: 'He has no objection to the slaughter of animals as such,' Shaw's printed card on vegetarian diet reads. 'He knows that if we do not kill animals they will kill us. Squirrels, foxes, rabbits, tigers, cobras, locusts, white ants, rats, mosquitoes,

---

★As far as I know there is no scientific research to back such a view, which is very common among vegetarians. On the whole, all excreta stink, but some stink more than others. Whether these are the meat-eaters' or not has never been established.

†The latest research worldwide into the health of vegetarians and meat-eaters gives overwhelming evidence that vegetarians are less likely to get cancer or have coronaries, the two most common afflictions of our society. This, it is thought, is due to the diet being high in fibre and low in fat and refined carbohydrate.

fleas and deer must be continually slain even to extermination by vegetarians as ruthlessly as by meat-eaters. But he urges humane killing and does not enjoy it as a sport.'[54]

At the end of 1881 Shaw caught smallpox. His friends thought his resistance was lowered because of 'those wretched vegetables'; for a time in his convalescence he resumed meat-eating, but then felt worse. He vowed to relapse never again, though his friends and doctors at every future illness would point to his diet as the cause, while Shaw claimed it was the diet that allowed him to recover so quickly.

Shaw's independence of mind, his rationalism and his radical thought were typical of many personalities in the vegetarian movement. He threw himself into a range of vegetarian and other causes – anti-vaccination, anti-vivisection, anti-blood sport, attacks upon the medical profession, dress reform, shorthand and spelling reform.

Though Shaw was an inveterate joker and made his vegetarian cult seem only another aspect of his eccentricity, the publicity he gave to the subject and its attendant issues throughout his life was considerable. In the public eye, however, vegetarianism through Shaw came to be seen ever more typically as the preserve of the crank and the beard, shorts and sandals brigade.

In 1898 Shaw wrote to Leo Tolstoy. Tolstoy scribbled on the envelope 'clever-foolish'. Shaw discussed God, and the problem of evil, but not the vegetarianism that they both practised.

## Wagner

We cannot leave the nineteenth century without including Wagner and his views, since some aspects of them were later incorporated into Hitler's own views on the new Aryan culture. Wagner hated vivisection (he claimed that the doctors were all Jewish) and in equating dissection with the armament factory he echoed the philosopher Schopenhauer's words: 'pity deeply-seated in the human breast is the only true foundation of morality.' Wagner believed that animals were the equal of human beings, but that meat-eating had corrupted the human race. His opinion of the human race was rather low: 'man was only superior to animals in his ability to deceive.'[55] Between 1880 and his death in 1883 he expounded his theories on vegetarianism and diet in a series of essays. He even ordered his followers to become herbivorous. The opera singer Lilli Lehmann was one who did as the maestro commanded. It is all the more surprising then that Wagner did not give up meat himself. Winifred Wagner, widow of his son, Siegfried, said in an interview in 1972 that 'Wagner would have liked to have been a vegetarian for ethical reasons, but his poor health prevented him from changing his diet. He suffered from a weak heart and eczema of the face.'[56]

## Croydon and the Simple Life

The Fellowship of the New Life in the mid-1890s moved to Croydon, which was a centre of free religious ideas; they welcomed 'atheists, spiritualists, individualists, communists, anarchists, ordinary politicians, vegetarians, anti-vivisectionists and anti-vaccinationists'.[57] They founded a co-operative store which sold vegetarian food and aimed to conduct their trade without profit. Tolstoy influenced them greatly. It helped that gathered in Croydon were several Russian exiles. Aylmer Maude, Tolstoy's translator, and Tcherkoff published Tolstoy's works through the Free Age Press. The Tolstoyan ideas that were of such profound influence were pacifism, a form of agricultural socialism whereby the land belonged to all, the brotherhood of man, labouring for food not money, the evil of the state, and sexual chastity as the highest form of life. Tolstoy felt that vegetarianism suppressed lust or at least boosted the spiritual nature of man. Various rural communes, in this spirit, were attempted before the end of the century (at Purleigh and Whiteway in the Cotswolds).

Not all socialists, by far, were vegetarian. William Morris thought it most peculiar. Shaw told a story of lunching with the Morrises at Kelmscott House, known for its excellent table:

> Mrs Morris did not conceal her contempt for my folly. At last pudding time came; and as the pudding was a particularly nice one, my abstinence vanished and I showed signs of a healthy appetite. Mrs Morris pressed a second helping on me, which I consumed to her entire satisfaction. Then she said, 'That will do you good, there is suet in it.' And that is the only remark, as far as I can remember, that was ever addressed to me by this beautiful and stately woman, whom the Brotherhood of Rossetti had succeeded in consecrating.[58]

One can well see how the communes also became part of the back-to-nature movement, which as an idea has its origins in antiquity and has never died. Rousseau and St-Pierre had revived it in the century before, Tolstoy was extolling simple labour and the goodness of the sweat of the brow. Another powerful spokesman, Thoreau, was also to add his voice. His book *Walden: Or Life in the Woods* was published in 1854. Its message was relevant to the rural socialist's view with its cry of 'Simplify, simplify, simplify.' Thoreau 'reduced life to its lowest terms in things pertaining to the body, that he might raise it to its highest possibilities in things of the mind and heart.'[59]

Edward Carpenter (1844-1929), author of a long Whitmanesque poem 'Towards Democracy', was foremost in this movement to return to the rural roots, but was giving voice to his anger at respectability as well: 'Law represents from age to age the code of the dominant and ruling class . . . today the code of the dominant class may perhaps best be denoted by the word respectability.'[60] This was the oppressive smokescreen of the bourgeoisie that hung like a pall over Victorian life. Carpenter wanted to discover the true nature of man, fired in some way by that Thoreau model at Walden pond. But instead he bought a market garden at Millthorpe, just outside Sheffield, and there he attempted to simplify his life. Apart from making sandals he advocated vegetarianism, lots of fresh air and a return to nature. He also worked for the socialist movement in Sheffield. Increasingly his books stressed the importance of individual emancipation, through spontaneity and mystical experience. Carpenter had been born into the upper-middle class at Brighton, seemed to be destined for the Church and went to Cambridge, where he even took orders and was for a short time curate to the Christian Socialist F.D. Maurice. But he rejected orthodox religion and orthodox society. He was homosexual, which placed him outside society anyway, and his sexual inclinations gave him insight into what was immoral and hypocritical.

He uses the metaphor of illness to describe civilisation, disease as a metaphor for the physical body and the social structure. Health, he tells us, means the whole self, mind and body. 'Whole', he points out, has the same derivation as 'holy'. Human beings must regain their unconscious instinctive nature and become one again with nature. His ideal was an image of cosmic humankind attuned to the universe. His home at Millthorpe

> became almost a centre of pilgrimage for many in the labour and progressive movements. Vegetarians, dress reformers, temperance orators, spiritualists, secularists, anti-vivisectionists, socialists, anarchists: all attempted to recruit, and some succeeded in recruiting, Carpenter to their cause. Sheffield artisans, pioneering socialists, Cambridge and London intellectuals like Lowes Dickinson and Ashbee, close political associates like Edith Lees, Olive Schreiner, Isabella Ford and Alf Mattison, the Whitmanite Charlie Sixsmith: all found a warm welcome and sympathetic political and social response at Millthorpe.[61]

Carpenter is a brilliant example of the social outcast, exemplifying how vegetarianism can be but one aspect of an individual who is outside contemporary society. Radical in politics, religion and sexual tastes, he spoke in his life to all those who were discontented and outraged by the facade of respectability which barely covered the moral vacuum at the heart of Victorian society. In 1904 his friend Hukin noted a visit to Millthorpe when Carpenter was away: 'two very pretty young ladies turned up with a donkey and cart and a dog. They had come all the way from Essex with bare feet and sandals and just a thin sort of Holland dressing gown – with no head gear. They said they were pilgrims and your disciples, they loved you and so sorry to have missed you.'[62]

## Animal Welfare

Vegetarianism did not really become involved in the welfare of animals until the 1870s and then it was the issue of vivisection that elicited passionate denunciation from all the most prominent campaigners. Vivisection was entwined with vegetarians' dislike of medicine and doctors. The body should, given the right food, be healthy enough not to need drugs, opiates, doctors or surgery. Therefore research and experimentation on live animals should be entirely unnecessary. Edward Maitland, who worked with Anna Kingsford, lecturing, writing and campaigning, wrote a letter to *The Times* dated 6 January 1885 in which he said: 'if proof be wanted of the dulling effect of a diet of flesh, whether upon head or heart, we assuredly have it in the opinions which find expression upon this subject.' Maitland goes on to attack the views of a distinguished physiologist, Dr W.B. Carpenter, who claimed that as animals have no moral nature, we have no moral obligation towards them, but may, without blame, treat them as cruelly as we please. Maitland counters: 'Which is to say that our rule of conduct is to be, not our own sense of right and wrong, but the sense of right and wrong we ascribe to those with whom we happen to be dealing. So that if they are murderers, thieves, liars or ruffians, we may be the same in our dealings with them and without disgracing our humanity . . .'[63]

Anna Kingsford began her medical training not for love of humanity – 'I do not love men and women. I dislike them too much to care to do them any good'[64] – but for animals and the knowledge she would acquire generally. Her degree thesis was called *The Perfect Way in Diet*. She suffered from tubercular consumption and first adopted the vegetarian diet on the advice of her brother, Dr John Bonns. Her illness in no way dulled her convictions or temperament. She married a clergyman, but they appear to have led separate lives. She joined the Church of Rome, but four years later founded the Hermetic Society in a desire to revive the study and spirit of mystic theology, and became President of the Theosophical Society in 1883. She refused to wear fur and feathers.

She was a remarkable woman, described by a friend as 'the most faultlessly beautiful woman I ever beheld,' she contrived to combine passionate feminism with caring for the rights of animals written in prose shorn of the customary flowery poetics of the time. How contemporary she sounds to us now. 'Of late, people have dared to ask why, in old times, wives and daughters were subjected to their male relatives, and practically denied the dignity of humanity. As a result of this enquiry we have the agitation for women's rights. Other people, again, have questioned the morality of flesh eating habits which have prevailed so generally in European countries, and, by consequence, the Vegetarian societies rise into being. Reform is the cry of the day.'

She died aged forty-two in 1888. Adverse comment in the press suggested that her early death was due to her diet. Her brother remonstrated and wrote to the editor of the *World*:

> Mrs Kingsford died of phthisis supervening on severe pneumonia, which she brought upon herself by getting drenched in the rain on her way to M. Pasteur's laboratory, in the winter of last year, and by remaining there several hours in her wet clothes, letting them dry upon her body. I have known several persons killed precisely in the same way who were not Vegetarians. Had she not been a Vegetarian, she would, in all likelihood, have succumbed to the primary inflammation at once.[65]

The campaign against vivisection did bring some form of parliamentary legislation in the 1876 Cruelty to Animals Act: 'It established that for each experiment authorization had to be obtained beforehand from a special board, which would grant it only if the absolute necessity of the experiment was proved. It further established that the animals had to be spared unnecessary suffering, and that the number of experiments had to be made public.'[66] But who was to decide what was 'unnecessary suffering'? The problem remains the same today. As Maitland put it:

> Exception is asked for experiments which consist in a scratch or a prick with a needle on the ground of their triviality. Here we find that we cannot depend upon them to tell us the truth. For the effect of these trivial wounds is apt to be terrible in the extreme, seeing that they are made for the purpose of introducing into the system some kind of poison, virus, or venom.[67]

Shaw, as usual, summed up the issue: 'Whoever doesn't hesitate to vivisect will hardly hesitate to lie about it.'

The *Vegetarian Review* also raised the issue of the agonies and terror suffered by transported livestock, particularly in the cattle ships. One of the problems was the ease with which shipowners could insure unseaworthy vessels which broke up in heavy seas:

> The steamer Iowa sailed from New York with 150 head of cattle on deck. Off the banks she encountered heavy weather. For two days she rolled and pitched, during which time her deckload of living, suffering beasts was thrown from side to side, goring each other with their horns. Scores of them were trampled underfoot, until finally a mighty wave struck the vessel, and the entire deck structure was washed away, and with it the 150 cattle. The shifting of the deckload caused the vessel to careen badly. In her hold, upon temporary platforms built upon each side, were 300 other cattle. In their struggles the staging was thrown down, and the 300 beasts were hurled to the bottom of the hold. For a while pandemonium reigned, and the tortured creatures bellowed and struggled, trampling and goring each other's lives out until the surviving ones sank exhausted.[68]

Horror stories abounded of ships afire at sea where the cattle were roasted alive, or of ships sinking:

> Cattle swam for the boats, and were with difficulty beaten off with hatchets and oars. One witness, George Pirrett, stated that in a ship in which he sailed, the firemen had all to help to get eighty dead cattle overboard after a gale; their bodies were in the 'tween decks – i.e. below the main deck – and they had been smothered by the closing of the hatchways. He says that they were lying dead, one upon another, up to the ceiling – i.e. the underside of the main deck, just where the last great lurch or 'send' of the ship had thrown them.[69]

To try and deal with such indifference to animal cruelty, Henry Salt (1851–1939) founded the Humanitarian League in 1891. Salt was a scholar and then master at Eton College, and a friend of Shaw, Gandhi and William Morris, a socialist and Fabian who saw vegetarianism as part of a much greater range of humanitarian values. The League existed to fight injustice, inequality and cruelty to all creatures including humans. Salt, who thought the RSPCA was too moderate, campaigned against flogging in schools and prisons, blood sports, vivisection, the fur and feather★ trade and private slaughterhouses.

The last decade of the century saw many protection societies begin, all part of the re-evaluation of nature which the spread of industrialisation had threatened. The League counted among its members Shaw, Carpenter and a popular Victorian novelist, Ouida.

## Tolstoy and the Dukhobors

Tolstoy's late espousal of vegetarianism and pacifism came out of his search for God. After the great novels had been published, *War and Peace* in 1868 and *Anna Karenina* in 1877, he wrote a treatise, *The Kingdom of God is Within You*, endorsing pacifism, and in a rewriting of the Sermon on the Mount came close to expressing a form of Buddhism: 'The ideal consists in having no ill-will . . . in calling forth no ill-will, in loving all. The ideal is not to care for the future, to live only in the present . . .'[70]

At the same time he wrote an essay, *What Then Must We Do?*, which contains religious ideas that 'go back to the heart of the Middle Ages – the Waldensian, the Lollard and the Anabaptist brotherhoods, who taught the invisibility of the sacraments and preached that the people should be free in relation to kings, magistrates and priests'.[71]

Tolstoy asks:

> How to combat the evil to which mankind is sinking ever more deeply? First, by rejecting all the machinery on which society is now founded. Turn one's back on the State, refuse to serve it in any way, take no share in the exploitation of others, give up money and land, abolish industry – a source of pauperism – flee the corrupting cities, tear the conceit of education out of your heart and return to a healthy rural existence. God wants everyone to work with his hands and be self-sufficient. The mind is improved by the body's fatigue. The truly wise are the 'peasant thinkers' on the Syutayev model, the muzhik in sheepskin jacket. Down with intelligence! Long live simplicity![72]

It is interesting to see that Tolstoy's concerns were all those which the English and American vegetarians had been involved in.

---

★This was still the heyday for feathers used extensively in women's fashions; even whole stuffed birds could be used on hats. It was out of the Fur, Fin and Feather Folk at Croydon that the Royal Society for the Protection of Birds developed.

For years Tolstoy had enjoyed hunting, but in 1882 he stopped and in that summer he began his new diet of water, porridge, fruit jellies and preserves. But he was inconsistent, sometimes eating nothing but vegetables, sometimes nothing but meat and sometimes drinking only rum diluted with water. Five years later, in 1887, he again took up vegetarianism. In 1892 the *New Review* published his article 'The Vegetarian movement ought to fill with gladness the souls of those who have at heart the realization of God's kingdom upon earth'.

Early in 1895 Tolstoy found a cause and wrote the preface to a new edition of *The Ethics of Diet* (see footnote, p.xiii): 'The precise reason why abstinence from animal food will be the first act of fasting and of a moral life is admirably explained in the book – *Ethics of Diet*; and not by one man only, but by all mankind in the persons of its best representatives during all the conscious life of humanity.' The cause was an oppressed minority, the Dukhobors, cruelly abused and suffering because they had read the great writer's works.

The Dukhobors, or 'spirit-wrestlers', were an old religious sect which Tsar Alexander I had exiled to the Caucasus. The Dukhobor leader, Peter Verigen, had become both vegetarian and pacifist. He had read Tolstoy in prison and told his followers to stop eating meat and to throw away their weapons. In the spring of 1895 the Dukhobors in the Caucasus, who carried arms to defend themselves against marauding hillsmen, determined, at the instigation of their spiritual leader Verigen, to destroy their daggers, pistols and rifles and publicly proclaim their refusal to serve in the army. The *auto-da-fé* took place during the night of 28-9 June 1895, in all the lands held by the Dukhobors. The sectarians gathered to pray and sing hymns around the huge bonfires in which their instruments of death were melting, crackling and exploding. Cossacks were sent to 'restore order'; they arrived at a gallop, circled the unfortunate worshippers and beat them with *nagayki* whips until they had disfigured them. Then, by administrative order, the Dukhobors' lands were confiscated and their houses pillaged. Four thousand of them were exiled to the mountain villages, and their leaders were put in prison.[73]

Tolstoy was horrified when he heard of this brutality. For he had no doubt that it was his books that had given these people their courage. One of Tolstoy's disciples, Biryukov, left for the Caucasus on 4 August to investigate. He returned with a story so shocking that it could not conceivably be published in Russia. Tolstoy had it printed anonymously in the London *Times*, under the title 'The Persecution of Christians in Russia in 1895'.[74]

Four thousand Dukhobors fled to the mountains; four hundred had already died of starvation. A manifesto was written by more of Tolstoy's disciples about their plight, signed by Tolstoy and sent to the Tsar. The disciples were arrested and exiled, but Tolstoy still felt personally responsible. Tolstoy was determined to collect funds in order to allow the Dukhobors to emigrate to Canada; one of Tolstoy's sons had contacted Quakers in Britain who had arranged a passage to Canada. Tolstoy finished his novel *Resurrection* and gave all the money he earned on the publication to the fund.

It is impossible to discover the origin of the Dukhobors as they believe the written word kills, so they pass on their traditions orally through hymns and psalms. But there is some similarity to the Bogomils: 'The Dukhobors have much the same Dualist beliefs. There was probably no continuous heretic church in Russia, but when circumstances brought about the birth of heresy, many of the heresiarchs made use of the Bogomil traditions embodied in the Palea and other old Slavonic sacred books.'[75]

A few Dukhobors remained behind in Russia, but most migrated to Canada where they farmed in the wheatlands of Saskatchewan and Alberta:

> Food had deep symbolical meaning to them: each religious meeting began with a large loaf of bread, a jug of water, and a dish of fruit on the table. They eat their meals with hand-carved wooden spoons, often starting with a dish of cabbage and borscht, mixed with cream. Various fruits, blinzes, kasha, pirogi, and green beans are other favourite foods, as are fresh vegetables, large tomatoes, salads, and sweet corn, which they are particularly fond of. Other staples are the wholewheat and black bread that are so closely associated with old Russia. Though milk products are used freely, eggs are rare. Tea with lemon is the standard drink, but huckleberry and redcurrant juices are common during the summer.
>
> Maurice Hindus, a Russian-American journalist, visited the Dukhobors in the 1920s and was certain they would feel a debt to Tolstoy.
>
> 'Tolstoy?' asked the head of the household where Hindus ate a vegetarian meal. 'Was he a general in the Czar's army?'[76]

If the vegetarian movement could count among its members the greatest living novelist of the time, they were also about to embrace a young man who would become a world statesman.

## Gandhi and the Danielites

Gandhi came to England in 1888. His father was the Diwan or prime minister of the tiny state of Porbandar on the west coast of India. His mother was the fourth wife of his father, who was fifty when Gandhi was born. The family were Hindu, of the sub-caste of Vaishyas (who rank third in the hierarchical caste structure) which comprise farmers and merchants. Gandhi was devoted to his mother: 'to keep two or three consecutive fasts was nothing to her. Living on one meal a day during Chaturmas was a habit to her.'[77] She was both vegetarian and ascetic, but Gandhi had a Muslim friend, Mehtab, who boasted that his bravery in not being afraid of either ghosts or snakes was due to eating meat. He was fond of quoting a piece of doggerel which explained the British Empire:

> Behold the Mighty Englishman
> He rules the Indian small,
> Because being a meat eater,
> He is five cubits tall.[78]

Gandhi longed to be both taller and stronger so he agreed to try and eat meat in secret, but his furtive experiments only distressed him and made him feel guilty as he could not endure to deceive his parents. His attempts at eating meat ended, never to begin again.

He sailed for England to study law only after promising his mother to abstain from wine, women and meat; on board the ship he found he was too nervous to enquire what dishes were free of meat so he refused to eat at the table, but hid in the cabin and survived off fruit and sweets, a supply he had brought with him.

He had conceived of England as a land of philosophers and poets, the very centre of civilisation. But at first he found it difficult to conform to Western ideas of etiquette, customs and dress and his friends thought his vegetarianism could wreck his studies at the law college in the Inner Temple as well as his health. He was permanently hungry and what little food he found to eat struck him as insipid and tasteless. But then the greatest stroke of luck occurred – he stumbled on a vegetarian restaurant in Farringdon Street and had his first big meal since leaving home. At the restaurant he was immediately impressed and influenced by what he read there,★ both Shelley and Henry Salt's *A Plea for Vegetarianism*, two writers who fused abstinence from animal flesh with much greater social reforms. He also read the *Bhagavadgita*, the most popular expression of Hinduism, in its English translation by Sir Edwin Arnold.† Gandhi wrote:

> A convert's enthusiasm for his new religion is greater than that of a person born in it. Vegetarianism was then a new cult in England. Full of the neophyte's zeal for vegetarianism I decided to start a vegetarian club in my locality, Bayswater. I invited Sir Edwin Arnold, who lived there, to be Vice-President. Dr Oldfield, who was the editor of the *Vegetarian*, became President. I myself became the Secretary.[79]

By 1889, Gandhi had met Salt and his group of like-minded vegetarian radicals, some of whom were members of the Fabian Society and the Shelley Society. He became a member of the London Vegetarian Society, attending its annual conference and contributing articles to its journals. While in London, Gandhi studied other religions. He was moved and impressed by the Sermon on the Mount; he 'learnt of the Prophet Mohammed's greatness and bravery and austere living'[80] through reading Thomas Carlyle's *Heroes and Hero Worship*; he even grappled with Madame Blavatsky's *The Key to Philosophy* and Annie Besant's *How I Became a Theosophist*.

When he was about to leave London, he hosted a farewell dinner for his friends from the London Vegetarian Society with a meal in the Holborn

---

★We know he also read *The Perfect Way in Diet* by Anna Kingsford and *The Ethics of Diet* by Howard Williams.
†This was to become his 'spiritual dictionary', the greatest single influence on his life. Arnold was also the author of *The Light of Asia*, a poem on the life of Buddha.

restaurant in Kingsway. He was so shy that he fumbled over his speech but the report in the magazine was kind: 'Mr Gandhi in a very graceful but somewhat nervous speech, welcomed all present, spoke of the pleasure it gave him to see the habit of abstinence from flesh progressing in England, related the manner in which his connection with the London Vegetarian Society arose, and in so doing took occasion to speak in a touching way of what he owed to Dr Oldfield.'[81] But it was not only vegetarianism that Gandhi shared with his new friends; concepts of civil disobedience and non-violence became clarified in his mind as possible courses of protest: 'Non-violence and non-violent protest by civil disobedience were ideas already planted by Shelley and Thoreau, though civil disobedience remained almost entirely untried.'[82] Could Shelley's poem 'The Mask of Anarchy' (inspired by the Peterloo massacre of 1819) have directly given Gandhi the ideas of mass civil disobedience and passive resistance?[83]

It was when he finally returned to India that Gandhi became deeply influenced by a brilliant young philosopher, Rajchandra, who eventually became his spiritual mentor and finally convinced him of the subtlety and profundity of Hinduism and *Ahimsa*. The keystone of Hindu ethics, *Ahimsa*, consists of consideration of life, both human and animal.

The vegetarian movement was particularly rich in ideas and personalities in this period. One cannot help wondering whether Gandhi in his London years met Lt. Col. T.W. Richardson, who founded a group called the Danielites, named after the prophet Daniel who had insisted on eating plain vegetables, refusing the meat at Nebuchadnezzar's palace. It was a group which took the Garden of Eden as their model, organising into gardens and groves with members titled Senior or Lower Gardener. It appears to have been mostly a social group with emphasis on fancy dress, dances, garden parties and theatricals. Their creed makes them seem quite dotty:

> In the beginning God created man to live for ever, for no sentence of death had been passed upon him. The food given to him by his Allwise Creator to enable him to keep his body in perpetual life, undiminished activity and supreme happiness, was living fruit and seed, for the art of destroying the life of the fruit by fire (cookery) was doubtless then unknown. His death was the result of his own action – still he lived 930 years. His descendants, with few exceptions, instead of lengthening their days, or possibly regaining immortality, continued to increase in evil doing and consequently, in shortening their days. The contrast between the delicious living food given by God, and the dead carcases fallen, depraved man delights in devouring, is enough to account for man's days being only a paltry 'three score and ten'.[84]

## The Flowering of the Ethic

What can explain not only the rise in vegetarianism but the organisation of it in the nineteenth century? It first flowered in the centre of industrial England and there can be no doubt that its main influence remained in the urban centres. The experience of living in these fast-growing towns and cities cut off from the countryside had a certain effect on human beings. Being divorced from rural life gave some people a continual yearning for it; the rise of the protection societies is obviously the expression of the need to protect what was left, so that it may not finally be lost. Nature study became a subject in primary schools; field studies and venturing out into the country by cheap public transport or cycling became the most popular weekend hobby.

For the first time in Britain a large majority of people were cut off from the earth and had no way of understanding the nature of animals, or the complex symbolism that they represented. Once the destruction of an animal was removed from view, animals could be both sentimentalised and idealised, seen as part of the simple life, a sort of rural furniture to decorate the landscape. When urbanisation came, within the years of 1750 and 1850 (and it has been growing ever since), the visible interdependence between humans and animals was broken and the life of the animals became inaccessible. Yet urbanisation also provided the foundation for the subsequent organisation of the vegetarian movement. Instead of vegetarians being isolated, flung far and wide over a rural landscape, they were now within a small area and likely to be going to the same public places, whether churches or markets. Besides, local papers had now given power to isolated voices to spread their views, their criticisms and protests, to people they might not know or meet who would then come to them. The quick growth of towns and cities collected the voices of protest and intensified them; without urbanisation there would have been no vegetarian movement, merely those isolated voices we have been hearing for centuries.

It is interesting to see that though the vegetarian movement with all its allied issues could no longer be called a heresy in the old Manichean sense, it was still a secular heresy to Victorian society. It verged upon the disreputable and in some of its practitioners, like Edward Carpenter, it was seen as downright scandalous and immoral. Vegetarians were therefore firmly outsiders and would remain so. The position that abstention from meat has always put its exponents in, without their having consciously sought it – that of questioning the validity of the foundations of society – is inevitable. It is these questions, nagging and insidious, which society has always resented; irritated too by the unspoken moral superiority of the practitioners of vegetarianism, its first defence is always ridicule.

The vegetarian movement also collected about itself a great number of sympathetic radicals who were not members of the Societies, because they were not completely vegetarian, yet who embraced many if not all of the issues: socialism, animal welfare, non-violence, pacifism, health and homeopathy. Throughout the century, and into the next, the radical vegetarian movement continued to make converts, while its message in the allied issues strengthened.

# 12

# Sunlight and Sandals

*Poverty and War*

It is no exaggeration to say that the opening of the twentieth century saw malnutrition more rife in England than it had been since the great dearths of medieval and Tudor times.[1] Such malnutrition had certainly been there since the rise of the urban society, but now social investigation, new in those first years of the century, revealed the true extent of the poverty and the diet of white bread and tea, which was all many families could afford to sustain them. At least in the old days they ate oatmeal and milk, which was nutritionally nowhere near as pitiful as the present diet. But why should the government bother to investigate the nation's diet now? The answer was war.

A memorandum from Sir William Taylor, Director General of the Army Medical Service, reporting that the Inspector of Recruiting was finding it difficult to find men of sufficient strength, physique and health to fight the Boer War had shocked the Government. Taylor had discovered weak hearts, inadequate sight and hearing, deformities and bad teeth. The Government reduced the minimum height for recruits for the infantry to 5 ft from 5 ft 3 inches. (In 1883 it had been lowered from 5 ft 6 inches.) Whitehall asked the Royal College of Surgeons and the Royal College of Physicians to look into the matter. Unwillingly they did so, believing that Sir William Taylor had exaggerated.

What they found was horrific enough (infant mortality of 250 per 1,000, boys of 10–13 at private schools were on average 5 inches taller than those in council schools), but the committee tended to attribute the ill health and poor physique to bad sanitation, alcoholism, factory conditions and ignorance, rather than admitting that these people were all on the edge of starvation. It was believed then that white bread was as rich in nutritive properties as wholemeal (even though Dr Allinson had lectured and treated patients on the advantages of bran and wholewheat for nigh on forty years). The diet was so inadequate that women could not breast-feed their babies; many could not afford cow's milk and fed them with flour and water. The dire state of the diet of manual workers, or even the slightly better diet of the semi-skilled workers (potatoes, suet puddings, milk and jam were extra to the bread and tea), amongst whom any scrap of food was fought over, could not encourage the idea of selectivity. The semi-skilled worker may well have been able to afford a cheap cut of meat once a month but that would have seemed luxurious, not a food to be lightly sacrificed.

At the beginning of the century the vegetarian movement had become solidly middle class and in its views and aims remained as it had been in the last quarter of Victoria's reign. One reason for its class limitations was these depths of extreme poverty which the working classes were now reduced to, a plight the rest of society appeared wholly indifferent to. Certainly the vegetarian movement had offered help and advice, pointing out not only the economy of their diet but its nutritional worth, but they had been ignored over this as over so many other issues and probably felt they had nothing else to offer.

Vegetarianism could only flourish where there was enough income to afford an abundance of food, so that some foods might be sacrificed. It began, as we have seen, in the lower-middle classes, a great number being young men and women who had read their Tolstoy and Shaw, their Henry Salt and Edward Carpenter, who were imbued with ideas of progress and of changing the world.

One of its idealistic expressions was in education and the founding of various schools. Abbotsholme was founded as early as 1889, by one Cecil Reddie, who had been influenced by Carpenter, while A.C. Badley, an ex-master of Abbotsholme, founded the co-educational Bedales. Both masters advocated diet reform and catered especially for vegetarian pupils. Then came the Quaker schools, which turned co-educational at the same time and also began to cater for vegetarians, though not until the twenties. Reddie was influenced by the spiritual tradition of Behmen, Blake, Kingsford and Maitland. He also saw meat as an inflaming ingredient, believing it led to loss of control among the boys and the inevitable 'vice'.[2] St Christopher's at Letchworth, which still flourishes, was specifically a vegetarian school. In the late twenties Eleanor Harris, then co-principal of the school, contrived to have the sentence, 'Let the law of kindness know no limit; show a loving consideration to all God's creatures', added to the revised edition of *Advice and Queries* – the book of principles suggested to all Quakers for their consideration – thus influencing the Quaker movement itself which was inevitably becoming more and more sympathetic to vegetarianism. Other schools were Pinehurst School, Heathfield, and the Garden School, High Wycombe. The schools tended to be built on the edge of towns or in the country as fresh air and the beauty of nature were important. Sleeping out in the open, sunbathing and gardening were all encouraged. Education was seen as a process of nurturing, leading to self-discovery; the whole child was involved, so craft and art work were important and the expression of emotions encouraged. Freud was an important influence: his work on liberating the child from adult repression, encouraging natural impulses and free expression. Competitiveness was frowned upon whether academic or sporting. The schools were always pacifist in inclination and loathed corporal punishment, criticising the public school system severely. The pacifist movement and the idea of world peace were seen as measures which would erase violence from the home and the school.

But world war came in 1914 and the recruits were again found wanting in physical health. The vegetarians among them would have to cope as best they could. One anonymous officer (initialled B.P.A.) wrote in the *Vegetarian News* an account of how he fared:

What I missed most was the wholemeal bread, and I felt the void of its absence sufficiently to have to consume other food in larger quantity than usual. Strange as it may seem, whilst in England, as the war progressed, the bread became darker and darker, the Army loaf kept fairly up to the pre-war standard of anaemia. On the other hand this bread was usually more than a week old, and not infrequently slightly mouldy about the crust and cracks. However, certain brands of Army biscuit, notably one of Huntley and Palmer's, approached the wholemeal. In fact, most of the Army biscuits were less decorticated than the bread, and they had the strange property of becoming soft on being warmed in the oven.

Bread or biscuit, margarine, sugar, cheese and jam were rations that were always well maintained. The cheese especially was a liberal and dependable supply. Other articles of diet occurred with varying degrees of frequency. Oatmeal and rice were usually issued or obtainable if wanted. We once had a butter ration.

Prunes, figs, dates, raisins and currants were occasionally given as substitutes for some article missing from the routine dietary.

Potatoes were a normal part of the rations, but never seemed sufficient. These were sometimes partly or wholly replaced by other vegetables, such as carrots, onions, cabbage or even cauliflower. I have calculated that during my period of Army service I failed to consume at least half-a-ton of meat that was due to me in rations, and at least a hundred and fifty pounds of bacon missed turning my stomach into a pig cemetery.

Other items of official diet sometimes reached us in the form of medical comforts, of which the most prized were packets of pea soup, cocoa, custard powder and flour, also extra tinned milk, and so forth.[3]

He was a doctor in the Medical Corps and probably coped better than others as he had some nutritional knowledge. He comments: 'I do not think that I met a single medical man in France who considered his daily dietary save from a gastronomic or temperance point of view.'[4]

Even if private soldiers had been sympathetic to vegetarianism it is doubtful that they could have survived upon army rations without meat when fighting trench warfare. Coming from the working classes they would have been pleased to eat adequately for the first time in their lives. Certainly after the war there was still no sign of vegetarianism in the working class. Fenner Brockway in the early 1930s in 'Hungry England' never encountered a fellow vegetarian amongst the people he met; nor did Leo Price, a vegetarian miner in South Wales who went to fight in the Spanish Civil War.

Towards the end of the war civilian rationing began on 1 January 1918 with sugar, then meat, butter and margarine. The Government used two vegetarians, Mrs Leonard Cohen and Dugald Semple, to spread their message, so as to eke out the rations and propose meat substitutes.* Recipes for nut cutlets, however, were not likely to make converts. Meat was rationed to three-quarters of a pound per person per week and bread progressively became darker as more bran was used in its making. These two improvements, applauded by the Vegetarian Society, were not received enthusiastically by the general public.

## Criticism and Ridicule

After the war, with the experience of rationing, the cult of vegetarianism proved still to be unpopular. The rivalry between the London and Manchester Societies had declined and so did much of the social reformist zeal that had been directed to the working class. Vegetarianism seemed to be in the doldrums. There was still Shaw, of course, always good for the cause's publicity, but the joker in Shaw still made the diet seem only to be food for cranks.

The diet continued to have fun made of it, as in Aldous Huxley's short story 'The Claxtons', in *Brief Candles* (1930). Orwell neatly summed up the public perception, and possibly still does for a majority of people, when he wrote: 'One sometimes gets the impression that the mere words "Socialism" and "Communism" draw towards them with magnetic force every fruit-juice drinker, nudist, sandal-wearer, sex-maniac, Quaker, "Nature Cure" quack, pacifist, and feminist in England.'[5]

But this extract does not do justice to the virulence of Orwell's dislike. He recalls being on a bus in Letchworth with two 'short, pink, chubby, hatless' sixtyish men dressed in pistachio-coloured shirts and khaki shorts 'into which their huge bottoms were crammed so tightly that you could study every dimple'. Orwell tells us that the ILP (International Labour Party) were holding their summer school there. He goes on:

> The man next to me, a commercial traveller I should say, glanced at me, at them, and back again at me, and murmured 'Socialists', as who should say, 'Red Indians.' But the point is that to him, as an ordinary man, a crank meant a Socialist and a Socialist meant a crank. Any Socialist, he probably felt could

---

* *Vegetarian Cookery* by Florence A. George was published in 1913. Her recipe for a nut cutlet sounds rather more delicious than many. In fact her recipes are not overloaded with carbohydrate and she does use some flavourings – onions, parsley, salt and pepper – but there are frightful simulations of roast chicken made from butter bean paste and roast goose made from lentils. Odd, the hatred of dead animal flesh on the table and then the aping of it in vegetables. Florence George taught at King Edward VI's High School for Girls, Birmingham.

be counted on to have something eccentric about him. And some such notions seem to exist even among Socialists themselves. For instance, I have here a prospectus from another summer school which states its terms per week and then asks me to say 'whether my diet is ordinary or vegetarian'. They take it for granted, you see, that it is necessary to ask this question. This kind of thing is by itself sufficient to alienate plenty of decent people. And their instinct is perfectly sound, for the food-crank is by definition a person willing to cut himself off from human society in hopes of adding five years on to the life of his carcase; that is, a person out of touch with common humanity.[6]

This passage seems rather shocking nowadays, but it shows how the public image of vegetarianism had been distorted and could so easily be profoundly misinterpreted. That Orwell can call a vegetarian 'a person out of touch with common humanity' is reasonable enough when one knows he means 'not able to relate to the working classes'. Yet the choice of the word 'humanity' implies that Orwell had never considered vegetarianism might be a more humane philosophy than his own meat-eating one. It is surprising how he trusts the view of a commercial traveller, 'the ordinary man', and not the Socialists who at least shared with him a common idealism. But it is clear that he hates the Socialists as they are all 'mingy little beasts' full of 'sniffish middle-class superiority', and perhaps it is the vegetarian bourgeoisie which so enrages him. If Orwell could have found a vegetarian coal miner he might well have written differently. The only one we know of, Leo Price, was soon off to Spain, but they did not even meet there, as far as we know.

Orwell was not the only writer who disliked the vegetarians. G.K. Chesterton loathed them. Devout Roman Catholic, medievalist and hugely obese, he considered vegetarians to be pagans and materialists, taking the medieval Church's view that they were Manichean heretics. Chesterton found an ally among the Church of England's orthodoxy in Dean Inge, who wrote a defence of flesh-eating:

the discoveries which are still rightly associated with the name of Charles Darwin have proved, beyond a shadow of doubt, that the so called lower animals are our distant cousins. They have as good a right on this planet as we have; they were not made for our benefit as we used to suppose. This discovery has certainly altered our way of regarding them; it has made us aware of moral obligations which were formerly unrecognised. The only question is how far the recognition of these obligations ought to take us. Some think that we ought to abstain from animal food altogether. But the whole nature, as has been said, is a conjugation of the verb to eat, in the active and passive; and if we assume that survival has a value for the brutes, no one has so great an interest in the demand for pork as the pig.[7]

Inge had a following, not only within the Church, and his views found wide acceptance. The Dean seemed both sensible and devout, showing up vegetarianism for what it was, an extremist view. A clergyman, Rev. Francis Wood, published in 1934 a reply to Dean Inge. Wood discusses at length what exactly the Dean meant, but the booklet had little readership outside the converted; even Christians did not much care whether Jesus, the Good Shepherd, ate the lamb cradled in his arms or not. The Church in the inter-war period was very much a structure which bestowed social respectability, and any controversial issue could easily puncture this façade. Wood ends his piece thus:

> Although then it may not be permissible to claim that Jesus, living long ages ago in far away Palestine, was a vegetarian; it is perhaps not unreasonable to cherish the idea that were he living amongst us in this Western World to-day, he would, in presence of the spectacle of so much selfish and senseless slaughter of the innocent, beautiful, and useful creature life of the world, be found in the forefront of those who are endeavouring, alike by precept and example, to put an end to the custom of killing and eating our fellow creatures. Certainly we can hardly imagine him as allying himself with those who – as Dr Inge – seek not merely to excuse, but to impart a specious and misleading aspect of use and worth to a system which is utterly and irredeemably harmful and evil.[8]

## Raw Foods

Though there was little acceptance in the realm of ideas for vegetarianism, the commercial potential from the beginning of the century had started to grow. Food companies like Mapleton's, Allinson's and Pitman's were known and trusted. Mapleton's had developed vegetable fats so that suet-like puddings and crusts could be made; Allinson's were famous for their wholemeal and stoneground flours,* which boasted on the packets 'nothing put in and nothing taken out'. Vegetarian restaurants were also just as popular as they had been in the last quarter of the century before. They offered value for money, and for lunch were peopled by many who found a vegetarian meal pleasantly different, as long as they did not have to eat it all the time. The diet of the nation had changed; more fruit and vegetables were being eaten, more milk drunk, the British farmer was producing more food from the land, while imported chilled fruit came from Australia and New Zealand. Vitamins had been discovered in the nineteenth century and the idea that fresh fruit and vegetables were not only good for you but essential to health

---

*It took some time for wholemeal loaves to be accepted by the vegetarians. When the movement first began in 1847, and through the fifties and sixties, white bread was preferred. It was in 1880 that Miss May Yates began agitating for wheatmeal bread and the Bread Reform League began. Rightly Miss Yates had condemned white bread as 'not containing mineral elements needed for human nutrition'. But there was an idea at the time that too many minerals led to indigestion, degeneration of the arteries and premature old age, a theory of Professor Gubler's (see Chapter 11).

had begun to seep into the national consciousness.⋆ Hence began a certain public suspicion that vegetarianism – though going too far – might not be quite as batty as had once been thought. The growing popularity of raw food helped; both the Swiss Bircher-Benner and the American Gayelord Hauser were influential. In 1895 Bircher-Benner lay in bed with jaundice, so unwell he fancied no food at all. His wife slipped into his mouth a sliver of apple that she was peeling at his bedside. During the next two days he slowly ate two or three more apples. A colleague a month later told him about a patient of his who was totally unable to digest any food and then he read a recipe by Pythagoras, a puree of raw fruit mixed with honey and goat's milk. Raw foods at the time were thought to be highly indigestible, but the doctors felt it was worth trying. The patient agreed and ate her first bowlful with appetite. No indigestion occurred and, what is more, the patient felt she wanted to eat more. After a few days he added a little raw vegetable and in a few weeks the patient had made a full recovery. Bircher-Benner went on giving raw fruit and vegetables to his patients over the next few months and found that raw food was *more* digestible than cooked.

But he needed to know why. He read and researched the subject for years, while opening various clinics which were hugely successful. He decided that meat threatened health because of the way it was prepared and cooked. If human beings ate the whole carcase raw, it was another matter. He eventually found the answer in the second principle of thermodynamics, which reveals that any alteration in plants (i.e. being cut up and cooked) means a diminution in the solar energy contained in them. Thus the plant wilts, and all kinds of cooking, smoking or fermenting squander the real food value. 'Eat living food,' he would say, 'eat green leaves every day.'[9]

> As with raw vegetables, Bircher-Benner reached his conclusions about the dangers of meat from clinical observation before he looked for the theoretical explanation and, over the years, scientific support for his views has accumulated. It has been almost entirely ignored. We still believe that Bovril will put beef into us, that athletes perform best on plenty of good red meat, that real men need steak to make them big and strong, rather than a bloodless diet of pulses and greens, and that a feast hardly deserves the name unless it features a fatted calf.[10]

It was his muesli which made his name and theories on raw food famous. The muesli recipe, it is said, he discovered from a shepherd on a long walk in the mountains. Coarsely ground wheat was soaked in milk, sweetened

---

⋆It is still not accepted in poorer parts of the UK. Folic acid deprivation in pregnancy can lead to babies suffering from spina bifida. Average per capita daily consumption of fresh fruit for the whole of the UK is 2 oz – the equivalent of half an apple. In Scotland research in 1991 revealed 15% of Scottish manual workers never eat green vegetables and 24% never eat fresh fruit (*Independent*, 18 January 1992).

with honey and eaten with an apple. Bircher–Benner began to serve it at the clinic for breakfast, where it proved an instant success.

Gayelord Hauser had immense influence because of his popularity with the 'smart set'. He opens his book *Diet Does It* with the story of how he almost died as a child:

> A boy lay dying in the Evangelical Deaconess Hospital in Chicago. Despite many operations, his tubercular hip refused to heal. One of Chicago's best surgeons told the nurse, 'Send this boy home. Just make him as comfortable as possible. There's nothing more that we can do.'
>
> So the unhappy and discouraged boy was sent back to Europe, to die in the serenity of the Swiss mountains. There, high up among the snow-capped peaks, a miracle happened. One morning as the boy was eating his usual breakfast, an old man who was visiting his family told him, 'If you keep on eating dead foods, you certainly will die. Only living foods can make a living body.'
>
> 'What are living foods?' asked the boy.
>
> The man described them vividly. 'Fresh, young growing things, especially the green and yellow vegetables saturated with the earthy elements; lemons, oranges and other tree fruits, full of sunshine and living waters.' He knew nothing about vitamins, minerals and the thirty other nutrients discovered since. But the boy started to eat enormous amounts of the designated foods, and wonder of wonders, the hip which had defied all sorts of treatment now slowly but surely healed. Through this amazing recovery, I discovered for the first time what a diet can do . . . for I was that boy. Only those who have had a similar experience can know the joy of such a victory. So eager was I to know more about the subject, that I decided to make it my life's study.[11]

Hauser was introduced by Adele Astaire, the sister of Fred who had married a Cavendish, to such key figures as the Duke and Duchess of Kent, then later, in Paris, to the Windsors. Hauser was not a vegetarian (if he had been, his success might have been more muted), but this allowed the raw vegetable diet to be even more enthusiastically embraced. Raw food was, of course, all part of the back-to-nature movement that had begun forty years before but now the urge towards sun- and sea-bathing, long hikes and organised physical exercise was much more pronounced. Nature clubs, the euphemism for nudity, also began in Britain, though naturism was far more popular in Germany, as were all these outdoor activities. The rise of the Nazi party was allied with concepts of the body beautiful – if the body was Aryan, that is. Though Wagner's music was loved and admired as part of the great Teutonic and Wotanic mythology of Germany's past greatness, the composer's idealistic views on vegetarianism and his hatred of cruelty to animals were dismissed. Hitler's own vegetarianism was a strange exception.

William Hickey (the columnist Tom Driberg), in the *Daily Express* in 1933, said: 'the four greatest dictators of the present day are all vegetarian –

Hitler, Mussolini, Gandhi and Shaw.'[12] As early as February 1934 the magazine *Health and Efficiency* expressed the hope that Hitler might extend the humaneness indicated by his diet in favour of the weak and the minorities he was oppressing. This was brave of the magazine as it was an early date for any disapproving remarks about Hitler to appear in the British press. During the Second World War many in the Society denied that Hitler was a vegetarian at all. Many vegetarians would still like to, for it is difficult to understand.

## Hitler

The association of a diet linked indissolubly with humanitarian feelings with an individual who committed such unspeakable crimes against humanity and genocide against a particular race seems at first profoundly bewildering. However, Hitler may have been following a pattern common to many vegetarians, that of individuals setting themselves outside society, to examine, find fault and attempt to rectify these moral lapses within society by the example of their own lives. Up to the outbreak of the First World War Hitler was a classic outsider. It seems he first adopted the vegetarian diet in 1911, at the age of twenty-two when he was living in Vienna, but he had idolised Wagner for ten years: 'At the age of twelve I saw *Wilhelm Tell* for the first time, and a few months later my first opera, *Lohengrin*. I was captivated at once. My youthful enthusiasm for the master of Bayreuth knew no bounds. Again and again I was drawn to his work . . .'[13] No doubt both Wagner's essays promoting the vegetarian diet and his anti-semitism would have predisposed young Adolf to be sympathetic. Adolf was the third, and first surviving, child of Alois Schicklgruber and his third wife, Klara. Alois was a cruel and unfeeling father. He beat his son every day of his life. Alice Miller compares the structure of Hitler's family to that of a totalitarian regime:

> His use of power paralleled exactly the way he had been brought up . . . Brute force represented the ultimate power, and it provided its own 'justification' for 'maintaining order' and for the 'legality' of its crimes; this practice, too, was borrowed from the structure of Hitler's family, in which everything – the stifling of feelings and creativity as well as the suppression of all the child's needs, indeed of almost every human emotion – was done in the name of a good upbringing.[14]

Alois died in 1903, when Adolf was thirteen, and he was left with his mother, whom he worshipped and adored, but he was a pale, thin, sickly lad and he soon collapsed from a lung ailment and had to drop out of school and convalesce for a year. He was then aged sixteen and obsessed with politics. He had become a fanatical German nationalist with a hatred of the Habsburg Empire and all the non-German races in it. His only friend, Kubizek, said the world's problems weighed heavily upon him: 'he saw only obstacles and hostility.'[15] In 1908, after being refused by the

Academy of Arts in Vienna, he returned to Linz as his mother was dying of cancer of the breast.

It has been conjectured that Hitler was fixated upon the oral stage.[16] He sucked his little finger when aggravated, he was overly loquacious, sometimes giving 1,500 speeches in a year, and was an exhausting host for his guests, giving repetitious lengthy monologues. At the oral stage, the infant perceives that a mother's breast is consumed along with the milk: thus Hitler's fear was that he would consume his own mother if he ate meat. Like Shaw, Hitler in later life would describe meat-eaters as corpse-eaters or carrion-eaters. However, his abstention did not halt there, for he loathed alcohol and smoking and in his youth and early manhood there is not a shred of evidence of any sexual activity. There is little afterwards for that matter – his love affair with his niece, Geli, could have been platonic, and nor does his later relationship with Eva Braun seem to have been fired by animal passion.

Between the years 1909 and 1913 he lived in Vienna, penniless and destitute, going from one odd job to another, shovelling snow, beating carpets, carrying bags outside West Railroad Station, or doing rough sketches of the Viennese sights to sell from market stalls. It is unlikely that he could afford meat in these years; in fact, Hitler had a pronounced sweet tooth and if he had a little extra money he would buy pastries and gorge on them or cook a large platter of rice in milk and cover it generously with sugar and grated chocolate.[17] The year 1911 gives us the first evidence of any deliberate dietary preference in a letter:

> I am pleased to be able to inform you that I already feel altogether well and have resumed my wanderings through the lovely countryside. It was nothing but a small stomach upset and I am trying to cure myself through a diet of fruits and vegetables. Since the doctors are indeed all idiots, I find it ridiculous to speak of a nervous ailment in my case . . .[18]

He had another favourite food, a kind of nutcake made at a canteen frequented by Jewish students. His longing for the cake would overcome his dislike of the company. He complained of stomach pains for much of his life, and no wonder, for his diet consisted of large quantities of sweets. In Vienna he knew other vegetarians – a man called Grill, who again, unfortunately for Hitler, was Jewish, but Joseph Greiner claims Hitler discussed vegetarianism with him. He was also influenced by Lanz von Liebenfels, a founder of the order of the New Temple, a monastery near Vienna which had strict dietary rules and where the brothers baked their own bread and made cheese and liquors. It is possible that, through a vegetarian diet, Hitler sought to separate himself from the masses. Discipline and self-control would help him to attain the superiority he sought. In passage after passage in *Mein Kampf* Hitler shows how low an opinion he holds of the human race, whose weaknesses must be exploited by lies and who can be terrorised into subjection. Hitler's vegetarianism had nothing to do with humanitarianism, but stemmed certainly from his desire to be set apart, to feel superior to the meat-eaters, fuelled by his hero worship of Wagner. But there is a further factor.

In September 1931 his niece, Geli, was found shot dead after a furious quarrel with Hitler. This was the niece who everyone considered was his great love. It was said to be suicide but there were rumours that Hitler physically assaulted her in anger and she was later shot by a henchman. Hitler was, however, inconsolable for months afterwards; in the Chancellery in Berlin he hung portraits of the young woman with fresh flowers placed around them at the anniversary of her death. Shirer writes: 'From this personal blow stemmed, I believe, an act of renunciation, his decision to abstain from meat; at least some of his closest henchmen seemed to think so.'[19]★ Hitler told Goering that on the morning Geli died, he looked at the ham that was served for breakfast and declared: 'It's like eating a corpse.'[20] This emphasises the oral fixation theory. (It is also interesting that the only women he loved were relations, reflecting his earlier adoration of his mother.) A journalist, Otto Strasser, met Hitler for the first time in 1920, when Hitler mentioned that he did not eat meat. However when he saw the trouble that Strasser's wife had gone to in preparing a lunch of sliced beef, he put aside his principles. It would be true to say that up to 1931 he preferred a vegetarian diet, but on some occasions would deviate from it. After Geli's death he never ate meat of any description on any occasion.

Hitler would tend to talk through mealtimes. He claimed that he was a vegetarian because it increased his working and intellectual capacities. Strangely the dictator did not insist that his dinner companions should abstain from meat. Martin Bormann pretended to while at table, then secretly ate meat in the kitchen. Meals at the Chancellery in the 'Merry Chancellor's Restaurant', a large 40 foot square room which could seat sixty people, always presented two menus, one with meat and one without. Hitler's tastes in food were mundane; his favourite dishes were Russian eggs, hard-boiled and covered with mayonnaise, soup with tiny dumplings in it, baked apple, and cauliflower. Hitler would take soup, a starchy dish, potatoes or pasta, vegetables, cheese and fruit. At his country estate at Berchtesgaden he ate breakfast before nine of oatmeal porridge and prunes, and wholemeal bread and honey; for lunch again two menus were offered. This food, in fact, looks no different from any dish you might have been offered the same year in a vegetarian restaurant in London. The Vega, for example, off Leicester Square, was founded by Walter and Jennie Fliess, who were refugees from Hitler.

In 1933 Hitler summarised Wagner's philosophical views for Hermann Rausching:

---

★Perhaps Shirer was unaware of Hitler's earlier commitment; he certainly does not allude to it in his thousand-page volume.

Did you know that Wagner had attributed much of the decay of our civilisation to meat-eating? I don't touch meat largely because of what Wagner says on the subject, and says, I think, absolutely rightly. So much of the decay of our civilisation had its origin in the abdomen chronic constipation, poisoning of the juices, and the results of drinkmg to excess. He [Wagner] did not touch meat or alcohol, or indulge in the dirty habit of smoking; but his reason had nothing to do with considerations of health, but was a matter of absolute conviction. But the world was not ripe for this advance . . .[21]

After 1941 notes were taken of Hitler's conversations, in which he expounded on many of the arguments for vegetarianism already discussed in these pages. He even speculated on how it all began: 'I suppose man became carnivorous because, during the Ice Age, circumstances compelled him. They also prompted him to have his food cooked, a habit which, as one knows today, has harmful consequences.'[22] Hitler was obviously thinking of the research and work of Dr Bircher-Benner. Goebbels wrote in *Hitler's Secret Conversations*: 'He believes more than ever that meat-eating is harmful to humanity. Of course he knows that during the war we cannot completely upset our food system. After the war, however, he intends to tackle this problem also.'[23]

At the end, within the Berlin bunker, his meals became more erratic. While vast amounts of pastries were eaten, he was also heavily drugged for an imaginary stomach condition. The cook, who had first come to him aged twenty at Berchtesgaden, was Fräulein Manzialy, who had been trained at the clinic of Dr Werner Zabel, and was very good at pastries. Along with Hitler's secretaries and personal cabinet, she refused to flee when the Russians had advanced into Berlin and died within the bunker.

One might think that, given Hitler's personal diet, once he had gained power the vegetarian movement within Germany would have gone from strength to strength, converting thousands every few weeks. Instead it was quickly snuffed out. Vegetarian societies were declared illegal and their magazine ceased publication in Frankfurt in 1933. Members of the former vegetarian societies were raided within their homes. The authorities feared that for Hitler to be associated with such societies would be too demeaning. Generally, the oppression of the movement amounted to horror for any group, however small, that they could not control. The vegetarians gave in without a struggle, though some like Walter Fliess and his wife fled.* Most kept quiet about their diet and the preferences of the Führer. But when rationing began in 1939 vegetarians were allowed to exchange their credit notes for meat for dairy products – and 83,000 registered.

---

*The first Vega restaurant was in the Beethoven-Strasse in Cologne. It was such a success that eight years later they opened a larger restaurant which could seat 200, but the Fliesses were Jewish and could see the persecution beginning. Jennie managed to flee while Walter hid for some months. He was told he was number 17 on the Gestapo's most-wanted list before he managed to get to England late in 1933.

Tom Driberg was not quite correct in calling his second dictator, Mussolini, a vegetarian; the truth was that a gastric haemorrhage suffered by Mussolini in 1925 led to his being placed on a restricted diet. Eventually he was allowed 'white meat' – chicken, rabbit and fish.

Hitler's vegetarianism proved the fallibility, without any shadow of doubt, of one claim which vegetarianism had boldly made since ancient times: that if eating meat led to aggression, the converse was also true, and vegetarians were therefore peace-loving, gentle people. After the Second World War this claim entirely disappeared from vegetarian literature, and with it claims that war would be ended if only humanity abstained from meat and the slaughter of animals. But between the wars the vegetarian peace movement was flourishing.

## Between the Wars

Pacifism and vegetarianism were very closely entwined and the First World War was a crucial issue for many vegetarians. The rabid jingoism of the time made the conscientious objector (CO) a loathsome figure, to be jeered at and derided. The organised peace movement had started a hundred years before and was inadequate to cope with many of the personalities of the early vegetarian movement like James Simpson and Brotherton, who were supporters of the various peace societies. The Quakers were the most prominent of all the voices heard throughout the nineteenth century, but neither the Crimean nor the Boer War tested the strength of the peace movement's opposition. When 1914 arrived, and the war was not over in six months, the peace movements were still unprepared. The naïve idealism of the period is caught in Rennie Smith, who believed that workers of the world would unite against the capitalist warmongers. Smith, later an MP, peace worker and vegetarian, had gone to Berlin in 1914 to work for the International Federation of Trade Unions, where he was horrified to discover that German nationalism infected the workers and the trade unions had become part of the war machine.

The war provoked new peace groups to emerge, some based on religion and others on political analysis. Fenner Brockway was notable in the latter group with his ILP associates, so much hated by Orwell. Conscription came in 1916 and united all the pacifist groups. The Government set up local tribunals to settle claims and most of the boards were hostile, tending to favour the religious objectors like the Quakers or eminent men of letters like Lytton Strachey, while those COs who opposed war on purely humanitarian and secular grounds were often failed and treated with great cruelty. A Quaker vegetarian and thirty-two others were sent to the army in France, where they were liable to be court-martialled and sentenced to death. There were obvious propaganda purposes in having these men paraded in front of the troops before their execution. The No Conscription Fellowship managed to secure a statement from Asquith that there would be no execution but life imprisonment instead.[24]

Though schemes of alternative work emerged, many of the COs maintained that all work was furthering the cause of war. Out of the 16,000 COs, 3,300 were non-combatant troops, another 3,000 in the ambulance division, 4,000 in alternative work at home and the rest, 6,000 in number, were imprisoned. Seventy men died in prison because of the harsh treatment, particularly abusive for vegetarians who could hardly survive on prison meals once they had abstained from meat, gravy and suet. Fenner Brockway led a food strike at Wormwood Scrubs and the authorities eventually allowed a vegetarian diet.[25]

From out of this struggle the peace movement of the twenties emerged, aided by anti-war poetry, journals, novels and plays. It flourished for a decade as the true nature of trench warfare became apparent. Yet as Hitler's war machine gathered power, the peace movement shrank. It seemed to people like Fenner Brockway that the Fascist threat must be fought as there was no other way to halt it. The Spanish Civil War was the turning-point and secular pacifism accepted that guns and bullets were inevitable. But the peace movement had made progress. At the outbreak of the Second World War over 61,000 registered as COs, which was a considerable increase on the 16,000 in 1914.

It was the Depression which more than anything else marked the inter-war years. The Vegetarian Society in 1926, at the time of the General Strike, sent food parcels to the distressed mining areas and continued throughout the thirties to fund such gifts to those areas of mass unemployment. Such practical help was gratefully received, for this was food given without any preaching against meat. The Society by that time knew that this was a better advertisement for their way of life.

Helped by the new research into diet and health in Europe and elsewhere, vegetarianism was beginning to gain the respect of nutritionists. They at least agreed that most people would benefit by eating a great deal more fruit and vegetables than they habitually did. The idea of the simple life and the love of nature that had sprung up in the last century now manifested itself in 'nature cures'. Health was primarily the responsibility of the individual, and other new therapies all had their vogues: osteopathy, chiropractice, the dowsing pendulum to trace diseased organs, homeopathy, Dr Bach and his flower remedies, and the Alexander technique. The Nature Cure Clinic was founded in 1928. Run by Nina Hosali, a vegetarian and animal rights campaigner, the clinic was involved in animal causes and antivivisection. It promoted fresh air, exercise and relaxation, as well as close contact with nature. The theory of the nature cure is that we are all naturally healthy, disease is unnatural, so we must live our lives to pre-empt the need for medical attention. It also treats the whole person, the emotional, intellectual and social factors. One significant aspect of the treatment is the elimination of toxins; fasting and a raw vegetarian diet are often prescribed. It is interesting how ideas first formulated by Mani or other Gnostic beliefs resurface, as in this comment by James Hough, Secretary of the Vegetarian

Society, in 1926 in a lecture to the Practical Psychology Club of Manchester: 'green vegetables and fruits are real blood and nerve builders, valuable blood purifiers, whereas flesh contains poisons.'[26]

Real dietary evidence of how people ate and the effect of diet on health emerged in the work of Sir John Boyd-Orr. He was the first to point out that the Great War was won on the kitchen front. As early as 1916 the German harvest had fallen well below expectation; in 1917 'people were physically and mentally enfeebled . . . they had completely lost the will to victory.'[27] Boyd-Orr was the Director of the Rowett Institute in Aberdeen, which brought out a report in the thirties entitled *Food, Health and Income* that proved that the poor could not afford fresh fruit and vegetables, milk, eggs and meat and so suffered from malnutrition. *The Times* said in February 1936: 'One half of the population is living on a diet insufficient or ill-designed to maintain health.'[28] Boyd-Orr was angrily aware that animals in Britain were better fed than people, an issue which the vegetarians had for long pointed out, meat-eating being a wasteful and inefficient way of human beings absorbing protein. One of the significant changes we find in the Depression is that vegetarians no longer suggest that their diet will solve the scourge of poverty. Because of increasing social awareness and Labour politicians' campaigns, average wages rose throughout the thirties by 15% and more money was being spent on milk, eggs, fruit* and vegetables. But by the time of the outbreak of the Second World War, Boyd-Orr estimated that 'the average dietary of about one-third of the population was above the standard required for health, the diet of about one-third nearly right and the diet of the remaining third below the standard'.[29] George Orwell believed that 'twenty million people were underfed'.[30]

> For most people the inter-war years were years of wider food choice, better health, and improved nutrition: for a minority – and in some years and some regions, a large minority – the progress was so frail, and started from so low a base, that it could easily revert to conditions of hunger, disease, and misery not seen since the turn of the century.[31]

In these years the public perception of the vegetarian diet grew a little kinder, though it was still commonly thought too extreme. The Vegetarian Society itself continued patiently dispensing the same information but not winning many converts, nor did it exert more power than in its heyday in the nineteenth century, even though it had within the House of Commons a scattering of vegetarian MPs.†

---

*Average consumption of fruit rose by 88% between 1913 and 1934, and of eggs by 46%.
†Fenner Brockway, Rennie Smith, Peter Freeman, Stafford Cripps and Ellen Wilkinson, the MP for Jarrow who led the march. She was not a complete vegetarian but largely so.

## The Order of the Cross and Mazdaznanism

We have seen how in the past the vegetarian diet has been one element in certain religious beliefs or dissident Christian groups. The twentieth century has been no different. The Order of the Cross, which still exists today, was founded in 1907 by the Reverend J. Todd Ferrier (1855–1943). In the early days he met with little success in gathering members but in the late twenties and early thirties Order of the Cross groups were established at Russell Square, Woodford Green and Streatham Common. In 1934 the order moved to 10 De Vere Gardens, Kensington, where it still exists. Ferrier felt very strongly about the ill-treatment of animals. The order emphasises the mystical and esoteric interpretation of Christianity.

Ferrier rewrote the New Testament, claiming that the Pauline message obscured the nature of Jesus (see Chapter 5). For example, Jesus and John the Baptist are one and the same, and his parents are Essenes who, at Ferrier's time, were believed to be both wholly vegetarian and natural healers. As proof of Pauline obfuscation Ferrier cites Christians through the centuries who have shown 'little reverence for life' by allowing the exploitation and slaughter of animals. Ferrier wrote a large number of pamphlets covering food reform, life after death, the Second Coming and re-interpretations of Biblical teachings and stories.

Another dualistic religion, an offshoot of Manicheanism founded at the end of the third century AD, was revived this century. After the fifth century it was named after Mazdak, its major Persian proponent, who sought to make both property and women common to all. Mazdakism infuriated the orthodox Zoroastrians and it was suppressed. Its members were slaughtered in AD 528.

Dr Otoman Zar-Adusht Ha'nish revived the sect as Mazdaznanism in America, then brought it to England in the early part of the century. Like the Order of the Cross they did not do well to begin with; secrecy surrounds the biographical details of Dr Ha'nish* and others involved in the movement. But Dr Ha'nish travelled and lectured widely and the religion spread in the inter-war years, in those same northern towns where vegetarianism had flourished seventy years before – Halifax, Harrogate, Huddersfield, Ilkley, Keighley and Leeds. Astonishingly there were thirty-nine Mazdaznan centres in 1931; by 1937 the number had risen to fifty-two.

Mazdaznanism's appeal might have been that it was a system which showed more concern over the body than the spirit, unlike the order. In the twenties and thirties Mazdaznanism was presented as a system of self-development through breathing, diet, exercise and prayer. 'Breath of life'† was their motto. The exercises were all based on yoga, known as Egyptian, which included humming and singing. Diet was highly significant and abstention

---

*Dr Ha'nish, who died in 1936, claimed in lecture asides to have been the colleague and inspiring spirit behind a range of people, from Nietzsche to Edison to Wagner.
†See Homer and early Hinduism.

from meat essential. Mazdaznans writing in their magazine emphasise the health and spiritual aspects of vegetarianism. Again, the historical Jesus is radically reinterpreted: Christ was taken down alive from the cross and restored by the healing gifts of his followers. Christ's true message has been lost or deliberately perverted by orthodox Christianity.

Another vegetarian religion was that of the Seventh Day Adventists, from the Latin *adventus* meaning 'coming'. It was believed that both changing the day of rest from a Sunday (the first day of the week) to the Saturday, the seventh, and giving up all stimulants – coffee, tea, tobacco, alcohol and meat – would bring Christ's Second Coming closer in time. The founder, an American, William Miller, actually gave two dates when Christ would appear, between 21 March 1843 and 21 March 1844. When the skies failed to rend and light up with the heavenly apparition, Miller, quite unabashed, gave another date, 22 October 1844. The quiet passing of this day led to what was called 'the Great Disappointment'. As Christ's appearance was to lead to the separation of the saints and the wicked, all those who were not Adventists must have been relieved. But some Adventists now persisted with the same theory but not based on precise dating. Led by James and Ellen White, the movement arrived in England in 1878.

Ellen White had received her message about evil stimulants in a vision and she was an exponent of the theories of nature cure and vegetarianism. Adventism grew in England but as an example of a vegetarian culture it is somewhat isolated, for it is fundamentalist and emphasises personal sin; this is unlike the Quakers, for example, who from the beginning of the century embodied a strong vegetarian movement but are solidly within the Gnostic tradition, emphasising the inner light within one.

## The Second World War

Rationing of food brought the ideal dream of Boyd-Orr to fruition; for now everyone, from no matter what class, had exactly the same amount of food, nutritionally adequate if for most people not very satisfying. That the working classes had enough to eat was reflected in the health of the children.

What rationing meant from day to day is reflected in the writing of the period. A book entitled *They Can't Ration These* by Vicomte de Maudit (1940) drew people's attention to wild foods and even to flesh such as squirrel meat. *A Kitchen Goes to War* was a ration-time cookery book with 150 recipes by famous people. Many of these were vegetarian because the meat ration was so small. Stella Gibbons (author of *Cold Comfort Farm*) contributed Savoury Rice, which begins by frying a clove of garlic in margarine – rather daring at the time as garlic was thought of as very anti-social. But the war tended to break down such social mores and inhibitions, including one on horse meat.

Theodora Fitzgibbon wrote: 'A horse meat shop opened in Chelsea Manor Street, called the Continental Butcher. At first it was hardly patronised, but later on when food was very scarce there were queues outside . . .'[32] Later she says how she made enormous horse-liver pâtés and jellied tongues but never confessed what the meat was. In Vicomte de Maudit's book there are recipes for stewed rooks and rook pie. Theodora Fitzgibbon says: 'I even made a rook pie one day which was eagerly devoured.'[33]

Fitzgibbon tells us how hungry they were:

> We were always hungry for the rations were meagre. One person's weekly rations consisted of one ounce of butter, four ounces of margarine, one ounce of cheese, and between one shilling and one and threepence worth of meat, with a few rashers of bacon. One egg weekly in summer; the winter was unpredictable. Egg powder, that is dried powdered egg, was expected to make up the deficit. The small amounts of sugar ($\frac{1}{2}$ lb) and tea ($\frac{1}{4}$ lb) we often swapped, illegally, for cheese which was of the uninteresting 'mousetrap' variety, and best made into Welsh rarebit with a little beer. Tinned fish and meats were on a points system, so many points being allocated each month. A tin of stewed steak or corned beef took two thirds of the allowance. Unless you were pregnant, or a child, milk was only two and a half pints per person a week. Vegetables and fruit were ration-free, but limited and seasonal (in 1941 I queued for an hour to get onions from the greengrocer).[34]

The complete disappearance of one ingredient was felt deeply by both meat-eater and vegetarian – the onion. German occupation of Brittany and the Channel Islands had stopped all the supplies which before had been taken for granted.* The Minister of Agriculture was forced to demand in 1941 a fifteen-fold increase in the onion crop, saying he hoped that now 'onions would be eaten and not talked about.'[35]

One would think such a struggle to find food for a meat-orientated diet would have driven many thousands, if not millions, to embrace a completely vegetable diet. (If they were registered vegetarians, meat was exchanged for cheese and fats, with a special allowance of nuts.) But this was not so; people become used to the types of food they consume, often claiming that it is preference when it is only habit. The snoek saga of 1948, which was a complete Government fiasco, and the wartime loathing of whale meat show how very conservative the British were at this time.

Jack Drummond was acutely aware of the public's conservatism and he organised a programme of dietary education. The Food Advice Division of the Ministry gave detailed information on the radio, through the press and with posters and leaflets. The Dig for Victory campaign was a huge success. 'Building on a long tradition of allotments and vegetables grown in back gardens, what more natural than that the population should set to and dig up every scrap of derelict land, together with road verges, golf courses, parks, school grounds, playing fields, and bomb sites?'[36] Our own flower garden at

---

*In February 1941 a $1\frac{1}{2}$ lb onion raffled among the staff of *The Times* raised £4 3s. 4d.

the back of the house where my family lived in Hove was dug up and planted with vegetables.

Lord Woolton created cartoon characters, Potato Pete and Doctor Carrot:

> 'Eat us,' they cried, in the same vein as the pills that tempted Alice in her Wonderland; and indeed the propaganda that if we ate enough carrots we'd be able to see in the blackout was as much a fantasy as anything dreamed up by Lewis Carroll, for we would have had to gorge ourselves silly to make the slightest difference. Still, it all helped to cut down imports, and children who had refused to eat any raw vegetables now took to an endless munching of carrots.[37]

The back-to-nature and 'find food for free' movements organised schools, Brownies and Cubs to collect nuts, berries, crab apples, mushrooms and rose hips. In 1943 the children collected half a million tons of rose hips, 'which made enough syrup for every single baby in the country'.[38] The Ministry dispensed slogans: 'Food or munitions. Eat potatoes instead. Thoughtful shopping saves shipping'; and: 'Turn over a new leaf, eat vegetables daily.'[39]

But though the amount of vegetables that were eaten rose, it was only because there was little else to eat and they were used so frequently as substitutes. Jam was made from carrots, swedes and marrows; potatoes were put into bread, pastry and cakes. Being forced to eat more vegetables did not make people like them any more, though the price, with other unrationed foods like flour, oatmeal and fish, was strictly controlled and kept low. Meat, simply because it was so unobtainable, became deeply desirable and when meat-rationing ended in the fifties there was no question of not buying it (all rationing ended in 1954).

It may seem surprising then that vegetarian restaurants did so well through the years of rationing, but they showed the public how an economical and tasty meal made from vegetables could be a satisfying and appealing one. The other popular range of restaurants was Government-inspired. The British Restaurants, started during the Blitz to feed the homeless, by 1944 served half a million meals a day. Inevitably they had many vegetarian recipes. Walter and Jennie Fliess* of the Vega Restaurant were interned. Then Walter was sent to Australia for a year, but relatives and staff kept the restaurant going.

In 1944 the Vegan Society was founded in Leicester. One of the founders, Donald Watson, a CO, has said that the word was chosen as the first three and the last two letters of 'vegetarian'. To many then and now veganism seems the logical outcome of vegetarianism, for in refusing all animal products, including eggs and dairy products – milk, cheese, butter – they are making a stand against modern farming and all animal exploitation. The

---

*Their book *Modern Vegetarian Cooking* (Penguin, 1964) very much reflects the Vega food, which was the very best of vegetarian cuisine at this time.

dairy herd is inextricably mixed up in the meat industry; three-quarters of beef production stems from it, and milk production entails the removal of the calves from their mothers when they are a few days old. The vegans broke away from the Vegetarian Society because they refused to publicise the vegan view. At first vegans were thought of as very extreme indeed and the diet was considered anti-social; most restaurants then could have managed an omelette or cheese salad, but this was unsuitable for vegans. It was also thought that vitamin B12 was completely lacking in their diet because it was commonly but inaccurately believed that this vitamin was found only in animal foods. A great fuss was made in the fifties and sixties about this dietary deficiency. B12, unique among vitamins, is made by micro-organisms such as bacteria reacting with algae, so all green grass and salad plants have it as long as they are not sterilised by overwashing. It is also in yeast and vegans usually eat plenty of excellent homemade bread, and in seaweeds and their products.* There is little risk of B12 deficiency in a vegan diet, nor was there ever any real one, but the myth continues. Veganism is much respected by vegetarians for many feel that it must be the next step forward. Veganism is an ideal to aim at. The diet certainly produces health and vigour and it is known as being the one with the lowest reports of the common afflictions like cancer and coronary complaints. Yet it is also spiritually ideal in that there is no exploitation of animals by humans.

We now know that the nation under a system of rationing and food subsidy attained far higher standards of health than ever before or since. Improvements were recorded in the birth rate, infant mortality and the general health of children.

> One further evidence of improvement is worth noting. Between 1940 and 1944 Dr E.R. Bransby of the Ministry of Health surveyed the growth of children in twenty-one areas of the country, comparing the heights and weights of standard age groups at the two dates. Despite the wartime dislocations of normal life, separated families, and evacuation (perhaps, because of it) the heights and weights of boys had improved in seventeen areas, and of girls in fourteen. Moreover, children identified by school medical officers as having 'bad' nutrition (Grade D) fell nationally.[40]

Surely vegetarianism needed to offer no greater proof that its diet was nutritionally completely adequate and far healthier? Evidence in the war pointed to a diet mainly of vegetables and cereals with very little fruit and small amounts of animal protein, and a big reduction in sugar; it also pointed to the fact that flour with a higher amount of wholewheat in it was more sustaining than refined white flour. Many vegetarians felt that the experiences of the war had helped the cause. No doubt they did, but there were other factors emerging in social life and it was they in the post-war

---

*Other foods rich in B12 are miso, shoya, tempeh, barley malt syrup and sourdough bread.

years that made themselves strongly felt. Everyone wished to forget the war and any lessons learnt; a diet without meat represented austerity and bleakness. In 1947 the average ideal meal began with sherry, then tomato soup, and sole followed by roast chicken, while in 1973 the preference was for prawn cocktail instead of the sole and steak instead of the chicken. Meat was as strongly entrenched as ever.

# 13

# Sentient or Machine?

In 1960 Ruth Harrison, a Quaker, received through the post a leaflet on veal production; she had been a vegetarian all her life and her first reaction was to think that any facet of the meat trade was nothing to do with her so she put it aside. But 'in doing nothing I was allowing it to happen',[1] so she sent the leaflet to every Friends meeting in the country; she received only twenty replies. All but two said there was enough suffering among humans without getting involved in animals'. A Friend then advised her that if she was going to campaign about animal rights she must learn about animal suffering.

She began to visit the farms and broilers, battery hens, veal calves and, steeling herself, the slaughterhouses. The farmers were astonishingly unaware that their methods were questionable, she says. Once she had collected all the information Mrs Harrison contacted one of the top television documentary film makers, who told her that he thought the subject was 'too slight'. So she wrote *Animal Machines* instead. On the day the book was published the Ministry of Agriculture called a press conference to answer the allegations of ill-treatment. The chief scientific adviser said that 'merely to deprive animals of light, freedom and exercise does not constitute an offence . . . nor, in my opinion, does it cause suffering'. Mrs Harrison says the word 'merely' stuck in a good many gullets.[2]

The majority of the British public were, at the time of the publication of *Animal Machines*, entirely unaware of what modern livestock farming entailed. In the almost thirty years since the book was published there has been a stream of information in the press and on TV, becoming a torrent, some would say, in the last decade. There is no doubt that the book opened the public's eyes to how the meat upon their tables came to be there. Glimpses into the rearing, slaughtering and processing now nauseated many and stimulated some to embrace vegetarianism, while others merely ate less meat.

A year after the publication of the book, in 1965, Brigid Brophy wrote a full-page article for the *Sunday Times* entitled 'The Rights of Animals'. She said that she 'picked the title by deliberate analogy with – or, more precisely and more pointedly, by deliberate extrapolation from – the title of Thomas Paine's book'.[3]

## The Counter-Culture

At the same time in the mid-sixties ideas were beginning to emerge which sociologists now refer to as the counter-culture. This was a movement among the young of revolt against the ruling Establishment, a protest at the fogies for the continuing process, it seemed, of spiritual devaluation; it was an attack upon science, technology, the nuclear age, colonial wars, oppression of the weak. It demonstrated hatred of the bisection of the globe into rich and poor, First World and Third, Communist and capitalist; of war in Korea and Vietnam, of CIA involvement in South America and elsewhere. The counter-culture embraced CND and socialism (though it was above party politics and socialism was seen as a broad humanising principle), free love, flowing robes, vegetarianism, soft drugs, the feminine principle, love, kindness and peace. But this was not quite all, for it also embraced, or endorsed and certainly approved of, white magic, the occult, the mystic and metaphysical, everything which science and the coldly rational had sneered at and derided.

Great stress was placed upon ancient wisdom. A new significance was discovered in the landscape with its ley lines, prehistoric trackways and megaliths. A movement to return to nature and to feel reverence and awe for the natural world and plant life began to grow. *The Findhorn Garden* shows how spirit and nature became fused. In the early 1960s Peter and Eileen Caddy together with friends moved to a caravan site on the Moray Firth. They were vegetarians and established a garden vegetable plot where with the co-operation of the spirits of nature (whom they called the *devas*) they grew giant flowers and vegetables.

What is particularly interesting in Eileen Caddy's account is the echo of Mani's voice after almost two thousand years:

> We were told that we were purifying the atomic structure of our bodies, transforming the dense physical substance into light and lightness that would be more receptive to absorbing energies from the sun, sea and air. . . Previously we had thought of food in terms of calories or energy needed for maintaining solid physical bodies. Now we were told what actually nourished us was a more subtle energy. Through our diet we were absorbing the light that made the vegetables and fruit grow – the light of the sun and the light of our conscious. Our bodies were becoming light.[4]

It was a movement of young adults and adolescents who had been born at the end of the war and grown up through the fear and tension of the Cold War, with the impending and ever-growing threat of the nuclear bomb, who now said by their extremely public lifestyle that enough was enough: 'We will now change the world.' Often itinerant, refusing work, surviving by anti-social methods like manufacturing and selling drugs, or by music, fringe entertainment activities and street entertaining, they bore in some ways a resemblance to the heresy of the free spirits, the Beghards and Béguines of medieval Europe. Orthodox and institutionalised religion was loathed and rejected for it had been found wanting. Images of gender separation and the idea that male was dominant and females a secondary sex were ridiculed. Nature was again reassessed for all its natural magic and wonder; life was transcendent and a sense of awe was valued. Jeff Nuttall's book *Bomb Culture* catches the iconoclastic rage of the sixties revolt, but it already had a soft mystical centre, and it was this aspect that came to the fore and emerged strongly in the seventies. It then became almost inseparable from ideas of holistic medicine, cooperatives, health and vegetarian food, the women's movement, Stonehenge and the New Age consciousness – almost a retreat into Voltaire's garden (that concern with the personal and the rural exemplified in the Findhorn Community) after the revolutionary hopes of 1968. This movement from revolution to rural was similar to Shelley's upsurge of Romantic political aspirations and the beginning of the Bible Christians: a quieter, more isolated, vegetarian movement.

Members of the counter-culture were either vegetarian or macrobiotic, but not necessarily members of the Vegetarian Society* anything so organised and with such a history would have seemed an anachronism for the New Age. The young adults of the sixties were growing older in the seventies and this too in itself changed the nature of the movement, so that it became more concerned with health and certain social issues like the women's movement; some members in fact borrowed capital and opened health food shops and restaurants, or started communes and co-operatives offering summer schools in Indian transcendentalism, alternative medicine and organic gardening.

There was no way, of course, in which the counter-culture could make such issues as vegetarianism acceptable for the rest of society. Far from it – the hippy image was again that of the outsider, and the counter-culture again is a graphic example of a group of people criticising the status quo and imposing a form of self-exile upon themselves. Yet because they were older in the seventies one finds a gradual merging into the edge of the social structure, as in the running of health food shops and restaurants† – the former being an area of slow but steady growth.

Also many elements within society though not conformist provoked curiosity; lifestyles were news and the media were interested in depicting the details of anything that seemed alternative. Magazines, newspapers and TV carried articles and programmes on alternative diets; people were interested

---

*In 1969 the London Vegetarian Society amalgamated with the original Society in Manchester. From 1959 their separate journals had already become one. The Societies' headquarters are at Altrincham, Cheshire, with an information centre and bookshop in London.
†In 1968 there were sixteen vegetarian restaurants in London and eighteen in the rest of the country. Ten years later there were fifty-two in London and eighty in the rest of the country. *Where to Eat If You Don't Eat Meat* (1988) lists over 750 restaurants in the UK. This guide is compiled by Annabel Whittet of Whittet Books.

and wanted more information. In 1976 the Vegan Society produced an *Open Door* programme on BBC which brought forth an avalanche of letters – 9,000– and at least 300 telephone calls.

## Modern Farming

What can explain a growing sympathy with vegetarianism and a corresponding decline in the consumption of red meat?

> The British did not become a nation of meat-eaters that some forecast, and the traditional joint of beef or lamb has continued to slide in popularity, particularly the latter, probably because of its high fat content. Were it not for the increase in pork, and the much more spectacular rise in poultry consumption following the mass-production of broiler chickens, total meat consumption would now be less than in the rationed days of 1950.[5]

Factory farming methods became bad publicity for the product, for the more the public learned, the more the public felt a distaste for carcase meat. For a time hormones were used to fatten cattle, accelerating their weight gain in the shortest time possible, and some of these hormone residues produced horrific side-effects when used by a very few unscrupulous farmers.* The over-reliance on antibiotics, which the great pharmaceutical companies had encouraged, can leave drug residues in some of the organs.† The greater the scientific knowledge and the technology, the greater the cruelty inflicted upon the livestock, it now seemed to the public; the chained sow in the concrete stall,‡ the four or five laying hens cramped in a cage, the great

---

*The most infamous growth promoter was diethyl stilboestrol (DES), which was banned in 1981 after some disturbing evidence was found in Italy of small children developing sexual features. It was discovered that residues of DES had been found in baby food made from veal. The DES had been injected into the calves' rumps instead of the ear, hence large amounts remained in the meat. There is also strong evidence which links DES with cervical cancer. When DES was banned the EEC proposed also banning five other substances used as growth promoters in the UK. There was much campaigning by the Ministry and the then Minister, Michael Jopling, to halt that proposal, claiming that these substances included three natural hormones and two artificial ones which were closely related to the natural ones. All five hormones were used in beef production. There were fears that the ban would produce a black market in the sale of hormones to farmers. The EEC went ahead and banned the five hormones from January 1988; this ban was reaffirmed in 1991 when it was challenged by FEDESA, the European Federation of Animal Health. They blame the ban for the present black market in the drug Clenbuterol, known as 'Angel Dust'.

Traces of this drug were found in eight herds in Northern Ireland in December 1990, where three farmers have died allegedly from contact with Clenbuterol while feeding cattle. If inhaled the drug can spark off a heart attack; residues in the carcase meat could cause palpitations, muscle tremors and pain. An outbreak of food poisoning affecting 135 people in Spain in 1990 was traced back to liver from cattle administered with Clenbuterol.

†More than a quarter of pig kidneys sampled by the Ministry of Agriculture in 1985 contained sulphadimidine residues at concentrations eleven times higher than government limits. Sulphadimidine is an antibiotic suspected to be a possible cause of thyroid cancer.

‡Phased out by 1998.

housing units with their locked doors, artificial light and ventilating shafts, but still reeking of ammonia and ordure when the door was flung open all reminded people of some fiendish animal hell. Whatever life is like in the wild – and it is often bleak – it could never match this for suffering and deprivation. Animals torn from their natural surroundings, limited to short lifespans, not allowed to move more than a few inches, given rich protein food so that they were obese when infants (a total perversion of the free creature because they were no longer considered animals but units of food production) – everyone who spared a few minutes to consider what was being done was sickened. But how had it happened? How had modern livestock farming been allowed to grow into this monster now covering so much of the landscape? No one could quite understand. To explain it by the need to make a profit on food-producing animals seemed too simple and too crude. A farmer in the fifties, leaving his yard with the hens pecking at his feet, shot forward in a time machine to the nineties and dropped in a unit with 30,000 caged hens, at the end of their lay, debeaked, deformed and defeathered, would have cried: 'Not for me, I don't care how much profit they make, I won't do it!' Yet intensive farming grew, until now the monster lives without any public sympathy; but because the products are cheap people still buy them and make the system economically viable. Factory farming grew because several factors had come together at the same time, not unlike the first agricultural revolution which started in the 1740s. There was a combination of research into cellular growth and DNA so that natural hormones could be extracted, then used to stimulate the desired characteristics; the ability of chemical companies to research and make a varied range of drugs; the availability of antibiotics which allowed farmers to keep greater numbers of animals than ever envisaged before; new building technology which could provide cheap housing units, concrete stalls and automatic feeders and timers, which made possible controlled feeding, watering and lighting. Fewer and fewer stockmen were actually caring for the animals, making it more and more difficult to see what was going wrong.

Agriculture in the fifties began to spawn a vast number of different but dependent industries,★ which involved the development and production of new equipment, fertilisers and seeds, and the storage, processing and preservation of the foods themselves – so that heavily mechanised farms with computer technology increasingly made individual farmers dependent on a host of other suppliers, and they were often unable to choose the way they produced their livestock because this was laid down by the particular supplier of the product to the farm. Once science entered the farm and monitored the soil fertility, the water control, the speed of crop growth, the span of time before livestock slaughter and the components of the animal

---

★Ruth Harrison, in particular, lamented the onset of large companies such as the pharmaceuticals which began to finance farming with millions of pounds of capital 'control from remote city offices'.

feed, the farmer took on more and more the role of a caretaker, losing close personal control. There were always plenty of arguments which suggested that animals did not suffer and that it was only anthropomorphic sentimentalists who said they did.★

We now have the experiences of people working in intensive farming. This was written by a stockman who at one time worked on a farm of 40,000 chickens, and sent to Chicken's Lib.† The chickens were bought in as pullets and sold at eighteen months:

> One of my jobs was removing dead birds. There was never any shortage. Due to poor light the bottom two tiers of cages were in darkness, and it was impossible to see if the birds were still alive. When the carcases were removed it was often a matter of a skeleton head and a few bones. I once took part in the clearance of a 10,000 bird shed. Ten other lads were brought in from local farms and the torture commenced. I recall being shouted at for my gentleness. Birds were dragged from the cages by their legs. Four birds were carried in each hand upside-down, down the shed to the door. The noise was deafening, the smell was putrid. Legs, wings and necks were snapped without concern. As I now look back, the whole system is incredibly cruel. After saying all this, this particular farm was good as far as battery farms go. The floors were swept daily and precautions taken against disease and pests.[6]

He gave up work in the poultry industry after nightmares.

Andrew Tyler a campaigning vegan journalist, visited a slaughterhouse in the south of England which disposed of 1,500 pigs weekly. It is one of the very few UK slaughterhouses which have an EC licence, hence is superior to the other 1,000 and more slaughterhouses that failed due to standards of hygiene and technique. Fifteen minutes are allowed per animal for electrocution, stabbing, degutting and dispatch to the chillers. Tyler comments: 'Speed, forced by a piece-rates system, was the essence and many a rule of welfare and hygiene was trampled on the way.'[7]

---

★The Athene Trust commissioned a report (October 1991), *Do Hens Suffer in Battery Cages?*, by Dr Michael Appleby of the Institute of Ecology and Resource Management at the University of Edinburgh. Appleby had been doing scientific research on the behaviour and welfare of hens in different husbandry systems for ten years. The report looked at the problems of pain, injury and disease, of thermal and physical discomfort, fear and distress and even hunger and thirst, which were only severe if techniques of induced moulting were used. The conclusions were: (1) 'Hens suffer in battery cages. Many aspects of suffering are chronic, and affect all individuals. Other aspects, which may be either chronic or acute, affect different individuals to a greater or lesser extent.' (2) 'Hens suffer more in battery cages than in well-run, alternative systems.' (3) 'Suffering is caused by specific characteristics of battery cages. It would be possible to legislate against such characteristics.' An earlier report by the Athene Trust on the dry sow stall system proved without doubt the extreme suffering and distress caused to the animals by the system. Both reports are available from Compassion in World Farming.

†Foremost in the campaign to end battery cages and all poultry intensive farming.

Tyler's account is vivid and horrifying. He concludes by reminding us that though those who work in the abattoir may seem callous and brutalised, they are in the end doing the work consumers bid them do.

Are Tyler's observations proof that killing animals brutalises? – which from Plutarch onwards, throughout these pages, has been a constant claim of the vegetarians. It is, of course, like the chicken and the egg. Only a fairly insensitive and probably aggressive personality would be likely to seek such work in the first place – as we have seen in the letter to Chicken's Lib, one stockman got out of the work because he could not endure the pain of the creatures. Whether further brutalisation is caused by habitually undertaking such bloody tasks it is impossible to say, though such a supposition seems reasonable. But Tyler is right – we can hardly blame the slaughterers when it is us and our society that demand the meat.

In 1984 a Government-appointed Farm Animal Welfare Council published a report. After studying conditions in forty slaughterhouses in Britain, Denmark and Holland, they recommended a hundred legal and practical changes to improve the lot of cattle, sheep and pigs on slaughterhouse premises. The report cast doubt on the efficacy of stunning before slaughter, and concluded: 'Local authorities should be more active in enforcing existing welfare laws, but the Ministry of Agriculture should step in to prosecute when authorities default on this duty . . .'[8] None of these hundred recommendations has been implemented by the Government since the report was published.

This is also true of the Brambell Committee, headed by two distinguished zoologists, which the Government hurriedly created immediately after the publication of *Animal Machines* in 1964. The Brambell Committee reported eighteen months later, stressing the importance of animal behaviour as a component of animal wellbeing. 'It laid down the principle: "An animal should at least have sufficient freedom of movement to be able, without difficulty, to turn around, groom itself, get up, lie down and stretch its limbs." Twenty-five years on the Government has still not achieved this for all species. Mrs Harrison is a remarkably patient woman. "If only a fraction of the effort, resources and ingenuity spent on ever greater intensification had gone into improving and developing humane alternatives and raising standards of stockmanship, we would be in a stronger position today," she says.'[9]

Though only some of this information percolated through to the general public in the seventies and eighties, enough did for the majority to know that intensive farming was wrong. Undeniably this was one factor in the decline in buying carcase meat, coupled with a growing squeamishness about buying anything that looked animal in origin. Butchers from the sixties onwards carved the carcases at the back unseen by customers and stopped displaying pigs' or calves' heads or anything else that was strongly reminiscent of the living animal. A definite move towards buying meat already cut and portioned, sealed and with absorbent paper to mop up the tell-tale blood, also began in the seventies. People preferred to choose their meat at the supermarkets, where they could pretend it was merely a packet of food like so much else there, rather than at the butcher's.

A large majority of people who turn to vegetarianism do so because they believe meat to be unhealthy. There is now powerful evidence on the nature and the amount of fat in livestock to back this belief. A well-fleshed fat buffalo shot in Africa for its carcase was analysed with other wild herbivores. These were all rich in the essential polyunsaturated fatty acids, a fact which astonished scientists who then believed that all cattle were high in saturated fats similar to the livestock reared for meat in intensive farming.[10] The Meat and Livestock Commission want farmers to aim for a 25% fat carcase, which means that a carcase carries 50% lean meat. But dissection of over 220 wild animals from sixteen different species showed that the average amount of fat was around 3-4% and that of lean over 75%. So if you eat meat, stick to wild game.[11]

Given the public image of factory farming, it was not surprising that the general public would become aware of the issue of animal rights. Brigid Brophy writes that when she coined the phrase, she was deliberately associating 'the case for non–human animals with that clutch of egalitarian or libertarian ideas which have sporadically, though quite often with impressively actual political results, come to the rescue of other oppressed classes, such as slaves or homosexuals or women.'[12]

Against that must be set Phil's statement: 'Your animal rights go out of the window if men can't get a living wage.'[13] Phil, eighteen years old, living in a depressed rural area, earned as a slaughterman, for a 12-14 hour day, £120 per week in the mid-1980s. His story of his first days as a slaughterman, of his hideously botched efforts to kill his first cow and his workmates' refusal to jeopardise their piece-rates by stopping to show him what to do, underlines Ruth Harrison's pleas for proper training.

Once domestication of livestock began, their control, breeding and slaughter by necessity inflicted barbaric cruelties upon them. Plutarch and many others after him have commented on this. There can be no difference in the degree of suffering experienced by animals then and now. The only difference now is one of sheer numbers: four billion four-legged livestock and eleven billion poultry are processed into food annually. It is the sheer scale of livestock farming which makes many feel that the crimes humans now perpetrate against the animal kingdom are horrific and unforgivable.

There are now three times as many domestic animals as people. China is home to 350 million pigs and two billion chickens. India has 107 million goats, 196 million head of cattle and 74 million water buffalo. Animals live much shorter lives in the First World than in the Third. Livestock in the USA tend to live only a third as long as livestock in China, so though at any given time China has more chickens than the USA, during the year the US raises and slaughters three times as many. The herds of the rich countries produce 61% of the world's meat, 55% of the eggs and 72% of the milk.[14]

At a global level meat is still the primary food and the most popular among those people able to afford it. More than a billion people now consume at least a kilogram a week. In the US per capita consumption is more than two kilograms a week. Meat consumption, in fact, has nearly quadrupled since 1950. The leaders in meat consumption per capita for 1990 were the US at 112 kg; Hungary, 108; Australia, 104; Czechoslovakia, 102; and France, 91.[15]

As modern farming techniques became more sophisticated and the numbers of livestock expanded, critics of the new farming methods were not slow to voice their feelings. In the early sixties an organisation was founded by Peter Roberts called Compassion in World Farming. Peter Roberts and his wife, Anna, ran a small dairy farm in Hampshire with 500 free-range hens.

> They had always been welfare-minded. Peter still recalls how, even in the snow, he would always let his cows out in the morning and they would charge out to the field, muck about for 30-40 minutes and then happily wander back to their clean, straw-bedded cow shed for warmth and comfort. But there were sides to their lifestyle which made them feel increasingly uneasy.[16]

These were aspects of factory farming they found they could not endure. Roberts wrote to a local paper questioning some of the factory farming techniques and was astonished when he received a massive response. Since then, Compassion in World Farming has been in the forefront of the movement to ban battery cages, tethered sow stalls, the veal crate, the export of livestock (particularly unweaned calves) and other cruel practices whenever they emerge. From the start CIWF equated world hunger with intensive animal feeding. In 1974 they published a pamphlet which graphically illustrated their message: it gave 'details of the feeding of groundnut meal, the basic protein of Indian Famine Relief Food, which was then being imported into the UK for cattle-feed – 190,000 tons of it – enough to carry over 13 million children through a famine at 40 grammes each per day'.[17]

CIWF has continued to be a pressure group of enormous significance up to the present, and will certainly continue. Many of the successes if not all, in animal welfare in the last two decades were due to their persistence. This may be due to the fact that each issue they take on is thoroughly researched; they always seek scientific backing for their claims and they do not ask the impossible; they do not campaign against killing livestock and eating meat (though the staff are all vegetarian or vegan) but simply work for more humane farming. ★

---

★Their 1991 Manifesto lists three headings: Bans on cruel systems and practices; Provision of minimum legal standards; Provision of strong regulatory mechanisms to prevent abuse.

## Caring for the Environment

Out of the counter-culture there slowly emerged a concept of humankind being the custodian of their planet. Much of the inspiration for this came from rediscovering the answer given by Chief Seattle of the Divamish Indians, when the US Government was forcing the purchase of his tribe's lands in 1855:

> We do not own the freshness of the air or the sparkle on the water. How then can you buy them from us? Every part of the earth is sacred to my people, holy in their memory and experience. We know that the white man does not understand our ways. He is a stranger who comes in the night, and takes from the land whatever he needs. The earth is not his friend, but his enemy, and when he's conquered it, he moves on. He kidnaps the earth from his children. His appetite will devour the earth and leave behind a desert. If all the beasts were gone, we would die from a great loneliness of the spirit, for whatever happens to the beasts happens also to us. All things are connected. Whatever befalls the Earth, befalls the children of the Earth.[18]

Now people were confused with the awesome knowledge that we were not only squandering the resources, but poisoning our soil, air and water.

> Never before in our history has the organic world around us been in so much trouble. We seem to be thriving – at least as a species we are replenishing ourselves everywhere – but not much else is. Whole forests in both the tropical and temperate zones are dying from acid rain, radiation, air pollution, timber harvesting, slash-and-burn agriculture. Harbours, estuaries, seas as broad as the Mediterranean, the River Rhine are all in decline from toxic wastes. Between now and the end of the century the extinction rate among higher vertebrates will be as much as 400 times higher than the average rate that has prevailed over the history of evolution. As these creatures that have evolved with us now disappear by our hand, many of the Earth's native ecosystems will go with them. We are creating an environment of gashes, wounds, disorganization, and death. The order of nature may be a difficult ideal to define precisely and follow, but we are simply disregarding it.[19]

Meat-eating and intensive factory farming are one factor which has several disastrous effects: 'Meat production dominates agriculture worldwide: everywhere domestic animals compete with forests and wildlife and the basic needs of people. Producing and consuming less meat, fewer dairy products and eggs would release land in the developing countries and enable people there to feed themselves better.'[20]

Out of a total of 19 million hectares of agricultural land in the UK, 15.3 million hectares, or more than 80%, are used either directly or indirectly for meat and dairy production. But it is the pollution caused by intensive farming of livestock which has a horrible and dramatic effect on our environment. In spring 1991 a dairy farm's storage tank released 25,000 gallons of slurry into the River Tamar on the Devon and Cornwall border killing 3,000 fish. There is a risk that silage used as cattle fodder, produced by keeping grass bales under plastic sheets, may be a significant source of listeria.

Unigate opened the biggest broiler-rearing and processing factory in the whole of Europe near Scunthorpe in January 1990. They rear 50 million birds a year and the Severn Trent Water Authority gave them permission to discharge 800,000 gallons of poultry-processing effluent into the River Trent daily. Two years later, the Unigate plant was up for sale. It has been bedevilled by protesters and had problems with local planners. Also, it could find no local breeding stock and had to transport fertilised eggs from the Midlands. It traded under the name of St Ivel Farm Foods and despite having a high turnover 'lost the money faster than any other poultry meat company in England and Wales . . . This example shows the value of opposing local planning proposals for broiler-rearing units in thwarting the expansionist intentions of the poultry industry.'[21]

The problem of waste is seen most dramatically in countries with small acreage and highly developed farming like Holland. Dutch farms produce 94 million tonnes of manure every year, but their land can only absorb 50 million tonnes. Illegal dumping of the waste produces clouds of ammonia which poison trees and plants and encourage nettles★ and brambles. Macdonald, writing in the *Scotsman*, pinpoints the ammonia 'produced by our burgeoning domestic livestock' as another primary source of acid rain.[22] The answer is possibly to process the waste into harmless and beneficial components. Research has been done but it is a slow business and should have begun thirty years ago, before the harm and pollution occurred.

But meat is consumed worldwide and affects the whole planet in a dramatic manner: 'It has been calculated that when rainforest is cleared for raising cattle, the cost of each hamburger produced in the first year is about half a tonne of mature forest, since such forest naturally supports about 800,000 kilos of plants and animals per hectare, the area of which under pasture will yield some 1,600 hamburgers. The price of that meal-in-a-bun is anything up to nine square metres of irreplaceable natural wealth − the richness and diversity of the rainforest which may never be re-created when the grazing lands are in due course abandoned.'[23]

A journalist visiting the Amazon forests writes:

On both sides of the road, the forest has been cleared as far as the eye can see. For the most part, it has been cleared for cattle ranching. Today, there are

---

★Nettles love soils rich in nitrogen. In the Scottish Highlands and Islands it was believed that nettles grew from the bodies of dead men and in Denmark the theory is that nettle clumps grow from the shedding of innocent blood. The truth is more prosaic: in a landscape they signal former human habitation as it is the toxic wastes of living creatures as they are chemically broken down within the soil that the nettle most enjoys.

over 8 million cattle in Brazilian Amazonia. Meat production is extremely inefficient (50 kg/hectare/year), making ranching an activity which is so wholly uneconomic that it would probably never have been undertaken on the present scale if the Brazilian Government, with aid from the World Bank and other multilateral development banks, had not poured $2 billion into subsidizing the cattle industry in Amazonia.[24]

Meat-eating worldwide produces environmental pollution on a massive scale. 'From the hundreds of algae-choked Italian lakes to the murky Chesapeake Bay and from the oxygen-starved Baltic Sea to the polluted Adriatic Sea, animal wastes add to the nutrient loads from fertiliser run-off, human sewage and urban and industrial pollution.'[25]

Ruminant animals also release about 80 million tons of gas each year in belches and farts, while animal wastes at feedlots and farms emit another 35 million tons. Livestock account for 15-20% of global methane emissions. There is no doubt that current methods of rearing these huge numbers of animals take a large toll on nature. The general public are slowly becoming aware that present-day animal agriculture is out of alignment with the earth's ecosystems.

No doubt statistics like these were considered by some meat-eaters who then modified their intake if not eschewing meat altogether, in exactly the same green spirit of recycling plastic bags or driving to the bottle bank. Certainly supermarkets at the end of the eighties were responding to the message by introducing environment-friendly foods. This entailed a deliberate move towards free-range products chickens and eggs, certainly, but also pigs. The latter decision, like the end of the slave trade, was due not to compassion but to economics. According to *Farmers' World*, 'now the return on capital with outdoor pigs beats that from even the most intensive system.'[26]

But exposing the trends towards a decline in the UK of red carcase meat-eating does not tell us much and tends to give us a distorted picture. Meat products and chickens are still both eaten in great quantities, so what is it we really eat and has there been a discernible trend towards vegetarianism in the last twenty years, or is it all a pipe dream of the animal rights campaigners?

As a nation we now eat less beef, mutton, and bacon, less sugar, bread and potatoes, less butter and jam, less fish and fewer eggs, and drink less milk and tea – that is to say, less of many of the traditional articles of English diet. No simple pattern emerges. Some of these, like bread and potatoes, were basic foods of the past and had been experiencing decline for many years, except when interrupted by war; others, like sugar, butter, and eggs, were relative luxuries to which previous generations had aspired as their standard of living rose. Similarly, the foods which have increased in recent times – pork and poultry, brown breads, margarine, cheese, pasta, breakfast cereals, and frozen foods – do not fit into a single category or explanation.[27]

The most significant change in our diet has been the growth in demand for convenience foods. These prepared dishes of labour saving foods are a constantly expanding range and include meat, fish and vegetable ingredients. The vegetarian convenience foods have also expanded from the late eighties to the present time of writing, twinned with an expansion of organic foods and ingredients. There has been no decline in convenience foods which contain meat or chicken – quite the opposite – so it would seem that feelings for animal welfare or the ecology of the planet do not operate when faced with a quick and easy dish to cook for the evening meal, or only among a small minority. But there is one other factor that has helped turn the public away from meat – that of health.

## The Concept of Pure Food

The founders of the Vegetarian Society in the middle of the last century had a strong concept of pure food. It was, of course, food untainted by previous life, food without death and without blood, but they went further and, recollecting the Hebraic dietary laws, wanted food free of fermented products; hence no alcohol could be drunk or mixed with the food (though unlike the Hebrews they did not forbid yeast in dough). However, they were very much against all flavourings, which were thought of as stimulants; that included tea, coffee, salt, spices and herbs, leading to the plain, bland food which one of their presidents, Francis Newman, complained of.

The concept of pure food that emerged in the 1970s was rather different. This was food untainted by chemicals, whether they were used in the life of livestock or added when the food was processed. Food, to be pure, had to have an unadulterated context; hence it had to be organically grown if possible, or at least in soil outside and not in greenhouses fed by nutrients in water. Such food was thought of as 'natural' and 'wholesome'. But such words are far from arbitrarily chosen, for if we examine them with more care, we find they have multiple meanings. A vegetarian diet is thought of as pure because it avoids the immorality of slaughter and exploitation; it is often organic and therefore free of chemicals; it is healthier, lighter and conducive to spirituality; it avoids the toxins in meat that may be produced at the moment of death from the adrenalin pumped through the terrified animal. While 'wholeness' means the whole grain and foods which are not refined, it has other echoes of psychic wholeness, meaning the complete entity of the person – mind, soul and body – and associations with holistic treatment. One can go further and suggest that wholeness means a unity with nature and everything that is alive on the planet, a communion and affinity between Gaia and humankind. The word 'natural', of course, is linked with 'wholeness' and 'pure'. The word has obvious connotations: pure spring water, green meadows scattered with flowering herbs and the fertilisation of the soil by the natural process of the animals that graze upon it dropping their manure. No wonder food companies in their marketing ploys have latched on to these three words and so misused them that any packet or carton bearing such a signal must be examined closely. They are, however, a strong trinity and a powerful force in selling the product, because the public believes in their mythical effect.

This is all the more so because many health anxieties attend the traditional foods and these have in the last decade grown ever more prominent and controversial. The dislike of unnecessary chemical additives being added to canned, frozen and processed food began in the seventies. In the following decade labelling was brought in, though at first the food companies had ridiculed the idea as being impossible, irrelevant and unnecessary because nobody would bother to read the labels. The Government frequently pointed out that the amounts of some doubtful chemicals added to certain foods were so minimal they could have no dire effects on the human body. But several were already having an effect. The Hyperactive Children's Support Group was formed in 1977. The group recommends first

> cutting out all food and drink containing synthetic colours or flavours, avoiding glutamates, nitrites, nitrates, BHA, BHT and benzoic acid. Second, for the first four to six weeks, foods containing natural salicylates (like aspirin, chemically) should be avoided and then reintroduced one at a time to see if they cause problems.
>
> Additives can hide the true nature of food. You can use polyphosphates (E450) to emulsify fat and to incorporate water, some 128 (Red 2G) to colour the fat so that it looks like meat, enhance the flavour with 621 (monosodium glutamate), so that the food has an addictive and chicken-like flavour. Add some BHA and BHT, E320 and E321, to make sure that the excessive quantities of fat do not go rancid, mix in some lean meat and salt, and surround the mixture with pastry of white flour and lard, then you have a meat pie which contains very little lean fleshed meat and lots of the sort of saturated fat that our government advises us only to eat in moderation. The additives make sure that our senses do not detect the fat.[28]

Shoppers have now got into the habit of examining the labels for the additives they refuse to buy and consume, and more and more products bear the words: additive-free. But in the eighties more frightening occurrences were to bedevil the public as outbreaks of food poisoning hit the headlines.

In May 1984, 631 British Airways passengers and 135 of its staff fell ill after eating foods coated in an aspic glaze contaminated by salmonella – two people died. In the same year 400 people at the Stanley Royd Hospital in Wakefield were ill from salmonella poisoning; this killed nineteen elderly patients. In 1985 sixty people were infected after consuming dried milk powder manufactured by Farley's.[29]★

---

★The publicity affected Farley's so badly that the company was bought by Boots at a knockdown price.

The cases of food poisoning in the eighties tripled. Salmonella from chickens and from eggs, listeria from a number of sources and lastly the BSE scare – the so-called 'mad cow disease' – bovine spongiform encephalopathy. But what most disgusted the public, all shades of meat-eater and vegetarian alike, was the exposure of the recycling of waste residues from intensive farming – the excreta and soiled straw, feathers and remains of dead birds, the unusable parts of carcases which were pasteurised and processed, then rendered into protein pellets, labelled animal protein and fed to all kinds of farm and domestic animals.* The herbivore cow was being fed chicken litter, pig's offal and infected sheep remains. Because we know that the BSE agent cannot be killed off through pasteurisation, this appeared to be an easy route by which one species of animal infects another. It is still not proven that the BSE agent in cows came from sheep infected with scrapie. But cross-infection occurs, not only between animals, but from animal to plant or vice versa: sheep with listeriosis in their manure had been used to fertilise a field where cabbages were grown; these were used to make coleslaw and the listeria had the right conditions to multiply. This outbreak in Canada in 1981 involved thirty-four pregnant women and seven other adults; in five cases the women miscarried, four had stillbirths, twenty-three gave birth to a seriously ill baby, and only two gave birth to a well baby.[30]

It has been estimated that at least 10,000 Britons suffer from food poisoning each week, 100 people die from it each year and more than 95% of the cases are meat- or poultry-related. The latest figures released in November 1998 were that about 9.5 million people a year, a sixth of the population, are affected by food poisoning. This costs the National Health Service the outrageous sum of £743 million per year. Though Government and the farming lobby did their best to suppress the facts, that from cattle, poultry, sheep and pigs we could catch E. coli 157 salmonella, campylobacter, listeria, toxoplasmosis, chlamydiosis and parasitic worms, while the accepted practice of feeding to animals its own and other rendered-down waste products was an obvious way of intensifying the risks of bacterial infection, in both animals and humans.

Could the vegetarian lobby have asked for a more vivid example to show how impure meat was? So impure in fact that it was a poison or threat to health and life. (Throughout history we have seen within the vegetarian movement the idea that meat is rotten.†) Here then, in this endless recycling of animal excrement with the survival of bacteria able to infect humans, was a graphic, blatant, living example of an almost unconscious assumption in the vegetarian lobby. The idea of pure food became by contrast even more desirable.

---

*It wasn't until 1990 that manufacturers quietly stopped using the material for dog and cat biscuits and tinned food. This is no guarantee that the practice has halted entirely.
†Of course, vegetarians have a significant point. Meat begins to rot immediately the animal is killed. Hanging meat to tenderise it is to allow the bacteria to break down the tissue and cellular walls. The more rotten a piece of meat the more it will melt in the mouth.

The heavy and continual use of pesticides and nitrogen fertilisers has induced a chemically engineered environment which inevitably has had its impact upon human health. 'There are now 450 active chemical ingredients approved by MAFF as pesticides (mainly insecticides, fungicides and herbicides). This number has increased more than 5 fold from 83 ingredients in 1965.'[31] In the UK we treat wheat, maize, linseeds and oilseed rape with Lindane which has been associated with damage to the immune system, birth defects and breast cancer. (Lindane in sheep dip was stopped in the mid 1980's). It is the crops grown for livestock – soya and maize – which undergo the heaviest use of this pesticide. Toxic residues from chemicals remain in the organs of the animals when they are slaughtered and some inevitably end up in the food we eat.

Perhaps the most notorious of these chemicals are the OP's, the organo-phosphates which have a direct effect upon the nervous system. It is very possible that the constant ingestion of OP's in our diet could be extremely dangerous, which has led to a rise in neuro-degenerative diseases, foetal brain tumours, Parkinson's, Alzheimer's, MS and ME. Farmers and other victims of chemical exposure have complained of identical symptoms: fatigue, problems of co-ordination, sweating, eye problems, muscle twitching, cramps, problems of temperature regulation and various forms of mild paralysis. These symptoms are consistent with a deletion of the cholinesterase enzyme in the nerves, precisely the enzyme which OP's are supposed to destroy.

Another tragic aspect of our chemical environment is that newborn babies can be either still born or suffer hideous birth defects from mothers who have been exposed to OP's and pesticides. Vegetarian mothers who have not eaten organic foods also can give birth to male children suffering from hypospadias, a malformation of the penis which can, thankfully, later be corrected by surgery. Recent studies have shown that sons of pesticide sprayers are at increased risk of urogenital malformations and that the rise in testicular cancer and decreasing sperm count in Europe and the US is another response to the chemical diet.

The flaw in the system which allows these dangerous chemicals to be used in the environment is in the licensing and monitoring of them by the governmental regulatory bodies, for they depend entirely upon the data presented to them by the chemical companies. Elizabeth Sigmund of the South West Environmental Protection Agency believes that: 'A body must be set up to be responsible for collecting, collating and publishing evidence on the effects, both acute and chronic, of OP's and the extent to which the population is exposed to them.'

There can be no doubt that in Britain the bad publicity* that factory

---

*Radical protesting groups have also attracted bad publicity. The rise of animal rights activists through the eighties is an interesting phenomenon. They resort to violence by attacking butchers' shops, freeing mink from fur farms, attacking vivisectionist laboratories because they claim that only destroying and attacking property will minimise profits from cruel trades and research projects. There is an element of naivety and insulated idealism in their beliefs but no doubt they are sustained also by a concept of purity which allows them to act above the law.

farming and chemical agriculture had at the end of the eighties increased the numbers of vegetarians. Throughout 1990, 28,000 people per week were converted to give up eating meat. In the last ten years the number of vegetarians in this country has risen from three million to seven million.

## Government Bungling

The immense power of the meat lobby and its investments is seen graphically in the ineptitude of Mrs Thatcher's government when they attempted to tackle the BSE crisis. For her government delayed for over ten years the commitment to the necessary research which would explore the likelihood of BSE passing into the human population.

They did nothing because they feared to dismantle a huge and profitable industry, which the taxpaper subsidises and whose products they ingest. If the government did not feel helpless, alarmed and in a state of panic, right from the beginning, why were the statistics from 1985 onwards fudged? In 1988 and 1989 the Ministry of Agriculture alleged that 7 cases of BSE had occurred in 1986, but in 1993 the 7 had grown to 60 cases, then suggestions were made that cases first appeared a year before- in the spring of 1985. Certainly those first cows would have been incubating the disease for anything up to six years.

Hence from 1980 cows which carried the infection, but did not yet exhibit signs of it were being processed into our food supply. This was food for human consumption, but also food for domestic pets, zoo animals and poultry reared for human consumption. In 1988 the government set up a committee chaired by Sir Richard Southwood to consider, among many other issues,the risks to human health. In July of that year a ruminant feed ban was imposed which forbade cattle and sheep to be given rendered protein pellets derived from animals. Then in August sick animals were excluded from the food chain and their carcasses burnt or buried. At the end of the year it was decided to also destroy the milk from sick animals. Up to then it had been going into the general milk supply. So for eight years both the meat and milk from sick cows had been consumed by the human population and these products were also being exported abroad. But offals were omitted from this ban, also calves eaten as veal and calves' brains, a so called 'delicacy' in French and Italian restaurants.

In the following year the report of the Southwood Committee predicted that the total number of BSE cases would be no more than 20,000, that the cattle would be the dead-end host and that the risk to humans was highly remote. Yet another committee, the Tyrrell, advised that the number of people succumbing to CJD (Creutzfeldt-Jacob Disease, the human form of BSE) be monitored over the next 20 years. At the end of 1989 offals: brain, spinal cord, spleen, thymus, intestines and tonsils were all banned from the food chain. This ban was particularly significant for all the cheaper meat products, for the offals had always gone into the slurry called Mechanically Recovered Meat (MRM) which had used up all the unattractive parts of a carcase which could not be sold across the counter. These were mashed up in a large vat, coloured and flavoured and then used as fillings in sausages, pies, meat pastes, dog and cat food.

Early in the nineties it was discovered that cats could also die from spongiform encephalopathy (caught from tinned food, 55 cats in all have died) ostriches at Hanover Zoo (infected feed was the source) and that pigs easily caught the disease. Bovine offals were banned from going into these animal feeds. In 1993 experiments which showed that tissues from dead cats which had died of BSE could infect mice, showed that the assurances from the Government that the disease could not 'jump' species was unfounded. In 1994 two dairy farmers who had tended herds infected with BSE both died of CJD. The government said that this was mere coincidence.

Early in 1995 a girl of 16 was diagnosed as having CJD in Wales, the youthfulness of this girl was unknown in the annals of the disease, because CJD was always thought to need at least fifteen years' incubation in humans. More evidence appeared which proved that vertical transmission of BSE, from cow to calf, was now appearing. But though farmers would call in Ministry vets to diagnose a sick cow or calf often the vets would deny that it was BSE and call the illness 'ketosis,' which merely means a pathological condition. Yet in June 95 there was a ban on the intestines and thymus from calves under six months old entering the food chain. At last it appeared that very young animals who did not show any signs of the disease might be infective. Oddly though, the brains among the offals were not banned. Nor was the meat, the infamous veal trade.

By 1996 the number of cases of BSE were now more than eight times the number predicted by the Southwood Committee in their 'worst case scenario.' Though the government admitted that calves could be a risk, they did not explain what the real risk was. For vertical transmission of BSE to occur between cow and calf, the infective agent (now called a prion) has to be in the blood and thus widely distributed in the animal and therefore in the meat that people eat. What is more, as there are cases of cows not exhibiting signs of the disease, but whose calves are born with it, we know that cows which seem healthy must be going into the food supply. Indeed,they always have done. Though critics of the government have repeatedly asked that specimens be taken in slaughter houses of seemingly healthy cows to ascertain whether they carried the infective agent, this has never been implemented. Nor do we still have any scientific proof that the agent or prion is the cause or that it stemmed from sheep scrapie, which was badly rendered down in the protein pellets given to the cows. It is still mere speculation. If that theory is true why is it that half the cows in a herd catch BSE while the other half are free of it, but all have eaten the same feed? Why is it that after the suspected recycled waste was forbidden from livestock feed that cows were still going down with BSE?

Dairy cows are culled at around six years of age; BSE has generally shown itself at around 4–5 years, but as there are no cows alive after around six years we do not know whether older cows might also die of the disease. The dairy cow, exploited for years for its milk, is an exhausted creature by the time it is culled, its meat goes into sausages, meat pies and burgers. Richard Belfield, producer of a TV enquiry Dispatches into BSE commented in a letter to the *Independent on Sunday* that 'It was clear from our research that few (if any) doctors or scientists working in this area eat burgers, sausages, or processed meat. If they would rather not take the risk, shouldn't they share their concerns wth the rest of us?' In fact, the burger empire could not exist without the dairy industry, as all the carcases from the clapped out dairy cows become mince meat. This is one of the significant keys to why government has not acted more stringently. Governments are nervous of getting into conflict with the great food empires of the world, for they are part of the international network within the multinationals which increasingly control our lives.

Thus, the people most at risk are children and pregnant women and all others who eat a high amount of cheap meat products, most of all burgers. This statement, the government and the meat industry, would view as alarmist, for there is no proof now that these foods could infect you with CJD. But the government did acknowledge the possibility, yet they did not bother to make CJD a notifiable disease until 1995, while in 1996 when there was at last an announcement that BSE and CJD were connected, CJD deaths were only registered after a post mortem which confirms the disease. There are many families now who claim their loved ones died of CJD, but no post mortem was performed and therefore such deaths are not in the official figures. Nor have figures ever been kept of the number of healthy cows from infected herds which have gone into the food chain. It is almost as if governments refuse to look closely at this controversial area, for fear of what they find, and if they do look, none of the information is ever released.

CJD has a long incubation period, but if infected food was being consumed as long ago as 1980, that incubation period of fifteen to twenty years is well-nigh up. Yet, we also now know that the new variant of CJD does not need long incubation. If CJD begins to rise dramatically within the population over the next few years, will we be told? Will we be warned to stop eating meat or milk? The most worrying aspect of this disease is the fact that more and more young people, often only teenagers, are now being struck down by the disease.

Why has there never been a major initiative to identify possible treatment of BSE or CJD? We do not know how much BSE infectivity would be needed to infect us by mouth. If we eat a small amount every day is this the same as eating a large amount in one go? No research has been done – why not? Why has there never been any debate or exchange of ideas between government scientists and other scientists? Why, in those early years, did we continue to export animals to other countries and so infect herds in Ireland, Switzerland, France, Canada, Denmark and Germany. Both in Canada and Germany the whole herd was culled, a measure Britain has always taken over foot and mouth disease, but refused to consider over BSE. We have now (February 2000) lost 170,000 cows to BSE and France, at long last, now admits that the disease has begun to infect its own dairy herds. It cannot fail to infect all the countries of the Common Market.

So far (March 2000) there have been 48 deaths from new variant CJD and around 10 more under investigation. Scientists at the recently created CJD Surveillance Centre in Edinburgh and at the University of California injected either BSE tissue (from cattle) or nvCJD tissue (from humans) into genetically engineered mice. They discovered that both sets of mice developed similar symptoms at the same time – around 250 days.[32] One of the world's leading BSE authorities, Stanley Prusiner, says that this experiment forces him to think that 'a large section of the UK population may be at considerable risk.'[33]

In my opinion the Tory government was devious, snide, crooked and incompetent, a responsible government would have resigned. The question now is, will New Labour with their Food Standards Agency put through policies which will protect the public? For such policies will be fought tooth and nail by the meat, dairy and pharmaceutical industries.

## Genetic Engineering

The great food issue which dominated the end of the nineties and which will undoubtedly continue to be obsessive in the new century is the safety or not of genetically modified organisms.

For years this issue has been creeping up on us and in that time the media have tended to take an alarmist view. After all, they coined the term, 'frankenstein's food' which played on public unease. In 1982 the American magazine *Business Week* prophesied a 'dairy cow as big as an elephant' capable of producing six thousand gallons of milk a year. Other ideas mooted were: beef cattle as long as a stretch limousine, square chickens all breast meat without feathers and turkeys as large as sheep.

The reality is not as garish, because genetic engineering is limited by the second law of Thermodynamics, so visions of hybrid monsters are unsound prophecies. Except that is for those creatures that live in water because fish are weightless in water. In 1994 the scientific journal, *Nature*, reported that scientists in Canada had genetically engineered a salmon 37 times its normal weight, this giant fish was created through the injection of a hyperactive growth hormone gene into Pacific salmon eggs.

But monster compound organisms do not have to be huge and unwieldly, they can be infintestimal and still be a terrible threat to the stability of our life on this planet. Where the public perception sees Frankenstein's monster stumbling through swirling mist towards us, the reality might only be a microbe, but that does not make the public's unease wrong or irrelevant. Especially when over the years the truth has been hidden from us or else fudged or deliberately distorted.

But how did the genetic engineering dream begin? Twenty-six years ago scientists met at Asilomar in the US near Monterey to discuss the potential of genetic engineering. They were horrified at the ethical implications and the possibilities of ecological disaster. They agreed on a two year moratorium before any decisions could be made. But the private business sector somehow got wind of the awe and fear generated at this conference and felt that herein lay a pot of gold. Genetic engineering was hyped up as the third technological revolution and the private sector was encouraged to see it as a bottomless gold mine.

However, to reach this fantasy of untold riches the vital matter of who owns what had to be clarified in law. Not only the patent rights but the plant breeders' rights must be enshrined in legislation. The latter was sorted out in most countries of the world by the mid-seventies, which prompted a huge buying spree among the pharmaceutical companies to absorb all family seedsmen of any commercial importance, so that these companies now control all the significant plant gene banks. But since time immemorial farmers once they sow a crop have always kept some seed back for next year. This, of course, makes seed companies irrelevant. Their obvious need being to sell more seed every year, but to do that they must have a seed monopoly.

It was corn on the cob that showed the way out of this dilemma. The hybrid maize is idiosyncratic, no seed ever comes out true, so farmers have to buy new seed every year from the seed merchant. This allows the seed manufacturer to possess effective control over the farmer and agriculture itself. So control over how plants pollinate is the key to making a profit from seeds. If a gene from another plant can be engineered to induce sterility in the male plant, this can only benefit the seed company and tightens control over the farmer.

Also, the more you can limit diversity in the varieties the simpler your task is and the greater your ultimate control. So what we saw happening through the eighties was a constant redesign of nature to fit the politics of monopoly and contemporary technology. For example, the Kelloggs factory outside Manchester only accepted three kinds of maize, for only that maize is compatible with their machinery. The lifetime of a factory is around 30 years, so for that amount of time only those three kinds of maize would be grown because of their commercial viability. Smith's crisps also can only use a few kinds of potato. So commercialism shrinks the range of crops we can grow and this process continues year by year.

Throughout the eighties all of the world's largest crops were scientifically studied to see how they could be genetically adapted to ensure a monopoly control over their cultivation, harvesting, production and distribution by one company alone. W. R. Grace, for example, a chemical and commodities company took out patents in India, China, Brazil, USA and Europe for all future innovations in genetically engineered cotton. The US patent was contested in the courts anonymously, but was thought by some to be the US government who, understandably, would have had cause to be greatly alarmed at such a cotton monopoly.

All this continued in secret behind the public's backs, the potential outcome being control of world commerce, which has almost occurred in the millennium year in the guise of the World Trade Organisation (WTO) that is, to my mind, akin to Big Brother. But before this happened warning bells sounded giving the uneasy feeling that this new technology was being foisted on us with the compliance of government. Take Bovine somatotropin, the genetically engineered gene which stimulates greater milk yield (BST): the manner by which this entered the general milk supply was scandalous.

BST boosts milk yield by more than 10 per cent per day, it causes feed nutrients to be diverted to the mammary glands for milk synthesis. This, of course, places enormous strain upon the cow's metabolism and weakens her. It is not surprising then that Montsanto sent out instructions to farmers with the drug warning of the harmful side effects and a possible decline in the cow's general health.

BST is surrounded by a murky area. It is a medical veterinary product, yet non-therapeutic, merely used to enhance production. It raises the body heat of the cow, so that cows can collapse in the summer months. The cow needs to consume more concentrated feed which means more protein rich foods (soya beans and peanuts) imported from developing countries – Brazil, Senegal and India.

No research has ever been conducted on the effect of BST milk upon humans. Children would be particularly vulnerable to any effects the BST milk might have. But how is the public to know if the milk goes on sale unlabelled? Which is exactly what happened. The British Government was aware that they could only get rid of the milk, if it was hidden in the general milk pool, fearing that milk labelled BST would remain unsold.

In the US there was already a revolt against BST milk. Swiss Valley Farms advertised their milk in grocery stores by saying that they did not knowingly accept milk from BST treated cows. Montsanto took them to court, claiming that such a statement implied that Swiss Valley products were somehow safer or better than milk products supplemented with BST.

In Europe we have a milk lake already which adds up to 92,000 tonnes of skimmed milk powder, EC subsidises the dairy farmer, which means we, the taxpayer are paying for the glut in milk and if BST is legalised in the EC the taxpayer will end up paying for Montsanto's billion dollar investment. When the EC discussed the matter in 1994, Germany and Luxembourg wanted an indefinite ban, while Ireland, Denmark, France, Netherlands, Greece, Spain, Italy and Portugal wanted a ban to continue until the end of the Milk Quota Scheme in the year 2000. Only we and Belgium wanted to allow BST to be used immediately. BST has now been banned by the EC completely, yet it is still used extensively in the US.

But throughout the eighties and nineties the public was kept alert to the GM threat by genetic engineering's spectacular failures. There was the onco-mouse that proved a flop for Du Pont, the chemicals giant, despite the fact

that it owns the licensing rights for lending this genetically engineered
creature which develops cancer so that anti-cancer drugs can be tested upon
it. All the pharmaceutical companies were nervous about using the mouse,
as it seemed chillingly inhumane. 'The principle seemed to be unacceptable
to the industry,' Du Pont said gloomily.

Then there was, at the end of the eighties, the superpig with the human
growth gene which the US Department of Agriculture's research facility at
Beltsville in Maryland came up with. This pig was intended to be fast
growing with lean and tender meat, destined to revolutionise the flavour of
pork. But the pig was excessively hairy, had bulging eyeballs was riddled with
arthritis, impotent, crippled and lay in a stupor for most of its short life. The
scientists went back to the drawing board, with the knowledge that the
public felt very sensitive, almost queasy over transgenic animals which have
human DNA.

The research scientists saw it happen in 1990 in Australia when 53
transgenic pigs were transported to market and sold for human consumption
without permission. Consumers who had bought and eaten pork began to
wonder if they might be accused of cannibalism? In Australia they worked
upon a self-shearing sheep that will simply shed its fleece.

At Beltsville, they tried again by injecting a suspected cancer gene from
chickens into another batch of piglets. The gene made their shoulders grow
big and meaty, but by the time they were three months old, their front and
rear legs hardly supported them – they couldn't stand up. There are further
ideas, that the genes in bears which induce them to hibernate could be
inserted into sheep and cows to save a fortune on winter feed. Or a 'third
sex' of cattle, sheep and swine which have been genetically engineered never
to develop testicles so that will do away with having to castrate billions of
farm livestock. In Britain, following the success of Israeli researchers, genetic
manipulation has been used to make 'naked neck' broiler chickens with 40%
fewer feathers. The theory is that because they are cool, these chickens will
eat more, put on weight faster and hence go to slaughter earlier.

Then there was Hermann, the transgenic bull living in a Dutch field
surrounded by a herd of 23 cows. Hermann, born in 1990 carried a human
lactoferrin gene which, it was hoped, Hermann would pass onto his female
offspring, so that they will carry the gene in their mammary glands and be
able to be the first cows to produce human milk proteins. But environmental
groups threatened to boycott all the products of the companies which had
invested in Hermann. Such an outcry was enough for Nutricia, a Dutch
producer of baby foods and powders, to pull out.

It became clear very early on that the name of this research was profit.
Questions of safety, welfare, concern for human health or the environment
never appeared on the agenda, all such areas were left unexplored. Research
continued on whether it was possible to place a mouse gene into sows so
that they produced 25 piglets per litter? If you get it right nothing makes a
quicker profit than a successful food product. Work went on at the

University of Wisconsin to make turkeys lay between 15 to 20 per cent more eggs by never going broody. The turkeys were genetically engineered not to produce the hormone prolactin which triggers their broody behaviour. Scientists seem unworried that such a hormone exists in order to protect the birds metabolism from excess. Science,it would seem, feels no respect for the complex intricacies of our physiology where protective mechanisms come constantly into play.

The goal is to produce an animal for food which will have increased growth performance, total disease resistance and carry in its carcase low fat content and an addictive flavour that the public find mind-blowingly delicious. Whatever such a creature is there is never a thought of what effect it might have within the food chain. Another bizarre idea stems from a scientist in Canada who has engineered pigs to produce human protein in their semen. Boars start to produce semen at 110 days old and ejaculate half a litre at a time. As there is more protein in semen than in milk can it be long before this becomes another food product?[34]

Genetically modified salmon developed by an American company A/F Protein, Inc. in Prince Edward Island, Canada can grow six times as fast as normal salmon. The Scottish Salmon industry rejects any use of transgenic salmon fearing their escape to lochs, rivers and seas and the risk of their gene transference to wild stocks.[35] Another American company set up by Johns Hopkins University, MetaMorphix have discovered a technique to block genes that limit animal's natural growth; this accelerates the rate of growth up to 12% and creates adult animals 29% bigger than usual with a much higher proportion of meat muscle. It is being used at present on shellfish.[36]

Transgenic animals can be divided into three sections, those destined for food, those created for research as in the oncomouse and those made for producing medical substances and replacement human organs. What we have seen in the last few decades are the birth throes of this new science. What is deeply worrying for vegetarians is this new giant threat that the animal kingdom now has to undergo. For the nature of animals which have evolved over millennia is now being raped and violated. There are no limitations on this work, no one speaks of having respect for a living creature, there are no moral values which would control how far an experiment can go. The scientific impulse is can it be done and will it be profitable. Such an impulse is demeaning to both human and animal.

The private sector now owns all research, a fact which strikes against the development of knowledge. For corporations refuse to do the research until they have a patent, which slows up or almost halts the scientific base of their work. Legislation continues over taking out patents for various products. The amount and pace of the research is hugely significant, for a patent lasts for twenty years and then goes into the public sector, hence a series of innovations has to be produced and patented for continuous income. There is incomplete information on the genomes of animals and plants, so the technology is very much a hit and miss affair. With greater knowledge the scientists might be able to avoid the ethical blunders and much of the bad publicity.

The last years of the old century saw a furore over the sale of GE foods in the UK. Critics of GE soya were furious that this crop grown in the US was finding its way into about 70% of processed foods which were being sold unlabelled. The 1998 crisis of the UK being inundated with GM products was a direct result of US policy. There, three federal agencies regulate GM crops and foods,[37] the heads of all three agencies have made rousing speeches in praise of this new powerful technology so they are far from impartial. They have set policies which affect us.

(1) No public records need be kept of which farms are using genetically engineered seeds.
(2) Companies that buy from farmers do not need to separate GM crops from others.
(3) No crops need to be labelled about their GM origins.

These policies meant that they have kept the US public in the dark about the spread of GM foods onto their dinner tables, these policies will also prevent doctors and epidemiologists from being able to trace any ill effects, allergies or new illnesses, because no one will know who has been exposed to GM foods or who has not.

Monsanto has claimed that without genetic engineering millions will starve, that the process is necessary to feed the world in the 21st century.

But if this was Monsanto's intention, surely they would by now have developed seeds with certain predictable characteristics?

(1) Ability to grow on substandard or marginal soils.
(2) Plants able to produce more high quality protein with increased yield, without the need for expensive machinery, chemicals, fertilisers or water.
(3) Monsanto would favour small farms over large farms.
(4) The seeds would be cheap and freely available without restrictive licensing.
(5) The crops would feed people and not livestock.

In my opinion none of the GM crops available or in development possess any of these desirable characteristics. In fact the opposite. GM seeds appear to require high quality soils. The crops seem to have been designed specifically to increase the sale of pesticides.

At least there is much black farce in this world. The saga of the Oxford scorpion pesticide is an example. This is the gene for scorpion venom spliced into a virus and made into a spray to kill caterpillars that eat cabbage leaves. No research was done on how many other species of insects it might also kill, or what the scorpion venom did on the cabbage leaves and whether residues of it might still linger on in the sauerkraut. Trials were to be performed not in the closed confinement of laboratory conditions but in a field of cabbages outside Oxford which happened to be next to Wytham Great Wood which contains five moths which are endangered species. The scientist, David Bishop, reassured any public anxiety by saying that as the cabbages would be covered with two layers of net and there would be a ditch of formaldehyde around the field it was unlikely that the pesticide could escape.

But what was particularly worrying was that the Advisory Committee on Releasing new Organisms into the Environment (ACRE) had agreed to this trial. Yet so outraged were they at the outcry against them that they reconsidered their decision but found they were satisfied anew. John Gummer, then a Minister of MAFF, approved the release of the scorpion venom. But the public remained unconvinced, knowing that birds eat caterpillars and every gardener knows that netting is no form of protection at all.

One of the main anxieties over GM crops is Gene-Flow, that organisms in the soil, bees, birds, insects and the wind itself can take pollen from GM crops and contaminate traditional crops which will breed more GM's. Any farmer or gardener will tell you this is inevitable, there are no safeguards that can possibly stop it. Monsanto and our government both insist that the safeguards will be an effective barrier. However we know that it has already happened. A report entitled *Investigation of feral oilseed rape populations: genetically modified organisms research report no 12*, carried out by the Scottish Crops Institute for the Department of Environment, have said that GM oilseed rape has already contaminated traditional crops in the trials done between 1992 and 1997. If the UK continues to plant GM crops the GM oil seed rape (which is inedible, grown for industry) will entirely wipe out the unmodified oilseed rape grown for margarine.

There is evidence that Gene Flow has occurred in the USA and Canada★. In 1999 the National Pollen Research found that maize pollen lives for twenty-four hours and in some winds can travel up to 120 miles. Dr Jean Emberlin of the Pollen Research Unit estimates that at 200 metres, one in every 93 kernels on an organic cob would be contaminated with GE genes.[38] A crop resistant to disease and drought could easily spread its resistance to weeds with the result that the mutated weed species could easily overrun millions of acreage. Then, if you have genetically designed a potato which automatically kills off the colorado beetle it will only be a matter of a few years before the beetle has grown a resistance to such a plant and you are back at square one. The same is true of any built-in resistance to fungus or viruses, the parasite that is threatened will mutate in a short time.

So eager are the companies for results that their scientists work under pressure and are often working in the dark. For example, the ice minus (a US term meaning refusing to freeze) gene from the flounder which has been put

★Triple resistant canola weeds found in Alberta.

into a tomato so that the tomato can be placed in a freezer without going mushy, might very well exist in a cabbage and therefore the tomato might be acceptable to vegetarians. But because the genomes have not been mapped out nobody knows whether ice minus genes exists in plants or not.

Then there was the new tomato hyped as the Flavr-Savr, which had been genetically altered to halt the rotting enzyme; it cost more than the common or garden tomato, and is still on sale in the US now. Over here the UK Advisory Committee of Novel Foods and Processes was concerned that the tomato's two alien genes might spread bacterial diseases. For the tomato was resistant to the antibiotic kanamycin and this resistance might well be passed onto the human gut. (Kanamycin here is used to treat TB.) The tomato was pulped and made into a paste which was sold in supermarkets in the UK. We were told that once the tomato was pulped the kanamycin was destroyed.

Ideas in the pipeline are fungus resistant lettuce, virus resistant melon with longer shelf life, peas with a high sugar content, and disease resistant tomatoes with high levels of the nutrients beta-carotene and lycopene. But these are just the tip of the iceberg, hundreds of genetically altered plants and animals are being developed in laboratories, 'biotechnicians circumvent natural cross breeding barriers by forcibly splicing a gene from one species into organisms of a distant, dissimilar species to endow them with a trait they do not normally possess, with the result that grains, fruits and vegetables are being implanted with genes from viruses, bacteria, animals and even humans. If the process continues as planned, the genetic blueprint of a majority of the world's edible plants and animals will be permanently reconfigured.'[39]

Billions of research dollars and sterling have been ploughed into these new animal and plant foods which the multinational companies like Monsanto, Nestlé, Unilever, Zeneca and a dozen others have backed. Various foods are now almost ready to be released into the market place, but the manufacturers are terrified that consumer reaction will be negative. This in turn makes them even more secretive about what they are doing and exactly what a product contains, which in turn makes the public more alarmed and suspicious. The way forward is the open society, but until the multinationals are controlled by government legislation they will never do it.

Then again the scientists and the food manufacturers find little common understanding; the former have a belief in a Newtonian rational world where the consumers must be a passive conglomerate which can be moulded to buy what they are given. Food manufacturers, on the other hand, like to encourage the irrationality of consumer demand, because it is by this means that they are able to compete with each other. So scientists resent and bemoan the fact that so much of their work becomes market led.

But if we really used our imagination there might be no need for the cow at all. Some critics of GM wonder why cows are not just pensioned off. We could make milk, they claim, by analysing and extracting the gene which is responsible for the enzymes which digest grass, then we could stuff grass into one end of a kiln and turn a tap at the other, and milk would pour forth which would organleptically taste the same as that from a cow. The same is true of meat muscle or goose liver or chicken breast; there is now no need for the creature itself, we could artificially create these substances in the laboratory.

This touches on the great irony about genetic engineering, that we are not using it in the right way. The tragedy is that we could feed the two thirds of the malnourished world by supplying plant foods for them to grow, which would have the full quota of amino acids and hence be rich in nutrients. But commercial exploitation of genetic egineering means the opposite, a decline in third world agricultural production. An example is Calgene who have genetically engineered rape seed and are developing it to produce stearic oil which is used in cosmetics. This oil is usually found in coconuts, but if rape can produce it then the coconut horticulture of West Africa will suffer dramatically. No research is being done on how to stop famine in the developing countries, instead the new technique is being used to make the multinationals even richer than they are, for it is being used to contrive new convenience foods for the affluent west. Or, the latest money spinner being, a genetically manipulated tobacco leaf which has 6% more nicotine than the usual tobacco. This has already been used in cigarettes in an attempt to strengthen brand loyalty. Those involved being indifferent, one supposes, to the fact that nicotine addiction can kill.

Governments worldwide seem as confused on the issues as commerce and science. Their special committees that sift the evidence are cautiously timid in their pronouncements, as if their main concern is not to disturb the flow or the stability of investment capital. The *Report of the Committee on the Ethics of Genetic Modification and Food Use*, was published in 1993. These are the findings of the Advisory Committee on Novel Foods and Processes led by the Rev Dr John Polkinghorne − a scientist as well as a Christian. This committee had consulted nearly 60 religious and other organisations to gauge feelings and concerns about transgenic foods. It found that Jews and Muslims were concerned about food which might contain the genes from pigs and other animals which their dietary laws forbade them to eat. Buddhists and Hindus found all transgenic creatures profoundly disturbing. While vegetarians and vegans were horrified at the idea of transgenic vegetables like the tomato with a flounder gene.

The Polkinghorne committee tended to dismiss all such worries, seeing no ethical dilemmas posed by such projects as cows which have been modified to produce 'human' milk. They found 'no overriding ethical objections to using copy genes of human origin in food.' Though they did stress that such food should be labelled.

In 1998 in the US, seventeen religious leaders representing a wide variety of faiths (spanning Roman Catholicism, the Eastern Orthodox Church, and Protestant denominations from Episcopalian to Baptist); three rabbis (orthodox, conservative and reform); a Hindu religious organisation; and a prominent Buddhist joined the Alliance for Bio-Integrity to protest against

GMO's which had infiltrated 70% of the diet without the American public being aware of what had happened.

Governments worldwide have shirked their responsibilities in not passing legislation which would control the creation of new life forms. We now have the power to change the living planet, it has begun in myriad small ways. One can argue that a species has always altered the environment in some form or other, but never before in such a radical way. And it is being done now with little government legislation at hand to limit and control the research or the release of the organisms. Must we wait until a genetically altered organism gets loose and creates havoc? Surely this is a time when the public's fears should be respected, discussed and listened to.

## Class

The effect on the public of these issues was dramatic, one of the most interesting results was the fact that going vegetarian was now freed from class boundaries. Vegetarianism's link with the working class died out before the end of Victoria's reign, though people like Carpenter could always make a convert of a single and special friend. The idea had lost its sense of progress, of being part of an ideology which could make an individual rise in society. It then became a solidly middle-class preoccupation, though rejected by the majority who were orthodox in all their beliefs. Certain sections of the middle class pursued it as part of a package of radical ideas. Thought of as the 'progressive middle class', they felt hostile to the industrial and increasingly the chemical aspects of society, tending to have creative professions or activities: designers and craftsmen, artists and writers, journalists, academics, people in the media, social workers, librarians and teachers. You tend not to find vegetarians among sales directors and managers, estate agents, shopkeepers and civil servants. The social base of vegetarianism is middle-class radicalism. Their protests are founded in humanitarian causes and they put a high value on education and reading.

The latter is, of course, vital, for through reading much of the information about food production is learnt; through reading, discoveries are made which lift vegetarianism out of a small parochial pursuit, the idea of cranks, into a holistic respect for all life. The counter-culture helped to break down the class barriers and, though still middle class at its centre, its converts came from across the range from working to upper. Research at the end of the eighties and beginning of the nineties* showed that converts

---

*Gallop for Realeat in 1988 and 1990 and a survey conducted by Bradford University for the Vegetarian Society: 'The 1990 Realeat Survey found that 24 million people, 43% of the population, are cutting back on the amount of meat they eat. 3.7% of the population are total vegetarians, 6.3% of the population avoid red meat. As before, women are more likely to be avoiding meat than men (12.8% compared with 7.1%) and for the seventh year running, women in the 16-24 year age group are most likely to eat little or no meat. Health was given as the main reason for reduced meat consumption (19.8%), followed by financial reasons (11.3%), taste (8.1%) and moral reasons (6%).'

were from the lowermiddle classes and lower-income groups.★

Another change was the ease with which the vegetarian diet had been accomplished; 67% found this and said they had no hassle at home from parents.†

There is no doubt that converts to the diet are growing across the class structure, though they are thinnest among the top income groups. People are slowly beginning to understand that one can bring up babies and small children on a meatless diet and they will not suffer nutritionally. On the contrary, without animal fats their physical foundation and well-being will very likely be strengthened and improved.

Membership of the Society itself doubled in the 1980s from 7,500 in 1980 to 14,970‡ in 1991 (13% of whom are associates). But the broad figures within society itself, where the term 'vegetarian' is ill-defined and allows for some consumption of fish, show the number of people who avoid red meat to have increased from around 2.2 million in 1984 to 8.2 million in 1991, which is 16% of the UK population. Historically, of course, in the West, this is the greatest number of vegetarians ever to exist within a meat-eating society who are not part of any one idealistic or religious group, who have abstained from meat for a variety of different reasons, though they broadly share the same view of society itself.

Another aspect of vegetarianism was that its definition became blurred. The word has now come to mean a refusal to eat red meat; it appears to be a diet which is mostly vegetables, but which also might include a little fish and a little chicken. These millions of people are, of course, people who it would never occur to join The Vegetarian Society. This diet seems to be much more popular with women than men, its adherents come from all classes, another of its attractions being that this particular diet is also politically correct, healthy and fashionable.

This vegetarian diet in the loose definition above is shared in the UK by conglomerate peoples. All races, creeds, professions and class, now share a common aim, they have become critics of the nation's diet and are determined to improve its quality. There is little doubt that the media, both TV, radio and the press, have encouraged this change by creating programmes which have explored the vile excesses of factory farming, its effect on the environment and the manner of disposal of its waste and slurry. What the big issues of BSE and GMO's did was to radicalise parts of society into a force for change, it moulded people into articulate critics of the way food is grown, reared, processed and sold.

---

★The C1 and C2 socio-economic groups are twice as likely to become vegetarians as ABs, while there was a perceptible trend for the diet from C2/DE, with 15% claiming to be vegetarian, compared to 5% in the 1990 Realeat survey.
†Nearly 60% described parents as being 'really helpful' or 'not minding', with only 5% describing mealtimes as a battlefield.
‡These figures do not include junior members, who are a separate category of the societies begun in 1987. In 1991 there were 5,410 junior members, bumping up the whole membership to 19,128.

## The Reason Why

In the early nineties the Gallop survey for Realeat, among adults the main reason for becoming vegetarian was health, though other reasons were not far behind; 75% hated the treatment of animals and methods of meat production, especially slaughterhouse practices. Among young people the most important reason was animal welfare, 76% citing concern over slaughter techniques and 75% the treatment of livestock. Many of them are also concerned about the wider global issues, the effect of food production on the environment, destruction of the rain forest and Third World malnutrition.

In the eighties there were a series of reports on diet, the first in 1983, by NACNE,* which the Government tried to suppress.[40] Its main findings were that a healthy diet should be very low in saturated fats (found mainly in animals), high in fibre (meat has no fibre), low in refined foods, salt and sugar, and high in fruit and vegetables. The amount of animal protein should fall, while vegetable protein should rise.

A Chinese study is the largest and most recent. It began in 1983 and was published in 1990. Scientists surveyed 6,500 Chinese, who each contributed 367 facts about their diet. The Chinese Academy of Preventive Medicine worked with a nutritional biochemist, T. Colin Campbell of Cornell University. One of their findings was that in those regions of China where meat consumption has begun to go up, it has been closely followed by the incidence of the diseases of affluence, including heart attacks, cancer and diabetes. 'People who eat mostly plant foods and a generous variety of plant foods . . . that is the kind of diet that is most likely to be associated with reduced risk of the kinds of disease that tend to kill us in this country.'[41] Meat was perhaps the most significant dietary contributor to disease that emerged when the massive amounts of data collected were analysed. Where meat consumption rose so did cardiovascular disease, sometimes fifty-fold over the rate for a more traditional Chinese diet in which animal fat provides only 15% of the calories. In a typical US diet animal fat provides 40-45% of the calories.

The report of the World Health Organisation (WHO), *Diet, Nutrition and the Prevention of Chronic Diseases* (1990), also concluded that the 'affluent' type of diet that often accompanies economic development is energy-dense. People have a high intake of saturated fat and sugar and a low intake of complex carbohydrates. This diet is linked with chronic diseases and premature death.

The 'affluent diet' is, of course, high in meat consumption and in saturated fat. In the Chinese study they found that the Chinese eat one-third less protein than the Americans and that only 7% of their protein comes from animal sources compared with 70% in the American diet. This research was clear in the conclusion that a large consumption of animal protein raises the risk of cancer and heart disease. Both studies were in agreement that the healthy diet is one which has a high-carbohydrate, low-fat intake rich in

---

*National Advisory Committee on Nutrition Education.

starchy foods (cereals, tubers and pulses) and includes a substantial intake of vegetables and fruit.

The Vegetarian Society welcomes these reports and research on health and naturally widely publicises them. They say that lifelong vegetarians visit hospital 22% less often than meat-eaters and for shorter stays; they point out that this saves the NHS something like £46,000 for every vegetarian. Other research indicates that vegetarians have 20% lower blood cholesterol levels than meat-eaters, that the diet reduces the risk of heart disease by 30%, high blood pressure is less likely, and the incidence of colon cancer is 40% lower among vegetarians, as are gall and kidney stones and various other common ailments. No wonder the adults in the survey gave health as their main reason for going on the diet. Recent research in effect seems to substantiate the claims of Dr Cheyne, Lambe and Newton, Cocchi, Cornaro and the writers of antiquity.

A new problem now besets animal welfare campaigners, for winning more humane legislation in the UK movement is only a small part of the battle. It is the Treaty of Rome and EC legislation which have to be radically altered. For example, at the beginning of January 1990 the UK banned the use of the veal crate; no longer could calves a few days old be imprisoned in a crate so small they could hardly move and be fed a liquid deficient in iron and fibre for those five months before slaughter. Instead the calves are exported out of the UK and imprisoned in the crates in other EC countries only to return as veal to the UK. If welfare is to merit its name, all the EC countries must obey the same rules in rearing livestock. The first step towards this is to change how animals are described in the Treaty of Rome. At the moment live animals are classed as 'agricultural products' along with crates of apples or cabbages. In 1988 Compassion in World Farming made the recommendation to the European Parliament that the new classification of 'Sentient Animals' should be adopted and that this term should be interpreted with a welfare code, comprising the following points:

1. Comfort and shelter.
2. Readily accessible fresh water and a diet to maintain the animals in full health and vigour.
3. Freedom of movement.
4. The company of other animals, particularly of like kind.
5. The opportunity to exercise most normal patterns of behaviour.
6. Light during the hours of daylight, and lighting readily available to enable the animals to be inspected at any time.
7. Flooring which neither harms the animals, nor causes undue strain.
8. The prevention, or rapid diagnosis and treatment, of vice, injury, parasitic infestation and disease.
9. The avoidance of unnecessary mutilation.
10. Emergency arrangements to cover outbreaks of fire, the breakdown of essential mechanical services and the disruption of supplies.

In the year 2000 the infamous sow stall where sows were chained and only able to move a few inches upon a concrete floor was at last banned in the UK. It is still extensivly used in all the countries of Europe from where however much pork and bacon is imported into the UK.

## The Future

These main reasons – health and the rising rate of food poisoning, animal welfare and ecology – will certainly, in the foreseeable future, continue to play a formidable part in influencing people's decisions on whether to turn to vegetarianism. A fourth reason continues to have weight with many people: the impact of the affluent countries' high meat consumption (Europe and North America in particular) on Third World countries. The EC is the largest buyer of animal feed in the world and 60% of the grain is imported from Third World countries, who grow the cereals as cash crops to sell to us (at the height of the Ethiopian famine they were still exporting cereals to Western Europe), when they could grow food crops for themselves and halt the malnutrition among their people:

> The rich white man, with his overconsumption of meat and his lack of generosity for poor people, behaves like a veritable cannibal – an indirect cannibal. By consuming meat, which wastes the grain that could have saved them, last year we ate the children of the Sahel, Ethiopia and Bangladesh. And we continue to eat them this year with undiminished appetite.[42]★

*How the Other Half Dies* attempts to explain and analyse the ways in which the strategies and concerns of the dominant countries and classes help to create and entrench hunger. In a new edition of this book (ten years after its first publication) Dr George explains that 'a further decade of utterly failed development strategies, the ravages of famine and ever-greater numbers of hungry and malnourished people' have shown that there was no improvement in the injustices of the status quo, and there is no sign of any change now, a further fourteen years on. Dr George's book, of course, explains that such inequality is not just due to the high consumption of meat but is far more complicated. However, meat is an important factor, and with a doubling in world population expected within forty years it can only become a greater and more demanding problem.

If the world's population is to be fed adequately then a far more efficient way of producing protein has to be adopted. A large percentage of the protein fed to cattle (94%), pigs (88%) and poultry (83%) is lost, mostly in their dung. The world's cattle alone consume a quantity of food equal to the calorific needs of 8.7 billion people, which is nearly double the population

---

★R. Dumont, quoted by Susan George in *How the Other Half Dies*. Dr George does not agree with this view, though the author does.

of the planet now. To halve the number of livestock reared would dramatically alleviate world hunger.★

It has been suggested that in the UK we could keep a large dairy herd of both cows and sheep, while pigs and chickens could become free-range again; livestock are needed to maintain fertility of the soil and some surplus animals could be culled. In this way the number of livestock could be brought down to one quarter of the present level.

> The rotation of a good mix of crops, including legumes, and the grazing of fallow fields one year out of every five, would reduce the incidence of soil-borne diseases of plants and animals while the regular input of manure from dairy animals and nitrogen from legumes would reduce the need for inorganic fertilisers.[43]

If the demand for meat continues to decline, would the Meat and Livestock Commission be likely to adopt some similar policy? Considering that the unsold meat is bought by EC subsidy (our taxes) and EC beef mountains continue to grow, for this reason alone one would expect a new meat policy to emerge. When Max the cat died from BSE in 1990 meat sales collapsed by a third overnight. Overall they have fallen by 6%; 25% of butchers since 1980 have sold up and gone to another trade; 50% of our slaughterhouses will close in the next few years.[44] But there has been no decline in the sale of meat and chicken products and unless that begins to happen, I cannot envisage a change occurring.

> Should the consensus of opinion in future society dictate that nature must be dealt with more sensitively, meat may well continue to be used as an expression of our relationship to our environment, and its social acceptability fall as a consequence. It is at least possible that, in this way, in some years' time meat eating could come to have a widespread image comparable to that of, say, smoking or drug addiction today – as a relatively vulgar, unhealthy and anti-social indulgence.[45]

I would like to believe this is true, but the meat lobby might well find other tactics to counter this and in using new techniques might bring down the cost of meat products, disguising the animal origin completely so that they would become an easily available supply of inexpensive food for the majority.

The changes in our diet that occurred in the last decade of the 20th century have been dramatic and unnerving leaving the general public confused and alarmed. The main issues have have been the infectious prion, Bovine Spongiform Encephalopathy (BSE) which has decimated the dairy herd and was then discovered to have infected the human population; and

---

★Ten acres of land will support 61 people on a diet of soya beans, 24 on wheat, 10 on maize but only 2 on meat from cattle.

crops which have been genetically engineered for certain characteristics, trials of which are now being monitored in the UK and inevitably changing the DNA structure of our environment. At one moment the British government and scientific authority have appeared to speak in unison on both these issues, lambasting their critics and much of the public as lunatic or hysterical, then later they have contradicted themselves, qualifying previous statements and even, at times, admitting to errors of judgement. The outcome of this is that the general public are suspicious and disbelieving of official reassurances as to the safety of their food. Scientists are no longer trusted as the final arbiter of the truth and with doctors, the public at long last seem to have concluded that scientific and medical knowledge is finite and that this once respected profession can be as ignorant and as misled as the rest of us. At least, the public appear now to come to the conclusion that scientists who work for the government or the food industry can not be trusted. This, indeed, is a step in the right direction.

When the outcry from British public in 1999 stopped GE foods from appearing in our supermarkets, it was a notable success. Such a setback for the powerful multinational companies who produce GE foods and for the New Labour government which had given support to this technology, shows us how the market economy works and how powerful the choice of the individual consumer is. If consumers are furnished with the correct information and allowed to make up their minds they can become a formidable force to improve the food we eat. In order for this to work it comes down to creating a means by which the consumer can receive relevant and unbiassed information and sadly, we do not live in an open society. We live in a society where profit is the goal and the consumer becomes a marketing ploy to be moulded one way or another. Yet we must not ignore the success consumer power had, in fact we should build on it and continue to fight for a food supply that is uncontaminated.

Will large numbers of people ever be able to give up that symbol of human domination over their planet, the slaughtered animal and its carcase meat? Will Leonardo have been right when he said that the time would come when men would look upon the murder of animals as they now looked upon the murder of men?

In evolutionary terms we have reached that Malthusian point where the rise in population has an effect upon the environment that begins to accelerate so that the earth is unable to replenish its resources as fast as they are used up: 'The upward surge in numbers and the downward plunge of resources lead to a crisis. The living systems have changed the chemistry of their environment beyond renewal, and by now their struggle for survival has become violent but futile. The fate of the dominant species is sealed.'[46]

It is profoundly ironic that the human need to prove our dominance is the driving force which exhausts the environment. If we had accepted other animals as our equals, neither killing nor exploiting them, but living in peace beside them, would the world's natural resources have been so depleted?

# Afterword

We do not adequately realise today how very deep within our psyche is the reverence for the consumption of meat or how ancient in our history is the ideological abstention from the slaughter of animals for food.

The precise beginnings of the vegetarian ethic are lost in the priestly cults of Ancient Egypt, but through the Orphic movement vegetarianism became one of the influences upon Pythagoras, who gave his name to the diet. After his death a clear thread can be traced from antiquity to present times. In the East, in India and China, as part of Hinduism and Buddhism, vegetarianism has flourished and numbers millions of converts. In the West the story has been one of persecution, suppression and ridicule. From the days of imperial Rome, when both Ovid and Seneca were equivocal in their vegetarianism, lying about their true preferences, to the Gnostic heretics, some of whom worshipped the creator as female and extended kindness and peace to all living things, to the most hated Christian heresy of all, Manicheanism and its progeny, the Bogomils and the Cathars, abstention from meat was seen as a sign of the devil's works, a clear rebellion against the word of God as revealed in Biblical text. Persecution began once Pauline Christianity started to colonise Europe, and wherever it spread vegetarianism was reviled.

In a very significant way the abstainers from animal flesh still are reviled, ridiculed and considered dangerous outsiders in our society at least by one Cabinet Minister in the Tory Government. The statements expressed by the Right Honourable John Gummer in a speech at the International Meat Trade Association on 1 May 1990 might have been said, word for word, any time in the last two thousand years by those who persecuted the Pythagoreans: 'I consider meat to be an essential part of the diet. The Bible tells us that we are masters of the fowls of the air and the beasts of the field, and we very properly eat them . . . If the Almighty had wanted us to have three stomachs (like grass–eating cattle), I am sure He could have arranged it, but He chose to make us omnivores instead.' Even though he was ridiculed in some quarters for these views (many critics correcting Mr Gummer on the fact that a cow actually has four stomachs) the remarks gladdened the Meat Livestock Commission and must have reassured that majority whose view is that eating meat is right and proper whatever anybody says. Later, in January 1992, Mr Gummer went on to launch Food Sense, a campaign against women who abstain from meat because it could damage their health. This campaign withered away with the demise of the government.

Never before in history has humankind produced such vast quantities of milk and meat, so that these foods have become part of the daily staple diet in the developed world. However much the dairy and meat lobbies strive to produce low-fat milk and leaner meat, the excess saturated fat has to go somewhere and almost certainly ends up elsewhere in our diet. In fact, subsidies are given to hospitals and schools that use saturated-fat products. Cooks at such establishments are encouraged to use more cream, butter, cheese and milk in their catering. Through such policies governments do not show the care due to vulnerable areas of our society, the very young and the infirm and elderly, and knowingly jeopardise their health. Governments are in league with the dairy and meat industries: though with one hand they dispense health advice on changing the diet from one high in sugars and fats, and low in fibre and unrefined carbohydrates, to one very low in fats and sugars and high in grains, legumes, fruits and vegetables, with the other hand they dig deep into Treasury coffers to propagate the present system of over-production in milk and meat.

Recently in the USA the Department of Agriculture offered the same healthy advice, but livestock-producers complained and the agency retracted its statement. In Britain, when the Vegetarian Society placed an advertisement in the press, under the heading 'Putting meat on your plate takes the food from theirs', saying that famine in the developing world is caused partly by grain being imported by developed nations to feed livestock, both the National Farmers Union and the Meat and Livestock Commission complained to the Committee of Advertising Practice (CAP). The Vegetarian Society substantiated every point in the advertising, showing that the UK imports each year from the developing nations £46 million worth of grain grown on land that could be better used to grow food for their own peoples, but the CAP decided the advertisement was misleading, that the image of famine was unacceptable and that the Society had oversimplified the issues.

Government subsidies need to be taken away from the meat and the dairy industries and transferred to fish, fruit and vegetable farming. Further, farmers should be helped not only to change from livestock farming but to grow a greater diversity of vegetable produce. Many hundreds of types of vegetables and fruits have been lost to us because growers have been encouraged by commerce to concentrate on a very few kinds, from an ever-narrowing range of species. This needs to be reversed.

What, then, could change the policy of governments? They are slow to act, as we have recently seen in the case of holes in the ozone layer even when there is a direct threat of disaster to our planet, governments tend to procrastinate. Many people consider that the feeding and slaughter of eleven billion fowls and four billion livestock each year are a growing environmental problem which needs immediate consideration. Livestock should be restored to its historical role as a boon to the environment and to enrich agriculture, or in their sheer numbers they will, in their slurry and carcase waste, overwhelm humankind and the earth we live from with insuperable ecological problems. But to do this, to cut down the numbers of livestock, will require dietary changes among the world's meat-eaters. As we have seen, this appears to be happening on a small scale in the UK and the USA. But this reduction is far outweighed by the rise in meat consumption in China, Hungary, the former Czechoslovakia and the Arab world. For, to the majority of nations, meat-eating is still irrevocably entwined with status and wealth, and it is these concepts, as well as Christian tenets of belief, that underpin the desire for meat.

It may be that the desire for meat is also a sensual, even an atavistic one – the texture of cooked muscle is unique and cannot be replicated by vegetables and may give a deep and mysterious satisfaction, stirring a race memory of a time when meat was the prize of arduous hunting. Such responses to food should not be underestimated, but they are also *habitual*. A change in diet away from meat can soon eradicate such a response and replace it with horror at the burnt corpse lying on the table. If we want to save ourselves, our children and their future, and this planet that we live on, we must alter our diet radically and rethink our concepts of the living world and the respect and consideration that is ultimately due to it.

It is tempting to conjecture what might have happened if Pauline Christianity had not colonised a large part of the world. What ideology was there to take its place? Manicheanism was a strong creed, yet its many critics would argue that its association of the material world with the Satanic was too bleak and negative to give spiritual sustenance. But the emphasis on guilt in Christianity and the idea of the Fall of Man is also bleak and negative and spiritually corrosive. What of Neoplatonism, which had captured many formidable thinkers in those first few hundred years of Christian expansion? The ideology contained much of Pythagoras as well as Plato and shared something of the Gnostic sects which proliferated at the time; it was probably too erudite to have been popular, but was firmly vegetarian, as were most of the Gnostic sects. It is likely that some syncretic ideology fusing pagan and Christian might have grown up valuing women as equal partners (so cutting itself away from any Hebraic foundation), and imbued with the ideas of the Classical Greeks and a creed of peace, non-violence and vegetarianism. Such an ideology would have made Western Europe and eventually the New World and Australasia into a culture that combined Buddhist and Hindu attributes; it would have made the world more cohesive, lessening the chance of war and strife. It certainly would have made the world a kinder place for animals. Some Christians are none the less concerned with animal welfare and become vegetarian, yet they lack in their faith a spur to re-evaluate the relationship between the animal kingdom and humankind. Two thousand years of 'speciesism' has left a void in Christian thinking; though there are lone Christian voices who urgently speak for animal liberation; they are not reinforced by any Christian-derived teleological structure and therefore sound hysterical and irrational, as does much of the animal welfare movement.

While the vegetarian lobby today is perhaps not so overtly ridiculed as it once was, vegetarians are still tainted with the image of the morally earnest and the downright cranky. (How many TV sit-coms get a laugh out of having a dig at the veggies? It is as prevalent as it was in Attic comedy in 300 BC.) But the issues that vegetarianism includes are profound and all-embracing, and this invites the scorn of the nervous and insecure. Today the diet has powerful millennial associations of salvation. For the believers it is the diet which will save the planet, halt the greenhouse effect, feed the Third World, banish malnutrition. It is the diet which heals the self, in both mind and body, halts the killer heart attack and the insidious growth of cancer. It is the diet which can feed the whole of the earth's population even if it doubles within the next forty years. It is the diet which Gaia approves of and, if the human race are her infants, it is the only one by which she will suckle her brood. Whether all this is true or not, these notions are passionately believed in by great numbers of people, many of them distinguished and articulate. And the number of adherents is swelling daily. Several facts are indisputable: as omnivores, human beings can easily survive and sustain themselves in full vigour on a diet without animal flesh; what is more, such a diet is on the whole healthier; and such a diet, without cruelty or unnecessary killing, is more humane.

The American naturalist Henry Beston, in his account of a year in the life of the Great Beach of Cape Cod, *The Outermost House*, first published in 1928, said: 'We need another and a wiser and perhaps a more mystical concept of animals. We patronise them for their incompleteness, for their tragic fate of having taken form so far below ourselves. And therein we err and err greatly. For the animal shall not be measured by man. In a world older and more complete than ours, they move finished and complete, gifted with extensions of the senses we have lost or never attained, living by voices we shall never hear. They are not brethren; they are not underlings; they are other nations, caught with ourselves in the net of life and time, fellow prisoners of the splendour and travail of the earth.' No one has ever summed up the mystery of animal existence so profoundly.

Think on that, then turn to a broiler shed of seven-week-old chickens: twenty thousand of them, about to be slaughtered, with legs so deformed and brittle they snap when the stockman picks them up; with the equivalent of bed sores suppurating on their thighs where they have inevitably rested on urine-sodden litter. All this for a cheap chicken dinner? Think on what Beston has said and turn to a calf crammed in a wooden crate for eight months unable to move, fed on a rich liquid diet of pigs' blood, chocolate and dried milk, deficient in iron so that its flesh will be white to please the gourmet. Look at the dairy cow who should give only five litres of milk a day to her calf but under intensive milking gives anything from 25 to 40 litres a day and after six or seven years is a broken creature, old long before her years, who goes to slaughter to make mince for burgers.

Our common humanity tells us that this is no way to treat animals, so eminently worthy of our respect and kindness. But worldwide, the exploitation of animals is a flourishing industry that grows more diabolic every day.

# Appendix 1:

# The Later History
# of Buddhism

It is ironic that Buddhism slowly died out in India, its homeland, and had to travel further east to colonise new countries. This was largely due to the rising strength of Hinduism and the Muslim invaders, who from AD 986 started to encroach into north-west India from Afghanistan. They smashed Buddhist images because of the Islamic dislike of idolatry and by 1192 the Turks had established their rule over north India from Delhi. Buddhists took sanctuary in the north-east and Kashmir but they were later persecuted and stamped out by Muslims in the fifteenth century. Refugees fled to the south, where Hindu kings were resisting Muslim power, and some continued southwards to Ceylon; others fled to the north, to the Himalayas. Between the Muslims, intent on a holy war, and the Hindus, closely identified with Indian culture, the Buddhists disappeared from central India.

Sri Lanka, however, became not a refuge but a flourishing Buddhist kingdom. The kings were all devout Buddhists active in social welfare. They were largely left in peace until the Portuguese and later the British arrived to try and import their Christianity.

From the time of the great Buddhist Emperor, Asoka, it is thought that a small Buddhist community had established itself in southern Burma/central Thailand. In the eleventh century a king, Anaurata (1040-77), unified the country, and impressed by the simplicity of the Buddhist doctrine made it the main religion of Burma, from where it spread to the Malay peninsula.

In the eleventh century Buddhism also became established in Tibet. By the fourteenth century the Tibetan Canon of Scriptures was completed. In the seventeenth century Buddhism also became established in Mongolia, pacifying a warlike people.

In China, Buddhism was present as early as AD 50, making inroads into Confucianism, the dominant ideology, and Taoism, but it had a slow and hard struggle to survive. 'To Confucian rationalists, there was no evidence for rebirth, there was nothing wrong with killing animals and the fate of individuals and kingdoms depended on the will of Heaven, not individual Karma.'[1]

But it did become the major religion of all classes in China. In the north more than 30,000 temples were built by the sixth century. The practical side of the religion was stressed, devotion, meditation and good works. The monks had a reputation for meditation-based psychic powers. Buddhism in the south first allied itself with Taoism, then began to flourish in its own right and to be seen as a unifying force which encouraged peace. It flourished in the T'ang dynasty (618–907), when monasteries grew into huge well-endowed institutions that fostered artistic creativity.

The Japanese monk Ennin wrote a diary of his visit to China in the 840s and tells us that millet was the daily fare in the north while wheat was considered a luxury. As an honoured guest it was wheat cakes and dumplings of various kinds which were brought out to greet him and his entourage or eaten as fancy food at the great feasts, here taking the place of meat, which the non-Buddhists would have eaten. This was before the wheat-gluten imitations of meat and fish. The Buddhists brought to China the Hindu taboo against the cow; though this was not dogma, if the Chinese continued to eat beef, they did so with a sense of shame.[2] They say the cow works too hard for humankind to be treated in such an uncaring way. Beef is not mentioned explicitly in the list of dishes for banquets, or by restaurants, which suggests that it was held in some disfavour and was eaten only for its novelty. Sung beef would not have been very tasty in any case: 'in south China oxen and water buffalo were used as draft animals . . . their flesh must have been tough, stringy and dry after a career of pulling a plough.'[3]

The Japanese too, more influenced by Buddhism, later ceased to eat beef entirely. ★

The religion reached north Vietnam from both China and India by the third century AD and it flourished there. Korean monks studying in China returned in the sixth and seventh centuries with Chinese Buddhism and it became the religion of the elite.† Buddhism reached Japan in AD 538, sent from Korea by a king who dispatched ambassadors with Buddha images, scriptures and monks. Prince Shotoku (573–622) made Buddhism the state religion.

The rapidity with which the religion travelled eastwards is quite astonishing. It was a civilising process. Monks acted as scribes and in travelling helped establish a system of road communication. As in China, there were several schools of Buddhist thought. The Zen form, introduced in the twelfth century, caught on in Japan, because the ethical discipline and indifference to death appealed to the Samurai.

Under successive ruling regimes in the various countries of Asia, Buddhism has maintained a strong and vigorous presence, quite unlike any Western vegetarian movement. Its abstention from killing and the

---

★Beef has now returned to Japanese cuisine because of the Westernisation of the last few decades. Heart disease and cancer have risen accordingly.
†The indigenous religion being a form of shamanism.

consumption of meat has always found acceptance among a population that might or might not eat meat itself. Buddhists have been taught to accept a portion of meat if it is given to them. This illustrates the generous spirit of both the alms-giver and the receiver.

When the Communists took over in China in 1949 the Buddhist monasteries had much of their income-producing land confiscated. The monks supported themselves often by running vegetarian restaurants. Down through the ages Buddhist temples always had their great temple kitchens where people came to eat at festivals. These kitchens would vie for custom, and it was rumoured that to enhance the flavour of their vegetarian meals they were not above cooking their noodles in a little chicken broth or having a cloth soaked in chicken fat with which to touch up a bamboo shoot and mushroom broth.[4] There was nothing new in such rumours. It was the Mahayana Buddhists who first made very credible imitations of chicken, pork and abalone out of wheat gluten.

There is a rather sad Ming short story which tells of an old Taoist gentleman who accepts an invitation to dine at a mountain retreat with a group of alchemists. After wine and canapes the two main dishes arrive in large tureens. In one, floating in broth, is the white, hairless body of a dog; in the other, that of a human infant. He recoils in horror, and refuses to eat, saying that all his life he has been a strict vegetarian. The host refers to the foods as special vegetables, but the old man still refuses while the rest eat. After they have finished they inform him that these were the roots of medicinal plants capable of imparting immortality to the eater. The old man replies that his state of enlightenment is not advanced enough to permit him the true recognition of the food, so he does not merit immortality.[5]

Today one can eat a meal called Buddha's Feast or the 18 Lohan, disciples of the Lord Buddha. It uses eighteen different ingredients and is eaten by vegetarians throughout the fifteen-day Lunar New Year season. Each of the ingredients is a symbol: hair vegetable (a dried seaweed) stands for prosperity, straw mushroom and lotus seeds for numerous progeny, lily buds for golden prosperity, leeks for riches and mange-tout for good health.

# Appendix 2:
# Manicheanism in China

Before expanding east into China, Manicheanism flourished for a while in the regions south of Samarkand in what was part of the Kushan Empire from the fourth to the sixth centuries, and known to the Greeks as Bactria, on a southern trade route between Iran and the Pamirs. It was here that the belief was much influenced by Buddhism and assimilated some of its features. The use of Buddhist terms began to appear in Manichean writings and the life of the Buddha was used by them as a teaching aid, especially on ascetical matters.

The silk road from China to Persia was reopened in the sixth century. Merchant and Manichean became almost synonymous – one of the titles for a leading saint was the Greatest Caravan Leader. Manichean miniatures depict them as scribes, musicians and entertainers. Empress Wu (684–704) granted an audience to a leading Manichean, Mihr-Ormuzd, who presented her with a work called *Sutra of the Two Principles*, which became the most popular Manichean work in China.

According to tradition, the Empress Wu liked her Manichean guest and asked him to explain his scriptures to her. As a woman she could not be a head of a Confucian system, which understandably enraged her, so she sought other scriptures to give her a theoretical base for her rule. She inaugurated the Chou dynasty but it died with her, and when the T'ang was reinstated her favourites, like the new Manichean cult, were unpopular. An imperial edict limited its practice to foreigners in China. Syrian refugees had already brought Nestorian Christianity, while the exiled Sassanian court had brought Zoroastrianism and this was practised in China almost exclusively by expatriate Iranians. The Chinese respected it, though they found some of the practices, like exposing the dead, highly distasteful.

The T'ang court in 755 was toppled by a revolt and had to abandon north China and take refuge in the mountains of the west. They turned to the tribes living outside their borders and asked for help. The Uighurs, a powerful barbarian tribe, a branch of the Turks, responded and attacked the rebels from the rear, put down the rebellion and in 762 liberated the eastern capital of Lo-yang. It was Manichean priests who greeted the victors and soon converted them. An inscription praises Manicheanism for being a civilising influence because it turned the Uighur lands from a territory where was practised 'the abnormal custom of blood sacrifices into a region of vegetarians, from a state which indulged in excessive killing to a nation which exhorts righteousness'.[1] The T'ang government now had to look favourably upon the religion and Manichean temples were built in the Yangtze Basin. The Buddhists, however, warned the faithful against associating with the religion. Uighur Manichean temples began to be seen as a symbol of foreign arrogance and Chinese military weakness. When the Uighur kingdom collapsed in central Asia the T'ang authorities closed the temples. The Japanese pilgrim Ennin wrote in his diary in the spring of 843: 'an imperial edict was issued, ordering the Manichaean priests of the Empire to be killed. Their heads are to be shaved and they are to be dressed in Buddhist robes . . . the Manichaean priests are highly respected by the Uighurs.'[2] Seventy-two women priests were slaughtered, others were rounded up and exiled, but half of them died from the hardships of the journey. Soon after, both Zoroastrianism and Nestorian Christianity were attacked and three thousand priests were defrocked. China turned in on itself and explored its own Confucianism.

Manicheanism now flourished in the Uighur kingdom. It was customary for three or four hundred Manichean priests to gather in the house of a prince and to recite the Books of Mani. It is from the ruins of a large Manichean monastery that thousands of fragments of texts were discovered in 1904-5. The calligraphy was of unparalleled quality. These flourishing centres continued with some inroads from Buddhism until the Mongol conquest in the mid-thirteenth century. The invaders brought Islam, which became the religion of the region.

From the discovered texts much has been learnt of Manichean ritual, dogma and theology. The founder Mani in these texts resembles more and more the Buddha of Light and even his autobiographical details started to share a similar royal parentage to Gotama's. On the slopes of Hua-piao Hill, thirty miles south of the Chinese city of Ch'nan-chou in the province of Fukien, there is a rustic shrine, the only Manichean building to survive. In its main hall is a stone statue of Mani as the Buddha of Light, donated by a worshipper in 1339. The figure sits crosslegged on a lotus, backed by a halo. The statue, bearded and with long, straight hair, stares straight at the spectator. At first glance it could be Buddha, but the differences are plain enough. In the courtyard there is an inscription dated 1445 exhorting the faithful to remember 'Purity, Light, Power and Wisdom – the four attributes of Mani'.

This shrine has a long history, for some Manicheans who had stayed in China after the suppression of 843 contrived to go underground and to assimilate Chinese manners and customs. They began to have a reputation as sorcerers and exorcists of evil spirits. They are then referred to as the Religion of Light. Under the Sung dynasty from 960 they set up places of worship under the guise of Taoism. These temples had extensive libraries.

They also became known as 'vegetarian demon worshippers'. At the time of the Fang La rebellion in 1120 an official wrote an account to give to the throne which referred to the Religion of Light setting up buildings that they call 'vegetarian halls'. There are constant complaints thereafter, often in another attempt at suppression. An edict of 25 February 1141 begins: 'All vegetarian demon worshippers and those who meet together at night and disperse at dawn to practise and propagate evil teachings shall be strangulated.'[3]

Under Mongol rule the Manicheans fared rather better. Foreign religions were given freedom of worship if they registered. When the Polos visited Fukien in 1292 they were told of a sect which no one could recognise, as they worshipped neither fire, nor Christ, nor Buddha, nor Mohammed. The Polos visited one of the meeting places and found its members reluctant to talk, but they were shown wall paintings and scriptures. When they were shown a book which seemed to be a psalter the Polos identified them as Christian. Marco Polo urged them to go to Kublai Khan and become registered, but the Nestorians and the Buddhists were arguing among themselves and in the mêlée the sect somehow became registered as Christian – not that this later gave them any protection against the Ming persecution of 1370. Shrines were destroyed and the followers expelled.

There were still Manicheans in Fukien when Ch'iao-yuan wrote an account of the shrine at Hua-piao Hill in 1600, but soon after they disappeared entirely. No one knows how. The Chinese scholars of the Ch'ing Dynasty (1644-1912) regarded the Religion of Light as a branch of Nestorian Christianity, the term 'vegetarian demon worshippers' perplexing them completely.

The shrine at Hua-piao is now preserved as a unique monument to a Gnostic world religion which had become so well integrated into Chinese society that few Chinese scholars were aware of its Mesopotamian origins until the Tun-huang discoveries of this century'.[4]

# Appendix 3:
# Modern Hinduism

Perhaps it is the Hindu religion which, more than any other belief, still reminds us of vegetarian commitment. India, without doubt, has the largest population of vegetarians in the world; it must also have in its cuisine the widest range and number of vegetarian dishes. Yet modern Hinduism does not necessarily mean abstention from meat (though it does from beef). It depends on which part of India you are brought up in, what caste you are born into (there are now over 3000 castes and sub castes) and what early influences that branch of Hinduism experienced. Of India's 680 million population 83% are Hindus and are practising vegetarians in some degree or other. Hinduism is based upon detailed codes of conduct, regulations and observances, and the Ahimsa cult which began in Buddhist and Jain thinking also turned a large section of Hindus to pure vegetarianism. Also, the well-known austerity of Jain ascetics had enormous impact on Hindu traditions. But, as in the West, there are degrees fish is allowed in some coastal regions, while eggs may be eaten in some provinces and not others.

Food observances help to define caste ranking; Brahmins being the highest caste must eat only food prepared in the finest manner, i.e., the least polluting. Meat is regarded as the most polluting as it involves contact with killed animals, therefore the highest caste of Brahmins are all vegetarians. They also forbid the eating of both garlic and onions as these are associated with meat.

'People who do not eat meat, look down upon those who do.'[1] This is in Maharashtra. Gujarat is another vegetarian province, famous for its pickles. Much khichri is eaten (two parts dhal and one part rice; this boosts the protein value). In Gujarat they also use many flours made from pulses which, according to Chakravarty, go back to 2,000 BC.

'On balance, the aversion to beef makes it possible for India's huge population to consume more rather than less food,' Harris argues, also quoting Gandhi on the cow: 'not only did she give milk, but she made agriculture possible.'[2] Perhaps in India we see an example of the equation of less meat, more food, which could apply in the future to the rest of the world.[3]

It is said that the pre-Aryan culture and the Indo-Aryan culture have survived in southern India without a break. In the north the culture and language were constantly buffeted by foreign influences, but in the south a pure form of Hindu culture managed to survive. This was the area too which originally had been most influenced by Jainism and Buddhism. Here the caste system is at its most rigid and they refuse to eat foods which are not indigenous to the area. The Muslims in this area and elsewhere in India, of course, eat meat, except for pork.

# Appendix 4:

# The Rise of the Vegetarian Cookery Book

Nothing is so illustrative of the popularity of the vegetarian idea than the publication of practical guides to its application. The vegetarian cookery book spent a long time in infancy and adolescence, and only in the last decades could one say it has reached its maturity.

Thomas Tryon published ten books between 1682 and 1702 which cover domestic matters, with a strong emphasis on diet and vegetarianism, but one cannot rightly call them cookery books.

In 1821 Mrs Brotherton's *A New System of Vegetable Cookery* was published anonymously 'by a member of the society of Bible Christians'. It must have sold well, for a new revised edition came out in 1829, published this time in Manchester. Another anonymous book was published in 1833 simply entitled *Vegetable Cookery 'By a lady'*, which also recommends abstinence from 'intoxicating liquors'. In 1847 *A Few Recipes of Vegetarian Diet*, 'accompanied by scientific facts showing that vegetable food is more nutritive and more digestible than the flesh of animals', also bore no authorship but it showed the influence of Liebig's work.

In America, William Alcott wrote a book on *The Vegetable Diet*, which included a system of vegetable cookery, published in New York in 1849. His friend and colleague, Henry Clubb, also published four books between 1855 and 1898, but these were collections of essays exhorting the vegetarian diet upon the reader and not plain cookery books. In fact there were plenty of publications from the middle of the nineteenth century of a proselytising nature. But many of the public vegetarian banquets of the 1850s financed by James Simpson were based upon Mrs Brotherton's book. In 1895 *Fast Day and Vegetarian Cookery*, by E.M. Cowen and Beaty-Pownall, was published in London, while in the following year Elizor Goodrich Smith wrote *Fat of the Land and How to Live On It*; it had chapters on nuts and vegetable oils and how to use them in cooking, milk, bakeries, feeding infants and various other subjects relating to the food problem. In San Francisco a Mrs Leadsworth published in 1899 *The Natural Food of Man and How to Prepare It*.

In 1904 *Substitute for Flesh Foods: Vegetarian Cookbook* by E.G. Fulton was also published on the west coast by the Pacific Press Publishing Company. Sarah Tyson Rover in 1909, in Philadelphia, published *Mrs Rover's Vegetable Cookery and Meat Substitutes*, while in London in 1910 Jeanne Jardine wrote *The Best Vegetarian Dishes I Know*, published by J.M. Dent & Sons. In the year of the outbreak of the First World War three books were published, two of which linked diet with health. *Meatless Cookery, with Special Reference to Diet for Heart Disease, Blood Pressure and Autointoxication*, by Marie McIlvaine Gillmore, was published in New York. In fact a good half of the cookery books in the first half of the century, both in America and here, intensified this link, which we tend to think of as such a contemporary one.

In the twenties and thirties the vegetarian cookery book still did not take wing. About twelve books were published in America and the UK. After the Second World War the movement did not do well, overshadowed by the austerity of rationing,★ but in the twenty years from 1960 to 1980 183 books were published in the English-speaking world. Thirty-five were published in the UK, most of them in the seventies.

The boom years began in the eighties, when hundreds of books upon the subject were published each year. The vegetarian and health aspect of every publisher's list began to loom large, and vegetarian cookery books are even written by meat-eaters, a strange anomaly that would have struck the founders of the movement as immoral but which now arouses no comment. In the last decade of the century almost every distinguished food writer and celebrity chef, all of whom are omnivores, wrote their own vegetable cookery books. Many of them emphasise the importance of vegetables in the meal and how they must be briefly but imaginatively cooked. This has undoubtedly improved the cooking and presentation of vegetable dishes, so that they can now be served and enjoyed without adverse comment. Vegetable cooking has lost that tone of moral earnestness which was there previously, even though at times it was enlivened with Shavian wit.

---

★The Vegetarian Society itself continued to publish pamphlets and cookery books throughout this time and, possibly helped by rationing, sold many copies of their books. During 1950, for example, the Society published *Chest Complaints: Their Cause and Cure* (4,000 copies), by Milton Powell ND, DO; *75 Vegetarian Savouries* (20,000 copies), by Ivan Baker, and reprinted his *Christmas Recipes* (1,000 copies). In addition the Society issued a new edition of *160 Meatless Recipes* (5,000 copies), making a total of 190,000 copies since the publication of the first edition.

# Notes

## Foreword

1. Letter of 3 March 1897 from George Bernard Shaw to Ellen Terry, quoted in George Bernard Shaw, *Collected Letters*, vol. 1, ed. Dan H. Laurence, Max Reinhardt, 1965.
2. *Meat, A Natural Symbol.* Nick Fiddes, Routledge, 1991. Fiddes explores the compound symbol eloquently.

## Chapter 1

1. Psalms 90: 5–6, Isaiah 40:6 and the First Epistle of Peter 1: 24–5.
2. Introduction by Sir Julian Huxley to Pierre Teilhard de Chardin, *The Phenomenon of Man*, Collins, 1965.
3. Michael Crawford and David Marsh, *The Driving Force*, Heinemann, 1989; rev. edn, Mandarin, 1991.
4. Karl R. Popper and John C. Eccles, *The Self and Its Brain*, Routledge & Kegan Paul, 1990.
5. *ibid.*
6. Professor Bilsborough, 'The diet of early man', *BNF*, 20, 1977.
7. Peter J. Wilson, Man, *the Promising Primate*, Yale University Press, 1983.
8. *ibid.*
9. Marvin Harris, *Good to Eat*, Allen and Unwin, 1986.
10. Wilson, *op. cit.*
11. Jane Goodall, *In the Shadow of Man*, Collins, 1979; rev. edn, Weidenfeld & Nicolson, 1989.
12. *ibid.*
13. Letter from a Meat Inspector complaining about Animal Aid, published in *Meat Trades Journal*.
14. Goodall, *op. cit.*
15. *ibid.*
16. John Hawthorne, *BNF Nutrition Bulletin*, vol. 63, September 1991.
17. *ibid.*
18. Ernest P. Walker *et. al.*, *Mammals of the World*, 4th, rev. edn: J.L. Paradiso and R.M. Nowak, Johns Hopkins University Press, 1983; 5th rev. edn: R.M. Nowak, 1992.
19. *Proceedings of the National Academy of Science USA*, vol. 85, p.2658. Researched by Glenn Gentry and three colleagues, using the 'molecular clock' referred to on p.5.
20. White D. Tim, *Nature*, vol. 371 (1994).

21. Michael Crawford and David Marsh, *op. cit.*

22. Letter from Professor Crawford to the author.

23. Elaine Morgan.

24. See Michael Crawford & David Marsh. *The Driving Force. Food in Evolution and the Future.* Heinemann, 1989.

25. *The Scars of Evolution*, Elaine Morgan, Penguin Books, 1990.

26. *The Descent of Man and Selection in Relation to Sex.*

27. Richard Dawkins promulgates the same theory in *The Selfish Game*, OUP, 1976.

28. Wilson, *op. cit.*

29. Reported in *New Scientist*, 9 September 1989.

30. Rosalind Miles, *Women's History of the World*, Grafton Books, 1989.

31. *ibid.*

32. Jon Wynne Tyson, *Food for a Future*, Thorsons, 1975.

33. Wilson, *op. cit.*

34. *ibid.*

35. *ibid.*

36. *ibid.*

37. *ibid.*

38. Popper and Eccles, *op. cit.*

39. Cohn Tudge, *New Scientist*, 13 April 1989.

40. Rupert Sheldrake, *Resurgence*, no. 111, July 1985.

41. Tudge, *op. cit.*

42. Robert Foley with Robin Dunbar, 'Beyond the Bones of Contention', *New Scientist*, 14 October 1989.

43. Most of these examples come from Indian tribes of the east coast of North America.

44. J.G. Hawkes, in P.J. Ucko and G.W. Dimbleby, *The Domestication and Exploitation of Plants and Animals*, Duckworth, 1971.

45. Donald Henry, *From Foraging to Agriculture*, University of Pennsylvania Press, 1989; new edn, 1992.

46. Letter from Peter J. Wilson to the author.

47. For example, B.A.L. Cranstone, 'Animal husbandry: the evidence from ethnography', in Ucko and Dimbleby, *op. cit.*

48. See Diamond, Jared, *Guns, Germs and Steel*, Vintage, 1998.

49. Ventris, Michael, Chadwick, John, *The Decipherment of Linear B*, Cambridge, 1970.

50. Pray Bober, Phyllis, *Art, Culture and Cuisine*, Univ. of Chicago, 1999.

51. Hillmann, Gordon, *The Collapse of Dietary Diversity with the Adoption of Agriculture*, Institute of Archaeology. Paper given on Wild Foods at Royal Society of Medicine, 1997.

52. Peter J. Wilson, *The Domestication of the Human Species*, Yale University Press, 1989; new edn, 1991.

53. *ibid.*

54. *ibid.*

55. Marcel Detienne, *The Gardens of Adonis*, Harvester Press, 1977.

## Chapter 2

1. Dalby, Andrew, *Siren Feasts*, Routledge, 1996.
2. Elizabeth Minchin, *Petits Propos Culinaires 25: Food Fiction and Food Fact in Homer's Iliad*. Prospect Books, March 1987.
3. Homer, *Iliad*, 9.209-17, trans. E.V. Rieu, Penguin, 1950.
4. *ibid.*, 5.899-904.
5. *ibid.*, 21.573-8.
6. Homer, *Odyssey*, 19.428-58. trans. E.V. Rieu, Penguin, 1946.
7. Emile Mireaux, *Daily Life in the Time of Homer*, Allen and Unwin, 1959.
8. Porphyry, *On Abstinence from Animal Food*, E.W. Tyson and Thomas Taylor, Centaur Press, 1965.
9. Homer, *Iliad*, IVV, 442-74.
10. The myth was probably first told by Hesiod, but it occurs in Ovid, *Metamorphoses*, 4.190-255. See also Marcel Detienne, 'The Spice Ox', *The Gardens of Adonis*, Harvester Press, 1977.
11. Marcel Detienne, *op. cit.*, 'The Spice Ox'.
12. John Wilkins, 'Public and Private Eating in Greece 450-300 BC', paper for Oxford Symposium of Food, 1991.
13. The most recent biography is Peter Gorman, *Pythagoras. A Life*, Routledge & Kegan Paul, 1979. Gorman bases his work on Iamblichus, *Life of Pythagoras*, trans. Thomas Taylor (1818); the biography by Porphyry which is available in English, M. Hadas and M. Smith, *Heroes and Gods*, Routledge & Kegan Paul, 1965; and two further biographies in German by Baltzer and Roeth. Other sources I have used are in the following notes.
14. Diogenes Laertius, *La Vie de Pythagore*, quoted in Gorman, *op. cit.*
15. *ibid.*
16. Michael Grant, *The Classical Greeks*, Weidenfeld & Nicolson, 1989.
17. Martin Bernal, *Black Athena*, vol. I, Free Association Books, 1987.
18. William J. Darby, Paul Ghalioungui and Louis Grivetti, *Food: The Gift of Osiris*, Academic Press, 1977.
19. Plutarch, 'Table Talk' from *Moralia 11*, 3, 365, trans. Harold Cherniss and William Helmbold, Heinemann, 1976.
20. Detienne, *op. cit.*
21. Quoted in Detienne, *op. cit.*, who cites both Porphyry and Lydus as having noted the experiment.
22. Howard Williams, *The Ethics of Diet*, John Heywood, 1883.
23. Pliny, *Natural History 18.72*, Loeb Classical Library,
24. E.R. Dodds, *The Greeks and the Irrational*, University of California Press, 1956.
25. D.A. Dombrowski, *The Philosophy of Vegetarianism*, University of Massachusetts Press, 1984.
26. Iamblichus, *op. cit.*
27. Gorman, *op. cit.*
28. Marcel Detienne, *Dionysos Slain*, Johns Hopkins University Press, 1979.

29. Quoted in Joscelyn Godwin, *Mystery Religions in the Ancient World*, Thames and Hudson, 1981.
30. Detienne, *Dionysos Slain*, Chapter 4, Note 2.
31. *ibid.*
32. Bertrand Russell, *A History of Western Philosophy*, Unwin, 1978.
33. Herodotus, *The Histories*, Book 3, trans. A.D. Godley, Loeb, 1932.
34. Bernal, *op. cit.*
35. Quoted in Godwin, *op. cit.*
36. Bernal, *op. cit.*, vol.3 (unpublished).
37. Detienne, *Dionysos Slain*.
38. *ibid.*
39. J.B. Bury and Russell Meiggs, *A History of Greece*, Macmillan, 1975.
40. Porphyry, *On Abstinence from Animal Food*.
41. Numbers, 19:2.
42. Deuteronomy, 14:12.
43. Herodotus, *op. cit.*, Book 2.
44. Darby, Ghalioungui and Grivetti, *op. cit.*
45. Herodotus, *op. cit.*, Book 2.
46. Plutarch, 'Isis and Osiris', *op. cit.*, vol. 9.
47. 'Prophecy of Neferrhu', quoted in Darby, Ghalioungui and Grivetti, *op. cit.*
48. Jonathan Barnes, *The Presocratic Philosophers*, Routledge, 1979.
49. W. Burkert, *Lore and Science in Ancient Pythagoreanism*, Harvard University Press, 1972.
    H. Thesleff, 'An Introduction to the Pythagorean Writings of the Hellenistic Age', *Acta Academiae Aboensis Humaniora*, xxiv, 3.
    H. Thesleff, 'The Pythagorean Texts of the Hellenistic Period', *ibid.*, xxxi.
    C.H. Kahn, 'Pythagorean Philosophy before Plato', *Mourelatos* (72).
    J.A. Philip, *Pythagoras and Early Pythagoreanism*, University of Toronto Press, 1967.
    C.J. de Vogel, *Pythagoras and Early Pythagoreanism*, Humanities Press, 1966.
50. Barnes, *op. cit.*
51. *ibid.*
52. Empedocles, *Purifications*, quoted in Barnes, *op. cit.*
53. *ibid.*
54. *ibid.*
55. *ibid.*
56. Athenaeus, *Deipnosophistai*, 1.3., trans. Charles Burton Gulick, Loeb, 1971.
57. Pindar, 'Olympian Ode II', quoted in Barnes, *op. cit.*
58. Russell, *op. cit.*
59. *ibid.*
60. Quoted in Gorman, *op. cit.*
61. Dombrowski, *op. cit.*
62. Athenaeus, *op. cit.*

63. Barnes, *op. cit.*
64. Detienne, *The Gardens of Adonis.*
65. Russell, *op. cit.*

## Chapter 3

1. Rig-Veda, 11:12, trans. from *The Sacred Books of the East*, ed. Max Müller, 50 vols., Oxford Clarendon Press, 1879–1910.
2. *ibid.*
3. Cyril Eastwood, *Life and Thought in the Ancient World*, University of London Press, 1966.
4. Rig-Veda, 10:129, from Müller, *op. cit.*
5. Juan Mascaró, Introduction to *The Upanishads*, Penguin Books, 1965.
6. Rig-Veda, 11:28.
7. *ibid.*, 10:129.
8. *ibid.*, 11:29.
9. A.C. Clayton, *The Rigveda and Vedic Religion*, Christian Literature Society for India, 1913.
10. I. Chakravarty, *The Saga of Indian Food*, Sterling Publishers, 1972.
11. Dr Rajendralala Mitra, *Indo-Aryans*, 1881.
12. I. Chakravarty, *op. cit.*
13. Manava Dharma-veras, 46, 48, 53, 56, from *The Pali Canon: Dialogues of the Buddha*, trans. T.W. Rhys Daniels, Oxford University Press.
14. Peter Harvey, *An Introduction to Buddhism*, Cambridge University Press, 1990.
15. Reported by Marvin Harris in *Good to Eat*, Allen and Unwin, 1986.
16. Edward Conze, *A Short History of Buddhism*, Unwin, 1982.
17. Reay Tannahill, *Food in History*, Penguin Books, 1991.
18. *ibid.*
19. Quoted in Buddhist scriptures, ed. and trans. Edward Conze, Penguin Books, 1959.
20. Danilo Dolci, *To Feed the Hungry*, MacGibbon and Kee, 1959.
21. Jivaka-Sutta, *Lawful and Unlawful Meats. Further Dialogues of the Buddha, Part 1*, trans. Lord Chalmers, Oxford University Press, 1926.
22. Maha-Sihanada-Sutta, 'The Long Challenge', trans. T.W. Rhys Daniels, *op. cit.*
23. Maha-Saccaka-Sutta, 'Saccaka Again', trans. T.W. Rhys Daniels, *op. cit.*
24. Anthony Christie, *Petits Propos Culinaires 35: Buddhist Attitudes towards Food: Aspects of Tradition and Practice in South-East Asia*, Prospect Books, July 1990.
25. *ibid.*
26. Reay Tannahill, *op. cit.*
27. Asoka Edicts, Amalyachandra Sen (ed.), 1956.

## Chapter 4

1. Plato, *Gorgias*, 462, Penguin Books, 1960.
2. *ibid.*, 5.01.
3. Plato, *The Republic*, 372, Everyman's Library, 1945.

4. D.A. Dombrowski, *The Philosophy of Vegetarianism*, University of Massachusetts Press, 1984.

5. Plato, *The Laws*.

6. Plato, *Epinomis*, trans. and ed. W.R.M. Lamb, Loeb, 1924.

7. Plato, *The Epistles*, 7, trans. R.G. Bury, Cambridge, Mass., 1946.

8. Several authors wrote books entitled *The Art of Cooking*, Glaucos of Locris, Eristratus and Heraclidus wrote books on Gastronomy, Vegetables and Pickles.

9. See Davidson, James, *Courtesans & Fishcakes*, Harper Collins, 1997, for a fascinating explanation of the terms.

10. Aristotle, *On the Parts of Animals*, Book 1, Chapter 5, ed. and trans. A.L. Peck, Loeb.

11. *ibid.*

12. Quoted in Dombrowski, *op. cit.*

13. *ibid.*

14. Athenaeus, *op. cit.*, 7.280.

15. Cyril Eastwood, *Life and Thought in the Ancient World*, University of London Press, 1966.

16. Pliny, *Natural History*, 8.7. Trans. W.H.S. Jones, Loeb, 1956.

17. Cicero, *Letters*, 7.1. Trans. W. Glynn Williams, Heinemann, 1965.

18. Seneca, *Letter IX*, trans. Richard M. Gummere, Heinemann, 1967.

19. Seneca, *op. cit.* X.

20. Introduction by E.J. Kenny in Ovid, *Metamorphoses*, Oxford University Press, 1986.

21. Ovid, *The Doctrines of Pythagoras*, trans. A.D. Melville, Oxford University Press, 1986.

22. *ibid.*

23. *ibid.*

24. *ibid.*

25. *ibid.*

26. Plutarch, 'Rules for the Preservation of Health', *op. cit.*

27. Plutarch, 'Symposiacs', *op. cit.*

28. Pliny, *op. cit.*, 11.117.

29. Plutarch, 'Essay on Flesh Eating', *op. cit.*

30. *ibid.*

31. *ibid.*

32. *ibid.*

33. Athenaeus, *op. cit.*

34. Plutarch, 'Essay on Flesh Eating'.

35. Peter Gorman, *Pythagoras. A Life*, Routledge & Kegan Paul, 1979.

36. Stephen MacKenna (trans.), *Porphyry's 'Life of Plotinus'*, ed. Turnbull, Greenwood Press, 1977.

37. *ibid.*

38. *ibid.*

39. Plotinus, *The Enneads*, 1, 4, 16. Trans. E.K. Emilsson, Cambridge University Press, 1988.

40. *ibid.*, 6, 7, 34.

41.  Howard Williams, *The Ethics of Diet*, John Heywood, 1883.
42.  Apicius, *The Art of Cooking*.
43.  Porphyry, *On Abstinence from Animal Food*, E.W. Tyson and Thomas Taylor, Centaur Press, 1965.
44.  *ibid*.
45.  *ibid*.
46.  *ibid*.
47.  Josephus, *Antiquities of the Jews*, trans. H.J. St Thackeray, Loeb, 1926–30.
48.  Porphyry, *op. cit*.

## Chapter 5

1.   Baigent and Leigh, *The Dead Sea Scrolls Deception*, Jonathan Cape, 1991. The authors base their theory on an academic paper by Eisenham, Meccatees, Zadokites, Christians and Quimran (Leiden, 1983).
2.   M. Black (ed.), *The Scrolls and Christianity*, SPCK, 1969, quoted in Baigent and Leigh, *op. cit*.
3.   *ibid*.
4.   Porphyry, *On Abstinence from Animal Food*, E.W. Tyson and Thomas Taylor, Centaur Press, 1965.
5.   *ibid*.
6.   The Gospel of Thomas quoted in Pagels, *op. cit*.
7.   The Gospel of Philip quoted in Elaine Pagels, *The Gnostic Gospels*, Penguin Books, 1990.
8.   I Corinthians, 8:13.
9.   Romans, 14 and 21.
10.  I Timothy, 4:1–5.
11.  Mark, 5:13.
12.  I Corinthians, 9:9–10.
13.  John, 10.
14.  Luke, 13:15–16.
15.  Luke, 14:5; Mark, 12:9–13.
16.  Genesis, 1:26.
17.  Genesis, 3:6.
18.  Genesis, 3:5.
19.  Genesis, 3:22.
20.  'The Semiotics of Food in the Bible' in *Food and Drink in History*, vol. 5, ed. Robert Forster and Orest Ranum, University of Michigan Press, 1979.
21.  Genesis, 4:4.
22.  Genesis, 6:20.
23.  S.H. Hooke, *Middle Eastern Mythology*, Penguin Books, 1963.
24.  Genesis, 4:11.
25.  Genesis, 9:2.
26.  Genesis, 8:21.
27.  Genesis, 9:4.
28.  Leviticus, 17:10–12.

29.  Deuteronomy, 12:15–16.
30.  See Exodus, 12.
31.  Leviticus, 17:11.
32.  Leviticus, 17:4.
33.  Robin Lane Fox, *Pagans and Christians*, Viking, 1986; Penguin Books, 1988.
34.  Galatians, 3:28.
35.  Tertullian, *On Feasting or Abstinence against the Carnal-Minded*, quoted in Williams, *op. cit.*
36.  Daniel, 1:15.
37.  Tertullian, *op. cit.*
38.  *ibid.*
39.  *ibid.*
40.  *ibid.*
41.  *ibid.*
42.  *The Writings of Clement of Alexandria*, trans. Rev. William Wilson, Hamilton & Co., 1867.
43.  Clement of Alexandria, *The Tutor*, trans. Wilson, *op. cit.*
44.  Eusebius, *Ecclesiastical History*, 2 vols., trans. H.J. Lawlor and J.E.L. Oulton, SPCK, 1927–8.
45.  St Augustine, *The Catholic and Manichaean Ways of Life*, trans. D.A. Gallagher and L.J. Gallagher, Catholic University Press, 1966.
46.  Clement of Alexandria, *The Tutor*.
47.  Clement of Alexandria, 'Miscellanies VII', trans. Wilson, *op. cit.*
48.  Plutarch, 'Essay on Flesh Eating', *op. cit.*
49.  Clement of Alexandria, 'Miscellanies VII'.
50.  Exodus, 23:19 and 34:26; Deuteronomy 14:31.
51.  Jean Soler, 'The Semiotics of Food in the Bible', from *Food and Drink in History*, vol. 5, ed. Robert Forster and Orest Ranum, John Hopkins University Press, 1979.
52.  Quoted in Mary Douglas, *Purity and Danger*, Routledge & Kagan Paul, 1991.
53.  Raymond Sokolov, *The Jewish American Kitchen*, Stewart Tabori & Chang, 1989.
54.  Mary Douglas, *op. cit.*
55.  Quoted in Jean Soler as cited in the *Dictionnaire Robert*.
56.  Exodus, 16:31.
57.  Exodus, 16:3.
58.  Exodus, 16:13.
59.  Numbers, 11:5.
60.  Numbers, 11:8.
61.  Numbers, 11:4.
62.  Numbers, 11:33.
63.  Quoted in William J. Darby, Paul Ghalioungui and Louis Grivetti, *Food: The Gift of Osiris*, Academic Press, 1977.
64.  Numbers, 11:31.
65.  Numbers, 11:19–20.

66. Numbers, 11:34.
67. Deuteronomy, 14:3-20; Leviticus, 11:2-42.
68. Deuteronomy, 17:1.
69. Leviticus, 2:11.
70. Leviticus, 19:19.
71. Deuteronomy, 22:10.
72. Leviticus, 19:19.
73. Leviticus, 19:19.
74. Deuteronomy, 23:3.
75. Acts, 10.
76. Acts, 10:14.
77. John Chrysostom, 'Homily XIX', from *Selections from St John Chrysostom*, Rt Rev. J.F. D'Alton, Burns, Oates and Washbourne Ltd, 1940.
78. John Chrysostom, *Homily XIII*, from D'Alton, *op. cit.*

## Chapter 6

1. Elaine Pagels, *The Gnostic Gospels*, Penguin Books, 1990.
2. II Corinthians, 12:2-4.
3. I Corinthians, 2:6.
4. Tertullian, *De Praesempkore Haereticorum*, quoted in Pagels, *op. cit.*
5. The Gospel of Philip quoted in E. Pagels, *op. cit.*
6. Pagels, *op. cit.*
7. Peter Brown, *The Body and Society*, Faber and Faber, 1989; new edn 1990.
8. Samuel N.C. Lieu, *Manichaeism*, Manchester University Press, 1985.
9. I Corinthians, 14:34-5.
10. Pagels, *op. cit.*
11. Quoted in Pagels, *op. cit.*
12. *ibid.*
13. *Codex Manichaicus Coloniensis*, quoted in Lieu, *op. cit.*
14. *ibid.*
15. Lieu, *op. cit.*
16. Quoted in Lieu, *op. cit.*
17. *ibid.*
18. Luke, 16:9.
19. Quoted in Lieu, *op. cit.*
20. Brown, *op. cit.*
21. Verse from *Psalms of Heraclides*, a Manichean work, quoted in Brown, *op. cit.*
22. Lieu, *op. cit.*
23. *ibid.*
24. Graham Greene, *The World of Dickens*, quoted in the *Guardian* obituary, 4 April 1991.
25. St Augustine, *Concerning Heresies*, Chapter 46, quoted in R.I. Moore, *op. cit.*

26. Steven Runciman, *Mediaeval Manichee*, Cambridge University Press, 1982.

27. Quoted in Dimitri Obolensky, *The Bogomils*, A.C. Hall, 1972.

28. *ibid.*

## Chapter 7

1. Procopius, *The Secret History*, Penguin Books, 1966.

2. *ibid.*

3. *ibid.*

4. See Samuel N.C. Lieu, *Manichaeism*, Manchester University Press, 1985.

5. Quoted in Edward Peters (ed.), *Heresy and Authority in Medieval Europe*, University of Pennsylvania Press, 1980.

6. Steven Runciman, *Mediaeval Manichee*, Cambridge University Press, 1982.

7. Cosmas, 'Sermon against Heretics', quoted in Dimitri Obolensky, *The Bogomils*, A.C. Hall, 1972.

8. Isaiah, 14:12-14.

9. Runciman, *op. cit.*

10. Reay Tannahill, *Food in History*, Penguin Books, 1991.

11. R.I. Moore, *Origins of European Dissent*, Basil Blackwell, 1985.

12. Obolensky, *op. cit.*

13. Tannahill, *op. cit.*

14. Matthew, 3:4.

15. *The Alexiad of Princess Anna Comnena*, trans. Dawes, Kegan Paul, 1928.

16. See Runciman, *op. cit.*

17. *ibid.*

18. Quoted in R.I. Moore, *The Birth of Popular Heresy* (Documents of Medieval History I), Edward Arnold, 1975.

19. *ibid.*

20. *ibid.*

21. *ibid.*

22. *ibid.*

23. *ibid.*

24. *Vita Norberti*, quoted in Moore, *op. cit.*

25. *ibid.*

26. *ibid.*

27. *ibid.*

28. *ibid.*

29. *ibid.*

30. *ibid.*

31. 'The Epistle of Barnabas' in M. Staniforth, *Early Christian Writings*, Penguin Books, 1968.

32. Erbstosser, Martin, *Heretics in the Middle Ages*, Editions Leipzig, 1984.

33. Brown, *op. cit.*

34. Baigent, Leigh and Lincoln, *The Holy Blood and the Holy Grail*, Jonathan Cape, 1982.

35. Quoted in Peters, *op. cit.*
36. Quoted in Martin Erbstosser, *op. cit.*
37. Runciman, *op. cit.*
38. Quoted in Gerald Carson, *Men, Beasts and Gods*, Charles Scribner's Sons, 1972.
39. 'Saint Antony's Sermon to the Fish', quoted in Peters, *op. cit.*
40. E.P. Evans, *The Criminal Prosecution and Capital Punishment of Animals*, Faber and Faber, 1987.
41. St Thomas Aquinas, *Summa Theologica*, II, I, Q.102, art. 6, Burns, Oates and Washbourne, 1922.
42. *ibid.*, II, I, Q. 64, art. 1.
43. *ibid.*, II, II, Q. 159, art. 2.
44. *ibid.*, II, II, Q. 25, art. 3.
45. *ibid.*
46. *Opuscula Varia*, quoted in *A Medieval Reader*, Penguin Books, 1977.
47. Quoted in Maria Dembinska, 'Fasting and Working Monks: Refutations of the Fifth and Eleventh Centuries' from *Food in Change*, ed. Alexander Fenton and Eszter Kisban, John Donald, 1986.
48. Barbara Ketcham Wheaton, *Savoring the Past*, University of Pennsylvania Press, 1983.

## Chapter 8

1. Dorothy Hartley, *Food in England*, Century, 1987.
2. J.C. Drummond and Anne Wilbraham, *The Englishman's Food*, new edn, Pimlico Books, 1991.
3. Quoted in C. Anne Wilson, *Food and Drink in Britain*, Penguin Books, 1984; new edn, Constable, 1992.
4. W. Nelson (ed.), *A Fifteenth Century School Book*, Oxford University Press, 1956.
5. Reay Tannahill, *Food in History*, Penguin Books, 1991.
6. Sir Thomas Elyot, *The Castel of Health* (1539), quoted in Drummond and Wilbraham, *op. cit.*
7. Erasmus, *Praise of Folly*, trans. B. Radice, Penguin, 1971.
8. Thomas More, *Utopia*, trans. R. Robinson, London, 1869.
9. *ibid.*
10. *ibid.*
11. Quoted in Williams, *op. cit.*
12. Montaigne, *Essays*, trans. J. Flono, Stott Library, 1859.
13. *ibid.*
14. *ibid.*
15. *ibid.*
16. *ibid.*
17. *ibid.*
18. *ibid.*
19. Sigmund Freud, *Leonardo da Vinci*, Routledge, 1984.
20. Leonardo, *Notebooks*, trans. Irma A. Richter, Oxford University Press, 1952.

21. K.R. Eissler, *Leonardo da Vinci: Psychological Notes on the Enigma*, Hogarth Press, 1962.

22. Leonardo, *op. cit.*

23. Eissler, *op. cit.*

24. Leonardo, *op. cit.*

25. Eissler, *op. cit.*

26. Leonardo, *op. cit.*

27. *ibid.*

28. Richard Barber, *Cooking and Recipes from Rome to the Renaissance*, Allen Lane, 1973.

29. Montaigne, *op. cit.*

30. Quoted in Colin Clair, *Kitchen and Table*, Abelard and Schuman, 1964.

31. Cornaro, *A Treatise on a Sober Life*, quoted in Williams, *op. cit.*

32. Quoted from Buckhardt, *Civilization of the Renaissance in Italy*, Phaidon, 1981; Penguin Books, 1990.

33. Russell, *op. cit.*

34. A.E. Waite (trans.), *The Hermetic and Alchemical Writings of Paracelsus the Great* (3 vols.), Bantam, 1990.

35. Keith Thomas, *Religion and the Decline of Magic*, Penguin Books, 1991.

36. Quoted in Alfred W. Crosby, Jr, *The Columbian Exchange*, Greenwood Press, 1972.

37. Quoted in Tannahill, *op. cit.*

38. *ibid.*

39. For a detailed account see Reay Tannahill, *Flesh and Blood*, Sphere, 1976.

## Chapter 9

1. Samuel Pepys, *Diary*, entry for 19 April 1665.

2. Quoted in Gerald Carson, *Men, Beasts and Gods*, Charles Scribner's Sons, 1972.

3. Descartes, *Treatise of Man*, trans. Thomas Steele Hall, Harvard University Press, 1972.

4. Fontanelle, *Plurality of Worlds*, quoted in Basil Willey, *The Seventeenth Century Background*, Ark, 1986.

5. E.A. Burtt, *The Metaphysical Foundations of Modern Science*, Routledge & Kegan Paul, 1980.

6. Letter to Van Helmont, quoted in Howard Williams, *The Ethics of Diet*, John Heywood, 1883.

7. *ibid.*

8. Gassendi, *Ethics*, quoted in Williams, *op. cit.*

9. Keith Thomas, *Man and the Natural World*, Allen Lane, 1983.

10. Quoted in Norman Cohn, *The Pursuit of the Millennium*, Paladin, 1957.

11. *ibid.*

12. *ibid.*

13. Laqueur, Thomas W., *Sexual Desire and the Market Economy during the*

*Industrial Revolution*. Discourses of Sexuality from aristotle to Aids ed., Domna C Stanton, Univ of Michigan Press, 1992

14.  Diary of John Evelyn, August 27th 1685, ed. William Bray, 1859.

15.  Tryon,Thomas, *The Way to Health and Long Life*, 1683.

16.  Earle, Peter, *The World of Defoe*, 1976.

17.  Tryon, Thomas, *A Memoir*.

18.  Mcendrick, Brewer and Plumb, *The Birth of a Consumer Society*. London, Europe Publications, 1982.

19.  Hume, David, "On Commerce." *Essays*, Moral, Political and Literary, T.H. Green and T.H. Grose,New York, 1898.

20.  Mcendrick, Brewer and Plumb.

21.  Misson, Henry, *Memoirs and Observations in his Travels*, trans and ed. by Ozell.

22.  Misson, Henry.

23.  Muffet, Thomas, *Healths Improvement*, 1655.

24.  Burton, Richard, *The Anatomy of Melancholy*, 1621.

25.  Verney, Francis P., ed. *Memoirs of the Verney Family*, 1892.

26.  Harvey, Gideon, *The Disease of London*; or a new discovery of the Scurvey, 1675.

27.  Cockburn, William, *Sea Diseases*, 3rd Edition, 1736. Quoted in *The Englishman's Food*, Drummond and Wilbraham, Cape, 1957.

28.  List Tryon's books in footnote on page 199.

29.  Williams, Howard, *The Ethics of Diet*, John Heywood, 1883.

30.  Tryon, Thomas, *Way to Long Life, Health and Happiness*, 3rd edition, 1763.

31.  *ibid.*

32.  *ibid.*

33.  *ibid.*

34.  *ibid.*

35.  Thomas Tryon, *A Treatise on Cleanness in Meats and Drinks, of the Preparation of Food* (1682).

36.  *ibid.*

37.  *ibid.*

38.  John Evelyn, *Acetaria* (1699).

39.  Germaine Greer (ed.), *Kissing the Rod. An Anthology of Seventeenth-Century Women's Verses*,Virago, 1990.

40.  Quoted in Basil Willey, *op. cit.*

41.  *ibid.*

42.  *ibid.*

43.  *ibid.*

44.  *ibid.*

45.  *ibid.*

46.  Keith Thomas, 'The Human Carnivore'. Lecture given to the Guild of Food Writers, 1990.

47.  P.C.D. Brears, *The Gentlewoman's Kitchen*, Wakefield Historical Publications, 1984.

48.  Philippa Pullar, *Consuming Passions*, Hamish Hamilton, 1970.

49. Keith Thomas, *op. cit.*
50. Milton, *Paradise Lost* (1667).
51. Bossuet, *Discours sur l'histoire universelle*, quoted in Williams, *op. cit.*
52. David Hartley, *Observations on Man, His Frame, His Duties and His Expectations* (1748).
53. Dr Cheyne, *Essay on Regimen* (1740).
54. *ibid.*
55. Hartley, *op. cit.*
56. John Gay, 'The Wild Boar and the Ram', in *Fables* (1727).
57. Gay, 'The Philosopher and the Pheasants', in *Fables*.
58. Gay, 'Pythagoras and the Countryman', in *Fables*.
59. Alexander Pope, *Essay on Man* (1733–4).
60. *ibid.*
61. Voltaire, 'Beasts', from *Dictionary of Philosophy*, quoted in Williams, *op. cit.*
62. Elizabeth Labrousse, *Bayle*, trans. Denys Potts, Oxford University Press, 1983.

## Chapter 10

1. Marcus Aurelius, *Martial Meditations*, 4.3, 23; 2.5, trans. Rev. R. Graves, N. Whitley, 1826.
2. John Howard, *The State of the Prisons in England and Wales* 1777.
3. John Locke, 'Some Thoughts Concerning Education', in *The Educational Writings*, Cambridge University Press, 1968.
4. Quoted in Harold Nicolson, *The Age of Reason*, Constable, 1960.
5. *ibid.*
6. *ibid.*
7. Quoted in Keith Thomas, *Man and the Natural World*, Allen Lane, 1983.
8. *ibid.*
9. *ibid.*
10. *ibid.*
11. John Wesley, *Works*, Vol.1, 1829–31.
12. Nicolson, *op. cit.*
13. *ibid.*
14. *ibid.*
15. Voltaire, *Elements de la Philosophie de Newton* (1738).
16. Voltaire, *Essai sur les Moeurs* (1756).
17. Voltaire, *The Princess of Babylon* (1768).
18. *ibid.*
19. George Trevelyan, *The American Revolution* (1926); repr. Reprint Services, 1991.
20. Gregory Claeys, *Thomas Paine*, Unwin Hyman, 1989.
21. *ibid.*
22. William Paley, *Moral and Political Philosophy* (1785).
23. *ibid.*
24. William Paley, *Of Population and Provision*, Longman & Co., 1838.
25. Adam Smith, *The Wealth of Nations* (1776).

26. Joseph Ritson, *Moral Essay upon Abstinence* (1802).
27. *ibid.*
28. *ibid.*
29. Quoted in Thomas, *op. cit.*
30. John Oswald, *The Cry of Nature: an Appeal to Mercy and to Justice on behalf of the Persecuted Animals* (1791).
31. *ibid.*
32. *ibid.*
33. *ibid.*
34. George Nicholson, *The Primeval Diet of Man: Arguments in Favour of Vegetable Food; with Remarks on Man's Conduct to Animals* (1801).
35. *ibid.*
36. *ibid.*
37. *ibid.*
38. *ibid.*
39. Wilham Lambe, *Additional Reports on the Effects of a Peculiar Regimen* . . . (1815).
40. John Abernethy, *Surgical Observations on Tumours* (1804).
41. William Lambe, *Reports of the Effects of a Peculiar Regimen* . . . (1809).
42. Quoted in Howard Williams, *The Ethics of Diet,* John Heywood, 1883.
43. Thomas, *op. cit.*
44. J.C. Drummond and Anne Wilbraham, *The Englishman's Food,* new edn, Pimlico Books, 1991.
45. Arthur Young, *A Farmer's Letters to the People of England* (1771).
46. Drummond and Wilbraham, *op. cit.*
47. William Ellis, *The Practical Farmer or the Hertfordshire Husbandmen* (1732).
48. Sir Frederic Eden, *The State of the Poor* (1797).
49. Quoted in Drummond and Wilbraham, *op. cit.*
50. Jonas Hanway, *Letters on the Importance of the Rising Generation* (1767).
51. Michael Crawford and David Marsh, *The Driving Force,* Heinemann, 1989; rev. edn, Mandarin, 1991.
52. *ibid.*
53. Jefferson Hogg, *Life of Shelley* (1858).
54. Percy Bysshe Shelley, 'A vindication of Natural Diet', Note 17 to *Queen Mab* (1813).
55. Newton, *The Return to Nature,* quoted in Williams, *op. cit.*
56. Richard Holmes, *Shelley: The Pursuit,* Quartet Books, 1974; new edn, Penguin Books, 1991.
57. *ibid.*
58. *ibid.*
59. *ibid.*
60. *ibid.*
61. *ibid.*
62. *ibid.*
63. *ibid.*
64. *ibid.*

65. *ibid.*
66. *ibid.*
67. *ibid.*
68. *ibid.*
69. *ibid.*
70. Hogg, *op. cit.*
71. Shelley, *Poetical Works*, ed. Thomas Hutchinson, Oxford University Press, 1968.
72. *ibid.*, Note 17.
73. *ibid.*
74. *ibid.*
75. Holmes, *op. cit.*
76. Shelley, *Prometheus Unbound, op. cit.*
77. Gandhi, *The Pacifist Conscience*, quoted in G. Ashe, *Gandhi*, Stein and Day, New York, 1968.
78. Quoted in Holmes, *op. cit.*
79. *ibid.*

## Chapter 11

1. Liebig, quoted in Howard Williams, *The Ethics of Diet*, John Heywood, 1883. Williams was a member of the London Vegetarian Society. This book, which was translated into Russian with a foreword by Tolstoy, is a history of all the vegetarian exponents since antiquity. It has been an excellent source book for these pages. Williams's style tends to the florid and the overblown, especially when writing about such heroes as Voltaire and Shelley, while Tolstoy is referred to as 'the most illustrious living advocate of the Higher Life'. Williams's passionate commitment to vegetarianism allows him to fudge and occasionally avoid mentioning an idol's lapse back into meat-eating habits.
2. William Cobbett, *Rural Rides* (1821).
3. Quoted in John Burnett, *Plenty and Want*, Methuen, 1978; 3rd rev. edn, Routledge, 1989.
4. *ibid.*
5. Quoted in Burnett, *op. cit.*
6. *ibid.*
7. John Wright, *Vegetarian Messenger*, August 1850. Copies of both *The Vegetarian Messenger* and the *Vegetarian Review* can be read at the offices of the Vegetarian Society in Altrincham, Cheshire. However, the Society sadly has not had the funds to keep archive material in a condition which would help research, so source material is often undated and not filed in sequence.
8. Bernardin de St-Pierre, *Paul et Virginie* (1787).
9. Julia Twigg, *Prospectus of Concordium. The Vegetarian Movement in England 1847-1981*, Ph.D. thesis for LSE (unpublished). This comprehensive and perceptive account of the modern history of vegetarianism was an invaluable help to these last chapters.
10. *ibid.*

11. Quoted in Twigg, *op. cit.* Taken from *Bronson Alcott: His Life and Philosophy* (1893).
12. Charles Froward in the *Vegetarian Review*.
13. *ibid.*
14. *ibid.*
15. *ibid.*
16. Quoted in Burnett, *op. cit.*
17. II Kings, 4:40.
18. Burnett, *op. cit.*
19. *ibid.*
20. *ibid.*
21. Samuel Smiles, *Self Help* (1859).
22. *Manchester City News*, quoted in *The Vegetarian Messenger*.
23. *ibid.*
24. *The Vegetarian Messenger*, March 1893.
25. *Leeds Mercury*, 6 August 1857, quoted in *The Vegetarian Messenger*.
26. *ibid.*
27. *ibid.*
28. Quoted in Keith Thomas, *Man and the Natural World*, Allen Lane, 1983.
29. Richard Phillips, *A Dictionary of the Arts and Civilisation*, Sherwood & Co., 1833.
30. J.L. Emary in the *Vegetarian Messenger*, 1921.
31. Alphonse de Lamartine, *Nouvelles Confidences* (1851).
32. *ibid.*
33. Letter from Dr M.L. Holbrook, New York, dated 21 July 1874, in *The Vegetarian Messenger*.
34. *The Vegetarian Messenger*.
35. Froward in the *Vegetarian Review*.
36. *ibid.*
37. *ibid.*
38. *Dietetic Reformer*, June 1890.
39. *The Vegetarian Messenger*.
40. *ibid.*
41. Quoted by Froward in the *Vegetarian Review*.
42. *ibid.*
43. *ibid.*
44. Percy Bysshe Shelley, *The Revolt of Islam* (1818).
45. Michael Holroyd, *Bernard Shaw*, Vol.1, Chatto and Windus, 1988.
46. *ibid.*
47. *ibid.*
48. *ibid.*
49. *ibid.*
50. *ibid.*
51. *ibid.*
52. *ibid.*
53. *ibid.*
54. *ibid.*

55. Janet Barkas, *The Vegetable Passion*, Routledge & Kegan Paul, 1975.
56. *ibid.*
57. Nellie Shaw, who published an account of this time and a later commune, Whiteway (1935), quoted in Twigg, *op. cit.*
58. Letter to Hall Caine, 21 September 1928 in George Bernard Shaw, *Letters*, vol.4, ed. Dan H. Laurence, Max Reinhardt, 1988.
59. Jupp, *The Religion of Nature.*
60. Edward Carpenter, *Civilisation: Its Cause and Cure* (1921).
61. Jeffrey Weeks, *Coming Out: Homosexual Politics in Britain from the Nineteenth Century to the Present*, Quartet, 1977.
62. *ibid.*
63. Kingsford, Anna and Maitland, Edward, *Vivisection and Vegetarianism: Addresses and Essays on Vegetarianism*, John Watkins, 1912.
64. *ibid.*
65. *ibid.*
66. *ibid.*
67. *ibid.*
68. Quoted in the *Vegetarian Review.*
69. *ibid.*
70. Henri Troyat, *Tolstoy*, W.H. Allen, 1968.
71. *ibid.*
72. *ibid.*
73. *ibid.*
74. *ibid.*
75. Steven Runciman, *The Medieval Manichee*, Cambridge University Press, 1982.
76. Barkas, *op. cit.*
77. M.K. Gandhi, *Autobiography*, Jonathan Cape, 1966.
78. *ibid.*
79. *ibid.*
80. *ibid.*
81. *The Vegetarian Messenger.*
82. Geoffrey Ashe, *Gandhi*, Stein & Day, 1968.
83. *ibid.*
84. Quoted in Twigg, *op. cit.*

## Chapter 12

1. J.C. Drummond and Anne Wilbraham, *The Englishman's Food*, new edn, Pimlico Books, 1991.
2. Julia Twigg, *Prospectus of Concordium. The Vegetarian Movement in England 1847-1981*, Ph.D. thesis for LSE (unpublished).
3. *Vegetarian News.*
4. *ibid.*
5. George Orwell, *The Road to Wigan Pier*, Victor Gollancz, 1937; Penguin Books, 1962.
6. *ibid.*
7. Dean Inge, *Outspoken Essays* (1922).

8.　　Rev. Francis Wood, *A Reply to Dean Inge's Defence of Flesh-Eating*, Daniel, 1934.
9.　　Quoted in Barbara Griggs, *The Food Factor*, Viking, 1986.
10.　*ibid.*
11.　Gaylord Hauser, *Diet Does It*, Faber and Faber, 1952.
12.　Quoted in Francis Wheen, *Tom Driberg*, Chatto and Windus, 1990.
13.　Adolf Hitler, *Mein Kampf* Houghton Mifflin, Boston, 1943.
14.　Alice Miller, *The Untouched Key*, Virago, 1990.
15.　Quoted in William L. Shirer, *The Rise and Fall of the Third Reich*, Simon and Schuster, 1960.
16.　Melanie Klein's theory elaborated in Barkas, *op. cit.*
17.　Janet Barkas, *The Vegetable Passion*, Routledge & Kegan Paul, 1975.
18.　*ibid.*
19.　Shirer, *op. cit.*
20.　*ibid.*
21.　Quoted in Barkas, *op. cit.*
22.　*ibid.*
23.　*ibid.*
24.　Twigg, *op. cit.*
25.　*ibid.*
26.　*ibid.*
27.　Griggs, *op. cit.*
28.　John Burnett, *Plenty and Want*, Methuen, 1978; 3rd rev. edn, Routledge, 1989.
29.　*ibid.*
30.　Orwell, *op. cit.*
31.　Burnett, *op. cit.*
32.　Theodora Fitzgibbon, *With Love*, Gantry, 1982.
33.　*ibid.*
34.　Fitzgibbon, op. cit.
35.　Norman Longmate, *How We Lived Then*, Hutchinson, 1971.
36.　Anne Valery, *Talking about the War*, Michael Joseph, 1991.
37.　*ibid.*
38.　*ibid.*
39.　*ibid.*
40.　Burnett, *op. cit.*

## Chapter 13

1.　Interview with the author.
2.　*ibid.*
3.　Brigid Brophy, 'The Darwinist's Dilemma', in Paterson and Ryder (eds.), *Animals' Rights: A Symposium*, Centaur Press, 1979.
4.　Quoted in Julia Twigg, *The Vegetarian Movement in England 1847-1981*, Ph.D. thesis for LSE (unpublished).
5.　John Burnett, *Plenty and Want*, Methuen, 1978; 3rd rev. edn, Routledge, 1989.
6.　Chicken's Lib.

7. *Independent*, March 1989.

8. *Guardian*, 26 June 1984.

9. In conversation with the author.

10. Michael Crawford and David Marsh, *The Driving Force*, Heinemann, 1989; rev. edn, Mandarin, 1991.

11. *ibid.*

12. Brophy, *op. cit.*

13. *Guardian*, May 1989.

14. Alan B. Durning and Holly B. Brough, Worldwatch Paper 103: *Taking Stock: Animal Farming and the Environment*.

15. *ibid.*

16. *Agscene*, 102, 1991.

17. *ibid.*

18. Quoted in Peter Bunyard and Fern Morgan-Grenville (eds.), *The Green Alternative*, Methuen, 1987.

19. Donald Worster, 'Man and the Natural Order' in Goldsmith and Hildyard (eds.), *The Earth Report*, Mitchell Beazley, 1988.

20. M. Frances, *Small Change: A Pocketful of Practical Actions to Help the Environment*, University of Edinburgh, 1990, quoted in Fiddes.

21. *Agscene*, 104, 1991.

22. Quoted in Nick Fiddes, *Meat: A Natural Symbol*, Routledge, 1991.

23. *New Internationalist*, 1987, quoted in Fiddes, *op. cit.*

24. N. Hildyard, 'Adios Amazonia?' in the *Ecologist*, quoted in Fiddes, *op. cit.*

25. Durning and Brough, *op. cit.*

26. *ibid.*

27. John Burnett, *op. cit.*

28. Maurice Hansson with Jill Marsden, *E for Additives*, Thorson's, 1987.

29. *Food Adulteration and How To Beat It*, the London Commission, 1988.

30. Dr Richard Lacey, *Safe Shopping, Safe Cooking, Safe Eating*, Penguin Books, 1989.

31. Turner, Jacky Dr, *Factory Farming & the Environment*: A report for Compassion in World Farming Trust, 1999.

32. *Agscene*: The Magazine of Compassion in World Farming, No. 137, Spring 2000.

33. *Daily Telegraph*, 27/12/99.

34. Bremner, Moyra, *GE: Genetic Engineering and You*, Harper Collins, 1999.

35. *The Independent*, 12th April 2000.

36. *The Sunday Times*, 23rd April 2000.

37. US Department of Agriculture (USDA), US Food and Drug Administration (FDA), US Environmental Protection Agency (EPA).

38. Bremner.

39. Alliance for Bio-Integrity. Web: www.biointegrity.org.

40. See Caroline Walker and Geoffrey Cannon, *The Food Scandal*, Century, 1984.

41. T. Colin Campbell, quoted in *Houston Chronicle*, 9 May 1990.

42.  Rene Dumont, quoted in Susan George, *How the Other Half Dies*, Penguin Books, 1976.
43.  Bunyard and Morgan-Grenville, *op. cit.*
44.  *Marketing*, 27 June 1991.
45.  Fiddes, *op. cit.*
46.  Crawford and Marsh, *op. cit.*

## Appendix 1
1.  For a full and detailed account see Peter Harvey, *An Introduction to Buddhism*, Cambridge University Press, 1990.
2.  E.N. Anderson, *The Food of China*, Yale University Press, 1988.
3.  K.C. Chang, *Food in Chinese Culture*, Yale University Press, 1977.
4.  *ibid.*
5.  *ibid.*

## Appendix 2
1.  Quoted in Samuel N. C. Lieu, *Manichaeism*, Manchester University Press, 1985.
2.  *ibid.*
3.  *ibid.*
4.  *ibid.*

## Appendix 3
1.  I. Chakravarty, *The Saga of Indian Food*, Sterling Publishers, 1972.
2.  Marvin Harris, *Good to Eat*, Allen and Unwin, 1986.
3.  For a detailed summing up of modern Hinduism, see Roger Owen's entry in *The Oxford Companion to Food*, edited by Alan Davidson, OUP, 1999.

# A Select Bibliography

Anderson, E.N., *The Food of China*, Yale University Press, 1988.

Apicius, *The Art of Cooking*, Barbara Flower and Elisabeth Rosenbaum (eds.), Harrap, 1958.

Aristotle, *On Parts of Animals*, Book 1, Chapter 5, Loeb Classical Library, Harvard University Press.

Ashe, Geoffrey, *Gandhi*, Stein & Day, 1968.

Athenaeus, *The Deipnosophists*, 7 vols., trans. Charles Burton Gulick, Loeb Classical Library, Harvard University Press, 1971.

Barber, Richard, *Cooking and Recipes from Rome to the Renaissance*, Allen Lane, 1973.

Barkas, Janet, *The Vegetable Passion*, Charles Scribner's Sons, 1975.

Barnes, Jonathan, *The Presocratic Philosophers*, Routledge, 1979; new edn, 1990.

Berman, Morris, *Coming to our Senses*, Bantam, 1990.

Bernal, Martin, *Black Athena*, vol. I, Free Association Books, 1987.

Boswell, John, *Christianity, Social Tolerance and Homosexuality*, University of Chicago Press, 1980.

Brown, Peter, *The Body and Society*, Faber & Faber, 1989.

Buckhardt, Jakob, *Civilisation of the Renaissance in Italy*, Phaidon, 1981; Penguin Books, 1990.

Burnett, John, *Plenty and Want*, Methuen, 1983.

Bury, J.B. and Russell Meiggs, *A History of Greece*, Macmillan, 1975.

Carpenter, Edward, *Civilisation: Its Cause and Cure*, 1921.

Carson, Gerald, *Men, Beasts and Gods*, Charles Scribner's Sons, 1972.

Cato, Marcus Porcius, *On Agriculture*, trans. William Davis Hooper, Heinemann, 1934.

Chakravarty, I., *The Saga of Indian Food*, Sterling Publishers, 1972.

Chang, K.C., *Food in Chinese Culture*, Yale University Press, 1977.

Churton, Tobias, *The Gnostics*, Weidenfeld and Nicolson, 1990.

Cicero, *Letters to His Friends*, 4 vols., trans. W. Glynn Williams, Loeb Classical Library, Harvard University Press.

Claeys, Gregory, *Thomas Paine*, Unwin Hyman, 1989.

Clair, Colin, *Kitchen and Table*, Abelard and Schuman, 1964.

Clayton, A.C., *The Rigveda and Vedic Religion*, Christian Literature Society for India, 1913.

Cocchi, Antonio, *The Pythagorean Diet (A Vegetarian Pamphlet)*, trans. R. Dodsley (1745).

Comnena, Anna, *The Alexiad of Princess Anna Comnena*, trans. Dawes, Kegan Paul, 1928.

Conze, Edward, *A Short History of Buddhism*, Unwin, 1982.

—, *Buddhist Scriptures*, Penguin Books, 1959.

Crawford, Michael, and David Marsh, *The Driving Force*, Heinemann, 1989; rev. edn, Mandarin, 1991.

Crosby, Alfred W., Jr, *The Columbian Exchange*, Greenwood Press, 1972.

Darby, William J., Paul Ghalioungui and Louis Grivetti, *Food: The Gift of Osiris*, Academic Press, 1977.

Detienne, Marcel, *Dionysos Slain*, John Hopkins University Press, 1979.

—, *The Gardens of Adonis*, Harvester Press, 1977.

Dodds, E. R., *The Greeks and the Irrational*, University of California Press, 1956.

Dombrowski, D.A., *The Philosophy of Vegetarianism*, University of Massachusetts Press, 1984.

Douglas, Mary, *Purity and Danger*, Routledge, 1966; new edns, 1978, 1991.

Drummond, J.C., and Anne Wilbraham, *The Englishman's Food*, Jonathan Cape, 1959; new edn, Pimlico Books, 1991.

Eastwood, Cyril, *Life and Thought in the Ancient World*, University of London Press, 1966.

Eissler, K. R., *Leonardo da Vinci: Psychological Notes on the Enigma*, Hogarth Press, 1962.

Erasmus, *Praise of Folly*, trans. B. Radice, Penguin Books, 1971.

Erbstosser, Martin, *Heretics in the Middle Ages*, Edition Leipzig, 1984.

Evelyn, John, *Acetaria* (1699), Prospect, 1982.

Eyton, Matthew, *Christian Ethics and Animal Rights*, unpublished thesis, 1989.

Ferrier, J. Todd, *On Behalf of the Creatures*, The Order of the Cross, 1983.

Fiddes, Nick, *Meat: A Natural Symbol*, Routledge, 1991.

Fox, Robin Lane, *Pagans and Christians*, Viking, 1986; Penguin Books, 1988.

Franklin, Benjamin, *Autobiography*, ed. John Bigelow, J.B. Lippincott & Co., 1868.

Gallagher, D.A., and U. Gallagher (trans.), *St Augustine: The Catholic and Manichaean Ways of Life*, Catholic University Press, 1966.

George, Susan, *How the Other Half Dies*, Penguin Books, 1976.

Godwin, Joscelyn, *Mystery Religions in the Ancient World*, Thames and Hudson, 1981.

Goldsmith, Oliver, *The Deserted Village* (1770).

Gompertz, Lewis, *Moral Inquiries on the Situation of Man and of Brute*, Centaur Press, 1992.

Gorman, Peter, *Pythagoras: A Life*, Routledge and Kegan Paul, 1979.

Grant, Michael, *The Classical Greeks*, Weidenfeld and Nicolson, 1989.

Griggs, Barbara, *The Food Factor*, Viking, 1986.


Hansson, Maurice, with Jill Marsden, *E for Additives*, Thorson's, 1987.

Harris, Marvin, *Good to Eat*, Allen and Unwin, 1986.

Hartley, Dorothy, *Food in England*, MacDonald, 1954.

Harvey, Peter, *An Introduction to Buddhism*, Cambridge University Press, 1990.

Hippocrates, *Hippocratic Writings*, trans. J. Chadwick and W.N. Mann, Penguin Books, 1978.

Holmes, Richard, *Shelley: The Pursuit*, Quartet Books, 1974; new edn, Penguin Books, 1991.

Holroyd, Michael, *Bernard Shaw*, Vol.1, Chatto and Windus, 1988.

Hooke, S.H., *Middle Eastern Mythology*, Penguin Books, 1963.


Kenney, E.J. (ed.), *Ovid: Metamorphoses*, Oxford University Press, 1986.

Knappert, Jan, *Indian Mythology*, Aquarian Press, 1991.


Lerner, Robert E., *The Heresy of the Free Spirit in the Later Middle Ages*, University of California Press, 1972.

Lieu, Samuel N.C., *Manichaeism*, Manchester University Press, 1985.

Louth, Andrew (ed.), *Early Christian Writings*, trans. Maxwell Staniforth, Penguin Books, 1987.

Luce, J.V., *Homer and the Heroic Age*, Thames and Hudson, 1975.


Mascaró, Juan (trans.), *The Upanishads*, Penguin Books, 1965.

Miller, Alice, *The Untouched Key*, Virago, 1990.

Mireaux, Emile, *Daily Life in the Time of Homer*, Allen and Unwin, 1959.

Mitra, Dr Rajendralala, *Indo-Aryans* (1881).

Momigliano, Arnaldo, *Alien Wisdom: The Limits of Hellenization*, Cambridge University Press, 1975.

Moore, R.I., *The Birth of Popular Heresy: Origins of European Dissent*, Documents of Medieval History I, Edward Arnold, 1975.

Morgan, Elaine, *The Scars of Evolution*, Penguin Books, 1991.

—, *The Aquatic Ape*, Souvenir Press, 1982, new edn, 1989.


Nelson, W. (ed.), *A Fifteenth-Century School Book*, Oxford University Press, 1956.

Nock, A.D., *Essays on Religion and the Ancient World*, 2 vols., Oxford University Press, 1972.


Obolensky, Dimitri, *The Bogomils*, A.C. Hall, 1972.

Ovid, *Metamorphoses*, Oxford University Press, 1986.

Pagels, Elaine, *The Gnostic Gospels*, Penguin Books, 1990.

Paterson, David, and Richard D. Ryder, *Animals' Rights: A Symposium*, Centaur Press, 1979.

Peters, Edward (ed.), *Heresy and Authority in Medieval Europe*, University of Pennsylvania Press, 1980.

Plato, *The Republic*, Everyman's Library, 1945.

Pliny, *Natural History*, 10 vols., trans. W.H.S. Jones, Loeb Classical Library, Harvard University Press, 1956.

Plutarch, *Moralia*, trans. Harold Cherniss and William Helmbold, Heinemann, 1976.

Popper, Karl R., and John C. Eccles, *The Self and Its Brain*, Routledge and Kegan Paul, 1990.

Porphyry, *On Abstinence from Animal Food*, E.W. Tyson and Thomas Taylor, Centaur Press, 1965.

Procopius, *The Secret History*, Penguin Books, 1966.

Pullar, Philippa, *Consuming Passions*, Hamish Hamilton, 1971.


Ritchie, Carson I.A., *Food in Civilisation*, Beaufort Books, 1981.

Rothschild, Miriam, *Animals and Man*, Clarendon Press, 1986.

Runciman, Steven, *The Mediaeval Manichee*, Cambridge University Press, 1947; new edn, 1982.

Russell, Bertrand, *A History of Western Philosophy*, Unwin, 1978; new edn, Routledge, 1991.


Salt, Henry, *The Savour of Salt*, Centaur Press, 1989.

Seneca, *Moral Essays*, trans. J.W. Basone, 3 vols. Loeb Classical Library, Harvard University Press.

Shelley, Percy Bysshe, *Poetical Works*, ed. Thomas Hutchinson, Oxford University Press, 1968.

Shirer, William L., *The Rise and Fall of the Third Reich*, Simon and Schuster, 1960.

Soler, Jean, 'The Semiotics of Food in the Bible', from Robert Forster and Orest Ranum (eds.), *Food and Drink in History*, vol. 5, John Hopkins University Press, 1979.


Tannahill, Reay, *Food in History*, Penguin Books, 1973.

Theophrastus, *Enquiry into Plants*, 2 vols., trans. Sir Arthur Hort, Loeb Classical Library, Harvard University Press, 1926.

Thomas, Keith, *Religion and the Decline of Magic*, Peregrine Books, 1973; Penguin Books, 1991.

—, *Man and the Natural World*, Allen Lane, 1983; Penguin Books, 1984.

—, *The Human Carnivore*, lecture to the Guild of Food Writers (unpublished).

Troyat, Henri, *Tolstoy*, W.H. Allen, 1968.

Turner, E.S., *All Heaven in a Rage*, St Martin's Press, 1965.

Twigg, Julia, *The Vegetarian Movement in England 1847-1981*, Ph.D. thesis for LSE (unpublished).

Ucko, P.J., and G.W. Dimbleby, *The Domestication and Exploitation of Plants and Animals*, Duckworth, 1969.

Valery, Anne, *Talking about the War*, Michael Joseph, 1991.
Varia, Opuscula, *A Medieval Reader*, Penguin Books, 1977.
Varro, Marcus Terentius, *On Agriculture*, trans. William David Hooper, Heinemann, 1934.

Weeks, Jeffrey, *Coming Out: Homosexual Politics in Britain from the Nineteenth Century to the Present*, Quartet, 1977.
Wheaton, Barbara Ketcham, *Savoring the Past*, University of Pennsylvania Press, 1983.
Willey, Basil, *The Seventeenth Century Background*, Ark Paperbacks, 1986.
Williams, Howard, *The Ethics of Diet*, John Heywood, 1883.
Wilson, C. Anne, *Food and Drink in Britain*, Penguin Books, 1984; new edn, Constable, 1992.
Wilson, Hilary, *Egyptian Food and Drink*, Shire Publications, 1988.
Wilson, Peter J., *Man, the Promising Primate*, Yale University Press, 1983.
—, *The Domestication of the Human Species*, Yale University Press, 1988.
Worster, Donald, 'Man and the Natural Order' in Goldsmith and Hildyard (eds.), *The Earth Report*, Mitchell Beazley, 1988.
Wynne-Tyson, Jon, *Food for a Future*, Thorson's, 1988.

# Index

Note: Where a term is mentioned in the footnote, the page number is followed by 'n'.